OF WOMEN BORNE

D1596235

Gender, Theory, and Religion

GENDER, THEORY, AND RELIGION

Amy Hollywood, Editor

The Gender, Theory, and Religion series provides a forum for interdisciplinary scholarship at the intersection of the study of gender, sexuality, and religion.

OF WOMEN BORNE

A Literary Ethics of Suffering

Cynthia R. Wallace

Columbia University Press   New York

COLUMBIA UNIVERSITY PRESS
Publishers Since 1893
NEW YORK   CHICHESTER, WEST SUSSEX
cup.columbia.edu

Library of Congress Cataloging-in-Publication Data
Wallace, Cynthia (Cynthia R.)
Of women borne : a literary ethics of suffering / Cynthia Wallace.
pages cm. — (Gender, theory, and religion)
Based on the author's Ph.D. dissertation, Loyola University, Chicago, 2012.
Includes bibliographical references and index.
Summary: "A new approach to the recent turn to ethics in literary studies
that emphasizes the gendered and religious syntax of suffering" —
Provided by publisher.
ISBN 978-0-231-17368-1 (cloth : alk. paper)—ISBN 978-0-231-17369-8
(pbk. : alk. paper)—ISBN 978-0-231-54120-6 (e-book)
1. Suffering in literature. 2. Pain in literature. 3. Redemption in literature.
4. Literature—Women authors—History and criticism.
5. Women and literature—History—21st century. I. Title.
II. Title: Literary ethics of suffering.
PN56.S742W35 2016
809'.93353—dc23
2015018091

Columbia University Press books are printed on permanent
and durable acid-free paper.
Printed in the United States of America

Cover image: Lucia Loiso © Gallery Stock
Cover design: Chang Jae Lee

For Darlene Yvonne Call

(1937–2008)

who knew what it is to suffer

but always underlined love at least three times

and for Miriam Elizabeth Wallace

who explores the world with joyful attention

and surprises us at every turn

Dry wafer,
sour wine:
this day I see
the world, a word
intricately incarnate, offers—
ravelled, honeycombed, veined, stained—
what hunger craves,
a sorrel grass,
a crust,
water,
salt.
—Denise Levertov, "This Day"

CONTENTS

PREFACE

If We Could Learn to Learn from Pain

> No "we" should be taken for granted when the subject is looking at other people's pain.
> —Susan Sontag, *Regarding the Pain of Others*

> Wagers are called for, again and again.
> —Richard Kearney, *Anatheism: Returning to God After God*

When I was a very small girl, I noticed that at family gatherings during the colder months, my mother and her sisters would often compare hands. They would raise their knuckles to each other's gazes, showing the reddened and roughened surfaces of their skins, tracing the fault lines where flesh cracked to expose thin red rivulets. They would chastise each other for their lack of self-care, challenge each other to put lotion next to the sinks where they washed so many dishes, near the cleaning supplies they used to scrub their bathrooms, next to the beds where they fell exhausted at night. They would discuss the relative merits of Jergens, Avon, and a peculiarly marketed green tin of "bag balm" intended for cows' udders but especially helpful for homekeepers' ravaged fingers. Their conversations were all about doing better at tending to themselves, but with the clarity of a young child, I sensed a measure of pride in their complaints, a strange competition to see who worked the hardest, whose skin was the most delicate, who suffered the most. These wounded hands seemed both a mark of their particular womanly fatigue and a trophy of their accomplished middle-class caring.

My story is prosaic, but its force is in its commonness. In Western culture, even as I write near the beginning of the twenty-first century, women continue to evince signs of socialized self-sacrifice; they—I should say *we*—continue to suffer in modes related to our cultural positions as well as our bodies. This suffering has seemed at times to be a soundtrack to my life in the city: Across the alley, I hear a domestic argument punctuated by the sharp warning of a woman's voice—"Don't you touch me!"—and underscored by her weeping. On the evening news, I am reminded again and again that globally, in countries torn by poverty and war, women are the most vulnerable, that even in stable nations they are often the poorest of the poor. In conversations, my friends and I discuss examples of suffering that are clouded by ambiguity: A dear friend, for instance, recently has been beset by awful morning sickness, but having experienced a series of nausea-free months before a painful miscarriage, she is thankful for her discomfort because it signifies a healthy pregnancy. She and others choose to sacrifice their comfort, their sleep, their unmarked abdomens in order to bring new life into the world, and in doing so they participate in a long tradition of women welcoming, or at least accepting, pain for the sake of the other that is their child. But then, their experience stands in contradistinction to that of many women who undergo the sacrifices of pregnancy, childbirth, and mothering not as a chosen good but as an inflicted pain. Their experience also bears only limited similarity to the sufferings of women oppressed by violent abuse, socioeconomic prejudice, or culturally mandated silence. There is no singular "suffering," only sufferings, of varying degrees and sources and with disparate meanings in different locations. In the multiplicity of these stories, ambivalence abounds.

How do we read such sufferings?

This is a book that examines the ambivalences of suffering in stories, and also in essays and poems, as it turns to late twentieth-century writing by women as a source for asking that important question. This is a book about suffering, and the apparently chosen suffering we often shorthand as self-sacrifice. It is a book about redemption, the question of whether suffering, whether accidental, chosen, or imposed, might bring about some good—the question of whether suffering has some positive ethical force. And it is a book about the act of reading suffering, about reading the signifiers "suffering" and "sacrifice" in contemporary literature and society, about interpreting texts and bodies in light of suffering. How ought we read and respond to suffering? And what role does suffering play in our own responsibilities as readers and responders?

My question of "ought" is not a new one. The end of the second millennium brought with it a noteworthy surge of interest in ethics on the part of literary scholars. This "ethical turn" has been widely mapped and debated in the more than twenty-five years since its inception: it has been a diffuse movement, meaning many things to many people. One of the most helpful delineations of the ethical turn, to my mind, is Andrew Gibson's in his "Ethics" entry for the *Johns Hopkins Guide to Literary Theory and Criticism*. In this article, Gibson differentiates the "new ethical criticism," which relies on a deconstructive or poststructuralist theoretical frame and tends to theorize the practice of reading, from the "moral criticism" that assumes the mimetic function of literature to shape readers through its content.[1] I am not the first to note that these two approaches map onto earlier arguments between high theory and multiculturalism or liberal humanism.

Entering the discussion two decades in, I am satisfied by neither side. The moral critics' forgetfulness of the strange literariness of literature doesn't do *justice* to such texts. Yet much of the new ethical criticism also seems forgetful of singularity, as theories of the reader-text relation— which often emphasize the limitless otherness of the textual other— ironically take on a formalist and universalizing tone.

Most disconcerting of all, however, is the apparent myopia, or per-haps forgetfulness, of many scholars who appeal to the popular ethical vocabulary of alterity and the Other, face-to-face relationship and respon-sibility, hospitality, and passivity. Drawing on the writings of the famously hyperbolic philosopher Emmanuel Levinas, many literary critics have contributed to a model of ethical reading that is fundamentally an ethic of redemptive suffering. By these accounts, the reader facing the text is endlessly responsible for it, for its well-being, for its coming-into-being, even to the point of suffering on behalf of that other (that is, the text). Almost wholly elided from these visions of literary ethics are key Western cultural associations of passivity, caring responsibility, and self-sacrifice: firstly, with women and also (not unrelatedly) with Christian paradigms of redemption through suffering.[2]

The elision of gender and religion in these influential visions of liter-ary ethics is not surprising. To begin with, philosophical ethics, gender studies, and theology are notoriously uneasy bedfellows, for reasons his-torical, political, and disciplinary. Add literature to the mix and the unease only intensifies. The sweep of secularization has much to do with this discord, as both literature and postmodern ethics have at various points been named the successors of Jewish and Christian religion as sources of moral development, or as feminism is held partly responsible for the fall of traditional religion or at least a beneficiary of its demise. Considerations of religion and spirituality were exiled from much literary scholarship during the mid- to late twentieth century, in much the same way ethics as such was exiled until "on or around 1987," if we follow Geoffrey Harpham's dating.[3] This exile may account for the deracinated version of Levinas many literary scholars appropriate by eliding his religious writings, as Adam Zachary Newton has aptly accused.[4] (A similar elision often hides Levinas's troubling gender talk in literary critics' celebrations of his work.) To compound matters, many of the most influential works in the ethical turn focus almost exclusively on male writers. The indexes of even the most recent monographs on literature and ethics—apart from those that distinguish themselves as specifically concerned with women writers—are heavy on male theorists whose work is not particularly attentive to gender. My purpose in naming this propensity is not to act as affirmative-action citation police but to emphasize that it should be no wonder that much ethical literary criticism is inattentive to gender. Our sources shape our outcomes, and even as I write, the masculine still seems to function as the neutral space from which to generalize and to theorize. Literary ethics holds no high ground in this respect.

In theorizing ethics, however, in reading suffering, gender and religion *matter*. What can suffering mean, as an abstraction? What good can ethics do, apart from the flesh-and-blood particularity of breathing bodies in untidy and unique circumstances? More negatively, what damage might an ethics of suffering do, if it reinstates an ideal of behavior that has been used to perpetuate disproportionate suffering among the disempowered? What wounding might an ethical model effect if it derives from ancient oppressive traditions but cuts away the attendant weavings of critique that have re-visioned and even redeemed those traditions? Attempting to snip and tug threads of the discourse out of the larger cultural textile in order to reconfigure a pristinely ungendered, unraced, unreligioned ethical subject is not just irresponsible, it is *impossible*. The echoes follow such a subject. The frayed threads trail along.

Nowhere is this impossibility more apparent than in contemporary literary writing by women. The texts I am thinking of—the texts I turn and return to in this book—are insistent in their exploration of suffering within a warp and weft of time and place, gender and race, religion and spirituality, and nation. These stories and poems and essays struggle with suffering, redemption, and responsibility, but they do so *as literature*, with its complex representations of the specific, particular, and multiple; its temporality of narrative emplotment; its reliance on metaphor and linguistic play that disrupts the illusion of straightforward communication; its affective engagement; its irreducibility to a singular, discursive *meaning*. They also often offer allegories of reading and interpretation, repeatedly suggesting an ethics of reading—what I call in these pages an *ethics of readerly attention*—that is not so different from the careful, hospitable, even self-giving stance propounded by the new ethical criticism. Indeed, such an ethics of readerly attention frequently parallels a tenuously positive appeal to redemptive suffering within the texts more broadly. Yet such a practice of reading—and such a potentially positive valuation of different modes of self-sacrifice—is inextricable from these texts' poetic grappling with suffering, with its risks as well as its possibilities. This literary incarnation is one of my intervention's primary offerings: in choosing texts with a certain *content* of suffering, always gendered and religiously inflected (a concern I come to call the *ethics of literary representation*), I am able to discern a literary ethics that neither refuses redemptive suffering altogether nor elides the history and dangers of such a paradigm.

Such a literary ethics refuses to celebrate a deracinated redemptive suffering, but it also refuses to condemn suffering as an inevitably negative force. Contra the contemporary Western uneasiness about suffering—the tendency to ignore it, medicate it, or elide it from public view, especially when it does not suit our purposes—the literary ethics I locate in recent women's writing recognizes the paradoxical dangers and powers of viewing suffering and sacrifice within a redemptive frame. This double-stance of critique and embrace is also present in the literary texts' engagements with the Christian tradition that stands in overdetermined relationship to the suffering of women, as the history of women's writing in English and of Western feminism inevitably highlights.

To do justice to these vexed imbrications, in the literary readings that form the bulk of this book, I turn intertextually to theology, and to feminists and theologians of color in particular, many of whom have already turned to the literary texts I read here. In other words, this book seeks to intervene in the ethical turn, not just as a sidelined feminist project but as a theoretical contribution of general interest. To reframe redemptive suffering within its context of gendered, religious, and raced implications, I rely on literary and theoretical texts by writers who deal with the mixed and mingled dynamics of gender, religion, race, and other particulars as they struggle with the syntax of suffering. This project, thus, is robustly interdisciplinary, seeking to join considerations of *how* we read with *what* we read.

This interdisciplinary reading—always circling around an interest in interpreting suffering so bound up with gender and religion in these texts—is not just the result of isolated research in my office or face-to-face time with a computer screen; it has been shaped by human voices, by conversations with philosophers and theologians and social workers, by reading discussions in my feminist theology group, by book and article recommendations garnered not just at conferences but through online social networking sites, by talks around my dining room table with academics and nonacademics. In other words, the emphatic textuality of this project does not begin in textuality but in embodied community, and that is where it ends.

Again and again, in the exceedingly particular readings of my chosen texts, I arrive at a structurally similar conclusion: First, that these texts, in their representations of the unique sufferings of women in specific cultural locations, seek to do justice to that suffering, to give it language, along with its complex web of causes and effects, in order to break a silence. These texts function to allow readers both to recognize themselves in the representations and to recognize their radical difference from those representations, textually suggesting thereby a tenuous dynamic of empathy, distance, and responsibility in the material world. Second, these texts manifest a paradoxical stance of both critique and embrace: of Christianity, of particular cultures, and of suffering itself as both bound up with oppression and source of empowerment for ethical action. Which is to say, repeatedly in these literary texts, I read a theorizing of suffering that both suggests a generalizable or universal paradigm of redemptive suffering *and* subverts that paradigm through the particularity of representation. Unlike theoretical discourses, therefore, literature both suggests a paradigm and challenges it through literature's uniquely incarnated form. Finally, I recognize in my literary texts the repeated implicit suggestion of a reading practice that itself is predicated on the self-giving, receptive, endlessly attentive reader that exists in an overdetermined relationship to the gendered, raced, and religiously mediated body of the suffering woman, a reading practice that is again paradoxically bound to a concurrent reading practice of suspicion and critical hermeneutics for the sake of justice: this is my ethics of readerly attention.

The book begins with a chapter thick with theory. Yet I interrupt my own proclivity to begin with heady abstractions by starting with a brief history that reads moments in women's writing in English. This constructed history highlights, from its beginning around 1400 to the present, the cultural-linguistic web of suffering, sacrifice, Christianity, gender, and redemption. From there I survey the twentieth-century interest in suffering's relation to literature and language, then introduce the role of redemptive suffering in poststructuralist literary ethics, feminist care ethics, and theology, as well as their vexed relations. This chapter is dominated by work from scholars located in privileged cultural locations: many of them white and highly educated, many of them male. It is so because these are the voices that have shaped the theoretical fields out of which my project develops, particularly the new ethical criticism that grew to prominence in the last decades of the twentieth century and relied extensively on male poststructuralist theorists—a reliance I seek here to disrupt. My reading practice throughout the book combines a feminist concern for context and materiality with a close attention to language and texts' allegories of reading that is shaped by poststructuralist theory. Yet after the introduction, I turn decisively *away* from that body of theory, in favor of careful attention to literary texts and theoretical intertexts that help inform my readings of those literary texts' disparate locations, their paradoxical engagements with the syntax of suffering in particular local vocabularies. In other words, although my reading practices are indelibly marked by my long study of this theory formerly known as "high," I am not interested in reading my literary texts "through" it or "in light of" it, not interested in "applying" it, but rather undoing the former hierarchical relationship in order to read the literature and theory "with" each other, to recognize resonances and challenges without reinscribing the authority of the theoretical. For readers who prefer the theory, this turn away may seem like a refusal of responsibility, even an injustice. I suggest such readers understand it instead as a reminder of the pragmatics of finitude and embodiment often not considered in postmodern ethics—the face-to-face relation with any one other means that I cannot at that moment be taking responsibility for an alternate other. In this project, I turn away from the relatively powerful poststructuralist theory that has dominated many discussions of literary ethics so that I may attend instead to women's literary writing, practicing my own suggestion that we consider power differentials and material social contexts as part of a literary ethics—focusing not just on *how* we read, but on *what* we read, and *why*.

The book's subsequent chapters—which look to Adrienne Rich, Toni Morrison, Ana Castillo, and Chimamanda Ngozi Adichie—participate in the typically told story of feminism by beginning with a white woman whose writing galvanized feminist activism in the seventies, even though I seek at points to undo this history. In chapter 2, I read in Rich's prose and poetry the ubiquity of the signifiers "suffering" and "sacrifice" in the midcentury women's movement and their presence in a semantic textile also woven through with Jewish and Christian religions. I also read Rich's related thematizing of language and its ambiguous status as both source of domination and tool of resistance, highlighting the fact that many insights typically attributed to poststructuralist theory also arose in literary political movements. Finally, I step back to read in the narrative of Rich's long career of poetic engagement a lesson in interpretive practice, one that is self-aware, radically open to the influence of otherness, and humbly willing to revise, but also committed to the risk of making claims for the sake of justice.

My turn to Morrison in chapter 3 highlights the agitation of women of color, especially in the late seventies and eighties, for recognition within the feminist movement as particular agents with experiences, insights, and concerns not addressed in a movement built around the presumably universal "woman" who was actually white and middle class. Of course, women of color were active in second-wave feminism from its inception, but the struggle for the recognition of differences among women gathered increasing momentum in the seventies in the writings of feminists like Audre Lorde and is often connected to the publication of major anthologies in the early eighties. This lesson of difference, of particularity, is an important contribution to a literary ethics of suffering. In this chapter I read such a lesson in Morrison's writings, arguing not just that Morrison seeks to represent specifically African American sufferings in literature in order to confront readers with questions of responsibility, but also that her texts' formal features, especially their stylized gaps and ambiguities, school readers in a practice of ethical attention that teaches the need for careful reading and interpretive humility. Reading Morrison's paradoxical portrayals of suffering and its relation to religion together with the black theological and womanist discourse of redemptive suffering, I locate in Morrison's recent novels *Love* and *A Mercy* a risky stance of redemption worked out in an ongoing negotiation between the general and the particular, between blind justice and context-bound mercy.

As chapter 4 reads Castillo, so this book continues to explore the importance of cultural location in interpretations of suffering. Castillo's literary and theoretical writings, I argue, represent the particular sufferings of Chicanas (and Chicanos) living within a system that combines sex and gender oppression with ethnic and class oppressions. Castillo's texts, again, evince a strong critique of women's culturally mandated suffering and self-sacrifice and their origins in Christianity, this time from within a Mexican Catholic frame. Yet the texts also manifest a paradoxical engagement with suffering and self-sacrifice, suggesting the practice of mothering—or of being a guardian, attending to the particular needs of an other, even sacrificing the self for the sake of hospitality—as an ethical ideal needed to resist the systems of oppression that cause suffering. This thematized suggestion is paralleled by a literary form that forecloses on conclusive readings that rely on readerly mastery and Western assumptions of rationalism, engaging readers in a practice of attention that parallels Castillo's description of mothering. I also read in Castillo's texts a repudiation of Catholicism challenged by a manifestation of its hermeneutic of liberation, which rereads texts and traditions in light of the experience of those who suffer, ultimately rewriting them and thereby forging a new reality. Castillo's writings thus contribute a paradoxical suggestion of hospitably open and suspiciously critical reading practices to my developing literary ethics of suffering.

Finally, chapter 5 on Adichie signals a move away from focus on the United States to a broader scope informed by the postcolonial theory that rose to prominence in the nineties and a concern with globalization that dominated scholarly imaginations as well as everyday practices in economic and technological developments after September 11, 2001. The vocabulary of "representation" has been especially important in postcolonial literary studies, particularly in the work of Gayatri Spivak, and this chapter is especially attuned to problems of representation in light of cultural location. In it, I argue that Adichie's exploration of suffering as arising from the postcolonial heritage of political turmoil as well as entwined familial and religious patriarchy—and her suggestion of critical fidelity to those broken systems through a proliferation of particular stories—offers a brave critique of unjust suffering paradoxically accompanied by a refusal to reject these specific histories altogether. I read Adichie together with postcolonial feminist theologians who forward a "critical hermeneutics" to give language to this paradoxical practice and end by reading in Adichie's novel *Half of a Yellow Sun* yet another thematic and formal lesson in recognizing the particularity of any suffering, and our limited understanding of it, even as we pursue a more-than-individual ethics of suffering.

Although the structure of my project supports this often-told narrative that begins with the West and the dominant white subject and moves out from there, I also seek to challenge that structure. For instance, Rich commonly is represented to students as a primary exemplar of second-wave radical white lesbian feminism; however, from her earliest stages of political radicalization she was in dialogue not only with Mary Daly, the philosopher-theologian whose writings often are cited as notoriously unattentive to racial difference, but also with Audre Lorde. In fact, Rich's feminist politicization developed, as she tells it, during her time teaching primarily black and Latino students with colleagues who were activists for racial and class justice. African American women, Latina and Chicana women, and West African women have been writing, theorizing, voicing, and influencing one another long before the tidy decades in which the common narrative's temporal structure might seem to place their contributions. I also seek to challenge the oft-repeated claim that postmodern or poststructuralist theory and "ethnic women" writers are opposed in their differing emphases on textuality (and inaccessible language) and everyday experience. Following Chela Sandoval's *Methodology of the Oppressed*,[5] I am convinced, first of all, that much poststructuralist theory is motivated by a profound desire for justice and that it, in an uncanny way, often parallels the insights of twentieth-century liberation movements. Second, I am convinced along with Sandoval and Barbara Christian[6] that such liberation movements also offer nuanced and sophisticated theorizing within their writings that often are read as simplistically expressive.

Thus, the conclusion is the chapter that most thoroughly (if tentatively) synthesizes my project's insights. In most fully elaborating my literary ethics of suffering at the project's end, I not only perform my own claim of self-revision and endless process but also invite my reader to undergo a similar experience of theorizing in and through the literary texts. Indeed, because the relationship between writer, text, and reader is such an important concern throughout the coming pages, it seems most appropriate to end this preface with an invitation: here and now, and not just for the abstract sake of "what ought to be," but for the sake of the texts and bodies crying out for response by their very presence before us, I ask you to join me in this reading, in this pursuit of a literary ethics of suffering.

ACKNOWLEDGMENTS

Writing a book is a long and at points isolating endeavor, but my experience also has been profoundly communal. Looking back over the years of work, I am overwhelmed at the number of people who have seen me through.

The project's unwieldy beginning would have been impossible without Suzanne Bost, Pamela Caughie, Micael Clarke, and Hille Haker: thank you for your willingness to wade with me into deep interdisciplinary waters, for your openness to stretched boundaries, and for your generous comments. Pamela, as a committee chair, teacher, and friend, you have exceeded my expectations time and again. I have been indelibly marked by your risky pedagogy of passing and your indefatigable, self-giving mentoring.

I am also grateful for Loyola University Chicago's fine English department and its hospitable theology and philosophy departments, particularly Diana Tietjens Meyers and her excellent reading recommendations and conversation. The Cudahy Library's collections and dedicated interlibrary loan staff were indispensible for the project's early stages. Finally, I appreciate the financial support of the Graduate School at Loyola University Chicago through an Advanced Doctoral Fellowship; a Research Mentorship stipend and assistant (thank you, Karissa Taylor!); and, through the generosity of the Arthur J. Schmitt Foundation, a Schmitt Dissertation Fellowship.

During those five years in Chicago, the people of Living Water Community Church kept me rooted in the real even at the headiest moments of my research and writing. Thank you to the whole beloved community, for potlucks, for music, for untidy multiculturalism and multitudinous particularity. Thank you to the women's storytelling group for gathering to construct our histories, to the senior high girls' group for sharing life and *Purple Hibiscus*, to the feminist theology group for humbly seeking to enlarge the horizons of our language for the most holy of Mysteries. Special thanks to Katherine Lamb, Nicky Owski, Sarah and Kirk Lashley, Meg Wallace, Sarah and Josh Harbert, Lisa and Mari Martin and Kyra Burke, Kacie Mulhern, Amanda Potter, Emily Venn, Peter and Liz Anderson, Tim and Patty Peebles, and Ruth Goring. Thank you, Andrea Hollingsworth, for being a soul companion on the writing journey. Thank you, Annie, Jason, Rivers, and Fern Gill-Bloyer for more than I can say.

The book took shape in its current form during my first years at St. Thomas More College, University of Saskatchewan, and I am very grateful for the support that allowed me to give it such attention, including a New Faculty Start-Up Grant, a Publications Fund Grant, and a humane teaching load. I am thankful for the smart, funny, and warm colleagues who have welcomed me and helped me acclimate to ridiculous winters. Among these colleagues, I owe a special thanks to Gordon DesBrisay, who soon after my arrival honored me with a treasure trove of his late wife Susan L. Blake's books. I never met Susan, but I have learned much from reading her work on African and African American writers, and in the final stages of writing this book I turned repeatedly and gratefully to the library I inherited from her. I am also grateful to the enthusiastic editorial staff at Columbia University Press, most particularly Wendy Lochner and Christine Dunbar, as well as Amy Hollywood and the anonymous peer reviewers, for their insightful and encouraging comments.

The tender early inklings of my concern for gender, religion, race, and ethics developed the wise care of other friends and mentors, and I must thank Don Deardoff, Kevin Heath, Jim Lamborn, Dave Mills, Julie Moore, and Peggy Wilfong, as well as Courtney Hahn, Katie and Mark Bentley, David Alenskis, Laura Werezak, and Brandi and Matt Molby. You were the community that began my thinking about community, faithful in a way that redeemed my own fraught faith.

Michele and Richard Rich, you are the ground in which I learned to grow.

Josh Wallace, I can imagine no better interlocutor, co-conspirator, and bookcase-sharer than you. You have bought my dreams at the price of many of your own, and I am unutterably glad—surprised, challenged, and comforted again and again—to find *my face in thine eye*, as *thine in mine appears*.

OF WOMEN BORNE

1

History (Herstory) and Theory, or Doing Justice to Redemptive Suffering

> *What are you going through?* she said, is the great question.
> Philosopher of oppression, theorist
> of the victories of force.
>
> We write from the marrow of our bones.   What she did not
> ask, or tell: how victims save their own lives.
> —Adrienne Rich, "For a Friend in Travail," *An Atlas of the Difficult World*

Dangerous Poetry

> . . . every time I think of the crucifixion of Christ I commit the sin of envy.
> —Simone Weil, *Waiting for God*

On the eighth of May, 1373, "a simple creature who could not letter" experienced a number of Revelations in response to her desire for "three gifts from God." These gifts were "mind of his passion," "a bodily sickness in her youth at thirty years of age," and "three wounds": "the wound of true contrition, the wound of kind compassion, and the wound of willful longing to God."[1] Dame Julian of Norwich, possibly our earliest example of a woman writing in English, asked her Lord for the gifts of spiritual and physical suffering, and she received them. *Revelation of Love* is her account of these experiences, the account for which she learned to "letter" so that she might share the gift of this revelation with her "fellow Christians" (18): she learned to write so that she could represent her suffering for the sake of her community.

Revelation of Love is a provocative mystical text: its pages recount Dame Julian's vivid visions of Christ's passion, God's answer to her agonized questions over the problem of evil, and powerful images of Christ as mother. Although she repeats the claim that her showings are entirely orthodox—insisting, for instance, "in the showing I was never stirred or led away from the Church's teaching on any single point" (91)—at moments it seems that the lady doth protest too much. The anxiety over possible accusations of heterodoxy indicates a latent awareness of the unorthodox nature of her theological claims.

When twentieth-century writer and lay theologian C. S. Lewis called *Revelation of Love* "dangerous," admitting, "I'm glad I didn't read it much earlier,"[2] he was probably not referring to the threat of Dame Julian's writing to established medieval church authority or to patriarchal control over speech. Yet Lewis's label does provoke thought on the danger of this text, and many possible dangers exist. From one perspective, Julian's famous answer from God about the problem of evil and the ongoing presence of sin threatens church tabulations of guilt and penance: "Sin is necessary, but all shall be well. All shall be well; and all manner of things shall be well" (55). Such an emphasis on blamelessness threatens creeds of punishment and death or at least threatens to skew the balance of justice and mercy.

Julian's portrayals of Christ as mother, similarly, are dangerous to reigning patriarchal and male-dominated images of God and to the structures of power that rely on such masculinist symbolism. "And our Saviour is our true Mother in whom we are endlessly born yet we will never come out of him," Julian asserts (127), relying on the bodily and feminine imagery of childbirth to convey a spiritual insight. She subverts gender binaries, combining the feminine title of Mother with masculine pronouns for Jesus, refusing the implicit valuing that would deem an association with femininity to be an insult for deity. And she draws on her understanding of women's experiences and virtues to describe God, rather than just men's experiences presumed to be universal or abstract virtues implicitly thought to be masculine: "Since Jesus Christ does good against evil, he is our true Mother; for we have our being of him where the ground of motherhood begins, with all the sweet keeping of love that follows endlessly. Even as rightly as God is our Father, so God is rightly our Mother" (131).[3] Reading this subversion, Liz Herbert McAvoy asserts that Julian "makes way for the feminine to assert its equal validity as part of the redemptive process."[4]

Revelation of Love threatens numerous comforts and authorities; it is dangerous to those who would prefer their theology from men, who would prefer to keep mind and body separated, and who would prefer rational argumentation over expansive and poetic narrative exploration. The text threatens those who wish for women to remain silent or who assert that women can have no real spiritual insight. So from one perspective, Julian of Norwich offers us a text that is dangerous to reigning masculinist binaries and to religious and social structures of punishment-meting patriarchal hierarchy.

Conversely, the text is dangerous in quite another way in its fascination with suffering, both bodily pain and spiritual anguish. Julian's specific request for the "gifts" of "mind" of Christ's suffering, "bodily sickness," and three "wounds" shows a desire to sacrifice both physical and psychological comfort. Even Julian's diction manifests a fascination with pain, as her choice of the word "wound" to describe "true contrition," "kind compassion," and "willful longing" is far from obvious. Julian *wants* to suffer, she wants God to *afflict* her, to take action and cause her to bear the burden: "I simply wanted his pains to be my pains, such was my feeling for him"; "I desired to suffer with him" (7). Julian wants understanding; she wants compassion; she wants spiritual insight. But is such desire masochistic? Must understanding come through wounding?[5]

Dame Julian does admit that a "loathing for pain . . . belongs to our nature" (43) and attributes such a loathing to Christ in his humanity. This natural turning away from pain contributes even more to Julian's appreciation for Christ's chosen self-sacrifice, so she does not seem to be claiming that a desire for suffering should come easily to all people. Instead, she links her appreciation for suffering with a higher end: "As our reward for the little pain we suffer here, we will know God himself without end, which otherwise we might never have. And the greater are our pains with him on his cross, the greater will be our reward with him when we come into his kingdom" (45). Both Christ's suffering and human suffering are associated with redemption, "endless joy and bliss" (51), purgation and closer relationship (55), and the ultimate answer of love.

Revelation of Love challenges its readers with a mysterious and paradoxical portrayal of suffering linked to love, self-sacrifice linked to redemption, passion linked to compassion, and pain linked to positive relationship. Herein lies another danger, for it is all too easy to favor one side of each paradox. Emphasizing love over suffering might have threatened a medieval Catholic church concerned with indulgences and penance, but emphasizing suffering over love threatens humanity with a sadomasochistic model of life and relation to divinity. A Christian emphasis on willing suffering like the one found in *Revelation of Love* is already dangerous—even literally fatal—if taken too far, if unbalanced by the paradoxically related poles of love and community. But such an emphasis is particularly dangerous for women who have been socialized to sacrifice themselves and suffer silently. One might argue that Dame Julian's text is revolutionary in that it does not link Christian suffering in particular to women but rather describes participation in Christ's cross as the calling of all believers, male and female. Diane Watt makes such a claim, pointing out that the figure of Eve, often associated with specifically female guilt and deserved suffering, is notably absent in Julian's text.[6] But it is also true that in associating the self-sacrificing Christ with the act of mothering, Julian does implicitly participate in the gendering of certain forms of suffering and in the spiritualizing of certain gendered experiences of self-sacrifice like childbirth and care. From a feminist perspective, the good in this case is in the honor accorded to women's particular roles and experiences; the danger is in the confirmation of an unhealthily gendered division of labor and pain.[7]

How do we walk this dangerous line, negotiating the tensions between life-giving and life-draining representations of divine and human sacrifice? *Revelation of Love* offers us no clear answer, only a poetic interaction with the paradoxical Christian paradigms of purgation and redemption. In doing so, the work stands at the beginning of a long history of women writing in English on Christianity, suffering, and self-sacrifice. Indeed, most of our earliest examples of women's publishing in English are explicitly religious and participate in a broader Christian attention to suffering.[8] In 1545, Katherine Parr's *Prayers or Medytacions* became the first instance of a woman author's name printed on the title page of an English book and includes a prayer "that I maie willyngly suffre for thy sake all maner of trouble and affliction."[9] Anne Lock, who in 1560 appended the first sonnet cycle printed in English to her translation of sermons by John Calvin, emphasizes the "sufficing sacrifice for all" of God's "swete sonne."[10]

Writing her *Salve Deus Rex Judaeorum* in the seventeenth century, Aemelia Lanyer links the men who cause women's suffering to those who caused Christ's suffering on the cross.[11] Lanyer also marvels at the very paradoxes

Dame Julian presents, the impossible opposites contained in a model of redemptive sacrifice:

> O wonder, more than man can comprehend,
> Our Joy and Griefe both at one instant fram'd,
> Compounded: Contrarieties contend
> Each to exceed, yet niether to be blam'd.
> Our Griefe to see our Saviours wretched end,
> Our Joy to know both Death and Hell he tam'd:
> That we may say, O Death, where is thy sting?
> Hell, yeeld thy victory to thy conq'ring King.[12]

Recognizing this emphasis on mysterious tensions inherent in Christian teaching, particularly as it relates in her piece to virulent critiques of misogyny, some have argued that Lanyer actually exploits the paradoxes themselves to undo a number of gender distinctions. Erica Longfellow argues, for instance, that in emphasizing Christ's "passive resistance," "patient suffering, generosity, and forgiveness," Lanyer exposes the way he "radically bridges gender and status" without risking any unorthodox interpretations of the biblical text itself.[13] In other words, Lanyer highlights the fact that Christ—the church's prime example of renewed humanity—is characterized by traits typically associated with women.[14] Once again, Lanyer's writing not only is dangerous to reigning patriarchal power systems and scriptural justifications of women's oppression but also participates in the dangerous association of women's suffering with Christ's as *good*.

Women writers in the following centuries continued the trend of religious and gendered motifs of suffering, and some engaged in more explicit critiques than others. As Helen Wilcox claims, many women in the years from 1500 to 1700 appropriated biblical discourse for their own purposes.[15] Versified Old Testament narratives were also popular in the eighteenth century, and those of Anne Finch, Anne Yearsley, and Elizabeth Hands expose the pattern of powerful biblical men causing women to suffer for men's benefit.[16] The eventual rise of the novel offered expanding opportunities to explore the psychological complexity of these situations: George Eliot's narrator in *Adam Bede* comments explicitly upon specifically female suffering, comparing the agony of the crucifixion to that of an unwed pregnant girl. The narrator concludes on the scene of the young woman's affliction, "No wonder man's religion has much sorrow in it: no wonder he needs a Suffering God."[17] Nineteenth-century poetry and essays also show interest in gendered redemption: famously, Christina Rossetti's "Goblin Market" presents a specifically female suffering savior,[18] and Florence Nightingale asserts in her treatise *Suggestions for Thought for Seekers After Religious Truth* not only that God causes suffering for the sake of learning but also that "at last there shall arise a woman, who will resume, in her own soul, all the sufferings of her race, and that woman will be the Saviour of her race"; "The next Christ will perhaps be a female Christ."[19]

An especially vivid nineteenth-century portrayal of this special connection between women and suffering or sacrifice appears in Elizabeth Barrett Browning's *A Drama of Exile*. In this dramatic retelling of the day after Adam and Eve's departure from Eden, Barrett Browning develops an Eve who is wracked by guilt, certain that she is entirely to blame for their fallen condition. Characterized by a groveling humility, Eve has to be repeatedly told that she is an important element of the promise of future redemption as the bearer of the "seed" that will one day be Christ. Thus, Eve's (and all women's) special punishment for sin is suffering, but suffering is also their special means of grace as "woman, wife, and mother."[20] Barrett Browning's Adam explains to Eve the "curse" outlined in Genesis 3:

> Something thou hast to bear through womanhood,
> Peculiar suffering answer to the sin,—
> Some pang paid down for each new human life,
> Some weariness in guarding such a life. (109)

He continues to detail further "peculiar suffering" for women, including a lack of thanks for hard work and "pressures of an alien tyranny / With its dynastic reasons of larger bones / And stronger sinews" (109)—plainly stated, patriarchal oppression. Nevertheless, although such suffering is mandated as woman's just punishment for eating the forbidden fruit, this curse is also connected to the promise of ultimate redemption, as a woman "in the set noon of time" will give birth to Christ (114). Thus, Eve is portrayed as taking on this responsibility of motherly suffering as a holy duty:

"I accept / For me and for my daughters this high part / Which lowly shall be counted" (111). Barrett Browning's Eve is therefore representative of a strong nineteenth-century ideology of the Angel in the House rather than an archetypal wicked woman, which subverts a long tradition of treating Eve as the sexual temptress and source of all wickedness. Eve's insistence on her own guilt takes the power to blame away from men: Adam's voice in the poem is often used to minimize rather than emphasize Eve's sin. In this way, the poem both participates in and undermines the tradition of blaming Eve and all women, and women's suffering through childbirth, constant service, and patriarchal rule are portrayed as both justly deserved and redemptively meaningful, even honorable.

The danger here is hard to overlook. The Victorian context in which Barrett Browning wrote was one that held women in a double bind of motherhood and its related suffering and expected self-sacrifice as both the punishment for their foremother's sin and the highest virtue and calling. In imagining and implicitly interrogating the origin of this role as wives and mothers, Barrett Browning at once dignifies and challenges her culture's relegation of women to the status of self-abnegating caregivers. She joins many other women writers in both participating in and challenging the reigning norm as it relates to women's suffering, and in so doing, she presents a text that paradoxically threatens multiple positions and resists final interpretation, frustrating later feminists' propensity to either embrace or repudiate literary forebears.

Furthermore, Barrett Browning connects suffering and self-sacrifice to the woman writer. She claims to have taken up her topic because it was previously unconsidered and best suited to a woman: "with a peculiar reference to Eve's allotted grief, which, considering that self-sacrifice belonged to her womanhood, and the consciousness of originating the Fall to her offence, appeared to me imperfectly apprehended hitherto, and more expressible by a woman than a man" (vi). Later in her preface, Barrett Browning explains that in another one of the collection's poems, "Vision of Poets", she "endeavoured to indicate the necessary relations of genius to suffering and self-sacrifice" (ix). Whereas earlier women writers justified their writing—typically a man's task—by appealing to their religious responsibility and downplaying their gender, by the nineteenth and twentieth centuries, women writers were recognizing a parallel between the rhetoric of self-giving in motherhood and self-giving in the creative process.

Christians as sufferers, women as sufferers, writers as sufferers—what do we make of these associations in the twenty-first century? Annie Dillard makes a great deal of them in her creative nonfiction book *Holy the Firm*. In three sections that narrate three consecutive days, it introduces the beauty of the world, grapples with the problem of evil, and proposes a mystical-artistic substitutionary redemption as an answer to the agonizing question of why, if God exists and is good, "Julie Norwich seven years old burnt off her face" in a freak plane accident.[21] Dillard's answer is a self-emptying, Christ-like artist. "A life without sacrifice is an abomination," claims the speaker. The writer—in the case of this book, the specifically female writer—like a "nun," must choose to undergo suffering to bring something good to the reader and the world.[22] For Julie to be saved, a woman who looks like she could be the little girl's mother must self-immolate, like a moth in a candle flame. Describing the artist with masculine pronouns, but implicitly referring to herself as writer-protagonist, Dillard exults,

> His face is flame like a seraph's, lighting the kingdom of God for the people to see; his life goes up in the works; his feet are waxen and salt. He is holy and he is firm, spanning all the long gap with the length of his love, in flawed imitation of Christ on the cross stretched both ways unbroken and thorned.[23]

Nearly 600 years later, Julie Norwich's salvation may be as dangerous as her namesake's.

Amnesia, Genre, Redemption

> Can a poetic text accomplish what philosophy and theology cannot?
> —Harold Schweizer, *Suffering and the Remedy of Art*

Dillard is just one of the many contemporary women writers whose literature explores and exposes the gendered and religious dynamics of women's suffering and self-sacrifice, and it is to a number of these writers that this book turns. From Adrienne Rich's poetic critique of motherhood as institution to Chimamanda Adichie's narratives of imbricated postcolonial, religious, and patriarchal complexities, women's writings in the past fifty years have insistently challenged their readers with representations and interrogations of suffering. My own reading of women writers—in research, in preparation for teaching, in quiet Saturday afternoons with volumes tugged down from the library's new acquisition shelves—confronts me with this repetition, with this obsession, with the weight of this concern. Women continue to write about suffering in ways that grip and haunt their readers, offering no easy answers, just a strangely mingled loveliness and sorrow that raises profound questions about the relation of ethics and aesthetics, the interaction of the literary and the material world, of suffering and language, flesh and word.

I have begun a book on contemporary women writers with an overview of their forebearers for several reasons. First, I do so to counteract the amnesia Rich, Mary Daly, and others have recognized working to erase the history of women's thought, so that each generation thinks it must begin anew. Women have been exploring questions of suffering and redemption for as long as they have been writing in English, and doubtless longer. Second, I begin the book in this way to provide a contextual framework for the ongoing presence of the religious—and the specifically Christian—in conversations of suffering and self-sacrifice, whether explicit or latent. In the West, such conversations, and their interactions with the particularity of gender, are indelibly marked by this religious history. Third, I do so to set up the complexity of questions surrounding suffering and redemption and to introduce the repeated structuring force of dangerous yet inescapable paradoxes.

And these *are* complex questions. Suffering is everywhere. We know suffering, many of us, in our bones. We know suffering in our psyches, in our bodies, in our friendships. We know suffering in the strange vivid drip of chemotherapy, in the images accosting us on the evening news, in the mass graves of Rwanda, in the memory of the Shoah, in the speakouts and Take-Back-the-Night rallies of second-wave feminism. And we know suffering in our poems, in our novels, in our plays. Suffering plays in ten thousand places. Yet, as numerous commentators have noted, contemporary Western society displays an unprecedentedly negative view of suffering and pain, leaving us with few resources for understanding its ubiquity and power—and raising the question at the heart of this book: how *ought* we to read suffering? This aversion to suffering has been variously linked to an Enlightenment optimism about social and scientific developments that could mitigate or even abolish human suffering; secular attacks on a Christian imagination that valued suffering as redemptive; technological developments that overwhelm Westerners with stories and images of suffering; and late-capitalist proliferations of choice, myths of achievement, and even heavily marketed pharmaceuticals. Whatever its cause, the widespread view of suffering as straightforwardly and universally *bad* has led, I argue, to a foreshortened cultural view of suffering in its complexity and nuance.

It is against this backdrop of widespread negative views of suffering that a number of contemporary discourses dealing in ethics, including philosophy, feminism, and theology, have forwarded redemptive suffering as a model of admirable response to (or responsibility for) some other in need. These paradigms of chosen suffering, or self-sacrifice, as ethical behavior have not gone uncontested; as I will highlight in the rest of this chapter, in some locations they have been subject to serious debates. The fact that such paradigms of redemptive suffering have been offered in the past fifty years in various disciplines indicates another side to the contemporary views on suffering, one that seeks to embrace rather than repudiate suffering as a possible ethical choice. But if the dangers that attend a wholesale rejection of suffering include flattening its meaning and leaving subjects with a limited capacity to interpret and respond, a danger that attends these ethical models of redemptive suffering is their forgetfulness: of specific vulnerable others and also of the history of redemptive suffering in Western culture and its myriad religious and gendered connotations—and implications.

In the following pages, I explicate two troubling and related dynamics I recognize in the current state of literary ethics, namely the prevalence of a deracinated redemptive suffering and the argument between approaches that emphasize the structural relationship of text and reader and those that emphasize narrative content. These dynamics ultimately lead me to turn away from theory to the women's writings that are the focus of chapters 2–5, but to do justice to those literary texts, I take a detour through twentieth-century feminist theory and Christian theology. This interdisciplinary rapprochement guides me, in the final section of this chapter, into a meditation on suffering and language. Seeking to do justice to the relationship between word and flesh, I lay out the hypothesis that guides this book—that contemporary literary writings by women challenge and correct the ethical systems of redemptive sacrifice appearing in numerous recent theoretical discourses and most especially in the new ethical literary criticism, and that they do so by engaging in a dynamically related ethics of literary representation and ethics of readerly attention.

For-the-Other

> It is perhaps thus that the for-the-other—the most upright relation to the other—is the most profound adventure of subjectivity, its ultimate intimacy.
> —Emmanuel Levinas, "Useless Suffering"

Near the end of *The Singularity of Literature*, Derek Attridge describes the reader's relationship to the literary text: "Being responsible for the other involves assuming the other's needs (if only the need to exist), affirming it, sustaining it, being prepared to give up my own wants and satisfactions for the sake of the other."[24] In a monograph that moves from theorizing creativity to reading to performance to ethics, this claim about responsibility arrives as a sort of climax, a strong vision of the ultimate role of the reader faced with a book.

Taken out of context, however, the characterization is redolent of *other* roles. "Assuming the other's needs," "affirming," "sustaining," "being prepared to give up my own wants and satisfactions"—these are all traits commonly expected of mothers in Western culture. Clustered together as they are in Attridge's sentence, the words suggest a portrait of self-sacrificing femininity. Or—and this second possibility is not unrelated to the first—the characterization of readerly responsibility might call to mind the Christian ethical ideal of being one's brother's keeper: *Greater love hath no man than this.*

Attridge, however, fails to acknowledge the gendered and religious connotations in this passage—and, indeed, fails to acknowledge them in his entire monograph. In this forgetfulness (for I do not assume it is a willful elision), *The Singularity of Literature* exemplifies two trends in the late twentieth-century turn to ethics in literary criticism. The first is a fascination with suffering-for-the-other, or redemptive suffering. The second is a persistent lack of engagement with the gendered and religious echoes that reverberate around an ethics of suffering and a lack of engagement with the particulars of suffering more generally. In this book, I take great pains to correct this erasure, to *do justice* to suffering and to literature.

The turn to ethics in literary studies has been documented widely by scholars from Lawrence Buell to Robert Eaglestone to Marjorie Garber, in the introductions to special topic journal issues, essay collections arising out of conference themes, and a spate of monographs.[25] As many have noted, one of the few shared characteristics of these accounts of the ethical turn, other than the claim that such a turn began sometime in the eighties, is an admission of cacophony, of critical dissonance over what precisely is meant by "ethics" and what exactly brought about this renewed interest among literary scholars. Generally, commentators recount that after decades of formalism and more recent postmodern suspicion of normative ethics as another disciplining domination, the political atmosphere and global events of the eighties, developments in numerous disciplines, late-in-life stock-taking by several theorists (including Michel Foucault and Roland Barthes), and even anxieties over the social importance of literary studies led to an increased interest in ethics as such among literary critics. And changes in the philosophical discourse of ethics itself—brought about, as sociologist Zygmunt Bauman explains, not only by philosophers' linguistic turns and the rejection of Enlightenment norms but also by rapid changes in technology, altered political structures, and the force of globalization—resulted in overlapping concerns for philosophers, scholars concerned with a variety of marginalized positions, and literary critics more generally.[26] Amid all these changes, many critics admit that while the term *ethics* was not a favored one in the mid-twentieth century, African American, Marxist, and especially feminist scholars were engaged in profoundly ethical critiques all along, and twentieth-century literature itself thematized any number of ethical concerns, often arising from human suffering: contemporary literature, for many, is "literature after Auschwitz." Finally, a concurrent move by numerous philosophers who began to appeal to literature for their ethical reflections, including Martha Nussbaum, Richard Rorty, and Alasdair MacIntyre, further confirmed the sense that as of the end of the twentieth century, ethics and literature were bound in a project of mutual discovery.

As Andrew Gibson tells it, this ethical turn in literary criticism had two main camps.[27] "Moral criticism," predicated on a mimetic understanding

of literature as an exemplary source for ethical reflection in its representation of human particularity and complexity, emphasizes narrative and
experience. This moral criticism is popular among neo-Aristotelians like
Nussbaum and literary scholars like Wayne Booth, who argues in *The
Company We Keep: An Ethics of Fiction* that authors are like wise friends.[28]
The "new ethical criticism," by contrast, is much more influenced by
poststructuralist theory, focusing on the formal features of literature and
the relationship between the reader and the text-as-other, rather than on
the content of literature as representing ethical dilemmas in the material
world. The new ethical criticism draws selectively from the discipline of
philosophical ethics, relying heavily on continental philosophers. Arising
from these theorists, the ethics to which late twentieth-century literary
studies turned is marked by a noncodified attention to specificity and difference (as opposed to universality), embodied relationship and affect (as
opposed to abstract, rational mental exercises), and limitless responsibility
(as opposed to laws of justice). Terms like *difference, alterity, other(ness),
relation, face-to-face, intersubjective, endlessness, passivity, hospitality, openness,*
and *responsibility* are repeated and echoed. Although not all the writers
who use these terms call their ethics "postmodern," "postmodern ethics" is the label under which these writers' works typically are subsumed.
Thus, key texts in the new ethical literary discourse—including J. Hillis
Miller's *Ethics of Reading,* Adam Zachary Newton's *Narrative Ethics*, Robert
Eaglestone's *Ethical Criticism*, Jill Robbins's *Altered Reading,* and Attridge's
The Singularity of Literature—all deal extensively in these vocabularies and
cite their poststructuralist origins.

This concern with the *ought* in literary theory does not primarily focus
new ethical critics' attention on thematic issues of justice and ethical relating within narratives; even more characteristically, it focuses critics' attention on readers' relationships to texts themselves. In other words, "literary
ethics" for new ethical critics is typically an *Ethics of Reading,* as Miller's
1987 study was aptly titled. In this way, the new ethical literary criticism
participates in deconstructive reading practices, following Miller's proposal that "there is a necessary ethical moment in the act of reading as
such."[29] The culture wars of the eighties often painted poststructuralist
theory as a radically disengaged, even antihumanist, play within the fragments of a sensible world, but many scholars have emphasized the ways
in which poststructuralism was engaged implicitly in an ethical project

all along, particularity in its uncovering of domination and its reappraisal of difference.[30] Although some continue to vilify postmodern theory as unconcerned with real-world problems,[31] practitioners of the new ethical criticism are more likely to agree with John Caputo's claim, "Postmodernism . . . is not relativism or skepticism, as its uncomprehending critics almost daily charge, but minutely close attention to detail, a sense for the complexity and multiplicity of things, for close readings, for detailed histories, for sensitivity to differences."[32] Even Jacques Derrida insists in an interview from the nineties that "close reading" is necessary for "political, ethical and juridical responsibility," that deconstruction is a project that should "not simply stay in the library."[33]

To do justice to a text parallels doing justice to a person in a postmodern ethical mode: it is a discipline, as Attridge highlights, of openness and attentiveness, the suspension or emptying of the self and the receptive alertness to the otherness of the text.[34] This self-emptying receptivity to otherness arises in large part from the influence of Emmanuel Levinas, whose importance it would be hard to exaggerate. As Simon Critchley notes, "In the English-speaking world, Levinas's name [had by the late nineties] an awesome, almost talismanic, power in contemporary theoretical debate."[35] Levinas claims in his major work *Totality and Infinity* that the face-to-face interaction is one of limitless, nonreciprocal responsibility for the well-being of the other and that this relationship constitutes subjectivity.[36] His influence is apparent in critiques by the likes of Derrida and Lyotard that question modern philosophical norms of totalizing narratives and the privileging of control, full knowledge, and freedom. In fact, Levinas's implicit influence is at least partly responsible for the shift in late twentieth-century thought to the privileging of difference and otherness. In the words of Norman Ravvin, "As I write [in the late nineties], and possibly still as you read, Levinas is a kind of prophet. Through his interrogation of the Western philosophical tradition he has become the source of one of the key paradigm shifts of postmodern culture: a return to ethics, a remaking of our tradition in the direction of the other."[37]

Levinas's metaethical paradigm, especially in his later work, is virtually obsessed with passivity, suffering, and self-sacrifice. His ethics is fundamentally a "suffering for the suffering of the other."[38] Levinas writes of the twentieth century as one "of unutterable suffering . . . in which the suffering of suffering, the suffering for the useless suffering of the other, the just suffering in me for the unjustifiable suffering of the other, opens suffering to the ethical perspective of the inter-human"; such a suffering-for-the-other becomes the "supreme ethical principle."[39] This ethical paradigm of suffering for the other is unremittingly asymmetrical: I am endlessly responsible for the Other whom I face, even to the extent of being responsible for that Other's wounding of *me*. Levinas's terminology in *Otherwise Than Being* even turns toward that of the hostage situation.[40] This is a radical ethics that arguably seeks to upend the structures that allow those in power to bolster their power by relating to others as resources or nonentities.

Such a description of ethical interactions is appealing for many reasons. As Ewa Płonowska Ziarek explains, the hostage metaphor isn't intended to place the victim in a situation of responsibility but rather to undo the Hegelian claim that alterity is a negation of the same in ongoing competition.[41] Instead, Ziarek argues, "By displacing the judging subject into a position of an addressee, the performative effect of obligation also restores a paradoxical possibility of an address for a victim"—the one who in most situations has no chance to voice requests or demands, in this situation, has a chance to do so and to "[call] the subject to responsibility for the social wrongs."[42] Levinas's paradigm, in other words, offers the hope of inversion, that the responsibility to care for the other in a self-sacrificial way will be taken up by the one who does not usually suffer: it challenges "egology," or a self-centered emphasis on consumption and competition.

Yet one wonders: what are the chances? Erin Biviano argues that Levinas's "is really an ethic for the offender who should be restrained but is most unlikely to listen to the summons of the other. Victims who are trampled by the heedless or cruelly powerful need hardly be exhorted to consider the other."[43] On the basis of this concern and of concern for Levinas's dubious gender talk, his writing has been subjected to numerous feminist critiques within the discipline of philosophy. Simone de Beauvoir, Luce Irigaray, and more recently Tina Chanter among others have noted the dangerous dynamics of Levinas's propensity to align his philosophy with the gendered symbolic, locating "otherness," "home," and "hospitality" in the feminine and speaking of the womb as an ethical site par excellence.[44] He writes in *Otherwise Than Being*, for instance, that "maternity" is "a bodily suffering for another, the body as passivity and renouncement, a pure undergoing."[45] Feminist debates tend to center on questions of whether women can be subjects in Levinas's ethical paradigm or just "others"; whether Levinas's "feminization" of philosophy through its emphasis on responsibility, intersubjectivity, and embodiment dignifies women and grants significance to their suffering or overlooks the need to change their situation; whether the tendency, rather than upsetting the hierarchical binary, is to further subject the already-subjected with a command that will be better heard by the vulnerable than by the powerful to whom it is aimed.

This gendered dimension of Levinas's writing—the gendered origins of sacrificial suffering as an ethical paradigm—is generally overlooked in literary appropriations and celebrations of his philosophy. Literary critics borrow selectively from *Totality and Infinity* and *Otherwise Than Being*, emphasizing the face-to-face encounter or the heady concepts of the Saying versus the Said. Thus, although the new ethical criticism is marked by a vocabulary of receptivity, openness, hospitality, responsibility, and care that is represented explicitly in Levinas's writing by the figure of the motherly woman and implicitly gendered feminine in a Western cultural imaginary, literary practitioners of the new ethical criticism have tended to show a marked oblivion to these gendered dynamics. But the gendered dynamics *matter*, because they highlight the dangers of celebrating passivity and care as an ethical ideal; they underscore the cultural norms and histories that have asked for more passivity and care out of some than others. They mitigate against the strange propensity to theorize ethics around a decontextualized, genderless and raceless and classless subject who is actually implicitly male and white and privileged. The new ethical criticism champions difference, but at points it seems to overlook what a difference difference makes—a generalized disavowal of freedom may not sound so appealing to a slave; a celebration of passivity may not be convincing for one who suffers violent abuse; an idealizing of chosen suffering may not inspire one who faces chronic pain.

Of course, theory travels. Edward Said first made this claim in 1983, writing of both the inevitable diminishment of radical ideas as they move from their original context and the necessity of borrowing, although nearly ten years later Said suggested in "Traveling Theory Reconsidered" that theory might not just be domesticated by the travel but also reinvigorated.[46] In *Shadows of Ethics*, Geoffrey Harpham asserts that theory *is* travel, elucidating the process of theorizing in terms of movement: "if a fact is to become theoretical, it must travel beyond its original context, suffering a decay or degradation in the process, losing something of its original context-specific solidity."[47] The suffering language is important here: Harpham translates Said's earlier claims into a late twentieth-century critical vocabulary that celebrates the ethical good of passivity and sacrifice. The concrete particular must *submit* to suffering and loss in the process of becoming theory, sacrificing its specificity for the sake of the *other*, in this case valuable generalization within another context.

Yet the question of what is lost continues to haunt. In the case of Levinas, what is sacrificed as his concepts travel into literary criticism is not just the particularity of gender that textures his original writings but also their theological origins. As Ravvin points out, Levinas's emphasis on redemptive suffering may be linked to his Judaic conception of the world,[48] and Levinas was prone to cite the biblical origins of his concept of ethics as care for the vulnerable other. Yet as Newton argues, literary critics on the whole have tended to ignore Levinas's Judaism, the fact that he wrote as both a philosopher and a theologian, the way even his philosophical texts were marked by Hebrew Scriptures and tradition.[49] There are, of course, reasons for this elision. If postmodern ethics rises to replace religious systems of ethics in a secular age, Levinas's ethics (divested of scriptural source materials) suggests a nonfoundational, nonnormative paradigm for ethical relating as an attractive alternative. Thus, to emphasize its origins in the biblical call to welcome the stranger and care for the widow and orphan would have undermined the suitability of such an ethics as a secular alternative in literary studies. To travel as theory into another context, Levinas's ethics had to sacrifice its religious particularity—an immense and ironic injustice, in Newton's perspective.

Considering the new ethical criticism's inadequate concern for the risks and dangers of infinite welcome and idealized sacrifice, we do well to heed Rich's warning in *Of Woman Born*, "From a thoughtful woman's point of view, no ethical ideal has deserved our unconditional respect and adherence, because in every ethics crimes against women are mysteriously unnamed or glossed over."[50] A certain hyperbolic, almost manically poetic, energy underlies Levinas's rhetoric, emphasizing the ethical good of self-sacrifice for others' suffering in a way that discourages questioning of the potential dangers of such a system. This has led some to critique

Levinas, in particular, as too reactionary to the ethical structures that pre-ceded him and not quite concrete or practical enough to account for the everyday ethical challenges of particular human beings.[51] I am less con-cerned with critiquing Levinas than with challenging his literary appro-priators; and even then, I am less concerned with showing what other literary ethicists have done *wrong* than with suggesting an alternative.

The elision of gender and religion from the new ethical criticism is not solely the result of a travel-weary Levinasian theory; it is also traceable to the sorts of literary texts scholars have tended to privilege in their ethical readings. Henry James, Joseph Conrad, James Joyce, Charles Dickens, J. M. Coetzee, and Fyodor Dostoevsky hold pride of place in books by Andrew Newton, J. Hillis Miller, Derek Attridge, Andrew Gibson, and others, not to mention the many edited collections and journal articles that contribute to the ethical turn. Nineteenth-century novels, which are also particularly popular among moral critics interested in their realism, and the difficult novels (and to a lesser extent poems) of high modernism, most of them by men, seem to occupy ethical critics, along with a smattering of avant-garde experiments. These preferences are not surprising, but they do shape the theorizing of literary ethics that arises from them, helping to explain the strong emphasis on form and the infrequent references to gender, race, or religion. It is not accidental that one of the few literary-ethical contributions that engages with feminist responses to Levinasian suffering reads Jean Rhys and Anaïs Nin, although the chapter that does so stands out as distinct.[52]

Along these same lines, it is also not accidental that most of the contem-porary writing by women I turn to in this book fall under the rubric of what Linda Hutcheon calls "historiographic metafiction" in *A Poetics of Postmod-ernism*.[53] I seek, with the new ethical critics, to theorize not only an ethics *of reading* (following my question, "How ought we to read [literary texts]?") but also an ethics *of suffering* ("How ought we to read suffering [in texts and bodies]?"). I am entering a discourse that has championed redemp-tive suffering as an ethics of reading, which in many of its theoretical texts bears a metaphorical, or perhaps microcosmic, relationship to broader questions of ethics and responsibility—a troubling fuzziness about the ways in which passivity, hospitality, and limitless responsibility between reader and text are different from the same stances between two embodied humans. The most helpful texts for thinking with as we struggle over how an ethics predicated on readerly suffering relates to an ethics of human suffering more broadly—the challenge of linking word and flesh, form and content—are those that both thematize suffering and allegorize reading. Historiographic metafiction, according to Hutcheon, "challenges . . . both any naïve realist concept of representation but also any equally naïve textualist or formalist assertion of the total separation of art from the world"; "postmodern fiction challenges both structuralist/modernist formalism and any simple mimeticist/realist notions of referentiality."[54] Hutcheon names in such texts' relationship to representation the double move of embrace and critique I recognize in my literary texts' approaches to religion and redemptive suffering: they don't deny representation altogether but contest it, "invoking" yet also "problematiz[ing]."[55] Hutcheon also insists that postmodern literature is "inescapably political," that it highlights the inseparability of aesthetics and ideology, an insight marginalized groups have known all along.[56] Rather than a primarily formalist reading of high modern literature's challenges or a referential reading of earlier realist fiction's character-driven narratives, I read in this project's literary texts *both* allegories of reading *and* references to enfleshed suffering: in fact, I read these two as indivisible.

The Language of Suffering

> The need to lend a voice to suffering is a condition of all truth.
> —Theodor Adorno, *Negative Dialectics*

Suffering gives rise to full libraries and apparently endless conversations as individuals forward competing definitions and distinctions. These distinctions often rely on comparisons of suffering and pain: for instance, for some, "suffering" signifies an ongoing state, whereas "pain" signifies an acute moment; for others, "suffering" signifies a psychological reality, whereas "pain" signifies a physical one; and some sources treat "suffering" as negative, but "pain" as positive. Needless to say, these disparate definitions *matter* in the theoretical, medical, and popular discussions. In this book, I adopt a broader sense of suffering as undergoing—or actively allowing oneself to be affected by—some outside force, most often pain or distress. Furthermore, "suffering" may be understood as both the action and the pain or distress itself.

As such, suffering frequently involves passivity, and passivity typically takes the female gender association in the Western binary that associates activity with maleness. The etymological roots of the adjective "passive" link it to suffering, so that to be "passive" is not only to be subject to outside forces or to be unresisting but also, in earlier uses, to be subject, specifically, to suffering. Importantly connected to the adjective "passive" is the noun "passion," which shares its Latin root and therefore also has its origins in concepts of suffering: the first *Oxford English Dictionary* (*OED*) entry for "passion" is "senses related to physical suffering and pain," which links its history of usage to both the theological vocabulary for Christ's suffering during his last days ("the Passion of the Christ") and the specific suffering of martyrs. The word also has a long history of use to signify not suffering in particular but any "senses relating to emotional or mental states," especially strong ones, whether they are anger, love, sexual desire, or enthusiasm. The English language, thus, shaped as it is by the Christian tradition, bears not only a gendered stance of passivity but also a semantic link between Christ's Passion and *all* suffering, between openness to suffering and openness to any feeling at all, positive or negative. Passivity and passion, to their etymological cores, remind us that human receptivity is a profoundly ambivalent phenomenon. Although we may distinguish between the actively chosen suffering for some good end and the passively experienced suffering of bodily frailty or human oppression, their overabundance of semantic possibilities reminds us of the paradoxical presence of potential goodness within passion and passivity as well as the pains and dangers.

"Self-sacrifice," a helpful shorthand for the chosen suffering that generally seeks to prevent or redeem the suffering of an other, is even more closely related, etymologically, to religion. The *OED* offers as a first definition for "sacrifice, *n*.":

> Primarily, the slaughter of an animal (often including the subsequent consumption of it by fire) as an offering to God or a deity. Hence, in wider sense, the surrender to God or a deity, for the purpose of propitiation or homage, of some object of possession. Also applied *fig.* to the offering of prayer, thanksgiving, penitence, submission, or the like.

Indeed, the Latin *sacrificium* means "to make holy." Common usage of the term "sacrifice," including in the phrase "self-sacrifice," works by way of metaphor, originating in the long history of animal offerings to deities that plays both a literal and figurative role in Jewish and Christian thought.

This focus on the language of suffering and sacrifice also highlights its contextually determined and nuanced meanings in different cultural locations. Which is to say, while the *OED* may offer a handful of definitions, the actual, embodied experience of suffering has a boundless series of significances, shaped by the particularity of each individual person who suffers as well as the cultural location in which she does so. As Arne Johan Vetlesen argues throughout his book *A Philosophy of Pain*, cultures mediate the *meaning* of any pain, physiological or psychical (if there can be any such distinction), arising from inevitable or avoidable "natural causes" or from violence or injustice.[57] Thus—and this distinction will be important as this book progresses—the very pangs of childbirth, even if the muscles contract in precisely the same way (and one wonders if they do), may have a different meaning, a distinctly understood significance, for a woman in contemporary Detroit, Michigan, and a woman in contemporary Lagos, Nigeria, not to mention the challenge of history. This cultural mediation further highlights the role of literature in exploring suffering, as the particularity and complexity of literary representations emphasize the *difference* as well as the symbolic (or linguistic) meaning of pain even in incarnate life.

While "suffering" is difficult to define, categorize, or standardize across locations and times, it is also notoriously difficult to describe. Numerous scholars have asserted that suffering cannot be represented in language, even as it demands representation. This phenomenon is perhaps most famously propounded by Elaine Scarry in *The Body in Pain*. Physical pain, Scarry argues, isolates individuals in silence: it "ensures this unshareability through its resistance to language" and further "does not simply resist language but actively destroys it."[58] Decades ahead of Scarry, Simone Weil insisted that those who are "afflicted" (her term for profoundly mingled physical, emotional, and social suffering) "have no words to express what is happening to them" and become "anonymous."[59] Dorothee Sölle draws on Weil in her landmark work *Suffering* to argue that suffering inevitably leads to silence and isolation.[60] With more optimism than Scarry, Sölle provides a model for the amelioration of profound suffering that requires the sufferer, who in phase one is "numb and mute," to find "language of lament, of crying, of pain."[61] This language, in phase two, can lead to the conflict and action necessary for change in phase three.[62] Many critics since Weil, Sölle, and Scarry have drawn on this model of suffering's resistance to language and the mysterious power of reclaimed language for suffering (which often takes shape as literature), including Harold Schweizer, who also notes the rich recent medical discourse exploring the need for suffering patients to give word to their complaints.

"Suffering," as a sign, sets off a signifying chain. It is enmeshed in complex histories, histories complicated by particularities of gender, sex, race, politics, class, religion, and justice, and although this complexity is often overlooked in discursive treatments of suffering, it is radically apparent in much contemporary women's literary writing. Because the very idea of suffering implies not just an is but an ought, it functions by way of contrast: suffering is value-valenced, contextual. Suffering by many definitions is pain, ongoing pain, whether it is physical or psychical, emotional or spiritual. Suffering is not well-being; it is not health; it is not happiness or wholeness or good. It is a teleological inversion. Self-sacrifice, in that it is a chosen form of suffering or of acute pain or loss, muddles the equation, because it claims a certain goodness for the badness, a certain buying-back of the state that should be by capitulation to that which ought not be. This is the paradox of redemption, the tension found in Norwich, Lanyer, Barrett Browning, Dillard, and countless other recent women writers.

Yet another layer of complexity surrounding suffering and self-sacrifice—beyond definitional debates, religious connotations, unrepresentability, and incommensurability—is contemporary culture's noteworthy aversion to suffering itself. Not only do writers like Vetlesen and Susan Sontag locate a pervasive negative view of suffering in contemporary Western society, but subjects within that society evince a marked difficulty attending to suffering.[63] Sölle argues that the twentieth century has witnessed an astonishing "indifference to the suffering of others," founded in a class-privilege-based apathy that protects by leveling out human experience, diminishing both the highs and lows of emotional life, and resulting in a "banal optimism" that disallows the perception of sufferings.[64] Sharon Welch describes a similar phenomenon among the middle classes who, faced by disappointments in past efforts to relieve human suffering and lulled by the relative comfort of their lives, have traded hope for cynicism.[65]

According to some, this aversion to suffering is rooted in its association with death, which is another reality contemporary Western society has a hard time acknowledging. Difficulties with taking in the full measure of human suffering and the full complexity and challenge of self-sacrifice perhaps also arise, as I mention earlier, from a century of unheard-of violence and agony, the rise of a consumer-driven culture of pain management, and technological developments that have exposed us to an unprecedented number of images and stories of global human suffering.

Ironically—or perhaps not surprisingly—this era of Western culture's disavowal of suffering is the one that produced a postmodern theory fascinated with revaluing it. At the same time, the disavowals challenged other traditions that had championed passion and passivity, sparking debates within feminist ethics and Christian theology. It is to these two discourses we now turn.

Suffrage and Care

1. Prayers, *esp.* intercessory prayers, intercessions. *Arch.*
10. A voice or voting power in a matter. *Obs.*
—"suffrage, n.," *Oxford English Dictionary*

The history of Western feminism is a history of reevaluating suffering both imposed and ostensibly chosen in self-sacrifice; through the years, many of its rallying cries and central debates have crystallized around these vocabularies, and first-wave feminism participated in (and doubtless contributed to) the widespread contemporary disavowal of suffering. Matilda Joslyn Gage famously asserted in 1893,

> The whole theory regarding woman, under christianity [*sic*], has been based upon the conception that she had no right to live for herself alone. Her duty to others has continuously been placed before her and her training has ever been that of self-sacrifice. Taught from the pulpit and legislative halls that she was created for another, that her position must always be secondary even to her children, her right to life, has been admitted only in so far as its reacting effect upon another could be predicated.[66]

Gage calls these "lessons of self-sacrifice and obedience" "fatal."[67] Her book *Woman, Church, and State* exposed a long history of women's oppression by church and state power, and she worked for years with Susan B. Anthony and Elizabeth Cady Stanton on women's rights in the United States. Stanton, too, spoke out against the common socialization of women to suffer for the sake of men, claiming in 1895, "Men think that self-sacrifice is the most charming of all the cardinal virtues for women, and in order to keep it in healthy working order, they make opportunities for its illustration as often as possible."[68]

Feminists have continued to struggle over the relationship between self-development and self-sacrifice. The most obvious site of this debate over the past thirty years has been in the realm of feminist care ethics, which posits a model of ethics predicated on self-giving service. Carol Gilligan's *In a Different Voice* set off a wave of work on women's moral reasoning and participated in a trend of looking at women's particular experiences as previously unacknowledged sources of insight into humanity. Gilligan's research attended to women's own descriptions of their moral decision making and led her to claim that developmental models like Lawrence Kohlberg's categorized women as coming up short in ethical development because they were based on men's experiences, presumed to be universal but actually particular to culture and gender. Gilligan thus presents a model of women's moral development that is much more attuned to narrative, relationship, and responsibility than justice- and rule-based anonymous models of morality.[69]

Gilligan notes that in many women's descriptions of their moral processing, the word "selfish" plays a key role as an undesirable label,[70] and in discussing this phenomenon, she looks to turn-of-the-century feminists like Elizabeth Cady Stanton, relating the history of their struggle to expose the ideology that led to women's expected passive suffering and self-abnegation. As women's rights are gained, Gilligan asserts, women's moral judgment is also altered, "seasoning mercy with justice by enabling women to consider it moral to care not only for others but for themselves."[71] The work of the early feminists increased women's ability to correct their endless self-giving with a degree of self-care, and further developments in women's rights could continue this process. Rather than idealizing a limitless giving of the self, Gilligan recognizes that just as male-dominated conceptions of ethics as justice and rights benefits from the corrective nuancing of an ethics of care and responsibility, so a typically feminine ethics of care and responsibility is nuanced by appreciation for justice and rights.[72] Thus, Gilligan suggests a risky dialectic, both asserting the underacknowledged value and legitimacy of self-sacrificial giving and relationality as a mode of ethical judgment and also questioning its goodness if unbalanced or unlimited by its other.

Intriguingly, Carol Gilligan's description of a specifically feminine ethics presciently predicts the postmodern ethics many literary scholars would soon embrace, emphasizing *others*, *responsibility*, and *attending*. Ruth Groenhout, one of the few scholars to note these parallels, lists the similarities between Levinas's ethics and care ethics as attention to the "relational self, embodiment, and the particularity of the other person."[73] Ziarek also offhandedly comments: "Levinas's distrust of the contractual community, his politicization of the seemingly 'private' virtues, such as love, patience, and relations to others, might be associated in an uncanny way with certain feminist alternatives to liberal citizenship based on the feminine 'ethics of care.' "[74]

As some feminists have questioned Levinasian ethics, however, they also have debated the good of a parallel ethics of care: some embrace an ethics of care because it champions women's experience, whereas others argue that women's role as caregivers is not natural to them but a deeply embedded expectation of patriarchy and that to idealize it or to look to it as a source of ethical insight is a simple capitulation to the powers that continue to oppress women. The typical counterargument is that such a devaluation of women's experiences is itself a capitulation to the masculine ideal of generalized justice, rationality, and rights, a desire to erase the difference of women's experience under the false universal of the masculine. And the argument continues.[75]

These debates have carried on for three decades with no sign of an end. Are women *naturally* self-givers, caregivers, self-sacrificers, passive welcomers? Does the fact that women's special propensity to suffer patiently for children and other loved ones is empirically observable mean that it is *good* for them, that it is best? How do we understand "natural"? In other words, is women's suffering and self-sacrifice rooted in the material or in the symbolic? Does it arise primarily, as Rich influentially asserts in *Of Woman Born*, from oppressive Jewish and Christian teaching, from the story of Eve's fall and curse? Or does Jewish and Christian teaching simply provide explanations of how things *are*, as stories of origin often do? Can the Christian paradigm of redemption through suffering offer women in their daily experience a certain dignity, or is its function more oppressive, more fatally dangerous? Have the rise of secularism and its critique of Christian tradition actually complicated these issues by unduly demonizing all chosen suffering? And how does the underacknowledged centrality of religious texts in the women's suffrage movement continue to affect feminist discourse?

Indeed, Elizabeth Cady Stanton worked energetically on a project called *The Woman's Bible*, a two-volume revision published in the 1890s that critiqued and removed misogynist and objectionable passages, asserted women's intrinsic value, and provided commentary from key feminist thinkers of the day on every biblical passage having anything to do with women. Engaging in a religious critique that was not quite a rejection, Stanton asserts that "from the inauguration of the movement for women's emancipation the Bible has been used to hold her in the 'divinely ordained sphere,' prescribed in the Old and New Testaments."[76] Ultimately, *The Woman's Bible* reminds us that first-wave feminism is steeped in textual and institutional religious critique and particularly critique of traditional Christian teachings on women's role as exemplary sufferer. The critical hermeneutics through which first-wave feminists approached culture and religious texts, allowing them to pursue resignification rather than outright rejection, will be an important feature in the later women's writing I discuss in this book.

Yet while first-wave feminists explicitly engaged with religious texts and traditions, influential second-wave feminists tended more toward virulent critique, a practice that is perhaps responsible for the contemporary silence in much feminist ethical theory around issues of religion, even when its language of suffering and care still echoes with the biblical already-said.

Hilde Lindemann offers a telling example of the ongoing presence of religious language but strange elisions within feminist discourse. In her chapter on "Feminist Ethics of Care and Responsibility," Lindemann tells a hypothetical narrative to convey the complexities of justice and care ethics that interrogates the ethical culpability of a Nazi's wife's care of her husband. Lindemann uses the phrase "not my will but thine be done" as shorthand for wifely submission in an ethic of care as "engagement with another's will,"[77] never acknowledging that this language is actually a quote of the Gospel writer Luke's account of Christ's words the night before his crucifixion (Luke 22:42). In her chapter, Lindemann does not relate feminist care ethics to Christian ethics or the religious history of Christianity, but her use of this phrase (and the strangeness of its King James language in comparison with the rest of the narrative) manifests a deep, linguistic cultural association of women's self-sacrificial giving to the Christian tradition and the figure of Christ.

Dangerous Memory: Surely He Hath Borne Our Griefs

> . . . in humility count others more significant than yourselves.
> —Philippians 2:3, English Standard Version

In a Western context, Jewish and Christian religion is perhaps the primary source of redemptive suffering as an ethical paradigm. As the brief history of women's writing that begins this chapter exemplifies, the narrative of creation and fall at the beginning of the Hebrew Scriptures has shaped conceptions of both suffering *and* the feminine. Likewise, the Christian narrative of redemption, one of a God who "emptied himself, taking the form of a slave" (Philippians 2:7, NRSV), suffered torture and death, and then returned to life to bring life to humanity, has proven a powerful paradigm in the Western imagination. As exemplified by Dame Julian's provocative text, a strong tradition of teaching suggests that Christians ought also to interpret their own sufferings as bound up with Christ's. These teachings have notably affected the cultural and linguistic force of suffering in the texts and contexts I address throughout this book.

It is against this backdrop of Jewish and Christian significance for suffering that many thinkers of the past three centuries have rebelled. Per Joseph Amato's account, "[Enlightenment] philosophers had among their most important goals the removal of suffering from human life and the mysterious from human consciousness."[78] Nietzsche, Marx, and Freud, Paul Ricoeur's three great demystifiers, likewise railed against Christianity as a disciplining force that keeps the masses piously passive in their suffering. And with secularization as the proliferation of possibilities for belief (or unbelief), Charles Taylor argues, the Christian view of suffering as redemptive has been charged with "den[ying] or hamper[ing] human fulfillment."[79] Not to mention the myriad ways in which Christianity (among many religions) has been exposed in the twentieth and twenty-first centuries as a powerful source of political oppression and cause of unjust suffering when married to nationalist or fundamentalist projects. The upshot of these and other developments has been, as Vetlesen recounts, that "for the modern sensibility, shaped as it is by the loss of religion's authority, in terms of both morals and interpretation, it is impossible to see anything else than the sheer negativity in pain, understood as human suffering."[80] Sontag similarly ascribes a shift in understandings of suffering to secularization and the reduced Western involvement in images of Christ's suffering.[81]

Yet this culture oriented against suffering is the context in which numerous theological positions, paralleling developments in postmodern philosophy, have retrieved suffering as the primary ethical good. Valerie Saiving Goldstein, writing in 1960, summarizes this popular theological view: "Sin is the unjustified concern of the self for its own power and prestige; it is the imperialistic drive to close the gap between the individual, separate self and others by reducing those others to the status of mere objects which can then be treated as appendages of the self and manipulated accordingly."[82] Over against such a view of sin, she writes, many midcentury theologians conceived of love (the ethical ideal) as "completely self-giving, taking no thought for its own interests but seeking only the good of the other," to the point of becoming "wholly receptive to the other": suffering (for) the other.[83]

This Christian ethic of self-sacrificing love, however, met with serious critique as feminist theology gained more practitioners in the sixties and seventies. Indeed, twentieth-century theology, continuing the tradition of women's engagement with the dangers of Christian paradigms of redemptive suffering, is one of the most provocative sites of feminist criticism of a generalized ethic of redemptive suffering. Saiving Goldstein's 1960 article was a groundbreaking response to this dominant current in theological ethics, as she asserts that considering the distinct experiences of women results in an importantly different view of the "human situation" than the view typically presented by male theologians as universal.[84] Rather than pride and selfishness like men, she argues, women are more prone to the sins of self-abnegation, of giving too much, of sacrificing the self too fully.[85] Ultimately, Saiving Goldstein's contribution is to challenge the concept of a generalized ethic predicated on self-sacrifice with the particularity of women's experience, and this contribution has been taken up by feminist theologians in the five decades since. This critique parallels the critiques of myriad liberation movements arising in the sixties and seventies that argued for consideration of the particular experiences of gendered, raced, and classed groups, challenging the so-called universal reigning human subject who was, in fact, implicitly white, male, middle-class, and heterosexual. Its methodology also parallels Gilligan's consideration of women's experience and self-articulation as a valuable source for ethical theorizing.

As in the case of Dame Julian's teaching, and poststructuralists' teaching, and care ethicists' teaching, the situation of the subject is key in Christian teachings about the sacrifice of the self: a call to give up one's life, to consider the interests of others more highly than one's own, to participate in suffering rather than cause it—these calls endanger power structures. They undermine the authority of the wealthy, the ruling class, the men of patriarchal privilege. Yet they also endanger the already vulnerable, those already expected to empty themselves, to "make themselves nothing." These teachings can easily be—and indeed have been—unevenly applied to protect the status quo and to ward off danger to those in control. Sölle succinctly names the critique: "most Christian interpretations of suffering . . . [lead] to a justification of masochism."[86]

More recently, however, many theologians have reconsidered redemptive suffering in light of these troubling dynamics of power. Johann-Baptist Metz, for instance, famously considers the Christian meaning of suffering in light of contemporary politics and the way later twentieth-century society prefers to keep suffering out of sight, particularly the suffering of those who have not been history's champions.[87] Rather than emphasizing suffering as a freely chosen ethical practice, Metz considers the reality of suffering as a result of injustices and oppression: remembering the suffering of Christ (the "Christian *memoria passionis*") grants a subversive significance to those who suffer from oppression. Such a perspective is subversive in part simply because of its refusal to participate in the wholly negative view of suffering that prevents subjects from attending to the suffering of others. Yet in Metz's view, "dangerous memory," stories of suffering typically unacknowledged by the politically powerful also, paradoxically, opens up the possibility of an ethic of suffering for the suffering other: "Even rebellion against suffering is fed by the subversive power of remembered suffering. In this sense, suffering is in no way a purely passive, inactive 'virtue.' It is, or can be, the source of socially emancipatory action."[88] Such an understanding of suffering finds its meaning, for Metz, in the scandalous Christian claim that Christ's passion, attested to in Christian memory, promises future hope,[89] resignifying all present suffering in light of its radical temporality. "Dangerous memory," therefore, is dangerous both to reigning political powers that seek to elide the sufferings of the oppressed and *also*, potentially, to the bearers of such memory who seek justice even to the point of sacrificing themselves.

Similar, explicitly political and even more purposefully particularized models of paradoxical Christian redemptive suffering are present in the writings of liberation theologians like James Cone and Dwight Hopkins, womanist theologians like Delores Williams and Emilie Townes, Latin American liberation theologians like Leonardo and Clodovis Boff and Gustavo Gutíerrez, and postcolonial feminist theologians like Kwok Pui-lan and Mercy Amba Oduyoye, all of whom feature in the following chapters. These theologians, like Metz, suggest the subversive power of remembered suffering understood in light of Christian love-as-justice; all, to some degree or another, forward practices of critical hermeneutics that retrieve elided stories, reconsider central Christian texts, and emphasize the particular locations of oppressed groups as significant sources for making meaning and doing theology. All are also subject to critique, not only for their participation in the dangerous Christian revaluing of suffering as redemptive but also for their blind spots to other locations. Just as Saiving Goldstein can be critiqued for her representation of "women" as a generalizable category with little regard for differences of race or class or culture, black and Latin American liberation theologies have been challenged repeatedly for their oblivion to gender. Many of these theologians also turn to literary texts for the dangerous stories they champion, with varying degrees of respect for the literariness of that literature, and in the chapters that follow this one, I will in turn engage them as sources for thinking through the particular paradoxes of redemptive suffering at work in the religiously engaged literary texts to which I offer my own ethical attention.

Writing, Reading: Representation, Attention

Other-Love is writing's first name.
—Hélène Cixous, "Sorties"

Seeking to forge an ethics of suffering that is attentive to gender, to religion, and to how suffering and language relate—seeking to forge an ethics that does justice to the complexity of texts and bodies marked by suffering—I turn to literary writing. I do so in part because literary writing uniquely incarnates its content in a certain form, so that its meaning is never reducible to propositional statements; this literary performance of meaning supports my interest in getting past too-easy distinctions between the material and the symbolic. I do so also because the literary writing I look to challenges the disciplinary distinctions I have discussed already, manifesting the tangled workings of gender, sex, race, class, religion, and other particulars that texture suffering. These literary texts disallow any overly simplistic diagnosis of suffering as resulting from a single cause or ameliorated by a single remedy.

The literary texts ultimately suggest an answer to my central question, *How ought we read suffering?* through a linked dyad I call "the ethics of readerly attention" and "the ethics of literary representation." "The ethics of readerly attention" refers to a practice of reading, one that is careful and close, alert to literature *as* literature, to the functioning of metaphor, to rhythm and repetition. The ethics of readerly attention is, at its core, an ethics of the relationship between reader and text, a description of how any given reader *ought* to approach a text. This reading practice of attention, in its form as a hypothesis I carry to the texts in chapters 2–5, originates in the new ethical criticism and the poststructuralist theory from which it learns. I value with Attridge the commitment "to work against the mind's tendency to assimilate the other to the same, attending to that which can barely be heard, registering what is unique about the shaping of language, thought, and feeling in this particular work."[90] The tentative reading practice is also informed by the Christian philosopher-mystic Simone Weil, whose claim, "attention consists of suspending our thought, leaving it detached, empty, and ready to be penetrated by the object,"[91] parallels Attridge's emphasis on a "remarkable openness of the mind to what it has not yet grasped."[92] For both the poststructuralist and the Christian, this mode of attention is a *creative* act, helping to bring the other into being, and Weil joins Attridge in linking such creative responsibility to self-abnegation, albeit in more strongly theological terms: "In denying oneself, one becomes capable under God of establishing someone else by a creative affirmation. One gives one-self in ransom for the other. It is a redemptive act."[93]

Yet the ethics of literary attention also originates in my feminist com-mitment to a politics of location, to joining Rich in "[picking] up again the long struggle against lofty and privileged abstraction," in questioning the assumed meaning of "we," in recognizing that while global sufferings do seem somehow related, the particularity of different locations disal-lows assumed mutual understanding.[94] In the essay I have been quoting from, Rich's "Notes Towards a Politics of Location" (1984), Rich names the importance of self-awareness about one's location and of serious, careful attention to *other* locations, and she exemplifies this practice by calling out white feminists who assume themselves to be "center" with-out realizing that the work of women of color like Audre Lorde and Bar-bara Smith does not simply derive from white feminism but from a rich tradition of African American activism and writing.[95] Rich's argument, like Attridge's, calls for a reading practice that resists the urge to interpret others only in light of the self. Reading Attridge, Weil, and Rich with Ricoeur, who asserts in *Time and Narrative* that the meaning made in the reading of any text arises from "the intersection of the world of the text and the world of the hearer or reader,"[96] I suggest an ethics of readerly attention that combines exceedingly close readings of literary language with contextual, intertextual readings that can expand "the world of the reader" through which she interprets the text. As I seek to practice such an ethics of readerly attention in this book, my reading is characterized by a wide-ranging interdisciplinarity. I read contextually in each chapter, drawing on feminist and theological texts that speak to the locations of production and representation for each of my literary writers. I read lit-erature and theory together, beginning in both places, turning repeatedly from one to the next.

My ethics of readerly attention arises both from theory and from literary texts themselves; in fact, as my readings in the following chap-ters illustrate, the ethics of readerly attention is both a reading practice brought to texts *and* a practice challenged, shaped, and taught by those texts. Caught in the strange temporality of the book, I must introduce my terminology in this early chapter, but it developed not in conversation solely with theoretical perspectives but rather in the process of reading the literary texts that make up the heart of the project. In other words, I began with a hypothesis that *attention* would be an important element of my literary ethics and questioned that claim in the test case of each chapter. Again and again, I find a confirmation of that practice, and not only (I believe) as a self-fulfilling prophecy. The poems and prose I read by Rich, and the novels and criticism of Toni Morrison, Ana Castillo, and Adichie, as instances of Hutcheon's postmodern literature, all thematize the act of reading and interpretation, the risky importance of language, and the centrality of self-giving (even self-sacrificing) care and hospitality. In their formal features, as well, these texts *school* readers in the practice of attention, challenging inattentive readings, provoking surprise and perplexity, foreclosing on easy conclusions, pivoting on ambiguity. They thematize and invite readers into a stance of creative attention that brings meaning into being, highlighting the responsibility of the reader.

It would be easy to read these texts simply as allegories of responsible, attentive reading, and if my project were just one more heady addition to the new ethical criticism, that might be the extent of my engagement. Yet I am concerned not just with the structures of ethical reading but also with the question of *suffering* as a theme, of women's suffering and sacrifice as a social phenomenon marking both texts and bodies. What of bones and flesh, of political rhetoric and labor relations, of the hands that hold the spines?

To answer these questions, I propose "the ethics of literary representation" as the other dynamic at work in my literary ethics of suffering, one always in tenuous and risky play with the ethics of readerly attention. Representation is a fraught term in contemporary literary discourse: it calls to mind debates over multiculturalism and formalism, over expression and textuality, over liberal humanism and high theory. Representation understood as mimesis, as I discussed earlier and address in chapter 2, also has structured key debates in the ethical turn in literary studies: per moral criticism, stories are "about us," rather than being about language or textuality.[97] Over against this perspective is the deconstructive reading of the new ethical criticism, which as I have argued often focuses more on the practice of reading than the content of literary texts. Practitioners of the new ethical criticism are often skeptical of the relationship between text and world and especially of literature as straightforwardly expressive of certain identities or positions. In his *Ethical Criticism*, Robert Eaglestone accuses moral critics (and especially Nussbaum) of under-reading, providing insufficient attention to the specifically literary nature of literature, and the new ethical critics (exemplified by J. Hillis Miller) of over-reading, being caught in an endless cycle of language's self-referentiality.

From an interdisciplinary perspective, another group of readers that often is accused of "under-reading" is the collection of theologians and feminists who have turned to literature in the past few decades for its affective engagement, particularity, and ability to introduce readers to "otherness." Of the theorists I cite in this study, examples of this use of literature include Kristine Rankka, Colleen Carpenter Cullinan, and Sharon Welch. Roxanne Harde notes this trend among feminist theologians, who draw on literary writing because it presents "a multitude of examples of women's experience, embodied experience in particular."[98] Significantly, Harde notes that one of the primary uses of women's literary writing by feminist theologians is to provide examples of suffering.[99] Harde acknowledges that a number of scholars, including Sheila Hassell Hughes, have questioned some feminist theologians' uses of literature, including their "selective quoting and critical misreading,"[100] even as she chooses to defend feminist theological appropriations of literature. Yet Harde herself manifests the common pitfall of identifying the value of literature for theory as its capacity to "reflect women's experience."[101] This vocabulary of untroubled mimeticism and appeal to experience recurs throughout Harde's article. Drucilla Cornell comments on this propensity as a willful or unintentional ignorance of the "specificity of literary language,"[102] and Heather Walton's books *Literature, Theology, and Feminism* and *Imagining Theology* both address the problem of feminist and theological under-reading in detail. In a sense, these scholars sacrifice the particularity of literary language on the altar of justice for embodied women.

This may in fact be a worthy sacrifice: literature may suffer such violence gladly for the sake of women's redemption. In this project, however, I take issue with such an approach, looking to literature not just for meaning but for performative insight into how meaning is made and arguing that literature's potential to do good in the realm of material justice is strongest when it is attended to as *literature*, when it is read closely, not "used" for some purpose but given open attention, with a heightened awareness to its singularity.

Still, I risk asserting that there *is* a content to literature, that literature *does* importantly point somehow to enfleshed reality, and that there are serious consequences of championing an ethics of readerly attention as openness, receptivity, and self-sacrifice without acknowledging the relation of such a grammar to gendered, raced, religious bodies. Even the most devoted proponents of deconstruction admit that readers ("we") inevitably make the leap of faith that takes literature as representative of reality. J. Hillis Miller names this move with Paul de Man as a sort of inevitable mistake.[103] In *Passing and Pedagogy*, Pamela Caughie similarly notes that "our impossible situation as readers of realistic fiction, conceived as the representation of the lived experiences of certain individuals" is to be "caught between the necessity and the error of taking it seriously or literally."[104] Attridge compellingly articulates the challenge when he asserts that literature's "mobilization of meaning by formal properties" means that "the text can never close down on a represented world, can never become solely the reflection of or a pointer to a set of existents outside language. The question of meaning and referring is kept alive *as a question*; referentiality is enacted—but not simply endorsed—in every literary act."[105]

I follow these theorists in understanding representation-as-mimesis not as an assumed function of literature but as a question it poses, inviting readers to take its language as referring to reality even while its own formal features, its metaphors and ambiguities and thematizing of language, interrupt that invitation. The texts I read in the coming chapters raise important questions of representation and location: who is speaking, and why, and to whom? What historical conditions have kept certain groups from representing themselves, and what conditions have kept certain sufferings from being represented? What good can come of such representations? Is the existing language, the existing symbolic, even adequate for representing nondominant groups, or is there always something more, some *differend*, that exceeds the given system of signs? Or, to borrow Lorde's haunting question, can the master's tools ever dismantle the master's house?

Representation, as W. J. T. Mitchell explains, is central to Western understandings of literature, beginning with Plato and Aristotle who emphasized the mimetic quality of art.[106] This mimetic understanding of representation is joined, as Ella Shohat notes, by religious and political connotations as well: religious in the sense of the second commandment of the Hebrew Scriptures, which forbids the creation of graven images, and political in the sense of modern democracy's demand for representation within government.[107] This second, governmental, aspect of representation is present along with the referential aspect in Gayatri Spivak's important essay "Can the Subaltern Speak?" In it, Spivak reads a passage from Marx to emphasize the distinction between *Vertregung* ("representation as 'speaking for,' as in politics") and *Darstellung* ("representation as 're-presentation,' as in art or philosophy").[108] Elision of the difference between the two does implicit work in theories of ideology, Spivak asserts, and theorists need to be more aware of the two different modes of representation. In a later interview she clarifies the distinction and how the two inevitably work together. *Vertretung* is representation by "proxy," and *Darstellung* is representation by "portrait"; however, "in the act of representing politically, you actually represent yourself and your constituency in the portrait sense, as well."[109] Which is to say, even representation by proxy, a standing-in-for, involves construction.

In writing of "the ethics of literary representation" I rely on Spivak's distinction, as I seek to get at the role literature can play within society, standing in for readers for some suffering or beauty that does exist in the material world, even though it inevitably does so through the re-presentation of language, which makes something new rather than pointing back to an original. The figure of legal representation may be helpful here, especially in a project concerned with justice, as it exemplifies the way these two modes of representation shade into one another yet how they also must be recognized as having different functions. The role of a lawyer within contemporary Western legal systems is to represent the client within a dispute of justice; "legal representation," as we often call it, relies on *Vertretung*, an act of substitution, perhaps most vividly at work in the term "attorney," which is defined in the *OED* as "one appointed or ordained to act for another." Within the scope of this project, this representation-by-proxy works as texts stand in for the realities they seek to represent, as language stands in for some material real. Yet a legal representative functions not just as an "attorney," or stand-in pointing back to some wronged subject, but also as an "advocate," "a person employed to plead a cause on behalf of another in a court of law": my literary texts argue for the importance of their own content, inviting readers to judge, to respond, and to become responsible.[110] But the work of a courtroom advocate is almost invariably reliant on the construction of narrative, and although the "truth" of the matter is typically what jurors and judges are supposed to discover, an advocate's success depends on her or his capacity to craft a compelling tale, with the generic features of truth, the subtle involvement of affect, and other formal features expected in suffering's emplotment. Thus, while "legal representation" functions by way of proxy, with the attorney substituting for the real person in the space of the courtroom, the task of advocacy relies upon a creative construction: there is no way to simply "represent" the facts without the mediating work of language (this is *Darstellung*).[111] Literature, I am arguing, functions in a similar way. It *does* represent some reality, standing in for it as a proxy for real life, and in the texts I have chosen for this study there is even a legal flavor to the representation, a sense of the writers' choice to challenge their readers with some instance of human suffering requiring ethical judgment and response. But literature represents that reality in language, language that also draws attention to its own poetic making and thereby disrupts readerly desire to take in only the first mode of representation (or readerly desire to be *taken in*).[112]

This understanding of representation sees it as an essential component of utopian activism, following Cornell's vision of "ethical feminism" as a future-oriented project of re-imagining, re-figuring, re-representing rather than succumbing to a pessimistic view of society as unchangeable and the material and symbolic as wholly separate. Because literature is never just a representation of what *is* but is always a creation of something new, even something that *might be*, along with Cornell, I believe that future justice is made possible by ongoing disruptions to the symbolic realm through women's writing: "ethical feminism turns us to what has traditionally been called the aesthetic, in order to fill out and make vivid our conception of wrongs women suffer."[113] Cornell's vision of ethics is clearly influenced by Levinas, but she also draws on Lacan, Kristeva, and Irigaray, in particular, to refuse the typical distinction between (and arguments over) symbolic and materialist approaches to feminism.[114] Rather, she insists that new forms of *representation*, new linguistic constructions of the symbolic, and new hermeneutic approaches to myth and mimesis can allow for "transformation" and "freedom," a future in which ethical relations are less impossible.[115] Literature, and particularly women's politically engaged writings, bears a terrific responsibility, for "woman and women cannot be separated from the fictions and metaphors in which she and they are presented, and through which we portray ourselves."[116] The power of these literary portrayals is in their capacity to imagine "the 'should be' of a different way of being human."[117]

The ethics of literary representation and the ethics of readerly attention function together within my literary ethics of suffering: Literary representation involves the ethical intentionality of the writer and the function of the text to wager an ethical meaning about the reality to which it tenuously refers. Readerly attention involves the practice of interpretation that seeks to give texts the careful, close reading that respects their otherness (the otherness of both language and social location). Within this dynamic at the heart of the ethics I propose, the specific representations of the literary texts—their tellings of stories about particular sufferings and their thematizing of language—challenge generalizations, comfortable conclusions, and even the unwittingly gendered and religious structure of the ethics of readerly attention. Yet they also invite such an ethics of readerly attention, invite interpretation and generalization and empathy even as they resist them. Thus, the mediating force between representation and attention—the mediating force that figures a response to suffering and sacrifice—is risk.

But I am getting ahead of myself. This book is structured by discovery, and the ethics of literary representation and readerly attention most fully work themselves out in readings of the literary texts themselves. And the risks—of occluding the linguistic and social otherness of any text, of giving too much of the self, of falling too far on the side of critique or embrace, of wagering an interpretation in the face of undecidability, of wagering an ethical response to the suffering other while knowing we may inadvertently do violence, of sacrificing embodied response because we are so enthralled by literature—these risks and others accompany us through the following pages. They are worthwhile risks, though, in the face of suffering, called for again and again by the marked bodies and books we face and read and hold. The ethics that develops in these textual encounters—this literary ethics of suffering—is itself a risk, a wager, an attempt to respond that, of course, never will be adequate. But these pages stand as an instance of responsibility, an instant of responsibility, a moment in the future-oriented struggle to learn to learn from pain.

2

Adrienne Rich and the "Long Dialogue Between Art and Justice"

Dear Stranger   can I raise a poem / to justice [?]
—Adrienne Rich, "Noctilucent Clouds," *Fox: Poems 1998–2000*

Adrienne Rich's groundbreaking 1976 prose work, *Of Woman Born: Mother-hood as Experience and Institution*, opens with the following epigraph on an otherwise blank page:

> . . . ma per trattar del ben ch'i vi trovai,
> diro dell' altre cose, ch'io v'ho scorte.
> (. . . but to treat of the good that I found there,
> I will tell you of other things I there discerned.)
> —DANTE, INFERNO, I:31[1]

Citing a canonical male poet of the fourteenth century, that imaginative poet of the mysteries of Christianity whose *Inferno* describes the sufferings of hell for his readers' benefit, Rich invites readers into her own "dark wood," where insight into the pain of twentieth-century Western motherhood may offer similar provocation. In quoting from Dante's opening, Rich both borrows the idea of an inevitable mixture of good and its "other" and implies a link between her subject and hell; she also invokes the Western literary tradition of poetry as an exploration of ineffable suffering in tandem with social critique and the tradition of poets relying on their forebears for guidance: as Dante turns to Virgil, Rich turns to Dante.

Yet in the pages that follow, Rich decisively turns *away* from Dante, as she names both the masculine literary establishment and Jewish and Christian religious traditions as structures that have contributed to the hellishness of women's lives on earth. This double move of embrace and critique or repudiation and engagement, this paradoxical both-and-ness, structures Rich's lifelong poetic and critical project, particularly in her treatment of motherhood as an institution of suffering and self-sacrifice and in her treatment of language as a source of oppression as well as ethical praxis. In this chapter, I trace this double move in Rich's work, first arguing that she wrote "suffering" and "self-sacrifice" into the center of second-wave American feminism through her literary representations in her pursuit of justice for women,[2] and then showing how her theorizing and performance of language and activism model an ethical attention and response to this phenomenon of suffering. Paradoxically, I argue, Rich both criticizes the cultural association of women with attentive care, suffering, and sacrifice, and also suggests such a stance of attention and care—even to the point of suffering—as an ethical response to the problem of women's oppression. The narrative of her own openness to change, in part manifested by her reappraisal of religion, exemplifies this stance.

But Rich's suggestion of an ethics of attention cannot be extracted from its poetic incarnations, which highlight the dangers that accompany self-sacrificial ethics as well as the importance of the symbolic for material justice. Reading Rich's poetry and prose in relation to religious feminists and the academic literary establishment, I demonstrate her writing's importance to these discourses as both a contributing and a challenging force in the field of ethics. Because of her prescience and her example of a risk-taking, re-membering, re-visioning practitioner at the interstices of literature, theory, and activism, however, I argue not just that Rich reminds us of the importance of women's literary writing for ethical questions of suffering but also that Rich's writing *in particular* needs to be critically reconsidered in present work on these issues.

Change and Time: A Brief History

Rich began her long career with the 1951 publication of her collection *A Change of World* in the Yale Younger Poets Series and remained ceaselessly productive until her death in 2012. Critics have a notable propensity to narrate the story of her work and to divide it into periods, and this critical tendency is not unwarranted. Rich's sixty-year history of poetic production lends itself to narrative form, as it is a story with a clear beginning point and a number of vivid plot twists. Indeed, as numerous critics have noted, Rich's repeated use of the word "change" helpfully illuminates her poetic project: "The one constant in Adrienne Rich's poetry," writes Cheri Colby Langdell, "has been change and successive self-transformation."[3] Or, to quote Liz Yorke, "Her work continuously evolves—revolves, re-visions, re-presents itself in different terms."[4]

In broadest strokes, the story of change goes like this: Rich, born in 1929, loved language from a young age and published her first volume as she was graduating from Radcliffe. Her early work, published in the fifties, was formally conservative and clearly influenced by her literary forefathers, and Rich was widely praised. Marriage and children in the fifties somewhat slowed her prolific output, but volumes in the sixties began to evince a stronger specifically feminine perspective and more experimental forms. Rich's political radicalization occurred in New York City in the late sixties, where her job teaching in the City College's SEEK/open-admissions program put her into contact with African American and female colleagues as well as underprivileged minority students who began to challenge her ways of seeing the world.[5] By the early seventies, Rich was publishing openly feminist and openly political poetry and researching the conditions of oppression that had affected women; in other words, she was diving headlong into the ethics of literary representation by seeking to present readers with socially unacknowledged sufferings in hopes of bringing about some justice. As I will discuss in greater detail, the publication of this feminist poetry, and particularly of her first prose work *Of Woman Born* in 1976, led to a clear shift in critical reviews as well as public and academic reception.[6]

Yet although she was hailed as a central voice of the radical feminist movement in the seventies, Rich began almost immediately to revise her early view. Many critics remain caught up in her brief period desiring romanticized androgyny (epitomized by *Diving into the Wreck: Poems 1971–1972*), followed by a period focusing heavily on lesbian experience (perhaps best represented in the much-debated 1980 essay "Compulsory Heterosexuality and Lesbian Existence"), but in fact, Rich continued to re-vision her own project, moving in the eighties into a careful attention to the particularity of race and class oppression; a complicating reappraisal of her past, including her religious roots; a critical reconsideration of Marx; and, ultimately, a turn to the enmeshment of global injustices. These changes are apparent not only in the prose and poetry but also very strongly in the introductions to her essay collections, in which Rich repeatedly turns a keen eye to her past and to her context to name gaps and failures and to articulate important reworkings.[7]

Until her death at eighty-two years old, Rich continued to write poetry of topical and formal innovation that grapples with ethical, political, and personal issues—and the inseparability of ethics, politics, and the personal. She continued to publish prose essays, particularly discussing the relation of literary production and language to problems of justice. She remained politically active and alert to the shifts of global and national politics. And she carried out her commitment to considering the oppression of women, the nature of relationships, and the centrality of the body to human experience.

Rich's writing compels its readers to a double move of their own: inviting the closest of readings, it challenges readers to hold the smallest detail of language in tension with a broader sense of the writing's development over time, to step back and witness the wide-scale sweep of change. In my treatment of Rich, I move between arguments about the development of concerns in her writings across the decades and detailed observations of brief passages, taking up both the diachronic and synchronic. As Craig Werner argues, Rich's poetry and prose are best viewed from within a framework of temporality, from a narrative perspective that also acknowledges the writer's commitment to recover the past, to be painfully open to the present, and to orient herself toward a better future.[8] In Rich's own words, "In order to change what is, we need to give speech to what *has been*, to imagine together what *might be*."[9] This is the temporality of feminism, and Rich's writing is a crucial exemplar of its shape and scope.

"The Suffering of Ambivalence": *Of Woman Born* and the Self-Sacrificial Mother

> Adrienne Rich reminds me that the source of my pain may also be the source of my power.
> —Krista Ratcliffe, *Anglo-American Feminist Challenges to the Rhetorical Traditions*

As the pivotal text of Rich's oeuvre—the text around which Rich's critics orient themselves and around which countless feminist conversations take shape—*Of Woman Born* is thick with references to women's suffering and self-sacrifice; indeed, the words "suffering" and "sacrifice" themselves ring like a refrain throughout the volume. My copy, a heavily underlined and annotated tenth-anniversary paperback edition, calls attention to these signifiers by my own markings, but even if one were to read it without a heightened awareness of suffering, one would be confronted insistently by the text's obsession. In emphasizing these concepts, Rich participates in the American feminist heritage of framing the ethico-political challenge for women's liberation as one of theorizing and mitigating suffering, including the ostensibly chosen suffering of self-sacrifice. She also effectively frames the second-wave feminist conversation in these terms so that to this day, debates about women's suffering and self-sacrifice, and their relation to motherhood, embodiment, and the symbolic, continue to unfold in an inevitable intertextual dialogue with *Of Woman Born* even when they do not explicitly cite it.

From its beginning, the book foregrounds questions of women's suffering, both chosen and imposed. The first chapter begins with an oft-quoted excerpt from Rich's journal of November 1960: "My children cause me the most exquisite suffering of which I have any experience. It is the suffering of ambivalence: the murderous alternation between bitter resentment and raw-edged nerves, and blissful gratification and tenderness" (21). Here, readers are plunged headlong into the double move, apparent not only in Rich's depiction of "alternation" between anger and delight but also in the very ambiguity of her language. This "exquisite suffering" is double voiced, as "exquisite" can denote both extraordinary beauty and extreme intensity or sharpness, carrying both positive and negative connotations. Similarly, the phrase "suffering of ambivalence" pivots on the tiny preposition "of": does ambivalence—two-sidedness, or mutually existing and conflicting thoughts or feelings—*result* from suffering? Does it cause suffering? Or is "suffering" here not an experience of pain but rather the reception or allowing of ambivalence (as in, "Suffer the little children to come unto me")? And why is the alternation itself "murderous," a word that colors the whole phrase with shades of violence, perhaps against the children or perhaps against the self? In these first lines of the first chapter, Rich establishes a dialectic of endless conflict, a paradoxical joy and sorrow in her experience as a mother, and she accomplishes this representation of undecidability through her use of evocative poetic language. Rather than clearly expressing her experience, the writing performs its ambivalence.

In the paragraphs that follow, Rich continues to describe her conflicted feelings as "a monster of selfishness and intolerance" (21) or "an anti-woman" (22), which arise from her desire for "privacy and freedom" (21) or "to be free of responsibility" (22) and her lack of "recourse to the normal and appealing consolations of love, motherhood, joy in others . . ." (22). In creating this image of conflict, Rich presents herself as one who cannot manage to "[act] the part of the feminine creature" (25) characterized by endless self-giving love. Yet it is not just in this conflict with prescribed roles that Rich locates her suffering: her own "sufferings lie" "in the enormity and inevitability of this love [for her children]" (22); her suffering is "with and for and against a child . . . because that child is a piece of oneself" (22). The suffering, then, seems to arise not so much from her failure to fit into a societal mold of womanhood or motherhood, but rather from the close relationship with her children, in the battle between impulses of anger and love, in the sameness and difference of herself and her children. The sufferings are both externally and internally derived: they are linked, in these first few pages, with both the institution of motherhood and the experience, undermining from the very start any clear distinction between the two that the book's subtitle might imply. To fit her understanding of a good mother, however, Rich's challenge is to "absorb the violence and make explicit only the caring" (22). In this series of quoted journal excerpts from a six-year span, which depicts the deeply personal challenges of her own ambivalence in the intersubjective space of mothering, Rich barrages the reader with honesty, with complexity, and with demonstrations of the inextricable linkage of maternal care and dark impulses typically kept silent, particularly at her moment in history.

Rich's choice to begin a book on the cultural institution of motherhood by sharing her own experiences, and in their (presumably unrevised) rawest literary form as journal excerpts, immediately alerts her reader to a generic subversion in the text, as Rich's first-person pronouns give rise to, embody, and at points implicitly undermine the academic research that makes up much of the book. In these early pages, Rich sets up a relationship between her own experience and her generalized claims, narrating her recognition of "the paradox contained in 'my' experience of mother-hood; that, although different from many other women's experiences it was not unique, and that only in shedding the illusion of my uniqueness could I hope, as a woman, to have any authentic life at all" (40).[10] Thus, the author expresses a highly personal motivation for her work on the structures of motherhood, which, in the central wisdom of second-wave American feminism, is also inseparably political. Beginning in her own experience, Rich works to explicate a number of personal and societal assumptions about mothering and women. These include the belief "that maternal love is, and should be, quite literally selfless" (22) and that women should possess "innate" qualities of "patience, self-sacrifice" (37). Central to her argument in the book is the claim that women's "passive suffer-ing" is foundational, not just accidental, to male-dominated society and its institution of motherhood: "It is as if the suffering of the mother, the primary identification of woman *as* the mother—were so necessary to the emotional grounding of human society that the mitigation, or removal, of that suffering, that identification, must be fought at every level, includ-ing the level of refusing to question it at all" (30).

Concern with suffering pervades the text not just in Rich's representa-tion of her own experiences but also in her research in history, anthropol-ogy, medicine, sociology, and psychology, and it is present as both social norm and verbal association. *Of Woman Born* functions as a compendium of past and contemporary sources (as of the seventies) of women's social-ization to suffer and sacrifice themselves and their symbolic association with these norms. In a sense, even this book exists in its present shape based on the parameters and vocabulary Rich set for twentieth-century Anglo-American feminism, not only in presenting her research but also in her synthesis and commentary. For instance, she writes, "Institution-alized motherhood demands of women maternal 'instincts' rather than intelligence, selflessness rather than self-realization, relation to others rather than the creation of the self" (44). Women are expected to "suffer" in general (50); specifically, the mother in labor is expected to "suffer," and throughout most of history is expected to "suffer *passively*" (128):

> Passive suffering and the archetypal female experience of childbirth have been seen as identical. Passive suffering has thus been seen as the universal, "natural," female destiny, carried into every sphere of our experience;

and until we understand this fully we will not have the self-knowledge
to move from a centuries-old "endurance" of suffering to a new active
being. (129)

Women are "socialized to expect suffering" (163), to accept "the self-
denying, self-annihilative role of the Good Mother (linked implicitly with
suffering and with the repression of anger)" (166), to take on the task of
"sacrificing herself for her children" (188), to participate in "maternal altru-
ism," or the "pressure on all women—not only mothers—to remain in a
'giving,' assenting, maternalistic relationship to men" (213), and to "[pass]
on her own affliction" to her daughters (243).

This concern with—indeed, this critique of—motherly and by extension womanly association with suffering and sacrifice is present not only in
Of Woman Born but also in Rich's poems, for just as she disrupted generic
expectations for theory by bringing poetic language and personal narrative into her researched prose, she also disrupted generic expectations for
poetry by bringing into it feminist political content and the particularity of
women's experience. "To Judith, Taking Leave" (1962),[11] for instance, speaks
of "all those women / who suffered ridicule / for us" in the earlier women's
suffrage movement and describes the experience of being "shared out in
pieces / to men, children, memories," yet newly engaged in the possibility of mutual friendship and hope for the future, "shared-out as we are."[12]
Uncollected in earlier volumes but printed in the 1994 *Collected Early Poems*,
this piece shows an early awareness of women's expected roles as self-givers.

The suffering of those in the earlier suffrage movement and the role of
women as self-giving carers also is treated vividly in "Culture and Anarchy" (1978).[13] This poem brings together past and present, juxtaposing the
everyday household lives of earlier feminists and the speaker's present as
well as their parallel political concerns. The textual brings them together,
both within the poem as the speaker describes the books and papers from
which she quotes earlier feminists, and in the materiality of the poem's
formal strategy, which uses a structure of overlapping columns, a sort of
collage that both unites and separates the present and the past. The present narration of the poem occurs in plain text, justified against the left
margin, while the italicized sections that begin near the center of the page
are quotations of earlier feminists' writings. This technique of quotation,
and also the listed names of earlier feminists, evokes a strong sense of

history, the culture of women; as Rich explains in the poem's notes, the title is "stolen" from Matthew Arnold's famous book *Culture and Anarchy*, which was published in the same era as many of the poem's named feminists but gave little attention to women.

A key turn of the poem occurs near the end, when the speaker misreads the titles of "heavy volumes" stacked on her table as "THE HISTORY OF HUMAN SUFFERING." The actual title is "THE HISTORY OF WOMAN SUFFRAGE," and the poem glosses this correction by quoting an earlier feminist on the frequency of historical erasure:

> I brush my hand across my eyes
> —this is a dream, I think—and read:
> THE HISTORY OF WOMAN SUFFRAGE
>
> > *of a movement*
> > *for many years unnoticed*
> > *or greatly misrepresented in the public press*
> > *its records usually not considered*
> > *of sufficient value to be*
> > *officially preserved*

"THE HISTORY OF HUMAN SUFFERING" is an easy mistake for "THE HISTORY OF WOMAN SUFFRAGE," requiring only a few letter substitutions, but this is no insignificant verbal replacement. Indeed, the poem goes on to explore the thematic links between the actual and misread titles:

> and conjure up again
> THE HISTORY OF HUMAN SUFFERING
> like bound back issues of a periodical
> stretching for miles
> OF HUMAN SUFFERING: borne,
> tended, soothed, cauterized,
> stanched, cleansed, absorbed, endured
> by women

The history of woman suffrage, here, is a history of human suffering, and women's long-standing role not just as sufferers but as the self-sacrificial respondents to suffering, as suffering is something that they have not only "borne" (a significantly double-voiced word that implies not only the passive acceptance of suffering but also the active work of childbearing), absorbed, and endured but also cared for in others. The poem emphasizes a continuity yet difference between past and present, seeks to re-present the *"records usually not considered / of sufficient value to be / officially preserved,"* and interrogates the linguistic as well as material associations of women's suffrage and women's suffering. It not only highlights the centrality of suffering to women's experience and to the resistance of women's movements but also thematizes (and performs) the importance of documentation and the linkages between public and private modes of suffering.

Such links between earlier women figures and the present, and between public and private, appear across the scope of Rich's feminist poetry. *The Dream of a Common Language: Poems 1974–1977* contains much of the poetry Rich was writing during the drafting, revising, and publication of *Of Woman Born*, and its pieces share many of the same concerns. "Power," the opening poem, explores the ambivalence of suffering in an earlier woman. "Living   in the earth-deposits   of our history" the poem begins, and then it speaks of the earth and the artifacts buried in it, invoking continuity with the past and a solid materiality.[14] The speaker goes on, contrasting this concrete image with a historical figure extracted from a text rather than the earth,

> Today I was reading about Marie Curie:
> she must have known she suffered   from radiation sickness
> her body bombarded for years   by the element
> she had purified

In the mingling of sight and sound particular to poetry, Rich uses the white space after "suffered," the visual and verbally temporal pause, to invite two meanings. If this poem is read within the context of Rich's other writing, Madame Curie "must have known she suffered" in the same way other women suffered, as a result of their gender. But the clarification that follows the space/pause particularizes this suffering: radiation sickness is the cause, and even more specifically, is brought about by Curie's own devotion to her science.

After detailing the physical ramifications of Curie's radiation sickness, the poem concludes,

She died   a famous woman   denying
her wounds
denying
her wounds   came   from the same source as her power

The paradox here—Curie's power, her scientific prowess, resulting from the same research and interactions that caused her crippling and death—is also intertextually overlaid with Rich's idea of the "token woman," a figure who functions within the male paradigm and is pointed to as an example of the fact that exceptional women do succeed.[15] Curie, no feminist activist, is here denying not only her bodily wounds but also her wounds as a woman (those "she must have known she suffered"), which come from a system predicated on male dominance, just as her power did. Again, the line spacing leads to both visual distance and verbal pauses, emphasizing the finality of death and the singular aloneness of "a famous woman." The repetition of "denying" and "her wounds" not only establishes the rhythm of lament, it also complicates the range of possible interpretations for these claims: first, the wounds themselves are what seem to be denied, but the final line—after yet another pause—links the denial not to the wounds themselves but to their source. The multiplicity of possible readings here, again, enacts the ambivalence of the wounding and empowerment of the token woman's experiences in a male-dominated society and Curie's scientific work, in particular. It is significant, at the end, to remember the poem's first line, "Living in the earth-deposits of our history": Curie's life and death as an exemplary woman achiever create the conditions for those who follow. Rich's use of the first-person plural possessive in this first line alone evokes a sense of community. The implicit question is one of power: at what cost do "we" achieve power, and how do our actions affect those who follow us? How do the small, mundane choices and responses to suffering—like the amber bottle unearthed in the second verse paragraph—create a history? How do women use the power available to them?

These questions of the paradoxical interwovenness of wounding and power are also of central importance to *Of Woman Born*; as I have mentioned, a deep sense of paradox and contradiction runs throughout the text. Echoing her epigraph from Dante, Rich writes of her early motherhood, "The bad and good moments are inseparable for me" (31). She writes, also, of the paradoxically combined power and powerlessness of the mother in her day (36), whereby mothers bear great responsibility for the rearing of children but typically lack the authority or means to make true choices, living as they do under male rule; she labels this state "powerless responsibility" (52).[16] Childbirth itself is also recognized as a paradoxical phenomenon, entailing both an experience of painful passivity and purposeful activity (160): it happens to women, bringing pain and a sense of helplessness, even as women engage in it as a form of active "labor." Rich turns to Simone Weil for help interrogating this paradox of pain and questions about its meaning, source, and purpose: how are physical and emotional pain different? What causes pain in childbirth? "Is there creative pain and destructive pain?" (158). Weil's distinction between "affliction" and "suffering" (which is developed in her essay "The Love of God and Affliction"[17]) helps Rich distinguish between "destructive pain" and "creative pain." Whereas "suffering" in Rich's gloss of Weil is "characterized by pain yet leading to growth and enlightenment," "affliction" is "the condition of the oppressed, the slave, the concentration-camp victim," repeatedly linked in Weil with "powerlessness, with waiting, disconnectedness, inertia, the 'fragmented time' of one who is at others' disposal" (158). Rich finds in these descriptions—which are not specifically connected to women in Weil's writing—an uncanny image of women's lives: "This insight illuminates much of the female condition, but in particular the experience of giving birth" (158).[18] Rich carries the argument further by problematizing the notion of all pain in childbirth as passive, inevitable, and linked to Eve. Instead, she seeks to consider the possibility that labor pain may not just be affliction but Weil's suffering, which allows that "where it is unavoidable, pain can be transformed into something usable, something which takes us beyond the limits of experience into a further grasp of the essentials of life and the possibilities within us" (158). In other words, appropriately understood, the pains of labor and delivery—and by extension, the pains of women's lives—if understood by a certain definition of *suffering* rather than *affliction*, can be a creative rather than destructive pain.

But Rich goes on to note that there is a danger here as well, because under patriarchy, "woman" *has* been told that suffering in childbirth is "purposive," even "*the* purpose of her existence," but that purpose is seized for the maintenance of patriarchy (159). Yet in the next paragraph,

she turns to *The Scarlet Letter* for an example of "defiance" against the patriarchal control of childbirth, asserting that while childbirth "may be pain,
dangerous, and unchosen," "it has also been converted into a purpose, an
act of self-assertion by a woman forced to assert herself primarily through
her biology" (160). In the following paragraph, Rich shifts her attention to
Doris Lessing's fictional character Martha Quest, a heroine among early
second-wave feminists, as an example of some twentieth-century women's
views that motherhood must be either embraced by patriarchal standards
or rejected altogether (160–161). In these sharp turns from one point to the
next, Rich offers no easy standing-ground. Engaging with a (religious) philosopher, an earlier American male writer, and a contemporary woman
writer, she weaves a web of increasing complexity surrounding the question of the pain of motherhood as creative or destructive. Rather than
providing any clear conclusion, she undermines the possibility of choosing one side or the other of the "either/or": she forwards the paradox as
paradox. This position on pain rings true to her original appeal to Weil and
the idea that although pain "is not to be sought," it can be "transformed."

In her afterword, seeking to conclude her synthesis and to name her
insights, Rich further emphasizes the contradictions of women's embodiment and emotional lives, commenting on the paradox of women's bodies as both powerful and powerless (283) and the ambiguity that arises
when one refuses to romanticize women: we are all destructive as well as
constructive, she argues, subject to violent impulses as well as loving ones
(283). It is in the negotiations of these tensions that we exist as embodied,
affect-driven humans. Even at the volume's end, Rich refuses to simplify
the ambivalence.

Rich's performance of paradox in *Of Woman Born* leaves it open to
accusations of going too far in one direction or the other. Rich's text has
been charged with essentialism, of claiming certain traits based on embodiment, motherhood, or other factors for women across time and cultures.
It has been accused of idealizing women's role as carers and givers of love.
It has also been accused of presenting women as unflatteringly monstrous.
And it has been accused of a too-focused critique of patriarchy, a hatred
of men.[19] What strikes me, however, is that all of these readings refuse to
attend to the ways Rich both explicitly and implicitly engages contradic-
tory and paradoxical elements of her complicated subject. As my reading
of her opening paragraph demonstrates, Rich's straightforward claims,

implicit rhetorical moves, and use of poetic language all emphasize the centrality of ambivalence. She contradicts herself, even as Ann Keniston claims, in the generic choice of combining an "I"-driven narrative of personal experiences with generalized and research-driven structural claims. Alice Templeton names this tension a "resistance between theory and practice" and insists that rather than weakening Rich's writing, it actually works to convey (in the senses of revealing as well as moving forward) feminist thought.[20] These different voices—the voices of literature and theory—conflict with and question one another, undermining any too-strong claims by once again performing the ambivalence at the heart of the ethical matter.[21]

As I note in chapter 1, however, the ambivalence at the heart of the matter of women's suffering is doubly confounded by the Western religious tradition, in which suffering and self-sacrifice are paradoxically considered both painful and redemptive and in which they also are associated problematically with the feminine gender. Although *Of Woman Born* is not typically discussed as a text dealing with theology, its treatment of suffering is inextricable from its pervasive concern with Christian religion as a historical social phenomenon and theology as a guiding force of culture. The book exemplifies the linkages of the gendered and religiously valenced signifiers *suffering* and *self-sacrifice* as well as the material effects of this symbolic linkage in patriarchal institutions. Indeed, Rich's project is shaped by her reliance on certain feminist theologians, and her early poetry and prose writing is marked by a repudiation of religion, first as part of a mid-twentieth-century intellectual critique informed by poetic modernism and then as part of her feminist critique. Yet this stance is complicated by the central importance Rich's writing has played in the history of feminist theology and by Rich's own later implicit reconsideration of religion as one possibly legitimate thread of identity. The story of Rich's engagement with religion in light of suffering, I argue, foregrounds the complex workings of gender and religion implicitly functioning in any contemporary treatment of the ethics of suffering.

Daughters of Eve? Rich and Religious Feminists

> as if she could believe in a / woman's god
> —Adrienne Rich, "Yom Kippur 1984," *Your Native Land, Your Life*

In *Of Woman Born*, the normative expectation of women's suffering in Western society is insistently linked to Jewish and Christian tradition. Like earlier American feminists, Rich recognizes the strong influence of religious practice and theological discourse on women's status in society. In presenting a contrast (and exploring the relationship) between motherhood as "experience" and motherhood as "institution," *Of Woman Born* links the "institution" of motherhood to institutionalized Western religion. In chapter 2, titled "The 'Sacred Calling,'" Rich recounts the social and historical forces that led women to be viewed as *naturally* and fittingly those who suffer and sacrifice themselves, emphasizing in particular the nineteenth-century archetype of the Angel in the House, which arose in part from the Industrial Revolution and the relegation of many women to the private sphere of the home. This role is linked in nineteenth-century discourse with the biblical figure of Eve, whom Rich treats in even greater detail in the chapters that follow. Drawing heavily on the work of feminist philosopher-theologian Mary Daly, especially her 1973 *Beyond God the Father: Toward a Philosophy of Women's Liberation*,[22] Rich levels a devastating critique against the history of church practice and normative theology that has empowered men to maintain the status of women as silent, passive sufferers. Monotheism and an all-powerful God underwrite patriarchy, Rich argues (67), and contribute to a global religious identification of women with evil (111). Participating in the mid-seventies' interest in an earlier goddess-worshipping era, Rich also follows Daly in citing early Yahwists (or Jews) as "savage" repressors of goddess worship (120) and thus forwards a history in which the long sweep of Jewish and Christian influence on the world has stifled women.

In chapter 6, Rich further explores Christianity's effects on childbirth over the centuries, arguing, "In Judeo-Christian theology, woman's pain in childbirth is punishment from God. (The notion of birth-pain as punitive is found, as well, in other cultures.) Since the curse laid on Eve in Genesis was taken literally well into the nineteenth century, the mother in labor had to expect to suffer" (128). Outlining the treatment of midwives as witches, the misogyny of Church Fathers, and death by childbed fever or "the curse of Eve" caused by eighteenth- and nineteenth-century male doctors' refusal to wash their hands (which claimed the life of feminist foremother Mary Wollstonecraft), Rich presents a story of the insidious effects of Jewish and Christian teachings for women's lives. Furthermore, citing nineteenth-century church leaders' resistance to anesthesia for women in labor because women are supposed to suffer (168), she explicitly connects her project to that of first-wave American feminists like Elizabeth Cady Stanton. In re-membering this past, Rich convincingly shows how religious rule and religious stories shape societies' expectations for women, and in quoting many documents from history, Rich also demonstrates how not just the ideas but also the signifiers "suffering" and "self-sacrifice" themselves have shaped women's realities.

As a radical feminist theological–philosophical source for Rich, Daly's *Beyond God the Father* offers her a methodology of engagement with religious practice and theology on the basis of their ongoing (often implicit) effects in society, one that seeks to critique in order to free readers from their insidious influences. Not only does Daly provide Rich with a compelling interpretation of the role of Eve and church teaching in the contemporary understanding of women's suffering, she also notes the connections between ancient and contemporary theologies of Christ and his followers as redemptive or salvific sufferers and the social situation of women. "The qualities that Christianity *idealizes*, especially for women, are also those of a victim: sacrificial love, passive acceptance of suffering, humility, meekness, etc."[23] She goes on to argue that although Christian teaching may promote such a stance among all its followers, it does not evenly expect or reward it: "A basic irony in the phenomenon of this 'feminine' ethic of selflessness and sacrificial love is the fact that the qualities that are *really* lived out and valued by those in dominant roles, and esteemed by those in subservient roles, are not overtly held up as values but rather are acted out under the pretense of doing something else."[24] While women are expected to actually follow the "passive ethic"[25] of meekness, long-suffering, and self-sacrifice, the church has tended to extol men whose "service" functions by way of power-plays rather than Christlike *kenotic* (or self-emptying) humility.

Daly's is one of many feminist voices that began in the sixties and seventies to raise warnings about the dangerous relation of women's social situation and Christian teachings on exemplary self-sacrifice. As I note in the introduction, an important precursor of later twentieth-century feminist theology is Valerie Saiving Goldstein's 1960 essay "The Human Situation: A Feminine View."[26] This piece, which draws on many of the same anthropological and sociological sources as Rich's *Of Woman Born*, is a groundbreaking instance of the by-now familiar critique of man's tendency to "identify his own limited perspective with universal truth."[27] The essay's assumptions about gender are clearly of its time, and many of its sources have since fallen out of favor, but its central thesis was essential for the feminist theology and philosophy that followed in its interrogation of the implications of contemporary theology for women so long associated with self-sacrifice. Saiving Goldstein explains that modern theologians, drawing on male experience, defined sin as a form of selfishness: "Sin is the unjustified concern of the self for its own power and prestige; it is the imperialistic drive to close the gap between the individual, separate self and others by reducing those others to the status of mere objects which can then be treated as appendages to the self and manipulated accordingly."[28] In contradistinction to sin, "Love, according to these theologians, is completely self-giving, taking no thought for its own interests but seeking only the good of the other," and "becomes wholly receptive to the other."[29] Yet this model of sin may be inadequate and even dangerous for women, argues Saiving Goldstein, who draws on contemporary sociological and psychological research to argue that women's experience is *different* from men's, particularly their experience as wives and mothers. For women, "the attempt to [love in the manner described by male theologians] can be deadly"; "a woman can give too much of herself, so that nothing remains of her own uniqueness; she can become merely an emptiness."[30] The sins that are structurally feminine, she further claims, "have a quality which can never be encompassed by such terms as 'pride' and 'will-to-power'" but rather are, "in short, underdevelopment or negation of the self."[31] Saiving Goldstein's argument—that men's and women's propensities to "sin" are not the same, and that any theology that claims to describe the human condition must consider the experiences of women as well as men if it is to avoid becoming "irrelevant"[32]—is a historically significant one. Rich's diatribe against the institution of motherhood takes its place in a discourse opened up by this early feminist theological exposure of the danger of women's "self-giving" and also is present in more recent feminist philosophers' critiques of redemptive suffering ethics.

Of Woman Born reminds us that any American feminist treatment of women's suffering must engage theological concepts and religious institutions because of their centrality in the Western vocabulary and imaginary. In this way, the book follows projects like *The Woman's Bible* in taking on long-held assumptions and biblical texts to critique their cultural power.

It also follows nineteenth-century feminists in recognizing the central paradox in Western conceptions of motherhood, which present women as both particularly guilty for Eve's sin and particularly important in bearing a redeemer (represented, for example, by Elizabeth Barrett Browning's *Drama of Exile*), or both predisposed to wickedness and predisposed to endlessly self-giving love. Rich names this phenomenon as a double bind in her introduction to the 1986 edition of *Of Women Born*, describing how mothers are both idealized and exploited (xxiv).

It is no accident that Rich and Daly illuminated each other's radical feminist projects in the seventies: not only was Daly's feminist critique of Judeo-Christian religion and theology groundbreaking and important for any work considering women's suffering and self-sacrifice in the West, but both women shared a strong reaction *against* the institutions of male dominance and their linkages to religion. Indeed, Rich's earliest poetry already evinces a grappling with religion; she arrived at her feminism with a critique of institutionalized religion already established. For instance, in the poem "Air Without Incense," published in *A Change of World* (1951), Rich presents not just a demythologized view of religious practice ("We eat this body and remain ourselves. / We drink this liquor, tasting wine, not blood") but ultimately a desire for freedom from the effects of a wearied or even damaging religion: "We seek, where lamp and kyrie expire, / A site unscourged by wasting tongues of fire."[33] In poems from the same volume, like "Reliquary," "By No Means Native," and "A Revivalist in Boston,"[34] Rich explores midcentury disbelief. This thematic concern persists in *The Diamond Cutters* (1955), in which Rich continues to play on, subvert, and critique Christian language and religious practices in poems like "Letter from the Land of Sinners," "Living in Sin," and "The Perennial Answer."[35] In "Lucifer on the Train," she goes so far as to write a prayer to the devil.[36] Rich's critique of religion before her feminist conversion is also apparent in her prose writings, for instance in her claims in "The Tensions of Ann Bradstreet" (1966) that Bradstreet wrote better when she wasn't writing orthodox theological poetry, which was "the fruit of pure convention."[37] Thus, it is not surprising that in *Of Woman Born* Rich names patriarchal religion as a key source of women's oppression. Indeed, throughout Rich's prose of the seventies and early eighties, religion and "the church" are named almost exclusively as sources of suffering for women and are soundly critiqued and implicitly renounced.[38]

In the essay "Split at the Root,"[39] Rich links her own critique of religion to her unique upbringing as the daughter of a secular Jewish father and nominally Protestant mother in the south who was both sent to Episcopalian church and subjected to diatribes against institutional religion. Her stance, however, is at once personal and public, as it exemplifies—and arguably contributed to—a certain antireligious stance among many second-wave feminists. As Charles Taylor articulates in *A Secular Age*, Western feminist movements of the twentieth century were closely tied to the rise of secularism, the complex forces of which resulted in the destabilization of longstanding institutions like male-dominated religion; widespread feminist critique both arose from the opening up of previously unavailable options of critique and belief and contributed to this opening.[40] Thus, both first- and second-wave Anglo-American feminism are complexly related to the sweep of secularization. The eventual embedding of Western feminism in the academy further complicates this relationship, as the twentieth-century academy and especially the study of literature also complexly relates to secularization. The result has been a widespread stance among feminist theorists, literary scholars, and academics more broadly of religious skepticism and critique.[41]

Within the secular age's proliferating possibilities, however, religious belief is still one available option, and some feminists have chosen this route. Others have chosen not belief, necessarily, but a more sustained interaction with traditional religious questions or more broadly spiritual questions. Although Daly could assert in 1973 that "few major feminists display great interest in institutional religion" and that many feminists were antichurch,[42] in the years that followed a number of feminists *did* begin to display great interest in institutional religion, reapproaching traditions and texts with new hermeneutics. Rosemary Radford Reuther, Elisabeth Schüssler Fiorenza, and Elizabeth Johnson, for instance, have taken paths more in keeping with the first-wave project of *The Woman's Bible*, by reapproaching religion through feminist interpretive practices and seeking, if possible, to re-vision or redeem the traditions.[43] What is perhaps surprising, given Rich's clear antireligious stance in the seventies, is her importance among many of these religious feminists. As Heather Walton notes, Rich's writings, both prose and poetry, have been central to religious feminist projects.[44] Early examples include Carol Christ, whose book *Diving Deep and Surfacing: Women Writers on Spiritual Quest* (1980) takes as its premise that creative women writers provide alternate sacred texts for women, whose "stories have not been told" within patriarchal religion.[45] She devotes an entire chapter to Rich, locating in her poetry deep spiritual insights for contemporary women. A more recent example is Roxanne Harde's article on the importance of women's creative writing to religious feminists, published in *Feminist Theology* in 2006, which draws on Rich to link women's creative writing, experiences of suffering, and the work of feminist theologians.[46] Publishing in the same journal the following year, Alison Jasper admits outright, "Adrienne Rich is not a Christian feminist yet her work is richly rewarding for the Christian feminist reader."[47]

Rich's importance among religious feminist scholars has a lot to do with her concept of re-vision, which she defines in "When We Dead Awaken: Writing as Re-Vision" (1972) as "the act of looking back, of seeing with fresh eyes, of entering an old text from a new critical direction"; she labels this process "an act of survival."[48] Such a practice underlies most Jewish and Christian feminist theological projects, which rely on a critical hermeneutics of re-visioning: indeed, this practice is central to my own project here. It also underlies Rich's commitment to openness, change, and self-re-vision, which explains the alterations in Rich's evaluation of radical feminism and her understanding of the role of religion in women's lives. During the eighties, as her first conception of radical feminism was challenged by a dawning sense of complexity among the women of the world, Rich began to examine her own origins, including her religious heritage. Rich interrogates these origins in the 1982 essay "Split at the Root: An Essay on Jewish Identity"[49] and in the powerful multisectioned poem "Sources," first printed as a chapbook in 1983 and then collected in *Your Native Land, Your Life* (1986). In this poem, Rich revisits the question of her father and his own suffering as a Jew, examining the multiple, interwoven strands of oppression that challenge the pride of place women's suffering had taken as paradigmatic in her earlier thought. At this point, Rich began to recognize that oppression did not just arise from religious institutions, but that it also was leveled against certain faith communities and those within them. Although Rich did not accept faith as such—as she asserts in an interview published in *Arts of the Possible* (2001), "I'm not a religious Jew. I'm a secular person"[50]—she began to recognize in faith traditions the inevitable paradox of wounding and healing, the ambivalent co-presence of oppression and possible meaning-making, community, and identity. This insight may have arisen in part not just from her rediscovery of Judaism (which she continued to name in poems and prose as a source of women's oppression as well as a source of social justice movements) but also from her engagement with African American women, many of whom, as I argue in the next chapter, have found paradoxical hope within Christian churches.[51] Even as critiques of religious institutions continued throughout her work, Rich, from the eighties on, began to show a softened stance, for instance in her claim in "Split at the Root" that she "learned nothing there [at church as a child] about spiritual passion or social ethics"; "Christianity as thus enacted felt like a theological version of a social world I already knew I had to leave."[52] The implication here, of course, is that there are multiple ways to "enact" Christianity, some of which offer "spiritual passion" or "social ethics" as positive contributions. Rich's later poetry also evinces more biblical allusion and, as critics like Nick Halpern have noted, a certain biblically sourced prophetic stance. Halpern points out that in the piece "On the Genesis of 'Yom Kippur 1984'," Rich admits to reading a lot of the Bible in the early eighties and that it changed her poetic rhythms.[53] Once again, Rich's history of relation to religion and its texts evinces her courageous willingness to reconsider earlier positions, as "change goes on."

This self-re-vision is important to my project in two registers: first, as it exemplifies the practice of an open attentiveness—an ethics of attention, even—that embraces the risk of changing one's own view based on the influence of an other. Second, Rich's reevaluation of religion as an oppressive and also paradoxically empowering force in subjectivity and society suggests the possibility of a rewriting of the work she did in *Of Woman Born*. Although that text functions primarily as an exposé and critique of the role of Jewish and Christian religion in shaping the unjust language and therefore meaning of women's suffering in childbirth and mothering, and in mandating its continuance, Rich's later writings on religion suggest another possible understanding of religion's role in women's suffering. That reinterpretation of religion does not appear in a revised version of *Of Woman Born*, but the texts that I will read in the following chapters do forward such a project of interrogating religion's role in suffering and sacrifice without quite repudiating it. As in the texts of her poems and prose, I read an incisive engagement with women's suffering and its sources, and in the narrative of Rich's own self-re-vision, I read a prototype of the stance of paradox that will work itself out in women's writing of the following decades.

In this history of change, Daly and Rich diverge, for even as Rich continued to reconsider and revise her earlier views in light of a dawning awareness of complexities, Daly remained committed to her radical feminist vision of women's oppression as the paradigmatic oppression and to her utter repudiation of Christian tradition.[54] Yet early on, their projects were united not just in their critique of patriarchal religious institutions and their explication of suffering but also in their profound critique of— and paradoxical hope in—language itself.

"Transformational Grammar": Language and Activism

> I have been wanting for years / to write a poem   equal to these / material forces
> —Adrienne Rich, "Contradictions: Tracking Poems,"
> *Your Native Land, Your Life*

As is commonly claimed, feminism is a profoundly literary movement, and religious feminism is no different, which in part explains Rich's importance among feminist theologians. The women's movement of the late sixties and seventies resulted in a concurrent "women's poetry movement," so that publishing and activism went hand in hand. Yet Rich's centrality is also rooted in her work as both a poet and a theorist: her prominence in some feminist religious texts, for instance *She Who Is: The Mystery of God in Feminist Theological Discourse* (1992) by Elizabeth Johnson, arises from scholars' propensity to cite both her poetry and her critical theoretical writings. The same is true in Daly's *Gyn/Ecology* (1978), where the seventeen indexed references could be divided between Rich, the poet, and Rich, the theorist. Working in both genres, Rich theorizes and practices the relation of human suffering to literary language.

Even just in the two major prose texts by Rich and Daly in the mid-seventies, the theme of language plays an important role. Daly speaks of the power of naming and the need for "new semantic fields," asserting, "The liberation of language is rooted in the liberation of ourselves."[55] In *Of Woman Born*, Rich argues that men's descriptions of the world are not necessarily true to women's experiences, "Yet any institution which expresses itself so universally ends by profoundly affecting our experience" (42).[56] She goes on to assert that the power of the fathers has "permeated everything, even the language in which we try to describe it" (58). This insight is powerfully performed, as well, in an often-discussed poem written in 1968, "The Burning of Paper Instead of Children."[57] This poem, which combines prose narration, free verse, and quotation, links through juxtaposition and the thematics of fire and language (as spoken and printed word) the sufferings of religious and gender oppression, class and race, colonization, the Vietnam war, and sexual passion. Among these concerns, the speaker claims "this is the oppressor's language / / yet I need it to talk to you."

Such an insistence on the necessity of impure language is present across the scope of Rich's writing. For Rich, an awakening to political activism also seems to have meant an awakening to this combined linguistic power and danger. In the essay "Teaching Language in Open Admissions" (1972), Rich describes herself as "a teacher of language: that is, as someone for whom language has implied freedom, who is trying to aid others to free themselves through the written word, and above all through learning to write it for themselves."[58] Yet Rich contrasts this apparently romanticized claim with her experience among underserved African American and Puerto Rican college students: "But my daily life as a teacher confronts me with young men and women who have had language and literature used *against* them, to keep them in their place, to mystify, to bully, to make them feel powerless."[59] At this moment for Rich, the answer is not to turn away from language altogether, but to modify educational paradigms and empower students with a critical awareness of its functions: "At the bedrock level of my thinking about this is the sense that language is power, and that, as Simone Weil says, those who suffer from injustice most are the least able to articulate their suffering; and that the silent majority, if released into language, would not be content with a perpetuation of the conditions which have betrayed them."[60] She also footnotes Paolo Freire to support that idea that "language can be used as a means of changing reality."[61]

Rich's claims about language from this era may recall poststructuralist claims about the constitutive nature of language, the way language mediates reality, disciplines subjects under the Law of the Father, and (borrowing the more optimistic readings of such dynamics by feminist theorists like Kaja Silverman[62]) the way resignification and the use of language can potentially transform reality. But in these early years of political and feminist writing, Rich's perspective seems to be slightly more optimistic about the expressive nature of language, emphasizing the importance of speech after centuries of women's silence. Rooting her analysis in activist practices like the speak-outs and consciousness-raising groups of the early women's movement, Rich develops a contrast between discovering and speaking one's own language and passively being described in the language of another. What is needed, first, is a powerful critique of the existing language, for "in the interstices of language lie powerful secrets of the culture"[63]; and, second, a new speaking, for "in breaking those silences, naming our selves, uncovering the hidden, making ourselves present, we begin to define a reality which resonates to *us*."[64] In other words, Rich proposes a nascent ethics of literary representation, suggesting the good of naming the unnamed, confronting the reading public with *other* realities of suffering and subjectivity. This process seems as simple as naming the power structures in dominant language and telling one's own stories. "Defining" a reality may signify constructing its meaning, a radical claim about the constitutive power of language, or it may signify describing it, a more conservative claim. As always, of course, there is the question of "us": which grandly unified "us" does Rich assume here?

Yet by the mid-seventies, Rich is questioning her earlier optimism. No matter one's intentions, words act on their own. In "The Images" (1978–79)[65] the speaker claims, "I can never romanticize language again / never deny its power for disguise for mystification," and later in the poem the speaker describes sitting near the sea, drawing in a notebook, silent: "I felt washed clean / of the guilt of words." This more ambivalent take on language continues through Rich's later writings, for instance in the poem "North American Time" (1983),[66] in which the speaker contemplates silence in the face of language's dangers, particularly the danger of being misunderstood and misused:

> It doesn't matter what you think.
> Words are found responsible
> all you can do is choose them
> or choose

to remain silent.   Or, you never had a choice,
which is why the words that do stand
are responsible
and this is verbal privilege

The long poem, which ranges over particular places in North America, directly addresses the "you" of a "Poet, Sister," and names its particular moment's difficult political context in which poets and others are oppressed and hungry. It emphasizes the dangers and responsibilities of the poet's role with words, the division between intention and textuality, the reigning symbolic or the source of language. Even the "choice" of using such words (or not) is called into question here, challenging an earlier optimism about the power of breaking silences and voicing sufferings: "verbal privilege," the capacity to name one's own reality, even, is indicated in the dangerous scope of words' origins in the grammar of domination and vulnerability to be used in contexts of oppression. The poem's speaker struggles with this question of "responsibility"—that is, the need for the poet to be incredibly attentive to details of difference (even the differences of women braiding each other's hair in different global locations)—even though representations of such particular scenes ultimately will "stand in a time of their own," being used for various purposes as divergent as *l'art pour l'art* and oppressive propaganda. Yet after the agony evoked by its nine sections of short lines meditating on particularity, the temporality of poetry's social use, and responsibility, it ends: "and I start to speak again." The poet faces the risks and impurities of language and still chooses, in the face of such particular injustices as "the toxic swamps, the testing-grounds," to engage the mixed dangers and possibilities of language. Tellingly, Rich chose this poem—and its simple last line, marked with the sure finality of a period—to end her collection *The Fact of a Doorframe: Poems Selected and New 1950–1984*: "and I start to speak again."

And she did. In the nearly three decades that followed this poem, Rich continued to grapple with language and its ambiguity, with its mingled ethical importance and danger, with the power of poetry to provoke change, even in a political context that devalues and flattens language, using it for its own oppressive purposes. Rich's thematic and performative engagement with language's ethico-political dimensions is widely acknowledged across the scope of criticism and underlies the book projects of Liz Yorke, Krista Ratcliff, and Craig Werner. More recently, Lisa Perdigao has noted Rich's persistent, even early, thematic concern with language.[67] Alex Blazer, likewise, compellingly argues that Rich recognized language as "the mean, medium, *and* mode of her pain" and thus "struggled to create a self-reflexive poetic that was fully cognizant of language's potential for psychic domination."[68]

Although some commentators, especially in the eighties, set up a contrast between heightened attention to language's functioning and real-world responsibility in debates over high theory, Rich's extensive engagement with the paradoxical power and danger of language is no retreat from material, activist concerns; in fact, her theorizing persistently interrogates the relation of language to the material, the relation of poetry to politics and literature to bodies, as numerous critics have noted. Liz Yorke, for example, recognizes Rich's explorations of the links between women's bodies, pain, and language[69] and cites a central passage from "Power and Danger: Works of a Common Woman" (1977): "When we become acutely, disturbingly aware of the language we are using and that is using us, we begin to grasp a material resource that women have never before collectively attempted to repossess. . . . Language is as real, as tangible in our lives as streets, pipelines, telephone switchboards, microwaves, radioactivity, cloning laboratories, nuclear power stations."[70]

Here Rich refuses the divide between language and the material, as well as a naïve view of language as neutral (it is "using us"). She also forcefully presents the paradox of language's danger and potential, associating language not just with apparently innocuous technology that structures our everyday realities but also the threatening recent technological developments hinging, in this list, on the middle item "microwaves," which mediates domestic conveniences and the military-industrial complex (or the personal and the political). Again, ambivalence.

For Rich, language both contributes to oppression, causing suffering and a self-perpetuating silence among the oppressed, and offers itself as a dangerous tool for resisting oppression. Poetic language, in particular, presents a prime source for subversive action: it offers the possibility of resignifying through metaphor, remythologizing (another key element of Rich's vision for the material effects of language), and bolstering the skills of imagination, which are necessary for envisioning a better future. And imagination, for Rich, is undeniably important and linked with the feminist temporality of hope in a future: "Poetry," she writes, "is not a resting on the given, but a questing toward what might otherwise be."[71] In this way, Rich predicts and supports the movement of later feminist turns to imagination and futurity, exemplified more recently by the work of Drucilla Cornell's postmodern utopian feminism.

Emphasizing, as I have said, an uncovering of past silences, a representation of elided sufferings, a sharp critique of present injustice, and a poetic weaving of possible futures, Rich both theorizes and performs the ambivalent power of language, and she does this in both her critical prose and her creative poetry—or should we say, her creative prose and her critical poetry. In doing so, Rich joins in a project shared by many feminist theorists—religious or otherwise—of exploring the profound paradoxes at the heart of women's suffering and their relation to language. At times implicitly, yet always insistently, this is an ethical project, and it is to ethics we now turn.

"No Mere will to Mastery / Only Care": A New Ethics

> It is clear that among women we need a new ethics; as women, a new morality. The problem of speech, of language, continues to be primary.
> —Adrienne Rich, *On Lies, Secrets, and Silence*

Rich's project, at least from her radicalization in the sixties onward, has been undeniably ethico-political,[72] even in an era when such commitments were considered inappropriate for, or antithetical to, poetry. Many critics in the late sixties and seventies reacted negatively against what they perceived to be a turn to "ideology" in Rich's poetry, what I am calling here her ethics of literary representation. Albert and Barbara Charlesworth Gelpi printed a number of these negative reviews in their 1975 Norton Critical Edition *Adrienne Rich's Poetry*, including Robert Boyers's assessment of a "decline" with *Leaflets* as Rich "falls prey to ideological fashions"[73] and Helen Vendler's assessment that Rich has traded "sweetness" for a new stance which is "nervous," "hardened," and "harsh."[74] Across the scope of negative reviews, one notes a propensity among critics to link ethico-politically valenced poetry with bad writing. Claire Keyes, for instance, asserts that in *A Wild Patience Has Taken Me This Far* (1981), "Rich's beliefs often take precedence over her commitment to the power of poetry."[75] Keyes insists that Rich's "good poems" show strong technical skill, but her writing becomes weak when Rich's beliefs take over.[76]

Rich discusses some of these difficulties in her essay "Blood, Bread, and Poetry: The Location of the Poet" (1984), admitting that "the reading of poetry in an elite academic institution is supposed to lead you—in the 1980s as back there in the early 1950s—not toward a criticism of society, but toward a professional career in which the anatomy of poems is studied dispassionately."[77] She goes on to analyze the both-and-ness of poetry's political power, how it is both feared and dismissed: "political poetry is suspected of immense subversive power, yet accused of being, by definition, bad writing, impotent, lacking in breadth."[78] Rich found a respite from this widespread attitude within the feminist movement, where a vision of the inextricable nature of the personal and the political opened up new possibilities: "we were also pushing at the limits of experience reflected in literature, certainly in poetry."[79] This testing of boundaries within community gave Rich the courage to write as she did, even if it couldn't protect her entirely against the negative reviews: "Working as I do in the context of a movement in which artists are encouraged to address political and ethical questions, I have felt released to a large degree from the old separation of art and politics."[80]

Rich's ethico-politically committed poetry may have found a home within the feminist movement in the seventies, but it also placed her in an unusual position in relation to the literary academy. Numerous critics have undertaken studies of the critical reception of Rich's work, demonstrating how the resistance of a powerful few within the academic literary establishment led to a certain elision of Rich's work among scholarly audiences. As early as 1977, Kathleen Barry asserted that "censorship" of Rich's publications had occurred on the basis of negative reviews, as bookshops and distributors pulled her volumes from the shelves.[81] Gretchen Mieszkowski convincingly demonstrates in a 1988 article that Vendler, a powerful figure in American poetry criticism, affected critical opinions by publishing numerous negative reviews of Rich's writing based on dubious readings and pop psychologizing.[82] Craig Werner names widespread academic resistance to Rich's political radicalization even as she achieved great popularity among a feminist and activist public.[83] Extending this argument, Alice Templeton provides a thorough reception history, demonstrating a critical split between "patriarchal" and "feminist" reviewers.[84] And Susan Sheridan takes up where Werner and Templeton leave off, detailing a history whereby the early Rich was embraced and then rejected by established critics with formalist assumptions, then championed by feminists, and finally reaccepted by some within the academy as feminism was ensconced in institutions of higher education.[85] Sheridan shows how some reviewers simply ignored the feminism of early feminist volumes, but she links the publication of *Of Woman Born* in 1976 to a notable demise in scholarly critical opinions of Rich's poetry.[86] Sheridan also notes that politically minded rather than literary-trained readers tended to ignore form for content, a tendency Walton also locates among religious feminist readers. Yet as many critics have noted, earlier literary critics were guilty of the same sin in reverse, ignoring content for form.

This reception history is important because it may help explain a puzzling elision. The "ethical turn" of literary studies in the late 1980s provoked many theorists, including poststructuralists, to a new reconsideration of the politico-ethical functions of literature. Yet although Rich's poetic and critical project was ethically engaged for at least forty-five years, and while her importance within the feminist movement (often admitted among practitioners of the new ethical literary criticism to have been the literary ethical mode *par excellence*) is undeniable, Rich's massive body of work has not played much of a role in the ethical turn in literary studies. Even more strange, Rich's writing parallels—even predicts— the postmodern ethics to which many ethical literary critics turned in the nineties.

As I outline in chapter 1, the movement of literary critics like J. Hillis Miller, Jill Robbins, and Adam Zachary Newton into an engagement with ethics was predicated on a reappraisal of the linguistic turn linked with poststructural theory. Although during the period of high theory (1968– 1987) "ethics" was rejected as a dominant mode of normative morality, theorists began to react against claims in the culture wars of the eighties that their postmodernism meant a turn away from serious questions of human need and value. Following Derrida, and taking up his championing of Emmanuel Levinas, a handful of literary critics began to argue for a mode of literary criticism that highlighted narrative form, the functions of language, or interactions between text and reader as always-already ethical. By the end of the twentieth century, an explosion of literary work in "ethics" occurred, although without any consensus on what precisely was meant by "ethics." Again, commonplace vocabulary includes *otherness, alterity, response, limitless responsibility, intersubjectivity,* and *the infinite.* In the stream of ethical literary inquiries most strongly marked by poststructuralist literary theory, deconstruction gained pride of place as an ethical practice of reading.

While Rich explicitly distanced herself from poststructuralist theory (and while many of its practitioners have also distanced themselves from Rich), numerous critics have recognized her work as remarkably similar to that of the theorists she criticizes and who have ignored her. In her prose collection *A Human Eye: Essays on Art and Society 1997–2008,* Rich expresses frustration with "poststructuralist jargon,"[87] and she asserts in *Arts of the Possible* (2001) that "in a country where native-form fascistic tendencies, allied to the practices of the 'free' market, have been eviscerating language of meaning, academic post-modern theory has to shoulder its own responsibility for mistrust of the world and attendant paralysis of the will."[88] Committed to language that a general public can understand (particularly those without the privileges of higher education) and to a dogged awareness of the political context, Rich is critical of any scholarship that turns a blind eye to the reality of the masses. As she puts it in "Toward a More Feminist Criticism" (1981), feminist criticism should involve "continuous and conscious accountability to the lives of women"[89]; or, in "Notes Toward a Politics of Location" (1984), theory may arise from the observation of patterns in the earth, "But if it doesn't smell of the earth, it isn't good for the earth."[90] As we have seen, Rich refuses to abandon the material for the linguistic or activist engagement for the academy.

The poem "Divisions of Labor," for example, printed in *Time's Power* (1989), narrates a sharp divide between real women's experiences around the world and the trends of academic theorizing and publishing, contrasting the actions of "revolutions" and "magazines," active subjects of the poem's opening lines, against the concrete actions of "women" who sew, iron, work in sweatshops, and raise children in wartime around the world.[91] While "an old magazine polishes up its act / with deconstruction of the prose of Malcolm X," "The women in the back rows of politics / are still" doing all their concrete labors under the rule of structural injustice. The textual and even political (with Malcolm X as a symbol of the masculinist activism of Black Power) are contrasted here against the embodied, everyday work of women who maintain human bodies and meanings. The poem ends by recognizing their power:

—the women whose labor remakes the world
each and every morning
    I have seen a woman sitting
between the stove and the stars
her fingers singed from snuffing out the candles
of pure theory   Finger and thumb; both scorched:
I have felt that sacred wax blister my hand

Even though it implicitly critiques the economic and social systems under which these women work, Rich's poem does not present them as victims but as active, creative forces: the verbs associated with them (licking, trading, splitting, producing, fitting, teaching, watching) are active, ongoing, and vivid. Here, Rich's poetic language again enacts her position, stated repeatedly elsewhere, that despite their oppressions women's activity has been remarkable and world-making. Here, too, she does more than present a contrast between theory and material women: she narrates a vision— and claims a personal experience—of active resistance to "pure theory," in the figure of a concrete, embodied woman's domestic task of snuffing out candles. Importantly, the poem links this resistance to "pure theory"—a resistance implicitly valued as good within the poem—to women's physical pain: her fingers, those fingers that do the work of world-making, are "singed," "scorched," "blister[ed]." Significantly, the hot candle wax of "pure theory" is termed "sacred," ironically associating theory (as deconstruction) with the religious image of prayer candles, some metaphysical rather than material hope. Yet "sacred" is etymologically connected to "sacrifice," and it is only through choosing pain (however minor) that the "woman sitting / between the stove and the stars" manages to snuff out those candles.

    Although critics have noted Rich's plain rejection of postmodern or poststructuralist theory as disengaged from issues of real-world justice,[92] a number of them also have recognized in Rich an engagement with theory and even a predicting of theoretical moves to come. As Liz Yorke argues, "These revolutionary calls [in Rich's early prose] for women to seize language and speak their way into a transformed subjectivity startlingly anticipate later, much more complex theorizing."[93] Werner further argues that despite Rich's self-styling as a "pragmatic American" rather than a "theoretical French" writer, several critics have recognized her project as deconstructive, including Charles Altieri and Rachel Blau DuPlessis.[94] Indeed, he goes on, many of Rich's commitments seem to align with American deconstruction,[95] and although "she perceives [deconstruction] as withdrawn from its actual social context," critics who take her claims at face value "seriously underestimate Rich's awareness of the underlying concerns and implications of post-structuralist thought."[96] His list of the shared concerns of poststructuralist thought and Rich's writing includes "decentering of dominant discourse," "recognizing that marginalized elements unveil the internal contradictions of dominant discourses," "understanding of the discrepancy between signifier and signified," an awareness of intertextuality, and a rejection of a concept of the self as essential or decontextualized.[97] Indeed, Werner goes so far as to argue, "in practice, Rich's poetry supports Derrida's concern with politics."[98]

Werner's argument is convincing, particularly in his recognition of this quasi-deconstructive movement in both Rich's prose and poetry, but I'm not sure I would claim that "Rich's poetry *supports* Derrida's concern with politics" (emphasis mine), which seems to presume a primacy for Derrida's concern with politics, for which Rich's poetry can work as a helpmeet. What I will say, instead, is that Rich's project uncannily *parallels* Derrida's and the work of those literary ethicists who consider him a major influence, in its attention to language; to the insidious effects of "dichotomies" (which seems to be a synonym for binaries) and the value of exposing their falseness; to the complex interworkings of the material and symbolic, or language and embodiment; to the dangers of mastery as an impulse of patriarchal power; to the need for careful attention, empathic relation, intersubjectivity, and openness to the other; to the importance of humility and revision in the face of radical complexity; and to the need for poets and readers to be responsive and responsible. These positions are apparent not just in Rich's critical writings but also in her use of poetic language, in her propensity for metaphor and metonymy, in her creation of dialogic situations through use of first- and second-person pronouns, and in her wide-sweeping eye for connections across difference. And none of these practices even begins to consider her thematic concerns with injustice—her ethics of literary representation—which range from gender to sex to race to class to any number of other enmeshed global oppressions. In what she says and how she says it, Rich is a poet and theorist of ethics, no matter one's definition of the term.

Several critics have recognized Rich's project as ethical, including Elizabeth Hirsch, who notes that although "critics with an interest in literary theory evince almost no interest in [Rich's] work [as of 1994]," Rich's writings parallel those of Luce Irigaray, who has been more popular with poststructuralist theorists.[99] Both, she argues, "envision an embodied dialogue in which human value inheres in a process of continual exchange between self and other. Expressing the inseparability of the ethical and the sexual, the category of the poetic contests normative definitions that identify ethics either with repressive rules of conduct or with abstract principles."[100] In this regard (and I agree with Hirsch's reading here), Rich's poetry challenges theory as the sole discourse of ethics. Abstraction disallows the necessary attention to particularity and embodiment that gives rise to an ethics that does justice to women's experience and its mediation in language, whereas poetry incarnates that material-linguistic reality and works through the representation of particular details to engage readers in an affective ethical negotiation. Rich's poetic theorizing challenges the reigning male–theoretical–abstract concept of justice, and thereby provides an important literary beginning for my contemporary literary ethics of suffering.

Most recently, Miriam Marty Clark published an article that explicitly names the ethical turn in literary studies and considers Rich's poetry in light of it. Important to Clark's argument is the unprecedented magnitude of contemporary ethical responsibility, which relates to the broader postmodern ethical sense of limitless responsibility for an infinitely other *other*. She explores Rich's formal and thematic choices, demonstrating how her later poetic strategies "figure ethical proximity" through translation, quotation, conversation, and metaphor.[101] Drawing on the work of Stephen White and the concept of "weak ontology," Clark shows how Rich's last decade's voice of "longing, perplexity, and an awesome awareness of her own finitude" actually functions to ground ethical responsibility:

"Rich's lyric probing of weakness and finitude raises the possibility that these states might themselves sustain an ethical engagement, providing a basis for recognition, attentiveness, and acknowledgment."[102] To reframe Clark's argument in the terms of my project (and recalling Rich's poem "Power"), it is shared suffering, rather than shared power, that underlies and paradoxically empowers ethical human interactions.

Clark's article highlights the ways recent literary ethical theorizing finally provides a critical vocabulary for discussing the ethical workings of Rich's writing, both formally and socially, and the refusal of a dichotomy between linguistic and material responsibility. Perhaps the most fitting label for this particular literary ethical work Rich has done is Perdigao's: Perdigao calls Rich's position "a material poststructuralism."[103] This term suits Rich's project in its apparently paradoxical union of the concrete and the linguistic, for while it is true that Rich refuses certain modes of poststructuralist and feminist theorizing on the premise that they abandon materiality,[104] I have already noted that she is hardly indifferent to the workings and concepts of language. Instead, her path seems (as usual) to lie in the exposure of an insidious dichotomy: language is key to the pursuit of justice, but it is dangerous and it is not the only element of the pursuit; materiality is also key, but it is perpetually mediated and shaped by language—which is itself material. Scholarship, writing, and education are utterly necessary in the pursuit of justice as well, but unlinked to the exigencies of real-world people and contexts, what good can they do? Rich writes this material poststructuralism into being, not just through her thematic theorizing of language or claims about the centrality of materiality, but also in her generic minglings, her creation of a poetic theory and a theoretical poetry.

There is also an element of gender justice even in these subversions of genre boundaries. As Heather Walton argues, twentieth-century theology and philosophy, or "theory" more generally—abstract, rational, logical, and empirical—has tended to be gendered masculine, whereas literature— concrete, affect-inducing, particular, excessive—has tended to be gendered feminine, and in the inevitable hierarchy of gendered binaries, among many recent turns to literature in theory and philosophy, the feminine has been used in service of the masculine.[105] (Case in point: Werner's assumption that Rich's poetry "supports" Derrida's political project.) In writing both poetry and critical prose, and at the same time in subverting some of the conventional distinctions between the two, Rich enacts a resistance to the binaries whose symbolic functions oppress women's bodies as well as their minds.

These interweavings of linguistic and thematic ethical interrogation, through interwoven genres, are what strike me as terribly important in Rich's texts. Critics have acknowledged her ethico-political commitment (even boundary-testing and risk-taking) either in terms of feminism or (more recently) in poststructuralist terms of linguistic performance, but they have not tended to consider the interplay of these dynamics. As an acknowledged foundational source for later twentieth-century feminist discussions of women's suffering, and as a prolific theorist and performer of the ethical dangers and possibilities of language in her material poststructuralism, Rich is an undeniably important source in any discussion of the contemporary *literary ethics* of suffering. In *Of Woman Born*, Rich forwards an ethics of suffering and self-sacrifice that is startlingly similar to the ethical paradigms embraced by many postmodern ethicists and practitioners of literary ethical criticism, critiquing mastery in favor of open attentiveness to the other for the sake of responsible, care-driven relationships (in my terms, an ethics of readerly attention); yet she concurrently and paradoxically critiques the gendered (and, in her later work, raced and classed) concrete and particular effects of this ethical paradigm in practice, and she does so through specifically literary writing. This complex formal and thematic both-and-ness is both Rich's unique and important contribution to a contemporary grappling with the ethics of suffering and, more broadly, an example of the singular role literature can play in ethical reasoning that seeks to attend to both structural and particular elements in a postmodern context.

Even as she critiques society's expectations that women should be suffering, self-sacrificial carers, Rich names these very traits as ethical ideals absent from the norms of a male-dominated society. Interrogating the concept of power and its centrality to patriarchy, she locates in sexual love—both in the East and the West—the assumption of "power *over* someone": "Once more, responsibility toward the other, genuine knowledge of the other person, is unnecessary. The language of patriarchal power insists on a dichotomy: for one person to have power, others—or another—must be powerless" (67). This notion of "power over," Rich notes, pervades human relationships, so that even power that arises from women's particular experiences is shaded and shaped by the patriarchal norm (68–69). Men tend to evince an "implicit sacrifice of human relationships and emotional values in the quest for dominance" (68). At work here is the idea that "responsibility toward the other, genuine knowledge of the other person," "human relationships and emotional values," and a mutual rather than dichotomous empowerment is the good against which this harmful norm of patriarchal power is defined. Thus, while Rich is at great pains in *Of Woman Born* to critique the expectation that women be endlessly responsible for children, open to the needs of others, relational, and self-emptying, and while she critiques the association of women with emotional rather than rational capacities, she locates in these particular, feminized traits an important corrective to the male norms of domination and self-aggrandizement. In other words, she both critiques (and even rejects) suffering and self-sacrifice as an effect of injustice and also embraces them as a source of social transformation. Near the book's end, she writes positively of women's contributions, naming not only the affective and embodied traits of "tenderness" and "compassion," but also the other-oriented "detailed apprehension of another human existence" and awareness of human fragility (280). It is in precisely the qualities that Rich critiques as being exploited in women under patriarchy that she locates hope for a better future, indicating that a self-offering ethic is both detrimental to women under patriarchy and potentially detrimental to the institution of patriarchy itself.

This is a dangerous paradox, and easily misread, as it is easy to read only the critique or only the embrace of an other-focused direction of being in this text. It is essential for readers to recognize that Rich's contribution, her praxis, is not so much in the critique of patriarchy's way of socializing women or in the proposal of an alternative, but in the profound sense of paradox that she represents and performs in the interplay of theoretical and autobiographical writing. Indeed, the refusal of dichotomies (or even, in other terms, the deconstruction of binaries) is the key wisdom of *Of Woman Born*, and she locates these dichotomies not just in practice but, as I have shown, in the "language of patriarchal power" (67). "Truly to liberate women," she writes, "means to change thinking itself: to reintegrate what has been named the unconscious, the subjective, the emotional with the structural, the rational, the intellectual; to 'connect the prose and the passion,' in E. M. Forster's phrase; and finally to annihilate those dichotomies" (81).

Even for women, even despite her passionate critique of the patriarchal institution, Rich does not decry self-sacrifice altogether. She explicitly rejects the proposed solution of feminists like Shulamith Firestone who seek through "technological revolution" to relieve women of the social suffering specific to their gender by promoting "artificial motherhood" (76). In her chapter on childbirth, called "Alienated Labor," Rich critically questions the passivity of drug-induced freedom from pain in modern parturition as adamantly as she questions the necessary association of women and suffering in childbirth. "This 'freedom from pain,' like 'sexual liberation,' places a woman physically at men's disposal, though still estranged from the potentialities of her own body" (171). Rather than mitigating or even eliminating the actual physical pain of labor and delivery, Rich argues that we need to consider the social and symbolic realities that lend significance to the material experience, to consider the language that grants such pain its meaning: "What we bring to childbirth is nothing less than our entire socialization as women" (182), again linking the symbolic and the material. The actual physical suffering of women is not precisely the object of Rich's critique; paradoxically these experiences may be a profound source of women's strength, as Rich emphasizes in her afterword and links to Weil's distinction between suffering and affliction. What is necessary for an ethical relation to the complexities of women's suffering, for Rich, is a keen critique of the patriarchal institution and a capacity for vivid imagining and poetic writing of other ways of being, resulting in a "new relationship to the universe" (285) and, doubtless, a new relation to the binaries that structure Western imaginations. She implicitly calls for a new *language* of suffering and sacrifice in women's embodied experience, a new interpretation brought about by new poetic figurations, an alternative social meaning brought about through the transformation of the cultural vocabulary.

Ultimately, Rich locates her praxis in women's creative agency, even (again paradoxically) the choice to undergo experiences that entail some degree of passivity and pain. She advocates, in this embrace of the painful act of childbirth, a refusal of "passive suffering" as well as its equation with "the archetypal female experience of childbirth": "Passive suffering has thus been seen as the universal, 'natural,' female destiny, carried into every sphere of our experience; and until we understand this fully we will not have the self-knowledge to move from a centuries-old 'endurance' of suffering to a new active being" (129). Following this stance of critique, she advocates "the conversion of suffering into activism" (129), joining a number of feminists and political scholars, including Daly and Dorothee Sölle, in arguing that only the suffering that leads to the mitigation of oppression should be embraced. Countering many of her not-so-carefully-reading critics, Rich claims near the book's end "To destroy the institution of motherhood is not to abolish motherhood. It is to release the creation and sustenance of life into the realm of decision, struggle, surprise, imagination, and conscious intelligence, as any other difficult, but freely chosen work" (280). Rich does *not* argue for an end to motherhood, but a new language for it, a new meaning for its suffering and sacrifices. Her language here, of "decision," "struggle," "surprise," "imagination," and "conscious intelligence," suggests an active, ongoing, dynamic that combines agency (in "decision" and "conscious intelligence") with an interaction with otherness (in "struggle" and "surprise"), or control and a lack thereof ("imagination" could be said to combine the two, as it is both a chosen activity and an experience of the subconscious's alterity). Again, Rich figures the ongoing and at points paradoxical negotiation of sameness and difference, activity and passivity, in her utopian revision of motherhood.

The poem "Splittings," written in 1974, beautifully exemplifies Rich's embrace of paradox in the question of suffering as passive experience or active engagement.[106] It also highlights her specific awareness of women's association with and experience of relationality and suffering, and her related project of interrogating dichotomies. Its lines embody the "splittings" of her title, as most of them are broken into two or more fragments by white space, though enjambment also creates a certain unity across divisions, as in the first two lines:

My body opens over San Francisco like the day-
light raining down   each pore crying the change of light
I am not with her

The "her" of this opening phrase appears to be a "lover" in Manhattan, but it is also, in the double voice of the poem, "the mother" referred to in section 2 and implied in section 3. Separation from the mother/lesbian lover here is linked to a pain that arises not just from "absence but / the presence of the past destructive / to living here and now." The pain of separation—the psychologically powerful "primordial" separation of child from mother, the distance from a lover that takes its shape, perhaps particularly in the case of a lesbian relationship, from those early structures of woman–woman separation—is the speaker's interlocutor in this poem, her challenger. The struggle is not to submit to these "configurations of the past," which turn the lover from a particular being into an archetypal figure, but rather to resist the "myths of separation."

The speaker grapples with pain, this pain that arises—perhaps—from the primary mother–child relationship, a pain that appears to be inevitable, and the speaker seeks neither to ignore it nor to succumb to it but to learn from it:

> . . .   Yet if I could instruct
> myself, if we could learn to learn from pain
> even as it grasps us   if the mind, the mind that lives
> in this body could refuse   to let itself be crushed
> in that grasp   it would loosen   Pain would have to stand
> off from me and listen   its dark breath still on me
> but the mind could begin to speak to pain
> and pain would have to answer:

Actively engaging the pain—acknowledging the suffering and wounds as Curie did not—is the central project of this poem, where splittings, including the splittings of child from mother, lover from lover, even self from self, are seen as inescapable but possibly productive. Indeed, not all splittings in the poem are viewed as negative: in section two, the speaker chooses "to separate her   from my past we have not shared." Splittings and divisions are viewed as both causing and resulting from pain, and they are viewed as both possibly harmful and possibly helpful. Indeed, the speaker repeats no less than three times, "I believe I am choosing something new / not to suffer uselessly"; "I choose not to suffer uselessly"; "I am choosing / not to suffer uselessly." The choice is *not* to refuse suffering or pain; indeed, the negative phrasing of choosing "not to" highlights the implicitly negative tenor of such pain and suffering. But the choice is to refuse to succumb to the suffering without engaging it. In the first occurrence of the phrase, the speaker claims, "I believe I am choosing something new / not to suffer uselessly   yet still to feel": the suffering is not rejected in favor of an anesthetized existence. Again, in the second instance, the speaker claims, "I choose not to suffer uselessly / to detect primordial pain as it stalks toward me," naming a goal not of rejecting the pain but of recognizing and making something of it. In the third and final utterance, the speaker insists, "I am choosing / not to suffer uselessly   and not to use her." Although the suffering is not a passive acquiescence, the seeker in engaging with it does not wish to "use" her (the mother/lover), which according to Rich's definition of patriarchal power in *Of Woman Born* is the norm of active patriarchal love.

Indeed, an engagement with suffering rather than passive acceptance is inextricable, in this poem, from a refusal of the normative dichotomies of patriarchy. In the poem's third section, the speaker describes an existence as an object in the world that leads her to seek either an infantilized or masculinized position of hiding, using her mother/lover as a refuge as children and men tend to do, as described in *Of Woman Born*. Here is the final section in its entirety:

> The world tells me I am its creature
> I am raked by eyes   brushed by hands
> I want to crawl into her for refuge   lay my head
> in the space   between her breast and shoulder
> abnegating power for love
> as women have done   or hiding
> from power in her love   like a man
> I refuse these givens   the splitting
> between love and action   I am choosing
> not to suffer uselessly   and not to use her
> I choose to love   this time   for once
> with all my intelligence

The splittings here are, primarily, between power and love, between action and love, between passivity and activity, between affect and intellect. The speaker refuses these gendered binaries, seeking neither passive suffering nor an active repudiation of suffering, but instead a meaningful engagement *with* suffering. The irony, of course, is that in refusing the splittings, the speaker also must enact her own splitting, as she must *not* seek wholeness in the child-like or man-like hiding in union with the mother/lover figure. In choosing "not to use her," the speaker in effect chooses a certain autonomy and separation, which is in fact the source of the original pain with which the poem begins.

This paradox of union and separation is present not just in the content of the poem but also in its form. The lines themselves are split by white space, but they cohere across line breaks, so that phrases carry on for large stretches. For example, in my first long quotation from the poem (". . . Yet if I could instruct"), the implicit "then" that follows the "if" of this first line does not occur for another five lines. To end the excerpt earlier (for instance, after "crushed") would elide part of the phrase and thus alter its meaning. This is a fairly common technique in Rich's poetry: the line breaks and internal white space open up multiple readings, as we have seen in "Power." It also works uniquely well in "Splittings" to embody the poem's theme, doing the peculiar work of literary language to both mean and perform meaning, and here we are reminded of one of Rich's key contributions to the discourse of ethics, for she not only expounds on ethico-political concerns but also performs them in poetic language, reminding us of the indissoluble togetherness of symbolic and material oppression and the materiality of both language and silence.

The dangers of Rich's ethical paradigm—which both critiques and forwards an ethics of chosen suffering, with the key goal of dissociating it from women and reassigning it to all—are strikingly similar to the dangers of Christian *kenosis* ethics and Levinasian postmodern ethics. To forward an ethics of self-giving openness to the other, an ethics that promotes activist suffering at either a political or interpersonal level, results in a certain vulnerability for those among whom such self-sacrifice and suffering are already the norm. This is also a critique of care ethics, some proponents of which draw on Rich's work. Interestingly, these shifts in ethical norms have been tied to a widespread "feminization" of culture that has led to different ethical models for all people, but the question remains as to whether they have been good for women. Yet Rich's ethical paradigm in *Of Woman Born* and the poems of its moment parallel much poststructuralist-driven ethical literary criticism *with a key difference*. Most theorists of ethical literary criticism (with a few exceptions) forward a strangely contentless structuralism as an ethical paradigm: face-to-face relation with an other (text or person), devoid of context, always resulting in limitless responsibility. In doing so, they tend to elide the implicit gendering and

religious history of the terms "suffering" and "self-sacrifice." Rich's project is to make them explicit. Hence, Rich's ethics of suffering in *Of Woman
Born* makes even more plain the paradoxes and dangers at the heart of a
self-sacrificial ethic of openness to the other and limitless responsibility.
What Rich uniquely offers is a practice of the chosen other-focused, contextual, self-sacrificial ethics that is inextricably entwined with a critique of
women's associations with these actions, attitudes, and signifiers as well as
a critique of their religious origins. This entwinement is not just thematic,
but formal, as *Of Woman Born* is a hybrid text in which scholarly research
in the social sciences is woven together with first-person narrative, literary
criticism, and lyrical writing. These are profoundly destabilizing moves,
and they correct a striking weakness among postmodern ethical models
that fail to account for the particularity of certain ethical situations as well
as the religious and gendered workings of the terminology and phenomena of suffering and sacrifice.

Attention, Undecidability, Risk: The Lessons We Carry from Here

> I choose to walk at all risks.
> —Elizabeth Barrett Browning, *Aurora Leigh*

In the years after *Of Woman Born*, Rich's ethical project morphed and
shifted, ever subject to the endless process of re-vision. In poetry and prose,
Rich turned in the eighties away from a narrow critique of patriarchy to a
broader critique of "solipsism," which Werner defines as "the tendency to
treat only the self or a group, sharing specific characteristics with the self
(gender, race, religion, class, nationality, etc.), as real and to establish fixed
poles for those defined as 'other.'"[107] Such a broader vision encompasses
patriarchy but also locates it within a global web of linked injustices, and
Rich explains this movement in terms not only of her dawning awareness
of complexly layered oppressions but also in an analysis of the Reagan era's
(and later the Clinton era's) economic and moral realities and the capitalist forces that took the early energy of second-wave feminism and turned
it around into marketable "lifestyles" and "self-absorption": "my thinking
was unable to fulfill itself within feminism alone," she admits in 2001.[108]

In Rich's poetry of the nineties and the new millennium, she continues to evocatively interrogate suffering, self-sacrifice, women's oppression, and language's ethico-political relation to the material. She insistently explores the body—its pain as well as desire—as a site for ethical insight, and her technique increasingly engages the paradoxical double move of concrete specificity (alluding to specific news events) and the alikeness of certain disparate modes of oppression. She does this through juxtaposition, spacing, pronouns, metonymy, and the ambiguity by which poetic language always means more than it says. She thematizes these tactics in "Contradictions: Tracking Poems"[109]:

> remember: the body's pain and the pain on the streets
> are not the same   but you can learn
> from edges that blur   O you who love clear edges
> more than anything   watch the edges that blur

This excerpt is a powerful reminder of one of Rich's primary contributions to a literary ethics of suffering: any given subject's body, the pain and suffering of human experience in any given location, is importantly *not* the same as anyone else's. There is no "suffering," there are only sufferings. But a feminism, or an ethics, that can only see difference fractures into a paralyzing nonethics, as Misha Kavka argues. These "blurred edges" of different pains (concretized in the poem as a waving column of white internally dividing its lines) can embolden a reading of other pains, but such a reading practice requires humility and risk, especially in an era obsessed with "clear edges" between self and other and, as Sharon Welch asserts throughout *A Feminist Ethic of Risk*, an era also obsessed with getting everything right.

Perhaps Rich's most important contribution to a literary ethics of suffering, however, isn't located just in her writings: it is located in the text of her embodied life. In writing and in living, Rich theorizes and performs the paradoxes of ethical problems, offering not a straightforward liberal feminist action plan or a radical retreat into sameness, but a contextual, dialogical, endlessly revisable paradigm of paradoxical pain and creative power: in suffering and self-sacrifice, in language and literary production. She theorizes and performs as well, in her poetry, prose, and life, the subversion of insidious dichotomies—between love and power, between emotion and intellect, between theory and practice, between symbolic and material, between form and content, between activism and writing, between unity and particularity. Even more strongly than in her beautiful, challenging, and evocative writing, Rich's lifelong commitment to re-vision exemplifies an ethical paradigm of careful, even loving attention, which leads to a sense of profound particularity and complexity, followed by the inevitable risk of response, followed by an openness to correction, revision, and endless reengagement. Her practice manifests what I am calling the ethics of readerly attention, the open and welcoming interpretation that brings meaning into being and keeps the self vulnerable to responsive change.

My experience of reading Adrienne Rich for this project—*all* of Rich, chronologically and repeatedly—has been one of perpetual surprise. My choice to include her in this book was based on a hypothesis that arose out of typical exposure to her work in graduate school: excerpted chapters from *Of Woman Born* and anthologized poems. On the basis of this somewhat-limited reading and some research at the outset, I suspected that a gender- and religion-conscious treatment of contemporary literary ethics should begin with her. When I began reading Rich in earnest, I was surprised by the prevalence of the signifiers "suffering" and "self-sacrifice" in *Of Woman Born* and across the scope of Rich's work. I was surprised by how very much she had managed to write and publish. I was surprised by the breadth and depth of the work on poetry and (in)justice in its myriad forms done by one who I primarily had heard caricatured as a radical white lesbian feminist separatist. On that note, I was surprised by how early and insistent Rich was in her learning from and championing of black women writers and their criticisms of white Western feminist generalizations. I was surprised, overall, by Rich's commitment to be open to correction, to re-vision her own project, to *change*. And I was surprised by how clearly her project resonated with poststructuralist ethical literary criticism (and how infrequently Rich's writing, prose or poetry, featured in it).

Two of the most provocative books that bring together postmodern or poststructural ethics and feminism are *Beyond Accommodation: Ethical Feminism, Deconstruction, and the Law* by Cornell (1999) and *An Ethics of Dissensus: Postmodernity, Feminism, and the Politics of Radical Democracy* by Ewa Płonowska Ziarek (2001).[110] Both of these books seek to overcome divides between materialist and linguistic or symbolic approaches to

ADRIENNE RICH AND THE "LONG DIALOGUE BETWEEN ART AND JUSTICE"   83

ethics (and particularly to feminism); both emphasize the importance of the imagination, myth-making, and poetic language to a feminist project; both highlight the workings of feminist temporality, with its emphasis on a better future; and both relate their arguments to feminist scholarship and the pragmatic, concrete awareness of legal and political systems. Ziarek, in particular, highlights embodiment, desire, and sexuality as keys to stalled debates in ethics and feminism. On every single one of these counts, Rich has been theorizing—and poetically performing—for more than thirty years. Yet Ziarek's book does not name or cite Rich a single time, and Cornell's book includes just one index entry for a page on which she quotes another feminist theorist who cites Rich.

I'm not deriding Cornell and Ziarek for their failure to engage the work of a feminist foremother; none of us can read everything or cite everything we've read, and doubtless any reader of this book will wonder why I have left out one source or another. Nor am I saying that there are no good reasons for Rich's absence in these more recent feminist texts; Cornell and Ziarek both work in a discourse that is much more French than Anglo, and so it makes perfect sense for them to turn to Irigaray and Kristeva rather than Rich, who explicitly distanced herself from French theory.[111] It is also true that Rich's work *is* implicitly present throughout their books in their reliance on writers like bell hooks who have been influenced strongly by Rich: but still, this is an unnamed presence, and a significant one.

Indeed, I would like to suggest three points of significance relating to Rich's absence from these two texts. First of all, her absence suggests the continuing force of a phenomenon Rich herself described in the seventies, the erasure of earlier feminist thought and the bizarre sense of repetition, starting over again, and rediscovery. Second, it suggests that critics' hypotheses about the effects of reception history are true: Rich's erasure due to politics and the expectations of the literary establishment have had long-standing effects on her status within the academy, even after the institutionalizing of women's studies and widespread acceptance of a moderate feminism. Third, and most important, it highlights an important gap in both Cornell and Ziarek's projects that engagement with the wide body of Rich's writing could correct. For while Cornell and Ziarek both forward the importance of the imagination, poetic language, and women's literary writing, neither of them is a poet. Both are, rather, trained in the logical styles and norms of theoretical writing. Although their books assert hope in creative literary production, neither provides many examples of the concrete practice of reading or writing in these transformative ways. Rich, by contrast, always does both, in poetry as well as prose. She writes creatively, reads creatively, articulating her responses to other writers in her critical writing as well as her poetry, even using quotations of her own poems to illustrate her theoretical claims, consistently demonstrating what it means to be both a reader and a writer inching toward the edge of tomorrow. The next generations of feminist scholarship and writing will be much weaker for having forgotten her, and she warned us of the consequences of such forgetting.

My greatest surprise of all has been the overwhelming presence, across the scope of Rich's writing and the critical writing surrounding it (and, as I have shown, in the text of her life), of precisely the critical vocabulary I had laid out for this project before extensive interaction with Rich's writing. Not only suffering, but also the feminist refusal of a dichotomy between the symbolic and material or linguistic and concrete (which I had located in Cornell's "ethical feminism"), as well as an emphasis on *attention, undecidability* or *radical complexity*, and *risk*. Again and again, these words appear in her writing and in interpretations of her writing, supporting my hypothesis of their importance in pursuit of a more nuanced literary ethics of suffering and predicting their continuing importance in the chapters that follow this one. In a sense, they may even suggest the degree to which Rich's writing has influenced that which has followed it, even as its source has been forgotten.

I narrate the surprises of my research experience because unless I do so their lesson will be elided: the temporal workings of a large-scale writing project (and the erasures that good writing entails) mean that the appearance of these terms in my first chapter and throughout the book could be the result of revisions *after* my sustained interactions with Rich's writing. They are not. They are uncanny hypotheses. More important, they are evidence of the profound and wide influence of Rich's work on those writers whom I had studied before I began this project. They are also evidence of the richness further critical engagement of Rich's writing has to offer those who are interested in how literature, feminism, ethics, theology, and theory have anything to do with systemic injustice in the material realm, how beauty and pain and goodness meet and argue and mingle in the twenty-first century.

I had thought, in beginning with Rich, that as I moved through the following chapters into engagements with other writers whose concern with other particulars of difference complicated an earlier white radical feminism, I would leave her work behind. And here lay another surprise, for I was wrong. Rich's writing, rather than maintaining a solipsistic commitment to generalized Woman, was challenged and changed by the writings and activism of African American, Chicana, religious, working class, and women of the Global South, leading to an increased attention to location in Rich's work that is especially important to my developing ethics of readerly attention and ethics of literary representation in later chapters. Likewise, Rich's writing contributed to a critical turn to African American, and Chicana, and global concerns in feminism; it also continued her engagement with the question of belief, traced an increasingly complex web of intermingled injustices, and continued the formal experimentation, at the interstices of literature and theory and life, that later women writers carried out. In moving ahead into this history in the coming chapters, interrogating the literary interactions of suffering with religion, literary theory, and feminism—or in the fitting trinity of Rich's poem "Necessities of Life," Jonah, Wittgenstein, and Wollstonecraft[112]— I do not leave Rich behind as a foremother, after all, but rather continue to read the text of her life—the narrative of her engagement—as a provocative source.

3
Love and Mercy

Toni Morrison's Paradox of Redemptive Suffering

The revolutionary artist, the relayer of possibility, draws on such powers, in opposition to a technocratic society's hatred of multiformity, hatred of the natural world, hatred of the body, hatred of darkness and women, hatred of disobedience. The revolutionary poet loves people, rivers, other creatures, stones, trees inseparably from art, is not ashamed of any of these loves, and for them conjures a language that is public, intimate, inviting, terrifying, and beloved.
—Adrienne Rich, *What Is Found There*

Power at its best is love implementing the demands of justice. Justice at its best is love correcting everything that stands against love.
—Martin Luther King, Jr., *Where Do We Go From Here?*

I stand on moral ground but know that ground must be shored up by mercy.
—Toni Morrison, "James Baldwin: His Life Remembered;
Life in His Language"

Over the nearly fifty-year span of her career as a writer, Toni Morrison has been a loving conjurer of language that is public yet intimate, inviting yet terrifying, and "beloved" in at least two senses. First, Morrison repeatedly and insistently thematizes language, and love for language, as a response to human suffering. Second, in writing *Beloved*—which stands at the apogee of Morrison's eleven-novel oeuvre—Morrison has *conjured* the figure Beloved as an embodiment only possible in language: in a certain sense, Beloved is a word become flesh who exists in response to the enfleshed pain of millions of enslaved Africans. Her indeterminate identity arises from several possible links to suffering: Is she a ghost of Sethe's killed baby? The flesh-and-blood young woman rumored to have been locked for years in a white man's house?[1] An ancestral visitor bearing witness to the horrors of Middle Passage? A desperately needed but dangerously needy reminder of the forgotten past of suffering? This Beloved language-act conjured by Morrison exists at the apogee of Morrison's work, forever in conversation with the novels that preceded and followed, forever in conversation with anyone who reads *Beloved*, haunting with questions of justice and love. Indeed, as many have noted, an exploration of love also plays across the scope of Morrison's writings: its presence, its absence, its limits, its aberrations, its multiplicity. And this question of love is often joined by a question of mercy: from the twisted affection and hatred in the Breedlove family and its town's merciless scapegoating of Pecola in *The Bluest Eye* (1970) to Pilate's passionate cry for "Mercy!" at her granddaughter's funeral and the resounding conclusion, "And she was loved!" in *Song of Solomon* (1977) to two of Morrison more recent novels—the primary focus of my analysis in this chapter—fittingly titled *Love* (2003) and *A Mercy* (2008).

If Morrison is one of the most prominent examples of contemporary women writers' interrogation of suffering, it is also her attention to specifically black women's suffering (although all of her novels focus on male as well as female characters) that has garnered Morrison's most vitriolic critiques.[2] But I would argue against commentators who claim that Morrison presents stereotypes and sentimentally manipulative victim stories. On the contrary, Morrison's engagement with suffering in her novels is complex and specific: she makes no sweeping generalizations, asserts no broad categories of victimhood. Rather, Morrison depicts characters whose unique situations and personalities affect them just as plainly as their subject positions within oppressive systems of gender, race, and class; she presents characters who are mixed, endowed with agency while also constrained by context. This mixed exploration troubles any categorical systems of moral judgment or final argument about cause and effect. Morrison's texts at once invite readers to interpret characters as representative—of African Americans, of women, of black men—and also undermine that possible representative status by the characters' particularity. Likewise, her texts both encourage readers to take them as reflective of material reality and also emphasize their own textuality, even to the point of performatively theorizing the relation of language to suffering.

Morrison's writings raise important questions about what it means to speak of a literary ethics of suffering that does not elide material sufferings: how do the acts of bearing witness and speaking unspeakable things (which imply both authorial agency and the function of a text in its social context of publication) relate to the formal, text-bound conception of ethics popular in the new ethical criticism? How do interpretive vocabulary and readerly responsibility (which imply an ethical relationship between reader and text) interact with these other, authorial and textual, modes of intention? How does the specifically racialized and gendered institution of chattel slavery, and its troubling relation to institutional Christianity, challenge and complicate paradigms of redemptive suffering?

In this chapter, I locate Morrison's literary ethics of suffering in a risky paradigm of redemption: first, in the function of her particular stories in their sociopolitical contexts and their explorations of the complexly intermingled sources of characters' suffering, which work together as her ethics of literary representation; and, second, in the narratives' thematization of language and interpretation in paradoxical relation to suffering, often in allegories of reading and writing (their ethics of readerly attention). I read in her work a performance of justice that is categorical and structural, as her novels school readers in their formal play of unassimilable otherness, aligning Morrison's texts with the poststructuralist ethical turn in literary studies. Yet this structural justice is *always* attended and subverted by a particularity in the text, as the representational raced, gendered, religious, and historical narratives invite readers into an ethical relation more closely akin to mercy, which is always context bound, than blind justice understood as a generalized structure. This textual dynamic repeatedly manifests the dangers of abstract redemptive suffering paradigms. Endeavoring to learn the texts' lesson in particularity, and recognizing the elision of gender, race, and religion in much postmodern ethical literary criticism, I look to the black theological discourse of redemptive suffering as an interlocutor for Morrison's texts, and within that stream I turn to womanist ethics (the major proponents of which have already turned to Morrison) to locate a more adequately contextualized critical vocabulary for the texts' ethical insights. Still, as my reading of womanist ethicist Emilie Townes will demonstrate, this theoretical discourse in itself does not provide a complete ethical system; the literariness of Morrison's texts still escapes womanist theory's systematizing impulses, offering an ethics that is at once material and textual, experiential and theoretical, in a paradoxically redemptive interplay of literary language and (black) (women's) suffering.[3]

Experience and Theory: Black Women's Writing and Literary Representation

> I finally want to express how much easier both my waking and my sleep-
> ing hours would be if there were one book in existence that would tell me
> something specific about my life. One book based in Black feminist and Black
> lesbian experience, fiction or nonfiction. Just one work to reflect the reality
> that I and the Black women whom I love are trying to create. When such a
> book exists then each of us will not only know better how to live, but how
> to dream.
> —Barbara Smith, "Toward a Black Feminist Criticism"

A tension between "experience" and "theory" structures a number of
debates in the humanities. This tension is famously invoked in Barbara
Christian's 1987 essay "The Race for Theory," in which she argues that "a
takeover in the literary world by Western philosophers" was "coopt[ing]"
the more beautiful, accessible, and concrete theorizing of marginalized
writers and scholars.[4] She insists that "people of color have always theorized . . . often in narrative form,"[5] and she points out that just as "minority" literature was finally moving into "the center," its political power
was diminished by the rise of theories that emphasized abstractions and
reading practices over literature's content and questioned language's relation to reality.[6] In other words, Christian and others assert that during
the seventies, when feminists and other writers outside the mainstream
were drawing on their unique experiences to challenge the false univer-
sals of white male thinkers, those same thinkers began to undermine the
category of "experience." In making these claims, Christian also articulates the key tension in the ethical turn in literary criticism between the
new ethical criticism's poststructuralist emphasis on reading and moral
criticism's claim that literature schools readers in real-life ethics through
mimesis. It is not surprising that in his introduction to the 1999 *PMLA* special issue on ethics, Lawrence Buell links moral criticism to multiculturalism, as both emphasize experience.[7]

Christian asserts near the end of her article, "My response, then, is
directed to those who write what I read and to those who read what I
read—put concretely—to Toni Morrison and to people who read Toni
Morrison (among whom I would count few academics)."[8] At that time,

Morrison scholarship was primarily the project of feminists. In fact, Morrison's writing was central to the work of black feminists in the seventies and eighties who had begun to assert the specificity of their experience over against black male and white female hegemony. Important examples of this critique include the groundbreaking volumes *This Bridge Called My Back: Writings By Radical Women of Color* (1981) and *All the Women Are White, All The Blacks Are Men, But Some of Us Are Brave: Black Women's Studies* (1982).[9]

These two volumes are widely acknowledged as instigating a turn in feminist scholarship, as they fractured the façade of sisterhood that had dethroned the false universal white male subject only to replace him with the false universal white female. It became increasingly clear that if feminists wanted to *do justice* to women's experiences, finding ethical paradigms in support of a project to end gender-based oppression, they would have to take into account the intersecting dynamics of race, gender, and class. In the famous words of the Combahee River Collective, printed in both *This Bridge* and *All the Women*, "the major systems of oppression are interlocking."[10] Foundational to the approach in Hull, Scott, and Smith's collection were both the recognition that black women experience "multilayered oppression" *and* the recognition that black women had nevertheless "created and maintained our own intellectual traditions,"[11] manifesting a "creative, intellectual spirit" and a "practical ability to make something out of nothing,"[12] a remarkable knack for survival. From its founding, Black Women's Studies was predicated on a double-pronged assertion that black women experienced particular modes of suffering and, at the same time, manifested particular modes of creativity rather than passive victimization. This interpretation of black women's experiences—the assertion that black women's suffering, while its source could never be celebrated, had offered those who experienced it a certain moral edge—assumes the structure of redemptive suffering popular with black theologians, whereby suffering leads to some good.

Black women's literary writing is central to the Black Women's Studies project forwarded by *All the Women*. The volume includes myriad sociological, pedagogical, theological, and other theoretical approaches to black women's experiences, but again and again the contributors turn to literature: Zora Neale Hurston, Alice Walker, and Morrison are among the most often-cited sources. Barbara Smith's pioneering essay included in the collection, "Toward a Black Feminist Criticism" (first published in 1977), takes Morrison's novel *Sula* as its primary text.[13] Smith insists that the literature, in its specificity, invites its own theory. This essay has provoked so many responses and debates over the past thirty years, Farah Jasmine Griffin argues, that tracing responses to "Toward a Black Feminist Criticism" allows one to chart the development of black feminism.[14] Literature—and particularly literature as trustworthy representations of black female experience—played a crucial role in the early black women's movement, and Morrison's writing in particular received notable attention.

This critical attention is frequently framed in the vocabulary of "breaking silences" and "bearing witness," much like the poetry of Adrienne Rich. The questions of *whose stories are told* in the media and in official histories, *whose stories are printed* in the industry of literary publishing (and who has access to the conditions necessary for writing), *whose stories are taught* in classrooms—material and pragmatic questions—were raised by white and black feminists in the seventies and eighties who recognized their ethico-political significance.[15] The assumption was that *recognition*, or attention, was a necessary component of justice, whether justice was conceived of as fair respect for diverse identities or redistribution of material resources. In most of these treatments, it is the telling itself that is necessary and good, both personally and politically, and "voice" stands metonymically for language employed for self-representation. This emphasis on telling the elided stories of marginalized subjects' suffering in order to engage readers in some form of responsibility is what I am calling the ethics of literary representation.

Scholars looking for examples of women's stories often turned to literature in the seventies and eighties because of gaps in historical archives and the fact that even when autobiographies were published by male and female former slaves, there was a noted tendency to elide the more traumatic experiences of suffering for the sake of "propriety." In her essay "The Site of Memory" (1987), Morrison roots this tendency in earlier writers' awareness that they would not have an audience if they were too honest in their portrayals, that they would be read, unlike martyrs whose narratives of extreme suffering "are and were read for the eloquence of their message as well as their experience of redemption," as "'biased,' 'inflammatory,' and 'improbable.'"[16] And so Morrison asserts in this essay that her practice as a novelist is to *imagine* the truth of the past and present sufferings, and to represent this truth through fiction.[17] Morrison's responsibility to represent—in the legal sense of pleading for justice and in the aesthetic sense of constructing a referential text, the two of which work together—arises from her conviction that the elision of certain past and present sufferings from the social imaginary is an injustice and may perpetuate more injustices. The telling of such stories—their construction, even in fiction—confronts readers with the question of responsibility for such particular sufferings and the challenge of ethical interpretation more generally.

For nearly two decades Morrison's novels were important primarily to scholars interested in black women's experiences. Yet the same year Christian published "The Race for Theory" in Cultural Critique's special issue on "The Nature and Context of Minority Discourses," Morrison published Beloved, which catapulted her into international fame, first with a Pulitzer Prize in 1988 and then, in 1993, the Nobel Prize in Literature. When Christian wrote of Morrison's unpopularity in the academy, she accurately described the broader established academy's lack of welcome for literature it took to be too "political,"[18] which also shaped Rich's reception. Yet since 1987, Morrison has risen to such stature within the academy that she is now commonly heralded as the most critically discussed living author writing in English.[19] This shift can be variously attributed to the institutionalization of feminist theory and gender studies, the increased concern with race in academia, the cooptation of black women writers as a hot commodity among scholars in the humanities, and the rise of critical vocabularies opening up discussions of ethics and politics in literature. It has produced an incredible range of critical approaches to Morrison's writing.

Morrison has invited and applauded a turn from exclusive attention to the "what" of her writing to an added interest in the "how." Whereas in a 1983 interview she could say, as she often did early on in her career, that she longed for criticism that would read her books in light of "the black cosmology,"[20] in interviews she gave after the publication of A Mercy in 2008, Morrison claimed to be glad that after years of being read as "black world novel[s]," her books now were considered for their poetics and participation in a discourse.[21] This movement to considering Morrison's literature as literature has been nowhere more apparent than in critics' propensity to highlight her novels' postmodern features over the past two decades, particularly in the mode of the new ethical criticism and its heightened attention to language.

L as Language: *Love* and the New Ethical Criticism

> I was just a girl coming slowly into womanhood when I read Adrienne Rich's words, "This is the oppressor's language, yet I need it to talk to you." This language that enabled me to attend graduate school, to write a dissertation, to speak at job interviews, carries the scent of oppression. Language is also a place of struggle. . . . The oppressed struggle in language to recover ourselves, to reconcile, to reunite, to renew. Our words are not without meaning, they are an action, a resistance. Language is also a place of struggle.
> —bell hooks, "Choosing the Margin as a Space of Radical Openness"

Although "voice" as a category and "breaking silences" as a practice can be too simplistically celebrated, Morrison's ethical literary praxis functions not only by way of her books' achievement of recognition for otherwise under-regarded stories, but Morrison also insistently performs and thematizes the structural relation of language to suffering. This performance is especially apparent in the novel *Love,* which I read here in concert with her 1993 Nobel Prize Acceptance Speech, an explicit articulation of Morrison's theorizing of language.[22] Critics have naturally emphasized the centrality of love as a concept in the 2003 novel.[23] Most also read the mysterious character whose comments make up part of the narration, L, to mean that her name is in fact "Love" when she mentions that her name is taken from I Corinthians 13. It should be noted, however, that while I Corinthians 13 is famous for its attention to love ("love is patient, love is kind . . ."), the biblical chapter is bookended by attention to others among the novel's concerns: childhood, interpretation, and *language.*

Indeed, language is a key concern in *Love*: its power and failures are dramatized by the third-person narration, and its importance is explicitly addressed in L's comments. She begins the novel with a discussion that entangles ideas of language, gender, race, music, sex, and change over time. *"The women's legs are spread wide open, so I hum. Men grow irritable, but they know it's all for them. They relax. Standing by, unable to do anything but watch, is a trial, but I don't say a word."*[24] Beginning with this connection between language and social norms, L asserts that she hums rather than speaks *because* the women's legs are spread wide open: her verbal silence is a response to perceived sexual affront. She also claims that while she was never one to speak much, there was something good about *"meaning much by saying little,"* and that words could have real effects: *"I could make a point strong enough to stop a womb—or a knife"* (3). L accords well-used language a certain power and authority.[25]

The third-person narration that follows also dramatizes issues of language, particularly its absence or failure, exemplifying the connection Simone Weil and Dorothee Sölle make between suffering, silence, and isolation. The moment preceding the young character Romen's "rescue" of a gang-raped girl is characterized by "silence," and after getting her out onto the porch, Romen finds himself incapable of speaking to her: "He thought her name was Faye or Faith[26] and was about to say something when suddenly he couldn't stand the sight of her." Faye/Faith doesn't speak either after her experience, not to Romen ("she didn't say a word") or to her friends, who repeatedly question her only to be met by silence: "Pretty-Fay! Say something, girl!" (47). Another violent trauma is followed by the loss of language when the young girl Junior's uncles run over her foot and then claim to have rescued her: "Day after day she lay there, first unable, then refusing to cry or speak to Vivian [her mother], who was telling her how thankful she should be that the uncles had found her sprawled on the roadside. . . . In silence Junior watched her toes swell, redden, turn blue, then black, then marble, then merge" (59). For both Junior and Fay, speech is an impossibility after their violent treatment by groups of men; both young women also choose to leave the context of their victimization (Fay doesn't return to school; Junior escapes the Settlement where her family lives) rather than continue to interact with the perpetrators of violence, removing them from their previous sites of community and the possibility of restitution in those spaces.

Importantly, both of these examples of silence preview another silence, present through the entire narrative but not explained until its end. This silence originates after parallel sexual violations are perpetrated by the novel's mysterious central figure Bill Cosey himself. When Cosey touches his granddaughter's friend Heed's prepubescent nipple and then is viewed masturbating by his granddaughter Christine in her bedroom window, the girls feel too guilty to tell each other of their experiences: "Heed can't speak, can't tell her friend what happened. She knows she has spoiled it all" (191), and "When Heed finds her, Christine doesn't explain the bathing suit, why she is wiping it, or why she can't look at Heed. She is ashamed of her grandfather and herself" (192). The narrator links the girls' inability to speak to their perceptions of unique dirtiness or culpability: "It wasn't the arousals, not altogether unpleasant, that the girls could not talk about. It was the other thing. The thing that made each believe, without knowing why, that this particular shame was different and could not tolerate speech—not even in the language they had invented for secrets" (192). The narrator points to this sexual initiation and the accompanying silence (and implicit lie) as the beginning of the silence that breaks down Heed and Christine's relationship and features prominently throughout the novel as the source of their isolated suffering.[27]

Healing in Christine and Heed's relationship is brought about precisely *by* language: after decades of silence, their unplanned interaction in Cosey's long-abandoned hotel eventually breaks the cycle. "Wordlessness continues" at first, but then a change occurs:

> Still, they avoid rehearsing accusations, a waste of breath now with one of them cracked to pieces and the other sweating like a laundress. Up here where the solitude is like the room of a dead child, the ocean has no scent or roar. The future is disintegrating along with the past. The landscape beyond this room is without color. Just a bleak ridge of stone and no one to imagine it otherwise, because that is the way it is—as, deep down, everyone knows. An unborn world where sound, any sound— the scratch of a claw, the flap of webbed feet—is a gift. Where a human voice is the only miracle and the only necessity. Language, when finally it comes, has the vigor of a felon pardoned after twenty-one years on hold. Sudden, raw, stripped of its underwear. (184)

The dialogue that follows is choppy, without quotation marks or tags to indicate the speaker; it has a passionate, immediate quality. The women suddenly begin to discuss their childhoods, their pains, precisely the "sad stories" L refers to in the beginning pages of her narration, the stories about "dragon daddies and false-hearted men, or mean mamas and friends who did them wrong," which cause them to "open their legs rather than their hearts where" "the sugar-child, the winsome baby girl" is curled (4–5).

Susana Vega-González sees this final dialogue as a convergence of love and language, the site where the "magic" of language allows them to reconnect and finally express or enact their love for one another.[28] This is language as a profoundly healing response to decades of suffering.

Even so, the story that precipitated their silence is the one we are not sure if they actually manage to tell. "Even in idigay,[29] they had never been able to share a certain twin shame. Each one thought the rot was hers alone," we are told: "with everything and nothing to lose, they let the phrase take them back once again to a time when innocence did not exist because no one had dreamed up hell" (190). The story of their sexual violation that follows is told in third-person present-tense narration, first focalized through Heed and then through Christine. It is not clear whether the women are discussing these memories or simply remembering them separately, especially as the passage ends as follows: "Now, exhausted, drifting toward a maybe permanent sleep they don't speak of the birth of sin. Idigay can't help them with that" (192). Is "the birth of sin" the experiences just narrated, or is it something beyond those experiences? In other words, have they managed to verbalize the early traumatic sexual violations, or are these experiences exactly the stories that still refuse language? This unanswered question emphasizes the depth of their pain, questioning the final redeeming power of language. "Voice" does not necessarily equal healing.

L ultimately asserts that her intervention in the Cosey story—her poisoning of Bill Cosey and substitution of the 1958 menu-will that named the indeterminate "sweet Cosey child" as beneficiary—connected Heed and Christine in the act of endlessly contested interpretation and taught them a lesson about the importance of language:

> My menu worked just fine. Gave them a reason to stay connected and maybe figure out how precious the tongue is. If properly used, it can save you from the attention of Police-heads[30] hunting desperate women and hardhearted, misraised children. It's hard to do but I know at least one woman who did. Who stood right under their wide hats, their dripping beards, and scared them off with a word—or was it a note? (201)

L's thematic connection of this act of hers, the importance of language, and the figure of Celestial, that mysterious "one woman" who scared off the Police-heads, continues the narrative's consistent dramatization of language as fragile, particularly in the face of sexual trauma, but also potentially powerful for healing and resistance. In this passage, L recalls an earlier time when she saw Celestial—about whom the narrative is notably reticent—dive into the ocean where "Police-heads were on the move," and then return to the beach and make some sort of linguistic—or at least oral—statement: *"Then she—well, made a sound. I don't know to this day whether it was a word, a tune, or a scream. All I know is that it was a sound I wanted to answer. Even though, normally, I'm stone quiet, Celestial"* (106). The indiscernibility of speech from music recalls Morrison's fascination with music as literary form and interactive process, particularly as L desires to answer Celestial in a form of call-and-response. We could also read this as Celestial's beginning of a verbal dialogue. In any case, her use of language saves her from the Police-heads' punishment, removes her from the position of "guilty" or "victimized" woman, and inspires something in L and initiates a relationship. Her speech act is real-world powerful, inviting response.[31] L's use of language is similarly powerful, for not only does it bring Heed and Christine into deeper and continued contact, but also it eventually results in their reconciliation, however fragile.

Language and narrative are also the central themes of Morrison's 1993 Nobel Lecture, which resonates in many ways with the novel published a decade later. In this lecture, Morrison tells the "Once upon a time" story of an old, blind, wise woman visited by children who ask her (she believes, in order to trick her) whether the bird they hold in their hands is living or dead. Morrison's old woman eventually responds, "I don't know whether the bird you are holding is dead or alive, but what I do know is that it is in your hands. It is in your hands" (318), emphasizing their extraordinary responsibility, that key word in both postmodern ethics and Morrison's oeuvre. In the passage that follows, Morrison reads this bird as language and the woman as a writer, and she goes on to express the dangers of dead language and the constructive power of language that lives. But Morrison then turns the story on its head, reapproaching it from the perspective of the young people, who are desperate for attention and advice from the old woman. They respond to her theorizing with an impassioned plea for concrete stories, stories of raced and gendered difference and history. The result is a dialogic partnership, a conversation that ultimately both forwards the generalizable ideal of a "just" language and questions it through the children's need for the particularity of mercy, exceptions to the rule of abstract justice.

In the speech, Morrison's writer conceives of language "partly as a system, partly as a living thing over which one has control, but mostly as agency—as an act with consequences" (319), much like Celestial's powerfully resistant language act and Christine and Heed's healing conversation, or, more negatively, like Theo's "trumpet blast" epithet that causes Romen agony (*Love* 47). "Dead" language is language used in the service of oppressive power structures, like the Police-head stories that keep women and children in line: "Unreceptive to interrogation, it cannot form or tolerate new ideas, shape other thoughts, tell another story, fill baffling silences" ("Nobel" 319). It prefers sameness over difference. This sort of language is as active and powerful as living language—it is violent and limiting (not just representing violence or limitation), used to silence the subjugated, including racial minorities, women, and children, to "render the suffering of millions mute" (320). Those harmed by these structures of power, too, are not only silenced but silencing: so boys express themselves in gang rape, poor young men harm and then lie about their niece, and a rich but racially demoralized man exerts sexual authority over very young girls. *This is the oppressor's language.*[32]

Yet "living" language asserts its power in the world in ways that create, heal, and forward knowledge, even forging a new reality. "The vitality of language," Morrison's writer says, "lies in its ability to limn the actual, imagined, and possible lives of its speakers, readers, writers." It is used in humble service of difference: "It arcs toward the place where meaning may lie"; "Its force, its felicity, is in its reach toward the ineffable" (321). Importantly, the writer in Morrison's speech notes a slippage between "language" and "experience": although language may seem to "displac[e] experience," language can never simply represent experience. Life exceeds language's attempts to master it, even as language itself is "generative" and thus can create something beyond that which presently exists as life (321).[33] The performance and theorizing of language at work here (and in *Love*) exemplify the new ethical criticism, particularly in their considerations of the power of language to privilege difference and the ineffable and the danger of using language to reduce all difference to an order of the same. J. Hillis Miller's 1987 *The Ethics of Reading* explores Paul de Man's ethics, which "erased from the reading subject every concern but respect for the text. A properly respectful reading or ethical reading, Miller had argued, lingered in the apprehension of textual 'undecidability.' "[34] As I discuss in chapter 1, following Miller's deconstruction and drawing on Emmanuel Levinas, many scholars have theorized the relation to text-as-other as parallel with our relation to people-as-others. The ethical responsibility—in any interaction with any other—is to resist the urge to contain, oversimplify, or use the other for one's own comfort or enlargement; to remain open to difference and insolubility; to respect alterity and to be submissive to the possibility of changing, oneself, as a result of the interaction. This is precisely the sort of ethical use of language for which Morrison's wise old woman writer commends President Lincoln for recognizing that "language can never live up to life once and for all" or " 'pin down' slavery, genocide, war. Nor should it yearn for the arrogance to be able to do so" (321).

The danger of an overgeneralized language is highlighted in the Nobel speech by Morrison's abrupt shift, more than halfway through, to another perspective. The children, hearing the command of their responsibility and the descriptions of "dead" and "living" language, "fill [the silence that follows her lecture] with language invented on the spot." They *respond*, asking their wise old woman why she has not attended to their specificity and materiality before telling them how to live: "Why didn't you reach out, touch us with your soft fingers, delay the sound bite, the lesson, until you knew who we were?" (322). "Is there no context for our lives?" (323). They demand of her,

> Think of our lives and tell us your particularized world. Make up a story. Narrative is radical, creating us at the very moment it is being created. We will not blame you if your reach exceeds your grasp; if love so ignites your words that they go down in flames and nothing is left but their scald. . . . Passion is never enough; neither is skill. But try. . . . Don't tell us. . . . Show us. (323)

The children's request for particularity, for narrative, for an aesthetically constructed truth, for risk could be read as a gloss on my whole project: they express a profound desire for an ethical practice of literary representation. At the same time, they do fall into some of the same generalizing they critique by asserting the radical, creative nature of narrative. This claim stands in the midst of impassioned pleas as a moment of theorizing, and it raises the familiar question, who is "us"? These speakers, in particular? The human population? The phrase highlights the tenuous play of literature and theory.

The children long for particular stories; they long for creation, for remembrance. They go on to describe the stories they want her to tell— stories of "ships turned away from shorelines at Easter, placenta in a field" and of face-to-face human mercy on a slave-trade wagon (particularly gendered, raced, historicized), and in describing what they desire from her, they actually take up the act of storytelling for themselves (323). The challenge of these particular stories does not altogether undermine the old woman's claims about language; indeed, it seems that her theorizing *invites* the children's response, in a dialogical encounter that promises not to end.

The speech is productively read as an allegory of justice and mercy and their ongoing negotiation. It is not insignificant that the woman is blind, a detail that invites an association with the traditional personification of justice. Her pronouncements before touching the children or hearing their stories suggest such a reading, although this reading certainly does not disparage justice: the woman's proclamations about language are compelling. But the children's longing to be known, in particular, and to tell and be told particular stories—their emphasis on context—suggests a dialogical relationship between justice as a generalized good and mercy, which is always a risky response to a particular subject or situation. By this reading, justice and mercy work in ongoing dialogue, as general and particular, theory and narrative, a lesson emblematized in the speech's final lines: "Look. How lovely it is, this thing we have done—together" (323). In its content and its form, the speech manifests the ethics of language's relation to suffering, its dangers and its necessity, the impossibility of mastery, and need for responsive dialogue and endless process.

Morrison's novels could be said to *teach* readers how to relate to them in this ethical way. Morrison has a long history of troubling easy readings: her novels are notoriously subject to multiple interpretations. Indeed, Morrison herself claims to purposely leave endings open and meanings indeterminate. In "Rootedness: The Ancestor as Foundation," she describes this interpretive openness as "space": "I have to provide the places and spaces so that the reader can participate. Because it is the affective and participatory relationship between the artist or the speaker and the audience that is of primary importance."[35] These gaps in the text invite the reader to contribute to the meaning of the text, as Morrison explains further in "Unspeakable Things Unspoken: The Afro-American Presence in Literature": "into these spaces should fall the ruminations of the reader and his or her invented or recollected or misunderstood knowingness."[36] Even though Morrison is willing to offer interpretations of her own novels, she has been known to provide competing readings and continues to insist on the importance of readerly participation. Indeed, the novels themselves refuse to "give up" their mysteries, and this structural relationship between text and reader is a mode of ethical practice.

Love carries on the trend of gaps and unanswered questions. The narrative's construction contributes to these uncertainties, evoking disorientation and tentativeness, not just at the conclusion but from the very first page. A first-time reader may ask, Who is this italicized "I" opening the narration? When and where is he or she speaking? Fairly early on we learn that "now" is the nineties, but the narrator's introduction of "Police-heads," mythical sea-creatures that arrive to punish "loose women and disobedient children" (5) knocks the reader off balance: is this story realistic or magical? Readerly disorientation continues as the narrative shifts out of italics and into apparently omniscient third-person narration, with focalization moving from character to character and presenting us with their competing limited perspectives on each other and the past. We are given imperfect glimpses, impressions, and memories, frequently with allusions to dates or historical events, and must fill in the gaps and make the connections to piece together a history that spans from 1890 with the birth of Bill Cosey to the mid-nineties. And many of the key pieces to the puzzle arrive near the end of the novel, suspending even partial understanding of the narrative and undermining our confidence in our own knowledge: we have to learn to wait for the text, to trust it to catch us up in its own good time as it teaches us humility and submission to its mysterious otherness.

In addition to the novel's challenging form, myriad details of the narrative remain ambiguous for characters as well as for readers. It is unclear, for instance, who is the "sweet Cosey child" of Bill Cosey's will, both for the characters fighting over its interpretation and for the readers who have access to more information. It also remains unclear whether L found this will or forged it.[37] Vega-González likewise notes that the C's engraved in Bill Cosey's silverware could refer to any number of characters.[38] Even the question of which woman dies at the end—Heed or Christine—is obscured by a mix of signifiers that seem to point to both women. Most critics assume Christine has lived and Heed has died, yet a careful reading complicates rather than clarifies which is which. This lack of closure is important for the narrative, undermining any possible implied vindication of one character over another. In a typically Morrisonian fashion, these gaps undermine any tidy moral system one might seek in the novel. In other words, the text schools its readers in an ethics of readerly attention, teaching through its own ambiguities the importance of careful reading.

The irony, of course, is that in blithely assuming Christine has died, professional readers highlight the way our training to read for narrative closure—the will to interpretation, the drive for "better" readings that prove professional clout—often works against an ethics of readerly attention. This is exactly the critical mode in response to which the new ethical criticism developed, as theorists recognized and sought to resist the "propensity to reduce everything fortuitous, foreign and enigmatic to conditions of intelligibility."[39] In ignoring textual ambiguity, critics refuse the lesson in ethical reading that *Love* seeks to engage them in, in a sense doing violence to the text, and the "proud but calcified"[40] readings produced are guilty of suppressing the generative power of language. In this textual lesson, Morrison shares the insight of the new ethical criticism, recognizing that the desire for full explanation, containment, and use of literature is related to the Western heritage of desiring full explanation, containment, and use of Africans, women, and other oppressed and marginalized peoples. The novel insistently reminds us that we "know in part and prophesy in part" (I Corinthians 13:9). This is the postmodern linguistic ethics of love, the ethics of readerly attention.

Yet reading *Love* as an allegory of ethical reading still leaves something to be desired. What difference does it make that *Love* does all this through a story that is about specifically gendered and raced dynamics? What difference does it make that these explorations unfold in a religiously inflected vocabulary (notable in *Love* but even stronger in some of Morrison's other novels)? The foregoing reading may very well participate in the new ethical criticism's tendency to produce abstractions that I am at pains in this project to challenge. In particular, as Ewa Płonowska Ziarek asserts, these contemporary ethical debates tend to elide "the role of sexual and racial difference."[41] In the words of womanist ethicist Emilie Townes,

> The irony is that postmodernist discourse often excludes although its theoretical intent is to call attention to and appropriate the experience of difference and otherness as legitimate discourse for critical theory and rigorous ethical reflection. Categories of otherness and difference can swerve toward abstraction at best and become tools for hegemony at worst.[42]

As we have seen in earlier chapters, gender makes a difference in ethical paradigms; the same is absolutely true of race. Endless openness and submission to the text's lessons are one thing in a certain social register; they're different when one has been socially, legally, or even physically bound to submit to another's rule. Critiques of "mastery," popular in poststructuralist ethics and Rich's midcentury poetry, take on a different tone entirely in the context of an enslaved people literally forced to call a man Master. Levinasian suspicion of "freedom" looks different in light of a group's historical longing to be legally and psychologically free. The material origins of our vocabularies of ethics remind us that there is more than one kind of difference, more than one source of suffering, more than one responsive mode.

Here is a prime example. Like Rich, Morrison writes repeatedly about mothering and suffering, but she does so with this important difference. Although the paradox posed by Rich is that mothering is both the source of many women's suffering and also a resource for ethical resistance to socially imposed suffering, Morrison seems much less concerned with the suffering *caused* by mothering and much more attentive to suffering caused by a *lack* of mothering, structural limitations on the right of the child and mother to an intimate relationship. As Andrea O'Reilly notes, mothers die or are removed from their children in all of Morrison's novels, which insistently depict "the suffering of unmothered children."[43] Central to an ethics of suffering arising from Morrison's work is the realization that the particularity of African American experience has meant a *different* relation of motherhood—and of sex and gender—to suffering for black women. This is not to say that black mothers never experience the oppression based on patriarchal family structures described by Rich and other white feminists, nor is it to say that other similarly encoded linguistic links do not exist between black women and exemplary self-sacrificial giving, especially within political rhetoric and the church. Black feminist and womanist scholars have raised many concerns about theologies of suffering and self-sacrifice and gendered expectations within the black church that parallel the concerns raised by white feminists like Mary Daly. Similarly, certain cultural positions have tended to subject black women to the same ideologies of sacrificial motherhood as their white sisters. Yet the history of chattel slavery and the ongoing reality of racism present a different set of causes of suffering for black women—specifically racialized causes. And as multiple critics have noted, these differences have not been adequately attended to in prominent contemporary ethical theory and ethical literary criticism, nor has literary critical language tended to accommodate the workings of the supernatural so prevalent in black women's fiction.[44] For a discourse that attends to the difference gender, race, and religion make in ethical considerations of suffering, one that will help me bring together representations of suffering with allegories of reading, I turn now to black theology and womanist ethics.

Redemptive Suffering and Womanist Ethics

> Black women have held, they have been given . . . the cross. They don't walk near it. They're often on it. And they've borne it, I think, extremely well.
> —Toni Morrison, in a conversation with Robert Stepto

There is a certain irony in locating the ethics of a literary text in its formal lessons of readerly submission and endless responsibility when that text itself dramatizes the dangers of submitting too fully—or being forced to submit altogether—to the whims of an other. The hyperbolic tendencies of postmodern rhetoric notwithstanding, limitless responsibility and substitutionary suffering are questioned as an ethical model by the particular overlapping dynamics of raced, gendered, classed bodies. Yet within the African American tradition, a similar ethical paradigm does hold sway in the concept of "redemptive suffering," which develops out of black experience and Christian teaching.

The questions of suffering and sacrifice in contemporary black ethics are insistently linked to theology and religious practice because of an important history of black faith that persisted into the twentieth century, especially among women, as well as the religiously grounded influence of such activists as Martin Luther King, Jr. Black theology, according to one of its key contemporary practitioners Dwight N. Hopkins, is "the interplay between the pain of oppression and the promise of liberation found in the Bible, on one hand, and a similar existence experienced by African Americans and poor people today."[45] Black liberation theology arises from a long history of African American appropriations of Christian scriptures and tradition. The discourse Hopkins represents began with figures like James H. Cone in the sixties as a response to the secularist and anti-Christian leanings of the Black Power movement. Cone insisted that the teachings of Jesus, rather than disciplining black people with a morality of submission and a pie-in-the-sky acceptance of injustice, were fundamentally political and liberatory.[46]

Like black and white feminists of the sixties and seventies, black theology privileged a methodology of reflection on experience. Cone argues in the essay "Suffering and the Black Tradition" (first printed as part of *God of the Oppressed* in 1975) that whereas white academic observations of suffering in mainstream ethics and theology have tended toward the abstract, "black reflections about suffering have not been removed from life but involved in life," rooted in specific racial experiences.[47] He claims that although numerous twentieth-century figures criticized Christianity as resulting in black passivity, particularly "poets and novelists" like Richard Wright and James Baldwin as well as members of the Nation of Islam and secularists like Frederick Douglass and the influential NAACP, many black people had been and continued to consider themselves Christians.[48] Furthermore, Cone argues, faith in Jesus had given countless black people courage, hope, and strength, not just personally but also politically: "no careful student of black history can say that their views on black religion and suffering led to inactivity, particularly when the black Church and its ministers were the visible activists against slavery."[49] This is a mysterious spirituality, he asserts, with an emphasis on a "future, apocalyptic imagination" emboldening a present of activism. He concludes:

> Suffering that arises in the context of the struggle for freedom is liberating. It is liberating because it is a sign of Jesus' presence in our midst. Black people, therefore, as God's Suffering Servant, are called to suffer with and for God in the liberation of humanity. This suffering to which we have been called is not a passive endurance of white people's insults, but rather, a way of fighting for our freedom.[50]

In presenting this concept of the relation of suffering, political struggle, and Christianity, Cone follows in the tradition of Martin Luther King, Jr., who articulated in his 1960 essay "Suffering and Faith" an understanding of suffering as a possible source of creative energy to use in the work of justice as well as a spiritually beneficial experience.[51]

"Redemptive suffering" stands at the center of many debates in black theology, and they often involve responses to Cone's theodicy (or theological attempts to justify God in light of human suffering). Two volumes that highlight these debates are instructive even in their titles: *The Courage to Hope: From Black Suffering to Human Redemption* and *Moral Evil and Redemptive Suffering: A History of Theodicy in African-American Religious Thought* both take up the question of specifically racialized suffering in terms of its redemptive purpose or value. In redemptive suffering theodicy, people understand their suffering as having some higher good or purpose. This approach to suffering can take myriad forms: one can assume suffering is redemptive because it teaches or provides special insight (good for either the individual or the collective society),[52] or one can understand suffering redemptively because it presents a deserved punishment.[53] The poet Phillis Wheatley exemplifies another tradition of redemptive suffering theodicy when she claims in "On Being Brought from Africa to America,"

'Twas mercy brought me from my *Pagan* land,
Taught my benighted soul to understand
That there's a God, that there's a *Saviour* too:
Once I redemption neither sought nor knew.[54]

Of course, Wheatley's thankfulness for the Christianizing effect of her enslavement is not a gladness for the enslavement itself, and she uses the second half of the short poem to critique the associations of the "sable race" with the devil, reminding "Christians" directly that "*Negroes*, black as *Cain*" can find salvation in Christianity, joining "th' angelic train." Indeed, we have numerous accounts of slaves finding redemption in their suffering in the belief that at least the continent of Africa was being introduced to Christianity, but this was no celebration of slavery itself, rather a "buying-back" of slavery's meaning by attributing to it some good.[55] From a different perspective, suffering can be understood as redemptive in the sense

Albert Raboteau asserts in his essay on American slaves as Christian martyrs whose subversive interpretation of the Bible "redeemed" it from the wicked misapplications of white masters. Finally, suffering can be understood as redemptive when it forwards the work of liberation: thus, inescapable suffering that can be translated into activist energy, as described by King, or suffering chosen in the name of the *eradication* of suffering can be redemptive.

These perspectives raise numerous problems, as I have been arguing that models that understand suffering as having some good effect are especially risky for the socially dispossessed. This danger/hope dynamic revolves around itself as ongoing paradox. Another strong critique of black liberation theology has been its inattentiveness to the specificity of black women's experience. Jacqueline Grant's essay "Black Women and the Church," printed in *All the Women,* is an early example of this critique: "My central argument is this: Black theology cannot continue to treat Black women as if they were invisible creatures who are on the outside looking into the Black experience, the Black church, and the Black theological enterprise."[56] Grant's insistence was taken up by other black women scholars. In her groundbreaking book *Sisters in the Wilderness: The Challenge of Womanist God-Talk* (1993), Delores Williams takes on James Cone and his colleagues directly, arguing that their methodological focus on "the black experience" was implicitly gendered *male* and had not taken into account women's voices.[57] Williams and others also note the tendency of the black community to relegate women to positions of particular suffering and self-sacrifice in the name of racial uplift.[58]

Yet many womanist theologians and ethicists join black male theologians in embracing the paradoxes of redemptive suffering. M. Shawn Copeland, for example, writes, "quite paradoxically, the suffering caused by evil can result in interior development and perfection as well as in social and cultural good."[59] Likewise, although Copeland recognizes the damage done to slaves taught caricatures of Christian virtues and the use of the Bible against black women in the past and present,[60] she also sees in Christianity an important resource for womanist resistance.[61]

I narrate this history to demonstrate that discussions of ethical approaches to (black) (women's) suffering arise out of a particular context of debates about redemptive suffering rooted in a particular raced as well as gendered history of oppression and theologizing. In Rich's terms, I seek not to interpret everything solely from the symbolic resources available in my own location, but to do the labor necessary to better interpret another location. I also narrate this history to demonstrate the work womanist scholars have had to do in responding to both white feminist and black theological discourses in their own writing.[62] Any conversation of suffering and redemption in Morrison is intertextually and communally related to this body of theoretical work on suffering and sacrifice.

The discourse of Christian womanist ethics arises out of this discourse of black liberation theology as well as (white) feminist theory. "Womanism," like "ethics," is a contested term. Layli Phillips, introducing the 2006 *Womanist Reader*, surveys the conflicting characterizations and ultimately defines it as

> a social change perspective rooted in Black women's and other women of colors' everyday experiences and everyday methods of problem solving in everyday spaces, extending to the problem of ending all forms of oppression for all people, restoring the balance between people and the environment/nature, and reconciling human life with the spiritual dimension.[63]

The relationship of womanism to feminism is a particularly difficult one with a history of debates beyond the scope of this project. The general view represented by Phillips, however, is that womanism's main distinction from (black) feminism is that it does not primarily emphasize gender oppression but instead emphasizes the linked workings of different systems of oppression.[64]

Womanism originates in the one-page definition Walker included in her collection *In Search of Our Mother's Gardens: Womanist Prose* in 1983, although she first used the term "womanist" in a short story published in 1979.[65] As it has been developed, womanism draws on standpoint theory, the idea that black women have shared a similar subject position and set of experiences and therefore share insights and capacities arising from that standpoint. Thus, womanists place a high value on black women's experiences, emphasizing not just their shared suffering but especially their capacity for survival and the skills they have to offer the community.[66] Womanists tend to emphasize community, plain speech, hard-earned wisdom, survival, and spirituality.

Such an integrated analysis of race, gender, and class resonates with Morrison's ethics of literary representation, manifested in the complex indivisibility of sufferings' sources in *Love*. This tension is particularly vivid in the scene of Heed and Christine's final conversation discussed earlier:

You sound sad.
    No. It's just. Well, it's like we started out being sold, got free of it, then sold ourselves to the highest bidder.
    Who you mean 'we'? Black people? Women? You mean me and you?
    I don't know what I mean. (185)

In this passage, Heed recognizes Christine's emotional responses to their memories, and then also recognizes the multivalence of Christine's reply, which utilizes the vocabulary of slavery. Christine's statement could refer to black people in general, particularly bourgeois black people "selling out" for their comfortable lifestyles—people like Bill Cosey's father, Dark, the sheriff-bribing Bill Cosey himself, and even Heed and Christine in their fight for Cosey's money. Her statement also could refer to women in general who respond to increasing twentieth-century freedom from gender constraints by insisting on serving and privileging men. Finally, as Heed realizes, Christine's statement could refer to the two women specifically, as women and as African Americans, in their relationship to Bill Cosey (even after his death). In claiming not to know rather than clarifying her meaning, Christine expresses the inextricable nature of the personal and political issues of class, race, gender, and particularity that have influenced their lives, but she also expresses regret for mistakenly reappropriating the role of slave: to racist ideology, to sexist ideology, and (or) to Bill Cosey.

Womanist ethics also provides a context for thinking through the fact that this scene between Heed and Christine, with its formal emphasis on dialogic intersubjectivity, readerly disorientation, and undecidability, also invokes Christian motifs. The juxtaposition of "innocence" and "hell" (190)—which implies meaning through a system of opposition—and the phrase "the birth of sin" (192), both apparently referring back to the childhood sexual initiation, imply an Eden–fall motif, further supported by the narrative's many references to apples and snakes. What is Morrison doing with these images? Why does she choose to invoke the guilty-Eve story of suffering's origins in a narrative populated by "wild women" and little girls turned old women whose suffering results from an impossible mix of raced and gendered victimization and their own choices? This is just one of many examples of Morrison's insistent intertextual play with Christian scriptures, even in a novel peopled by apparently a-religious characters. The Christian symbols still function for meaning-making, in this case allowing Morrison to probe female guilt at the heart of a male-dominated system, perhaps implying Eve as both a model scapegoat and a wild foremother. From a womanist perspective, Eve can be both, and Christianity can be both oppressive and liberating.

Such an undecidable representation of religion plays out across the scope of Morrison's writerly project. Her novels and essays rely on religious categories, biblical cadences and allusions, and the significance of faith in historical characters' lives as well as books' meaning-making in partnership with readers. Not all of Morrison's black folk are emphatically religious: while funerals draw characters in *Sula, Song of Solomon,* and *Jazz* to church, Morrison's novels set in the twentieth century tend not to emphasize the role of religion in their characters' lives. An important exception to this rule is *Paradise,* which is perhaps Morrison's most insistent exploration of the communal conflicts and dynamics of black faith—both its dangers and its possibilities.[67] Novels set in earlier eras, however—notably *Beloved* and *A Mercy*—present figures steeped in their religious traditions, characters whose imaginations and vocabularies are marked by their religious contexts and commitments. And all of Morrison's novels, in epigraphs and linguistic allusions, bear the marks of their author's engagement with Christianity and its scriptures in ways that often escape the explanatory power of critics socialized in a secular academy. The upshot of this insistent engagement with Christianity is that Morrison's novels do not only explore the specifically gendered and raced dynamics of suffering; they also emphatically—through comparisons between black women and Christ, for instance[68]—entangle these gendered and raced dynamics with religion, suggesting that these dynamics already are entangled.

Poststructuralist theory may provide a vocabulary for Morrison's paradoxical and open-ended ethics of readerly attention, but it does not do justice to the imbrications of religion with gender and race. Womanist ethics seeks to do such justice. Indeed, Phillips calls womanism "postmodernism at street level," noting their shared "concentrat[ion] on the circulation of

power" and respect for difference.[69] Yet Phillips also cites important differences, including use of language (womanism as accessible, theory as *not*,
as Barbara Christian argued) and womanism's commitment to spirituality.[70] Although Phillips's view of postmodernism does not strike me as
quite robust enough, I do believe that womanism gives us an alternative—
gendered, raced, and religious—paradigm for understanding features
of Morrison's writing, including paradox, dialogics, the deconstruction
of binaries, and undecidability, that otherwise requires us to appeal to a
body of theory that seems to have originated far from the lived experiences of the black women whose suffering Morrison's novels explore.[71]
Womanist ethicists, theologians, and literary scholars insistently explore
the workings of paradox and disrupt clear binary oppositions,[72] frequently
relying on the sentence structure "both . . . and" to express their ideas
and emphasizing the mixed or impure nature of much human experience
and language as well as the problems that arise from the privileging of
certain binary terms and segments of society. They trace these capacities
for complex thinking to African American women's experiences of working simultaneously within multiple systems (particularly under slavery),
black women's traditions of finding ways to thrive within severely limited
fields of choice and drawing support from community, and the paradoxes
inherent in Christianity: life through death, joy through pain, and, most
important, redemption through suffering.

Womanism's attention to paradox and challenged binaries—formal
features I find in Morrison's writing—interests me more here than looking to Morrison's characters for examples of womanist heroes, which has
tended to be the extent of literary critics' engagement with womanism
in Morrison's novels. Womanist ethics, continuing and correcting the
black theological tradition of redemptive suffering, offers an explanation
of the *textual features* at work in Morrison's writing—like ambiguity and
paradox—that is rooted in specifically raced, gendered, and religious *experiences*. In other words, the ethical theory derives from material reality,
highlighting the linked workings of ethico-political literary representation
and poststructuralist lessons in attention. It is this dynamic relationship
between "literature" and "theory" that is particularly interesting in reading Morrison and womanist ethicists together, a relationship that is further supported by the extent to which Morrison's writings have been a
source for womanist theorists.

Emilie Townes frequently relies on Morrison's work, especially in her three major invocations of the vocabulary of suffering: the edited collection *A Troubling in My Soul: Womanist Perspectives on Evil and Suffering* (1993), *In a Blaze of Glory: Womanist Spirituality as Social Witness* (1995), and *Womanist Ethics and the Cultural Production of Evil* (2006). The marks of Morrison's writing are all over the most recent monograph, which attends to both experience and theory, disrupting Barbara Christian's earlier division. Townes combines a materialist approach with a reading practice that recognizes the ideological and symbolic functions of signifiers. And she theorizes this approach through her appeal to Morrison's own theorizing, taken together with poststructuralist theorists, black writers, and womanist or feminist theologians and critics. Turning to alternative readings of familiar phenomena, like stereotypes of black women, to mobilize them as counterhegemonic imaginary forces, Townes models redemption, employing figurations that have been used against women in order to undo the evil. She both exposes the sinister workings of religion in the public sphere and unapologetically draws on a *different* mode of Christianity that seeks liberation. In the womanist tradition, her mode is hopeful and dialogic, exposing false binaries, seeking in her last chapter, through use of the second person, to forge a community of action that is future-oriented, much like Drucilla Cornell's utopian feminism.

Townes claims early in the book that her work relies on stories to provide examples of the "truncated narratives designed to support and perpetuate structural inequities and forms of social oppression" as well as examples of narratives that resist these goals.[73] She asserts, "Fine writers help us 'see' things in tangible ways and 'feel' things through intangible means. Their ability to turn the world at a tilt, to explore our humanity and inhumanity challenges me in ways that theories and concepts do not."[74] In fact, at one point near the end of the volume, Townes herself writes in poetry rather than prose in her attempt to convey the complexity of her argument, its emotional as well as rational, personal as well as political, imaginary as well as factual truths.

However, although *Womanist Ethics and the Cultural Production of Evil* is a thought-provoking and even inspiring text, it fails to deliver on its early promises in terms of engaging with literature. Townes does read numerous phenomena, even the narrative of history, through methods best characterized as literary, but her assertions about the role of narrative and literary language are undermined by her choice to turn primarily to critical essays by creative writers like Morrison and James Baldwin. In her one more sustained reading of a narrative, Harriet Beecher Stowe's *Uncle Tom's Cabin*, Townes seems to be dipping her toe in the textual ocean, drawing the most attenuated conclusions from her interpretation of Topsy. This critique is also true of the 1995 volume *In a Blaze of Glory*, in which Townes engages more with Morrison's novel *Beloved*. In this book, which provides both a fascinating historical and sociological overview of slave religion, nineteenth-century African American women's spirituality and political activism, contemporary intra- and interracial struggles, and a constructive theo-ethical response—all of which suggest a material history for the figurations of paradox at work in contemporary black women's fiction—Townes also manifests a strange propensity to decontextualize literature, both removing it from its social context and snipping literary elements out of their textual locations. Chapter 3, titled, "To Be Called Beloved: Historical and Contemporary Lynching in African America," begins with a poem by Townes and then an unidentified block quotation. Those familiar with Morrison's novel *Beloved* may recognize it as a portion of Baby Suggs's sermon, but Townes's text provides no explanation, narrative context, or citation other than an endnote that names the novel without any commentary.[75] Townes repeatedly refers to this epigraph as a source throughout the chapter, naming not Morrison but "Baby Suggs" to the extent that a reader who has not read *Beloved* might assume that Baby Suggs is a contemporary or historical real-life preacher, giver of speeches, or writer of inspirational self-help books. Townes writes, "Baby Suggs's words are pithy instructions for womanist ethical reflection,"[76] and in other sections implicitly and explicitly attributes insights about postmodernism to Baby Suggs's teaching.[77]

Townes is a formidable figure, and it would be difficult to overstate how important her work is for contemporary thought on the ethics of (black) (women's) suffering. She performs an exemplary interdisciplinarity, drawing together mainstream theology, sociology, feminist and womanist scholarship, political and linguistic theory, and black theology in a truly original critique and constructive theo-poetic-politico-ethics. Her writings, like those of many womanists, are read provocatively and helpfully together with Morrison's nonfiction and fiction, in part because they draw so heavily on Morrison's writing, offering materially rooted and spiritually attuned perspectives of postmodern redemption. The problem is that Townes's work occludes the singularity of Morrison's ethical offerings, the resource of her writing *as literary*, in its language and its ambivalences. In so doing, she unexpectedly aligns herself with the moral critics' understanding of literature as *too* representative.

The ethical challenge of *Beloved* is not solely in Baby Suggs's sermon; I would argue that the narrative's ethical dilemma occurs after Baby Suggs finds she can no longer offer the Word, after Sethe's unspeakable act: yet this struggle does not feature in Townes's ethics. In other words, Townes appeals to Baby Suggs's sermon by removing it from its narrative context. Of course, nothing is wrong with drawing wisdom from an inspiring sermon, whether that sermon be the speech of an enfleshed human or an imagined character: that is one of the rhetorical functions of the sermon as a genre. This use of Baby Suggs's speech, however, belies Townes's avowed interest in literature as a corrective to the generalizations of theory. The challenge of ethical thought offered by *Beloved* as a whole, as a work of narrative fiction, is much broader, much more difficult than the inspiring speech of one of its characters. Its tone is more wary: it emphasizes more strongly the dangers of the paradoxes, the struggle and difficulty, rather than naming them and then moving on. It helps readers feel them. It also leaves us asking, wondering, questioning, pondering the meaning of its ending refrain, *This is not a story to pass on*. That literary ambiguity suggests an altogether different ethics, a more tenuous and risky practice of judgment, than Baby Suggs's admittedly compelling command to "love your flesh."

Womanist ethical theory reminds us of the difference made by race, gender, history, and religion in ethical considerations. It gives us a material history for certain representational and formal linguistic features that characterize Morrison's writing: the invitation of readerly intimacy and participation that arises from a value placed on community, the moral undecidability of situations in which freedom is radically constrained, the strong emphasis placed on language, literacy, and characters' capacity to communicate. It reminds us that the paradoxes of religion and redemption require careful consideration, an explication of their dangers as well as possibilities, but not any elision of complexity and certainly not a refusal of the significant meaning-making of *then* in light of a superior secular *now*.

It gives us a vocabulary of *survival, hope,* and *particularity.* Then, at some point, it reaches the limits of its own genre, requiring its practitioners to write poems and stories of their own, or to read the poems and stories of others, to seek out stories "to pass on." Arriving at these limits, we find that it is time to put down the volume of theory and take up again the literature, aware of its singularity and its writer's poetic purpose, its allegories of reading enmeshed in representations of particular suffering. There is never any need to abandon the one or the other altogether—the books all remain at the ready, pressed in close together, waiting on the shelf.

Justice and *A Mercy*

> The Master's tools will never dismantle the Master's house.
> —Audre Lorde, *Sister Outsider*

Morrison's slim 2008 novel opens in an unfamiliarly cadenced first-person narration, a direct address: "Don't be afraid. My telling can't hurt you in spite of what I have done."[78] These words already imply a story, imply violence, imply a reason to fear. They hint at the past that will be unfolded in this narrative, and they raise questions of its narrator's motives and trustworthiness from the very beginning. This opening line also asserts a disconnect between telling and doing, between language and material reality, in the speaker's insistence that the telling can't hurt, but the very need to make this claim of words' inability to hurt already calls it into question. And the direct address raises the question, to whom is the speaker doing this "telling"? The reader seems to be the best guess, although an implied character is another possibility suggested by the pages that follow.

The narrator continues, on the first page, with a sudden shift in the middle of the paragraph, "One question is who is responsible? Another is can you read?" (3), framing the narrative in the very terms that frame this entire chapter and book. The question of responsibility, particularly in the context of violence and mystery the narrator evokes, is a question of ethics. This question is associated by proximity to the one that follows, so that responsibility and reading are implicitly linked.

An assumption of "reading" as verbal literacy is immediately challenged, however, by the narrator's example of reading, which has nothing to do with written words but with another semiotic system altogether:

> One question is who is responsible? Another is can you read? If a pea hen refuses to brood I read it quickly and, sure enough, that night I see a minha mãe standing hand in hand with her little boy, my shoes jamming the pocket of her apron. Other signs need more time to understand. Often there are too many signs, or a bright omen clouds up too fast. I sort them and try to recall, yet I know I am missing much, like not reading the garden snake crawling up to the door saddle to die. (3–4)

"Reading" here is interpreting natural phenomena, rather than language, for predictions of what will happen in the future. "Can you read?" is a question of understanding material signs, and the narrator admits both a capacity for such reading and also a difficulty, the undecipherable nature of semiotic complexity.[79] And the disrupted idea of "reading" as linguistic is hardly the only mystery here, as a first-time reader is left to wonder at the relation, the patterns of speech, and the unfamiliar language. (An Internet search—or contextual clues later in the novel—indicate that "a minha mãe" is Portuguese for "my mother.")

Yet the next few pages again challenge the strictly nonlinguistic sense of "reading," for we discover that the narrator is "lettered" on the next page (4), and only two pages later learn that she (for we know her gender now) had been clandestinely taught to read and write by a "Reverend Father" or Catholic priest, who hid weekly with her and her mother and mother's "little boy" (never called "my brother") near a marsh to teach them, risking imprisonment and fines (6).

This first section, fewer than six full pages long, introduces all manner of linked thematic concerns, casting the narrative to follow in terms of reading, different languages, responsibility, untold violence, sexuality (and "bad women"), Christianity, and mothering. It clarifies several elements—naming the main characters (the narrator Florens, Lina, Mistress, Sorrow, Sir, Will, and Scully), the date (1690), and the religious tensions across geographic regions of the day. But it also raises myriad questions—Florens the narrator expresses such longing for the addressee, but to whom is she doing this "telling"? Why do "mothers nursing greedy babies scare [her]" (8)? Who are all these figures, and how are they related? And what is the unnamed violence implied from the very first page? What is there to fear?

A Mercy takes shape, much like *Love*, in the interacting points of view of multiple characters, as third-person narration focalized through them takes turns with Florens's stylized first-person sections. Again, Morrison relies on a form that woos and destabilizes the reader in its opening pages and then presents the gaps and conflicts of a dialogical encounter of multiple points of view. This form sustains the thematization, indicated by those opening questions of responsibility and reading, of interpretation, demonstrating the inescapably partial nature of judgment and the difficulty of a final "reading." In another aspect of its postmodern ethical poetics, the narrative thematizes not only language and interpretation, dialogics and limited points of view, but also writing itself: for at the end of the narrative, we discover that Florens's telling relies on those lessons in reading and writing learned in secret from the Reverend Father, for she has been *writing* this story, at night, in the empty room of her dead master's newly built house, inscribing the words with a nail on the wooden floor and walls (158). The narrator's voiced telling is given material shape; the narrator becomes the *writer*, embodied and alone with a lamp in the dark of the master's house, assumed by those who see her light to be a ghost.[80]

Florens's literacy is again attributed here to the priest, though his tutelage is characterized in Florens's memory not by gentleness but by strict discipline: "Sometimes the tip of the nail skates away and the forming of words is disorderly. Reverend Father never likes that. He raps our fingers and makes us do it over" (158). The implicit pain in this mode of teaching is linked, again, by the apparent free association of the sentence that follows without a paragraph break: "In the beginning when I come to this room I am certain the telling will give me the tears I never have. I am wrong. Eyes dry, I stop telling only when the lamp burns down. Then I sleep among my words" (158). Florens's original belief that her "telling" would provoke therapeutic emotional release is false, as she tells her story—her mother's rejection of her in offering her to a faraway master she calls Sir, her growing love for the women in Sir's household, her hungry passion for the blacksmith and subsequent search for him and jealous violence against him—without the relief of tears. Thus she undermines the widespread popular and theoretical claim that giving voice to suffering provides release from that suffering. Giving voice to suffering, breaking silence, offers Florens no redemption.

Yet although Florens's act of telling, in her own estimation, offers her no cathartic release, does it do so for the reader? It becomes clear in the final pages of her narration that the "you" of her address has been her lover the blacksmith, the one against whom she acted violently, the one who needs her reassurance not to fear, but in the double move characteristic of Morrison, this addressee of the early pages also functions as the reader. Florens says (or, we might imagine, scratches the words with her nail) to the blacksmith, "My arms ache but I have need to tell you this. I cannot tell it to anyone but you" (160), again rendering her telling with a material force, not just of the words inscribed in the wooden surfaces but also in the aching (suffering?) of her body. But then:

> Suddenly I am remembering. You won't read my telling. You read the world but not the letters of talk. You don't know how to. Maybe one day you will learn. If so, come to this farm again, part the snakes in the gate you made, enter this big, awing house, climb the stairs and come inside this talking room in daylight. If you never read this, no one will. These careful words, closed up and wide open, will talk to themselves. (160–161)

"Or perhaps," she goes on, they need air, "to flavor the soil of the earth": perhaps she will get Lina to help her light the master's house on fire and burn it away, again disrupting the immateriality of language as words become ashes and dust (161).[81] The blacksmith "you" Florens addresses, we learn at the very end, does *not* hear her telling: no communion is created by their relating, because there is no relating in the present of the narrative. The reader is a sort of interloper, stumbling upon the story (in a material, typeset form of its own) in the liminal time between Florens's nail-scratch "telling" and any possible future reading (a near impossibility based on the blacksmith's raced or classed social position) or burning. Any sense of intimacy between narrator and reader, established by the dialogic second person, is subverted by this final realization that the reader is actually more of a voyeur, relying on her or his relative privilege of literacy to read what the blacksmith cannot. What is readerly responsibility, in this case? What ethics of readerly attention does this text teach?

A Mercy, in addition to exploring the linkage between suffering and language—both material and immaterial—persists in thematizing many of the topics Morrison has explored across her career as a writer. Florens's agonized hunger for mother-love and hurt at her mother's rejection of her joins the Mistress Rebecca's experience of bad parents in poverty-stricken London and devastating grief at the loss of her own three children, Lina's Native American myths of mother birds (a persistent motif through the narrative), and the orphan foundling Sorrow's refusal to drown her second baby as Lina did the first and her choice to become a mother and rename herself Complete. The interwoven experiences of this household of diverse women—Rebecca a white woman saved from poverty in London by an arranged marriage to a colonial settler, Lina a Native brought up by strict Protestants, Sorrow a "mongrel" found near the wreckage of a ship, and Florens the daughter of an African slave and a Portuguese master— with their myriad parallels and links, imply a universality to the mother–daughter bond and longing. Yet the particularity of Florens's desperate longing as the daughter of the only African chattel slave in the novel questions this universality: Florens is the only character removed from her mother not by death or choice but by men's economic dealings in human flesh. And Florens's agonized search for a surrogate love gains center stage in the narrative.

The novel similarly interrogates suffering's relation to religion, as Morrison paints the theological diversity of colonial North America, where different regions are home to Catholics detested as luxuriating "Papists" by nominal Protestants like Jacob Vaark, witch-hunting Puritans, splinter-sect Anabaptists, spiritually active Natives, and religiously unaffiliated settlers. Florens's literacy is explicitly linked to the priest's willingness to risk himself, his potential self-sacrifice, and recalling his journey accompanying her north to Vaark's homestead, she asserts, "Reverend Father is the only kind man I ever see" (8). The Catholic priest is by far the most sympathetic religious male character in the novel: another character remembers an Anglican curate's pedophilic "schooling" (153), a deacon from the nearby Anabaptist sect takes advantage of Sorrow (123), and a mother and daughter must wound the daughter to prove to their Puritan community that she is not a witch (129).[82] Yet while the priest stands in stark contrast to these other examples of oppression linked to religious (and gendered) power, even the priest's religious ideology is not embraced wholeheartedly by the text.

Just as characters' sufferings are differentiated on the basis of race, so too are the linkages between religion and suffering. Unique in A Mercy is Morrison's engagement with the biblical book of Job, which features prominently in white philosophical and theological treatments of suffering and evil but which is not a notable player in womanist and black theological engagements. As womanists explain, the tradition of black Christianity appropriated parts of the Bible that were of particular service. Because the widespread cause of suffering for blacks could clearly be traced to human agency (white people and the institutions of racism and slavery), the commonplace appeal to Job as a righteous man whose suffering seems senseless and to originate from God in white theology has been less important for black Christians. Instead, black Christians have tended to rely on the story of Exodus as a paradigm where it was clear that suffering came from a *human* oppressor and that God, above all else, was *liberator* (in the Exodus story) and *cosufferer* (in the prophets and in Christ), rather than the cause of anyone's suffering.

It is significant, then, that when Morrison brings Job into her narrative, it is as part of the *white woman's* grappling with her suffering. This makes sense in light of the fact that Rebecca's suffering results primarily from the natural causes, or "acts of God," of illness and frailty rather than human evil, although a good deal of her psychological suffering results from competing modes of religious practice. (The only accessible Christian church will not baptize her infants because of their Anabaptist theology, leaving Rebecca, raised to believe in infant baptism, to agonize over the possibility that her babies are burning in hell.) Rebecca Vaark interprets her suffering, the loss of her husband and children and her own illness, in light of Job's illness and the loss of all his family. Remembering her grappling with the story on the ship coming over to the Americas, Rebecca interprets Job's longing in the midst of his agony as a simple longing for "the Lord's attention," so that God's answer to Job's despair—asking him "Who do you think you are? Question me? Let me give you a hint of who I am and what I know"—was a satisfaction not of "divine knowledge" but of recognition by the divine (91). But Rebecca challenges the story's application to her own life on the basis of gender:

> But then Job was a man. Invisibility was intolerable to men. What complaint would a female Job dare to put forth? And if, having done

so, and He deigned to remind her of how weak and ignorant she was, where was the news in that? What shocked Job into humility and renewed fidelity was the message a female Job would have known and heard every minute of her life. No. (91)

Finding no comfort in the tale of Job, Rebecca gives herself over instead in her illness and to hallucinations of the refreshingly crude female shipmates who accompanied her on the journey to the Colonies.[83]

Yet while Rebecca's commentary on Job—and her rejection of it on the basis of her difference as a woman—exposes it as offering little hope to suffering women, and while suffering in the novel is attributed to natural causes, human intention, and human accident, in another sense the novel as a whole can be read as a redemptive theodicy, justifying God in light of human suffering. Until the final, epigraph-like section where Florens's a minha mãe speaks, the narrative could sustain competing readings whereby suffering is seen as redemptive—leading to some good, to some learning— or not. On the one hand, the suffering leads to a dissolution of the happy female household Rebecca, Lina, Florens, and Sorrow/Complete had constituted in their diversity: the novel ends with a fall from grace, a psychological and bodily separation on the basis of race, class, and religion that leads to the isolation of its characters and the downfall of its formerly productive household. Order gives way to chaos. On the other hand, Sorrow has become Complete, and Florens finds herself at the end of her telling with the sense that she has finished her task: in a sense, her own sorrow has also become "complete" as she has filled a room with its articulation, given language to her suffering. In a bold assertion of self-possession and identity, she claims, "I am become wilderness but I am also Florens. In full. Unforgiven. Unforgiving. No ruth, my love. None. Hear me? Slave. Free. I last" (161). Her one remaining "sadness" is her inability to know what her mother has been telling her (in dreams?) and her inability to express to her mother the change in herself, the hardened soles on her feet that signify her strength.

The novel could end here, and according to Morrison in one draft it did. Her publisher asked her to include the epigraph from Florens's mother, and while some reviewers have critiqued it as sentimental or heavyhanded, I argue that the end, which matches Florens's opening narration in length, does not foreclose on the narrative's ambiguity. In this last section, Florens's mother explains her choice to send Florens away with

Vaark—an act that Florens could interpret only as rejection, a refusal of responsibility and a favoring of her younger brother—as a removal of the maturing adolescent Florens from the master's sexual advances. Four times the mother repeats, "There was no protection" (162–163, 166).[84] Religious teaching didn't prevent the master's sexual use of his slaves, but Florens's mother pursued the priest's teaching for her children, ambivalent about Christianity but sure that "there is magic in learning" and the potential for future escape: language and literacy offered the woman's children hope (163). Recognizing in Jacob Vaark "another way," she explains, she boldly offered her daughter to him as payment for the master's debt because "to be female in this place is to be an open wound that cannot heal. Even if scars form, the festering is ever below" (163). This verbal association of femaleness and woundedness is a powerful reminder of the association of women and suffering, not only as a general Western norm in the cultural symbolic but also in the specific bodily experience of a slave-woman mastered by a sexually exploitative white man.

Recognizing that Vaark saw her daughter as "a human child" rather than a black commodity as she had been reduced to (166), recognizing Vaark's ethical attentiveness, Florens's mother explains, she leaped at the chance to remove her daughter from the situation where her specific blackness and femaleness rendered her vulnerable. The book concludes,

> It was not a miracle. Bestowed by God. It was a mercy. Offered by a human. I stayed on my knees. In the dust where my heart will remain each night and every day until you understand what I know and long to tell you: to be given dominion over another is a hard thing; to wrest dominion over another is a wrong thing; to give dominion of yourself to another is a wicked thing.
>
> Oh Florens. My love. Hear a tua mãe. (166–167)

The mother's voice is the final word, offering explanation and wisdom, narrating the horrors of her own entry into slavery and the reduction of her complexity to one identity marker, the color black (165). In terms of theodicy, the mother's speech to her daughter offers the final explanation, an incontrovertible view of the redemptive cast of Florens's suffering: her mother and Jacob Vaark (not God, she insists) partnered in an act of mercy. To Florens, it may not feel like justice, may not feel fair, and the daughter may struggle with the question of her mother's responsibility, see her as guilty of abandonment. But from this other perspective, it is out of her own love that the mother sacrificed shared life with her daughter to see that daughter taken to live as a human in the household of one who chose to extend a very human mercy of his own. The mother substitutes her own suffering (her heart perpetually in the dust) for her daughter's likely sexual and racial degradation. The act that Florens experiences as a debilitating rejection is actually, in the eyes of one who knows much more and much better than she does, an act of mercy. And so, in this perspective, the novel does offer an allegorical theodicy, even as Florens's mother rejects God's work in their story: the suffering you experience, when caused or allowed by the one who loves you and knows much better, is really for your good.

And yet—always and yet—the narrative also undermines this reading, for has Florens's desperate wildness, her longing for love, her willingness to give herself over to the blacksmith been better than the life she would have had on the plantation with her mother? To be a black woman on the plantation may be to suffer like an open wound, but her mother, at least, seems possessed of a more holistic wisdom, capable of a certain self-possession and self-giving love. The "wildness" that the blacksmith accuses Florens of, and which she herself embraces at her telling's end: Is it a good thing? Or a dangerous thing? Is Florens's ruthlessness healthy, in response to the traumas she has undergone, in light of the narrative's earlier positive portrayal of community and relationship? *Does* Florens ever get to hear her mother's message, or is it only there to assuage the reader's discomfort, providing us with a satisfyingly cathartic view of redemptive suffering, even if such redemption is unavailable to Florens? In which case, could it be said that Florens's (possible) ongoing suffering stands in for ours, in yet another configuration of sacrificial substitution?

To these questions, *A Mercy* provides no answer. It does, however, break a silence Morrison located in the contemporary public imagination, forwarding Morrison's ethics of literary representation in narrating the fictional truth of an historical era in our nation when slavery and race were not yet quite indissolubly linked, when black and white had not yet been established as the primary binary structuring America. In the peculiar economy of literature's relation to suffering, it brings to our attention a truth of complexity, a truth of both shared humanity and important difference, through both representational and formal features that invite us to identify and understand even as they disrupt those identifications and interpretations. In other words, it engages us in an ethical practice of readerly attention.

As I have been arguing, this paradoxical admixture of universality and particularity constitutes Morrison's literary ethics of suffering, and this is apparent even in that penultimate paragraph of Florens's a minha mãe's own telling, when she offers a pithy gloss on the whole narrative, "to be given dominion over another is a hard thing; to wrest dominion over another is a wrong thing; to give dominion of yourself to another is a wicked thing" (167). This statement functions as an interpretive paradigm for the whole novel, even an ethical model that might provide material for those intent on a memorable quotation. It is just the sort of speech that provides compelling material for womanist ethicists to build on. Indeed, Morrison herself has asserted in interviews that this lesson about mastery is the moral of the story, and it is one that aligns itself with her other novels, and with womanist theory, and with feminist ethics, and with Rich's stated concern with "mastery," and even with some versions of postmodern ethics. It is a hard-won insight that comes only at the end of a novel rife with suffering, but it is also broadly universal.

And yet—and yet—the statement's existence as *one character's speech* within a fictional narrative, a narrative full of ambiguities and ambivalences, undermines its final universality as a moral code. The particularity of Florens's experience as a black female slave, the concrete materiality of the master's dominion her mother feared for her, the questions regarding Florens's ultimate redemption, challenge readers, destabilize our pithy conclusions. Here we come up against Morrison's literary ethics, the ethics of the double move of form and content, textuality and materiality, as she reminds us both of our sameness with her characters and of our difference from them, as she invites both a common feeling of empathy and a distance, as she both enacts a universal questioning of mastery and reminds us that one ethical paradigm will never suffice in a world suffused with such particularity, where some have known the literal dominion of a man she must call Master, or "Senhor"—the same Portuguese word used in addressing prayers to God. Suffering must be named, exposed, critiqued, and, at times, chosen, in the name of risky but merciful love. Justice, universal and blind, is longed for and yet always challenged by the call for mercy, tentative, concrete, and narrative bound.

4
Ana Castillo, Mexican M.O.M.A.S., and a Hermeneutic of Liberation

Many [members of dominant society] do not understand or refuse to accept that today all women suffer, in one way or another, as a result of the prevalent misogyny legislated and expounded in this society.
—Ana Castillo, *Massacre of the Dreamers*

Perhaps like me you are tired of suffering and talking about suffering, estás hasta el pescuezo de sufrimiento, de contar las lluvias de sangre pero no has lluvias de flores (*up to your neck with suffering, of counting the rains of blood but not the rains of flowers*).
—Gloria Anzaldúa, "Foreword to the Second Edition,"
This Bridge Called My Back

Sometimes in the face of my own / our own limitations, in the face of such world-wide suffering, I doubt even the significance of books.
—Cherríe Moraga, "Refugees of a World on Fire: Foreword to the Second Edition," *This Bridge Called My Back*

Good Friday. The phrase tangles on my tongue, a mystery: how, I wondered as a little girl in a church of suits and silences, could we call this Friday good? An innocent person was killed on that day, by people who did not understand him: he was killed unjustly, even. Except we believed justly, somehow, both undeservedly and purposefully? This was a lesson of countless Sunday Schools and sermons, equipping my six-year-old vocabulary with all four syllables of *omnipotence*. What sort of child needs to know the term *foreknowledge*? What human still too small to cut an apple into slices needs to grapple with the problem of evil, the puzzle of free will? There were questions I knew better than to ask adults, when my knees were still skinned with maple-tree climbing, but I asked the trees just newly in bud: how could we call such a Friday good? The trees kept their own silence.

Three years into graduate school, I pass a Good Friday in reading, lying flail-limbed on my couch in a third-floor apartment. I am reading *So Far from God* by Ana Castillo, deciding on a quick breeze-through whether I want to focus my attentions on it for a term paper. I am intrigued by the cover, by the back blurb, by the first few pages with their miracle of a three-year-old's fanciful resurrection. The narrative's treatment of Sofi and her four daughters, Esperanza, Fe, Caridad, and La Loca, of religion and syncretism and gender and politics, compels me. But as I work my way through, I'm not sure I like it. The narrative feels uneven to me; its subplots don't seem fully conceived and connected; the tone is strange, the narrator's voice inconsistent so that I'm not sure whether to trust it; I don't know how to take the humor. The book throws me off-kilter, sends me mixed messages. Yet I keep questioning myself—perhaps these are purposeful moves? Perhaps I am meant to feel unbalanced? Perhaps the chatty narrator isn't meant to be trusted? Perhaps my outsider status, my location, colors my perception? Perhaps it would be different if I had been to New Mexico, or spoke Spanish? Perhaps my discomfort is part of the experience.

It is true that I don't know much about Mexican American culture as I read this novel. When I moved to this North Side Chicago neighborhood for graduate school, just two blocks east of a stretch of Clark Street famous for its *panaderías* and *taquerías*, I stopped once on the sidewalk to take in a massive painting that graced the brick side of a building. A gentle-looking woman, in a tall thin oval rimmed with spikes, looked down over a parking lot and fruit stand. "Who is she?" I asked my companion, who stared at me with raised eyebrows. "The Virgin of Guadalupe? You don't know the Virgin of Guadalupe?" I didn't know the Virgin of Guadalupe, or *elote*, or that tough-looking men could drive around proudly with Polka rhythms shaking their cars. There is a lesson in not-knowing. I work through Castillo's novel deeply aware of this lesson.

On this Friday, in that strange first-time-through-a-novel sweep of plot and character, I read of Sofi and her daughters, of their sorrows and joys—but mostly of their sorrows. I read of Caridad's brutal and mysterious rape, her healing and deep love, her stalking by an obsessive religious ascetic. I read of Esperanza's unsuccessful love life in the Chicano movement, of her capture and death as a reporter in the Middle East where she had hoped to do good. I read of Fe's body ravaged by the cancer she acquires working in faithful pursuit of the American Dream. I read of La

Loca Santa's wilting with an impossible case of AIDS after a cloistered life of prayer and care for her sisters. I read of Sofi's stubborn effort to maintain a crazy faith, hope, and love in the face of systemic injustice and personal anguish, her daily struggle to survive and thrive in her community.

The windows are cracked open after a long winter of stagnant radiator heat, and I hear as always the engines and horns of cars in Chicago traffic, the occasional siren from the fire station a few blocks away, the chatter of passing neighbors on the sidewalk. I live in a courtyard building with windows facing brick walls, not the street, and so I cannot see the sources of these sounds. Over the years I have learned to trust them as the unobtrusive backdrop to my life, which is very much a life of the mind. Now the book's weight is skewed to my left hand, only a dozen or so pages left in my right. Chapter 15: "La Loca Santa Returns to the World via Albuquerque Before Her Transcendental Departure; and a Few Random Political Remarks from the Highly Opinionated Narrator." I read its first line: "That year, Holy Friday was unlike all others" (238). The book is ending on this day I am living in, finishing with this day my body occupies unsure of how to conceive it. I am finishing this book about suffering on this day of celebrated suffering, and the book is ending in this same temporal space.

I hear an unfamiliar sound layered with the traffic. It is the sound of many voices raised, the sound of singing, far away and faint but growing stronger. I read the novel's narration of the Way of the Cross Procession, threaded and subverted with politics and the passion of concrete loss, perhaps the most powerful scene in the text:

No, there had never been no procession like that one before.

When Jesus was condemned to death, the spokesperson for the committee working to protest dumping radioactive waste in the sewer addressed the crowd.

Jesus bore His cross and a man declared that most of the Native and hispano families throughout the land were living below poverty level, one out of six families collected food stamps. Worst of all, there was an ever-growing number of familias who couldn't even get no food stamps 'cause they had no address and were barely staying alive with their children on the streets.

Jesus fell, and people all over the land were dying from toxic exposure in factories.

Jesus met his mother, and three Navajo women talked about uranium contamination on the reservation, and the babies they gave birth to with brain damage and cancer.[1]

The voices are closer, and I hear wailing. The sound is eerie behind my reading, distracting, even disruptive. Still, I am slow: I grew up among Christians for whom most embodied ritual constituted idolatry: we did not kneel or raise our palms, we did not countenance statues or pictures, candles or incense. The Catholics in my neighborhood were the middle-class great-grandchildren of German and Irish immigrants, private about their faith. To my unfamiliar ears, realization dawns later than one might expect: the sound is my neighbors' voices. They are singing in Spanish. They are walking the Way of the Cross.

I carry the book with me to the window, use all my strength to push the heavy wooden frame higher, lean forward against the screen. I can't see a thing but brick and pitiful early spring courtyard grass, but I hear them mourn. I hear their voices, which I do not understand, and yet I think I understand.

I am not making this up now in the writing. It is uncanny and true. I sit on the windowsill, holding *So Far from God* against my chest, my arms wrapped around my ribcage, staring at a wall but seeing nothing, only listening. They are walking down my street toward St. Jerome's at Lunt and Paulina, bearing in their bodies and voices the strange mystery of a day of suffering called Good and Holy. They are living it in their muscles, their faces open to the rest of us, their song rising to the rest of us, agnostic or iconoclastic or sympathetic or otherwise. They are unashamed, unabashed. I am tasting my own tears on my mouth.

I finish the novel with a salt-streaked face and burning eyes, reading of Castillo's Procession as the Chicago Procession passes and fades. I do not know what to make of this. The Procession seems incongruous: it follows two-hundred pages of dark humor, and after juxtaposing the pageant of Christ's painful final journey and the community's voicing of its own sorrows and injustices suffered, the novel ends with an irreverent account of Sofi's organization "Mothers of Martyrs and Saints." The Procession seems incongruous: daily life in my experience of the north side of Chicago is not magical, not mystical, but littered and gritty and noisy and secular. It is thick with suffering but offers little room for its expression.

I am unsettled and sure that I'm not ready to write on this novel for a term paper. I have some thinking to do, and I will have to do it while walking. My body is asserting its need to move.

I Will Lay My Body Down: The Chicana Feminist Literary Tradition

> Out of poverty, poetry:
> out of suffering, song.
> —Mexican Saying from Gloria Anzaldúa, *Borderlands/La Frontera*

In this chapter I return to *So Far from God*, recognizing in it and in Castillo's more recent novel *The Guardians* a subversively mystical-political ethics of representation that challenges readers' attention with troublingly paradoxical evaluations of religion and of sacrificial motherhood. Seeking to do justice to the particular locations of these texts, I read their ambivalent gestures in conversation with the mixed Mexican American traditions of sacrificial mothers and redemptive suffering and the interpretive method of liberation hermeneutics developed by Latin American liberation theologians. Castillo's writings repeat the dynamics I have recognized in both Adrienne Rich's and Toni Morrison's: her texts are attentive to complexity and particularity, insistently concerned with the sufferings of women tangled with sexuality, race, class, and religion. Yet even while Castillo critiques the expectation that women be self-giving sacrificers within Mexican American culture, she also forwards through both theoretical assertion and literary performance a model of ethics that is predicated on a self-giving stance. Once again, the novels I here examine challenge readers to pay closer attention through their gaps and mysteries, particularly their spiritual mysteries, engaging readers in an ethical practice of reading that asks them to think less of their own mastery and to respond to the texts on their own terms. Yet any generalized system of ethics—either in the novels' content or in their stylistic interactions with readers—is subverted by the inescapable particularity of the novels' representations and context. Castillo both invites us to generalize and also refuses generalization in the characteristic double move that structures my literary ethics of suffering.

So Far from God contributed to a richly growing tradition of Chicana literature when it was published in 1993.[2] It shares with that tradition an emphasis on mixture and the complexity of life on myriad literal and social borders, a reevaluation of culturally specific mythologies, an inter-rogation of religion and spirituality, and a stubborn attentiveness to suf-fering. These concerns are apparent not just in the fiction, drama, and poetry of Chicana writers but also in the groundbreaking essays that have framed Chicana writing since the early eighties. Castillo is joined by Gloria Anzaldúa and Cherríe Moraga as the triumvirate of widely cited Chicana writer-theorists whose work transgresses boundaries: creative/critical, experiential/theoretical, third world/postmodern.[3]

Although women of color have been active for the whole history of second-wave feminism, the literary expression of Chicana feminism often is narrated in terms of the landmark collection of essays and poems by "radical women of color" published in 1981 by Anzaldúa and Moraga.[4] *This Bridge Called My Back* began as a project in the late seventies out of a concern similar to the one that motivated Gloria Hull, Patricia Bell Scott, and Barbara Smith to produce *All the Women Are White, All the Blacks Are Men, But Some of Us Are Brave*, which appeared the following year. As with *All the Women* and *Of Woman Born*, *This Bridge* frames its ethico-political intervention explicitly in terms of women's suffering and sacrifice. Par-ticularly in their forewords to the second edition published in 1983, quoted in the epigraphs to this chapter, Moraga and Anzaldúa write of the "worldwide" nature of human suffering and of their own particular suf-ferings. Acknowledging this "endless reservoir of pain"[5] is fundamental to their project, yet the editors also challenge too total a focus on the pain, emphasizing the need to acknowledge one's own particular suffering even while opening oneself to concern for the suffering of others, the need to *act*. Anzaldúa writes in her foreword, "Basta de gritar contra el viento—toda palabra es ruido si no está acompañada de acción (*enough of shouting against the wind—all words are noise if not accompanied with action*)."[6] She and Moraga voice a call of hope for the future (the temporality of femi-nism), a hope located in interconnectedness as opposed to "privatism," accountability toward each other, and refusing "passivities and passing time" waiting for someone else to fix the problems. Such active work leads to their title image, which Moraga embraces in her preface: "For the women in this book, I will lay my body down for that vision [of freedom].

This Bridge Called My Back."[7] Yet this image is hard-earned: in the pages that precede it, Moraga narrates her struggle against feeling "walked over"—"over and over and over again."[8] "I cannot continue to use my body to be walked over to make a connection. Feeling every joint in my body tense this morning, used," she writes, describing her experience at a feminist conference dominated by white women who rely on her to bridge the gaps between dominant culture and women of color.[9] Moraga's narration of this struggle, this pain and resistance to allowing herself to be used this way, makes clear that to lay one's body down for others—allowing them to cross over on it—is a sacrificial gesture. In finally vowing, in a verb tense that implies not just an act in the future but also an act of will, of agency, to "lay [her] body down" for her sisters, for the vision of "a desire for life between all of us, not settling for less than freedom," Moraga clearly chooses a way of possible pain for the sake of love. She also undermines her own statements against passivity by representing the *act* of "being used" as an ethical ideal. Thus, with their titular image, Anzaldúa and Moraga frame their entire project not just in terms of attending to women's suffering (and particularly the suffering of women of color) but also in terms of a self-sacrificing activism.[10]

Moraga's language, her promise "I will lay my body down," echoes the rhythm of Christian language: Jesus's words rendered in the masculinist austerity of the King James Version are "Greater love hath no man than this, that a man lay down his life for his friends" (John 15:13). Moraga's phrase also echoes the black spiritual call to "lay my burdens down" by the river, the site for a bridge—or a baptism.[11] Indeed, she ends the preface, "In the dream [of a bridge], I am always met at the river,"[12] and the paragraphs leading to this end tell of her mother's faith in St. Anthony de Padua and a not-unrelated activist faith, "believing that we have the power to actually transform our experience, change our lives, save our lives."[13] The religiously resonant voicing here is not surprising, for as I have been arguing, in Western culture and the phrasing of the English language, discussions of suffering, self-sacrifice, and redemption tend to ring with the Jewish and Christian already-said even when they aren't intended to. Religion underlies not only Western experience and language but also, more specifically, the life practices of many women of color. *This Bridge* manifests not only linguistic evidence of Christian influence but also an emphasis on women's spirituality more broadly, Christian as well as indigenous and intuitive.

This Bridge calls repeatedly for attention to particularity within the collective body of "women." As multiple contributors articulate, when women of color speak out against white hegemony in the women's movement, the ensuing conversation often takes shape along binary terms: white and black. Non-African women of color may feel further marginalized by their black sisters.[14] As late as 2002, the editors of *A Reader in Latina Feminist Theology* name the black/white racial polarity in their introduction, noting that other anthologies that bring together women's "experience" and theology continue to be dominated by Anglo or African American concerns, so that their collection is a first in the field of theology.[15] They challenge both European American feminists and womanists to "rethink" their gender-race figurations and claim that Latina feminist theology is an emerging conversation in the twenty-first century.[16] Within the field of literature itself, this timeline is also supported by the objective fact of a generational shift: while Rich, Mary Daly, Audre Lorde, and Morrison were all born in the late twenties and early thirties, Anzaldúa was born in the early forties, and Moraga and Castillo in the early fifties.[17] These groups came into their own as activists in very different political contexts. Castillo has admitted in interviews that because of the dearth of Chicana or Latina writers, she looked to Morrison and Maxine Hong Kingston for models as a young writer.[18] Scholarly treatments of Chicana writing, similarly, show a propensity to cite black women's scholarship as precedent and support, even though, as mentioned, Chicana women have been active in the women's liberation movement since its inception.[19]

Yet although this reliance supports my choice in this project to follow a chapter on Morrison and a black liberation/womanist theology of redemptive suffering with a chapter on Chicana writing, it does not indicate a clear parallelism between the two cultural groups' experiences and representations of women's suffering. The Chicana heritage is not one of transcontinental captivity, chattel slavery, and the division of mothers from their commodity-bred children, miscegenation laws, or ambivalent conversion to the Protestant Christianity of one's owners. But it is a history with its own specific widespread sufferings brought about by conquest, rape, de-territorialization, and racism, as well as its own indigenous heritage, cultural changes, religious appropriation, and contemporary struggle. In light of these distinctions, it is important to address the particularity of suffering and sacrifice in the social location of Chicana writing, especially in relation to the religious and cultural heritage that so strongly emphasizes the role of self-giving women and an economy of sacrifice.

Mexican American Mamas

> We are tired of being your sacrificial lambs and scapegoats.
> —Gloria Anzaldúa, "Speaking in Tongues"

The widely acknowledged endlessly giving mother of Mexican culture has received scholarly treatment across disciplines, from history and sociology to theology and poetry, often in relation to Roman Catholicism, which, Castillo asserts in *Massacre of the Dreamers*, "permeates Mexican culture."[20] Indeed, Catholicism is often painted as the source of cultural expectations that women suffer for their husbands and children as gentle, patient, giving mothers, sacrificing themselves in emulation of Mary, Mother of God. "The culture and the Church," writes Anzaldúa in *Borderlands/La Frontera*, "insist that women are subservient to males. If a woman rebels she is a *mujer mala*. If a woman doesn't renounce herself in favor of the male, she is selfish."[21] Tey Diana Rebolledo further asserts, "followers of the cult of *Marianismo,* or Mariology, strive to emulate the Virgin's faith, self-abnegation, purity, care of her physical as well as spiritual child(ren), and passivity."[22] In a culture that highlights this model, the spiritual pressure on women to be "self-abnegating" and "passive" is arguably even stronger than in other cultural contexts: Anglo Protestant women may be given subtle instruction from their churches on how to be good wives in well-ordered households, and African American women may have a heritage of legally enforced servitude, but Mexican Catholic[23] women see their example in statues of a pious woman with downcast eyes and flowers at her feet. According to countless commentators, the Eve/whore and Mary/virgin dichotomy prevails, church teaching mandates only procreative sex, and women are relegated to a role of motherhood.[24] A mixture of veneration and blame accompanies women in this view of the world. Coupled with the more broadly present Christian emphasis on redemptive sacrifice, the added valuation of Mary results in a strong place for women's suffering—both acquiescence to long pain and passive receptivity—within the Mexican Catholic imagination. This imagination has been further strengthened, asserts Rebolledo, by the frequency with which prominent male Chicano writers and activists have represented the Virgin Mary as a model for Catholic women, portraying "dutiful mothers, wives, daughters, teachers, nurses, and other helpful, nurturing, compassionate figures of all kinds."[25] Such is the masculinist–nationalist literary tradition against which Chicanas have written their reevaluations of cultural myths and norms, and Castillo's Sofi, the mother at the center of So Far from God, is no exception.

Yet many Latina and specifically Mexican American feminist theologians are also quick to point out the empowerment of the religious tradition. A strong cadre of Latina feminist theologians argues that Catholicism offers women meaningful, life-giving spiritual practices. And even outside the realm of theology, many progressive Chicanas also claim their faith tradition as an integral part of their identity. María Pilar Aquino claims, "There is no doubt that our communities, whether by culture, by personal conviction, or by the mere human orientation to the transcendent, are constituted by a deep sense of the sacred. This sense involves the whole of our everyday lives. There is no doubt that religious faith is a major dimension in the life of grassroot Latinas."[26] And even those who abandon Catholicism and claim to have avoided a Catholic imagination still manifest fascination with Catholicism and its cultural effects. Castillo has repeatedly claimed in interviews to disavow Catholicism, insisting in an interview with Hector Torres, "I don't think like a Catholic at all."[27] Yet in another interview she admits, "I stopped following the Catholic Church when I was eighteen, but Catholicism is embedded in our culture, in our psyche."[28] One element of this cultural heritage among Chicanas in general is the radical re-visioning and remythologizing work undertaken around such figures as the Virgin of Guadalupe, La Malinche, and La Llorona, mining the cultural imagination for subversive examples of empowered and empowering female figures.[29]

Nor do Chicana writers and scholars who still embrace Catholicism shy away from critique. Such a stance is apparent throughout A Reader in Latina Feminist Theology. For instance, theologian Jeanette Rodríguez asserts, "Many Latinas' psychosocial religious development has been brought about, as well as hindered, by a legacy of culturally construed Catholicism."[30] The result is a profound ambivalence but also optimism. Latina feminist Christian theologians draw on liberation theology, with its class-analysis-inspired critique of the traditional church, as well as feminist theory, to re-vision Christian tradition and holy texts. This interpretive project relies on a "hermeneutic of liberation," seeking to reread or re-vision text and traditions through the perspective of the oppressed (more on this to follow), and it also tends to employ interdisciplinary methodologies that arrive at theological insight from a starting point of sociology, literary analysis, and interview.[31] For those *conscientized* Chicanas who do work through critique of Catholicism to arrive at any sort of ambivalent embrace, it is, like Moraga's bridge image, a hard-earned conclusion. But for many women, the process is not as conscious: Catholicism is revised and appropriated not so much through a purposeful individual process as through a communal history of syncretism and popularization. Aquino further elucidates the dynamic:

> Due to the blending of kyriarchal[32] European religious colonization with the kyriarchal indigenous religious traditions, religious faith has contributed to deepen our oppression and exclusion. However, there is no doubt either that throughout our history, popular religion has provided the liberating principles of Christian faith to support and validate the grassroot people's struggles of resistance and emancipation. Grassroot women are both the majority and the primary carriers or subjects of popular religion, and their various movements speak of their articulation of a religious faith aimed at the transformation of the kyriarchal domination.[33]

The argument generally follows these lines, recognizable also in the black liberation claims of James Hal Cone: Christianity has a history of contributing to injustice, but it also has been an empowering force, particularly among the dispossessed, providing both peace in trial and the courage for the oppressed to seek not only survival but also social change. Furthermore, theologians like Ada María Isasi-Díaz remind us that much Latina Christianity, as "popular religiosity," veers off official paths of Roman Catholicism, developed in the everyday life-practices of Latinas based on their embodied, pragmatic spiritual needs.[34] In an Anglo Protestant context, popular Mexican Catholicism can provide a unified identity; and in a skeptical modern world, the spirituality of Chicanas can even subvert Enlightenment inheritances of rationalism, attempted mastery, and dualisms that divide emotion from intellect and mind from body. Thus, Catholicism can be seen as both the source of women's suffering and culturally mandated self-sacrifice and also a source of strength for overcoming these expectations.[35]

Yet the question of women's suffering in Mexican American culture is further complicated by the fact that Roman Catholicism itself is not wholly culpable for a cultural emphasis on suffering and sacrifice. As Aquino asserts, kyriarchy structures not just Christian religions but also the indigenous religious traditions to which many Chicanas turn in their search for a more authentic spirituality. Anzaldúa references these dynamics in *Borderlands/La Frontera* with references to the "life-in-death and death-in-life" goddess *Coatlicue* and "Aztecan blood sacrifices."[36] Castillo in *Massacre of the Dreamers* explores the "war-oriented, conquest driven society" of the Aztecs that reigned at the time of the Conquest, asserting that one must look even further back to discover a nonphallocratic, Mother-oriented past.[37] Indigenous Mexican cultures are steeped in sacrifice, even human sacrifice, with creation stories that rely heavily on the premise of life-through-death and flourishing through suffering. Thus, many Chicanas who follow Castillo's advice in turning back from Catholicism to an indigenous spirituality and the wisdom of the grandmothers rely on interpretive work not unlike the critical hermeneutic theologians apply to Christianity to re-vision the tradition, uncovering or creating the positive feminine beneath layers of spiritual oppression. According to Castillo, "Xicanisma" (Chicana feminism) develops in this unearthing: "It is our task as Xicanistas, to not only reclaim our indigenismo—but also reinsert the forsaken feminine into our consciousness."[38] Ancient matriarchal and egalitarian origins may be mined, but the interpretive work to get back to them is not insignificant.

Nor is its effect entirely to deny the sacrificial economy found in both Aztec and Catholic heritages, if we take seriously the examples of Castillo and Anzaldúa. As Suzanne Bost argues in *Encarnación: Illness and Body Politics in Chicana Feminist Literature*, Anzaldúa, Moraga, and Castillo all manifest an attitude toward suffering that counters the dominant Anglo culture's attitude of resistance to and denial of pain. Bost locates the source of this perspective in "[both] Saint Teresa of Avila's stigmata and Aztec sacrifice rituals," which "both reflect an assumption that physical pain is a sign of regeneration, communication with the divine, and the crossing of spiritual boundaries."[39] Implicit in Bost's treatment of these writers is the possibility that reading their spiritual outlooks on their own terms, while not a common practice among academics, may provide insight into their writings and what those writings offer the public. Indeed, she links these writers' "incorporations of pain," which make sense in the context of both Catholic and Aztec religious traditions, to their "*mestiza* feminist politics: a politics that is strengthened by its mixing of cultures and its openness to continual change brought on by incorporating difference."[40] This approach to sacrifice and suffering, Bost argues, while countering the popular feminist repudiation of such expectations for women, can open up a radical postmodern politics of fluid identity and connection through vulnerability. Thus, although these three key writers of the Chicana feminist movement all roundly critique the gender, sex, race, class, and religious oppressions that lead to suffering, they also paradoxically reappropriate suffering for their own feminist purposes.

The result is that the religious resonance of self-sacrifice and suffering manifests just as much complexity and mixture as Chicana *mestiza* consciousness more broadly. There is no pure origin. Nor is it possible to single out one symbolic mode of oppression caused by religious cosmology or gender norms. Interwoven with many Chicanas' enculturated expectation of suffering are numerous concrete material sufferings that attend their raced, classed, and gendered subject positions: environmental racism, sweatshops and deathly migrant work, enforced sterilization, urban violence. Questions arise: Who is paying attention? How should we understand these phenomena? What ought to be done? These are ethical questions posed by social scientists and social activists. These are the questions posed by numerous contemporary Chicana writers, including Castillo. And these are the questions at the heart of liberation theology.

So Far from God and the Question of Liberation

> Dejemos de hablar hasta que hagamos la palabra luminosa y activa (*let's work not talk, let's say nothing until we've made the world luminous and active*).
> —Gloria Anzaldúa, "Foreword to the Second Edition,"
> *This Bridge Called My Back*

Castillo's novel troubled and challenged me the first time I read it, and it has continued to trouble and challenge me, not only with its mysteries of tone and spirituality but also with its devastatingly realist representations of social and economic injustices that lead to Chicanas' suffering. My experience is not unique: the critical dissonance surrounding this text suggests that its ambiguities have had broader effects, even among professional readers. I trace this dissonance in large part to the text's stance on Roman Catholicism and its curious practice of rereading (and responsively rewriting) earlier stories of saints and martyrs. Notwithstanding Castillo's open rejection of Catholicism and even feminist liberation theology in her essay "Saintly Mother and Soldier's Whore: The Leftist/Catholic Paradigm" in *Massacre of the Dreamers*, I suggest that the interpretive methodology of liberation hermeneutics provides explanatory force for the paradoxical combination of criticism and participation at work in *So Far from God*'s mystical-political ethics of representation and attention.

So Far from God, from its title and epigraph to its opening and closing scenes of communal religious practice, and throughout in its persistent engagement with both indigenous and Catholic spirituality, is incontrovertibly marked by religion. As Carmela Delia Lanza asserts, Castillo "focuses a great deal of attention on Chicana spirituality," which "involves intricate inter-connections regarding race, gender, and class issues."[41] These inter-connections are responsible for the novel's ambivalence regarding Catholicism. Many characters in the novel express Catholic faith: Sofi manifests devout habits like kissing her scapular after cursing and maintaining the local priest as her confessor, and people turn out en masse for funeral masses, pilgrimages, and Way of the Cross Processions. Yet Catholic religion is problematized from the very opening scene.

In the first pages of the novel, the child called La Loca's death and resurrection give rise to a depiction of a not-so-sympathetic priest concerned with the "decorum" of her funeral mourners. Holding the crowd outside the church in 118-degree heat, he sermonizes against questioning "our Father's fair judgment, Who alone knows why we are here on this earth and why He chooses to call us back home when He does."[42] Sofi finds little comfort in this teaching, letting out a cry and pounding the ground with her fists—it is this display of grief and resistance to the priest's instruction that gives way to the miracle of La Loca pushing the lid off her coffin and sitting up, then flying up to the church roof (22–23). Sofi's insult of the priest when he questions whether her three-year-old is a messenger of God or of the Devil, and the child's correction of the priest when he asserts his desire to pray for her ("Remember, it is *I* who am here to pray for *you*"), further challenge a stance of unquestioning respect for the Church hierarchy (23–24). The narrator tells us that after making this statement about her role as one who prays, La Loca "went into the church and those with faith followed" (24). The question is whether "those with faith" have faith in the Church generally or in La Loca and her claims more specifically: in either case those "with faith" follow a toddler in a ruffled chiffon nightgown so that she may pray for all of them—or for Father Jerome alone, depending on whether we understand her "you" to the priest as singular or plural. This vignette sets up the narrative in subversive terms: La Loca's spirituality does not explicitly transgress the parameters of Catholicism, and Sofi interprets her daughter's miracle as an answer to prayer, but the image of a baby girl leading a line of the faithful into a church to guide them in prayer subverts any typical picture of Catholic patriarchy. It also calls up the apocalyptic intertext of Isaiah 11:6, which foretells a time of peace and changed power relations when "the wolf shall live with the lamb, the leopard shall lie down with the kid, the calf and the lion and the fatling together, and a little child shall lead them."[43]

The ambivalence at work here has led to critical debates over how to interpret La Loca (who is given no other name in the narrative), and these debates are often related to how to understand Catholicism in the text. On the one hand, Gail Pérez asserts that *So Far from God* seems at first to manifest a "revisionist Catholicism" that aligns with Latina theologians like Isasi-Díaz but that ultimately in the novel Castillo "will reject the Catholicism of the mothers for the *curanderismo* of the grandmothers."[44] Ralph E. Rodriguez similarly asserts that Castillo rejects Catholicism in the novel, instead favoring Caridad and the indigenous spirituality she represents, and Laura Gillman and Stacy Floyd-Thomas share this view of Caridad as the incarnation of Castillo's ideal of Xicanisma described in *Massacre of the Dreamers*.[45] Lanza aligns herself with these positions when she argues that *So Far from God* demonstrates a rejection of Catholicism in favor of a cosmology more familiar as paganism or Wicca.[46] Perhaps most strongly, Rita Cano Alcalá argues that Sofi and her daughters represent a "female-identified spirituality and woman-led activism" in contrast to the "Eurocentric Catholic Church" represented by Francisco el Penitente.[47]

On the other side of this debate, some critics view *So Far from God* as a reconsideration of Catholicism rather than an outright rejection. Colette Morrow, for example, must take the Catholic elements in the novel as sincere to make her point that the narrative legitimizes lesbian identity for women of color by showing how they can fit into traditional religious scripts.[48] Michelle Sauer emphasizes medieval mysticism as a precedent for the powerful women within the novel, implicitly arguing for the legitimacy of the tradition's forms of sainthood that for a long time have subverted the religious institution from within.[49] Gillman and Floyd-Thomas, too, recognize in the Procession that ends the novel a model of Catholic liberation theology and in La Loca a possible re-visioning of Jesus Christ's death and resurrection.[50]

In perhaps the most robust perspective on the novel, a number of critics frame the question not as for or against Catholicism but in terms of how the Catholicism, indigenous spirituality, and activism in the novel relate to one another. Daniel Alarcón, taking up the oft-discussed topic of hagiography, avers that the novel critiques the Catholic church and its violence, but not to the extent of rejection: although Francisco el Penitente shows that not all syncretism works, Sofi and Esperanza demonstrate the practical good that can be empowered by a syncretic spirituality.[51] In a much-quoted essay, however, Theresa Delgadillo asserts that the novel demonstrates not "syncretic" spirituality, which implies a unified wholeness, but "hybrid" spirituality, which allows for more fluidity and disjunction. This hybridity allows the novel to demonstrate that spirituality does not have to stand in the way of political activism and can in fact empower it.[52]

In these readings, critics tend to choose a character as a heroic figure, often arguing that this figure represents Castillo's ideal, exemplifying her message about what *ought* to be, or how justice might be achieved: some of them emphasize Caridad and her indigenous spirituality, others emphasize Esperanza and her Chicana activism and work for global social justice, others emphasize La Loca and her mystical power of healing and sacrificial death, and still others emphasize Sofi, who gains wisdom through her daughters and demonstrates a community-oriented, hopeful engagement with concrete social issues in the face of serious suffering. Some of these critics highlight Sofi's traditional Catholicism, and others overlook it entirely. (No one idealizes Fe: she is most frequently taken as an example of what not to do.)

The sheer variety of critical perspectives on this novel—the dissonance among claims regarding its stance toward spiritual and political responses to suffering—says something about the ambivalence of *So Far from God* as a text, an ambivalence I struggled with that first Good Friday I read it and all the times I've read it since. The memory of those neighbors marching on that day of reading and witness, the memory of the pain in their voices, the tears on my lips as I held the book in my hands, reminds me, as well, that these questions about how one ought to understand and respond to women's suffering *matter*. They matter to the real-world impoverished Mexican Americans living on the diminished plots of land whose voices Castillo listened to and whose verbal patterns she emulated in the writing of this novel. They mattered to the mysterious yet flesh-and-blood women who provided Castillo's source material, martyred and sainted hundreds of years ago. They matter to the Mexican Americans living in my north-side Chicago neighborhood who work shift jobs, live in small overheated apartments, and wake up at the crack of dawn to haul their children's clothes to the Laundromat, whose voices I heard on that day. They matter to me. The way that these questions matter, coupled with the varied critical perspectives on Castillo's novel, reminds me of the place of desire in academic work: our scholarship expresses not just our assumptions and values and training but also our hopes and longings. Such longings— including the desire for closure instilled in scholars through academic training as well as subtle, more deeply personal desires—may be at the root of critics' tendency to isolate heroic figures as models in *So Far from God* and the disagreements that characterize its critical reception. Again, we read from our own locations.

Still, neither this awareness of the desire expressed in the literary criticism of *So Far from God* nor the volume and diversity of these critical assessments mean that some critical approaches are not better than others. Although it is almost certainly not intended as a narrative exploration of Catholic liberation theology, and although its liberation theological features do not precisely align with the claims critics have made to this date, *So Far from God* does as a whole engage readers in a *hermeneutical practice* that is not unlike liberation theology's practices. Translated into my own critical vocabulary, *So Far from God* establishes an ethics of literary representation and provokes an ethics of readerly attention, both predicated on the paradoxical dynamic of critique and embrace.

I take issue, first of all, with the claim that characters in the novel represent unmixed or uncomplicated stances toward Catholicism, either devout or resistant. As my previous comments highlight, the novel's first scene hardly rejects Catholicism altogether, although it certainly subverts it. Those critics who claim the novel denies Catholicism as a liberating force also tend to point to both Father Jerome (who plays a limited role in the narrative) and, especially, Francisco el Penitente as exemplars of the patriarchal religious institution. It is true that Francisco is an obsessive, unbalanced ascetic stalker and possible rapist. Francisco takes on an untoward degree of suffering *by choice*, for spiritual purposes, despises his own flesh, and seems misogynistic, highlighting the Western Christian dualistic devaluation of the material and women as well as the link between it and suffering (100). In these ways he might be said to "embod[y] the worst of male-constructed theologies."[53] But he is hardly representative of the "male-dominated Eurocentric Catholic Church," as Alcalá claims.[54] Indeed, while Francisco certainly privileges spirit over flesh and men over women, he does *not* privilege "his Spanish heritage over an indigenous or a mestizo one."[55] The Penitente Brotherhood of which Francisco is part is a *mestizo* group and a marginal group, Catholic but native to nineteenth-century New Mexico as a lay response to the need for spiritual and material care when the official church withdrew its priests for political reasons. Likewise, Francisco's occupation as a *santero*, carving wooden images of saints, is also a *mestizo* one, a practice that originated in the confrontation between Spanish colonizers and indigenous people. Francisco and his tío rely on the materials of their New Mexican world for their spiritual purposes, on the "straight and healthy" pines of the land where they live for wood, the "earths and plants and carbons from charcoal or soot" for paints, the "yucca fronds and chicken feathers" and "horsehair" for brushes (100–101). As Francisco's conversation with a Puerto Rican friend illustrates, *santeros* in different colonized locations engage in very different, place- and culture-specific practices.

Additionally complicating in the case of Francisco el Penitente is the foil his tío Pedro provides. While Francisco mixes ashes into his food, takes vows of silence, and even confesses as sinful the pleasure he takes in a cedar's shade and scent, his unbalanced devotion contrasts with that of his tío, who, while similarly having given his life to the prayerful work of a *santero*, has a longstanding and apparently happy marriage and is displeased by his nephew's extremes (199). Tío Pedro suggests a male Catholic piety that does not veer into the destructive territory Francisco's does. Such a view is further supported by the narrator's description of Francisco as a man with a complicated background, as Delgadillo notes:[56] hardly the Everyman representative of European patriarchal Catholicism, Francisco manifests signs of posttraumatic stress disorder after Vietnam (94, 99–100). Francisco's outlook on life—especially his outlook on women—is also linked by the narrator to his mother's and baby sister's deaths when he was six years old (97). The suffering he causes women, and the suffering he causes himself, seem to spring from a deep well of suffering in his own past and are only exacerbated by the spirit/body and male/female binaries he finds in Catholicism, not uniquely sourced in it.

Doña Felicia, the ancient and wise *curandera*, is another character whose complexity tends to be overlooked by critics pitting indigenous spirituality against Catholicism. Doña Felicia's story of faith sounds like a classic conversion narrative: as a young woman, "Felicia was a non-believer of sorts and remained that way, suspicious of the religion that did not help the destitute all around her despite their devotion" (60). But eventually she does "develop faith, based not on an institution but on the bits and pieces of the souls and knowledge of the wise teachers that she met along the way" (60). Many critics seem to stop reading here, pleased by doña Felicia's intuitive, noninstitutional spirituality. The narrator, however, continues: "But as the decades wore on, doña Felicia came full circle, reaching a compromise with the religion of her people when she became caretaker of the House of God in Tome. And finally, she came to see her God not only as Lord but as a guiding light, with His retinue of saints, His army, and her as a lowly foot soldier. And she was content to do His work and bidding" (60). After her children are grown and living far away, we are told, "doña Felicia, who as a child was said to have no faith, had nothing but faith left and devoted herself to healing with the consent and power of God, Tatita Dios en Sus cielos, the only lasting caretaker of her life" (62). Doña Felicia's ultimate relationship with the institutional church and the masculine, powerful God of capitalized pronouns is significant here: her practices of *curanerdismo* are syncretic, joining indigenous traditions with Catholic cosmology, and this is the wisdom she passes down to her student Caridad, who so frequently is celebrated by critics as exemplar of Xicanisma.

The overlooked complexity of these characters relates to the puzzle of the novel's relation to liberation theology. While numerous critics invoke liberation theology in their discussions of *So Far from God,* Caminero-Santangelo ventures a more sustained engagement, problematizing the trend of describing Castillo's work as magical realist and arguing that scenes that appear to be magical realist—or miraculous, to the faithful—are in fact scenes of passivity in the face of social suffering and injustice. These scenes stand in stark contrast to the realist depictions of the politically gripping communal Way of the Cross Procession at the narrative's end, or Sofi's organization as the "Mayor of Tome" of a cooperative land-sharing, food-raising, wool-weaving project for her community. Caminero-Santangelo links these realist depictions of organizing with liberation theology, understood as a theological perspective that forwards active work for justice in the here-and-now.[57] To support her claims about liberation theology, Caminero-Santangelo relies heavily on the writings of Leonardo and Clodovis Boff, including their 1987 *Introducing Liberation Theology,* especially their claims that the response to oppression should be protest and effective resistance.[58] Caminero-Santangelo's reading, unlike most critics', seems to have no room for spirituality, for ritual, for pilgrimage, for retreat, for prayer. It also ignores Rich's reminder in *A Human Eye* that literature is not "a blueprint."

This argument presents many problems. The first of these problems is that Caminero-Santangelo relies heavily on two relatively brief passages in a much larger narrative (Sofi's organization of the cooperative and the final Procession), appealing repeatedly to the "hormone-free meat" and "pesticide-free food" that result from Tome's community organizing as a litmus test against which all the other activities in the narrative are measured. This reading does not take into account the fact that the description of Sofi's organizing activity as "Mayor" is itself wildly idealistic, even miraculous. The narrator does remind the reader repeatedly of the difficulty of these changes, citing "many community-based meetings" and "debates"; naming the realization that "it would take YEARS of diligence and determination beyond this telling to meet their goals"; that "every step" "took a lot of effort, a lot of time, and mostly a lot of not only changing everyone's minds about why not to do it but also changing their whole way of thinking so that they *could* do it" (146). Still, in a 250-page novel composed in large part of descriptions of loss, survival, suffering, struggle, and the ultimately tragic demise of all four of Sofi's daughters, this three-page account of the community's massive-scale success, even with all the narrator's caveats about "untold challenges" (147), seems by its very brevity to emphasize its daydream-like quality. Caminero-Santangelo's interpretation also fails to account for the fact that even after Sofi pulls together her community, these physical provisions do not prevent all four of her daughters from further suffering and sacrifice to the systems that ravage their persons. The novel poses problems for which these activities are not the solution.

This interpretation seems to arise from its author's strong desire for a model of justice in the novel, a desire to find a materialist Marxist argument embedded in the text, and this desire also seems to have colored Caminero-Santangelo's reading of Boff and Boff. In *Introducing Liberation Theology*, they do present an active, resistant stance to injustice that emphasizes the agency of the oppressed rather than aid organizations or reform of existing structures: "In liberation, the oppressed come together, come to understand their situation through the process of conscientization,[59] discover the causes of their oppression, organize themselves into movements, and act in a coordinated fashion."[60] The Boffs emphasize participation, justice, and politics: "It is a theology that leads to practical results because today, in the world of the 'wretched of the earth,' the *true form* of faith is 'political love' or 'macro-charity.' "[61] There is no true Christian faith, they assert, without work for justice: in this way, liberation theology can be understood as a reevaluation of the Christian tradition and its central message that parallels the re-visioning work of feminist theologians. This emphasis on justice and action underlies Caminero-Santangelo's reading of the two community organizing passages in *So Far from God* as the bar by which the rest of the narrative's events should be measured.

Yet this reading widely misses the profoundly spiritual element of liberation theology Boff and Boff describe as equally central to its Marxist critique and materialism. In a section titled "Temptations Facing Liberation Theology," they list

Disregard for mystical roots, from which all true commitment to liberation springs, and overemphasis of political action. It is in prayer and contemplation, and intimate and communitarian contact with God, that the motivations for a faith-inspired commitment to the oppressed and all humankind spring and are renewed.

> *Overstressing the political aspect* of questions relating to oppression and
> liberation, at the expense of other, more supple and more deeply human
> aspects: friendship, pardon, feeling for leisure and celebration, open
> dialogue with everyone, sensitivity to artistic and spiritual riches.[62]

I quote at length because of the fittingness of this rejoinder—already present in the little book she herself quotes—to Caminero-Santangelo's argument. The final irony of that argument is that in its insistent materializing
of the oppression and justice work in *So Far from God*, it fully misses the
Xicanista valuation of indigenous spirituality, which finds a perhaps surprising ally in liberation theology as a subversive yet institutionally situ-
ated outgrowth of Catholicism.

I also quote at length because *Introducing Liberation Theology* can be put
into provocative conversation with Castillo's own treatment of liberation
theology in her essay "Saintly Mothers and Soldier's Whore." Although
critics often quote from *Massacre of the Dreamers* in their scholarly treatments of *So Far from God*, they have tended not to mention the nine-page
section in which Castillo takes on liberation theology. This avoidance isn't
hard to understand: Castillo roundly critiques "liberation theology" on
the basis of two textual examples. But although Castillo may not express
appreciation for liberation theology, her literary writing has, like Morrison's and Rich's, been important to feminist liberation theologians' work.
And, as I am arguing, while she does not paint a liberation theology blueprint in *So Far from God*, Castillo does exemplify and engage readers in
liberation theology's hermeneutical practices.

Castillo's critique of liberation theology (both "Chicano" and "Hispanic Women's") arrives at the end of an essay that explores the parallel
patriarchal structures of Marxist ideology and Catholicism. The "feminine
principle" is missing in both, she asserts, which means that neither can
lead to "true social transformation."[63] Both socialism and Christianity are
"male-dominated perspective[s]" (87); they share "the polarities of good
and evil," "a deference paid to a higher good," and "respect . . . for patriarchal order and hierarchy" (89). They also conflict with each other, she
asserts, because Marxism does not have room for spirituality (91). Castillo
sees liberation theology as "a blend of Marxist and Christian beliefs," but
since "both ideologies are male-centered, have hierarchical structures, and
significantly repress the feminine principle that is crucial to our spiritual
and material aspirations as Xicanistas," Castillo can find no room for them

within Xicanisma (96). She further asserts that both Marxism and Catholicism view women as commodities and as religiously subordinated (97).

To focus her discussion, Castillo relies on the example of *A Chicano Theology* by Andres Guerro, which is based on a series of interviews with nine Chicano leaders. The methodology of interview is key to Paulo Freire's pedagogy of the oppressed, but Castillo takes issue with the fact that Guerro chose *community leaders* to interview, implying a hierarchy, and that only two of them were women (97). Ultimately, Castillo's problem with the book seems to be that it hands down a mandate for resistance from leaders to the working-class women who make up the majority of both the religiously involved and the laboring population but who are also the most vulnerable to retaliation if they engage in leader-mandated liberation activism.

Castillo moves then into a discussion of *Hispanic Women's Theology* by Isasi-Díaz and Yolanda Tarango. This gender-inflected theology of liberation seems to offer more to Castillo's vision of Xicanisma, including a respect for the religiosity of Chicanas and an embrace of intuitive syncretism, a revaluing of women's strength in countercultural modes of survival (101), and a deep appreciation for women's own reality (102). Yet Castillo again calls women's liberation theology "problematic" because as a Christian theology, it is still rooted in the dualisms of spirit and body, transcendent and immanent, good and evil (102). Her criticisms arise not from the book itself but from a fundamentally negative stance toward Christianity not shared by all her feminist sisters. Castillo asserts, "we cannot make a blanket dismissal of Catholicism" (96), but her criticisms in this essay veer toward such a dismissal. Many of Castillo's assertions about Christian doctrine in this final section invite rejoinders from feminist theologians with a more hopeful revisionary outlook and even contradict what *happens*—regardless of its author's intentions—in the text she named *So Far from God*.

Faith, Hope, and Charity: The Hermeneutic of Liberation

> Theology, as a critical reflection in the light of the Word adopted through faith on the presence of Christians in a tumultuous world, should help us to understand the relationship between the life of faith and the urgent need to build a society that is humane and just. It is called upon to make explicit the values of faith, hope and charity that that commitment involves.
> —Gustavo Gutiérrez, "The Task and Content of Liberation Theology"

Latin American liberation theology[64] begins with the experiences of the majority of people in a divided society whose lives are affected by material and social deprivations. As Christopher Rowland puts it, "A constant refrain in all the different approaches which are grouped together under liberation theology is that the perspective of the poor and the marginalised offers another story, an alternative to that told by the wielders of economic power whose story becomes the 'normal' account."[65] The editors of *A Reader in Latina Feminist Theology* bring together this liberation theological perspective with Moraga's explanation of the title image of *This Bridge*: "We do this bridging by naming our selves and by telling our stories in our own words."[66] The beginning of work for justice that results from the sharing of such stories, according to Boff and Boff, is "Compassion," or "Suffering with"[67]: a commitment to recognize, even from a position of relative privilege, the vast suffering of many throughout the world whose suffering—whose sacrifice to the systems of late capitalism—often goes overlooked. I have been writing in this book of the ethics of literary representation, the question of which themes or topics warrant exploration in literature, which sufferings writers (and publishers) choose to bear witness to. A correlating concept might be the ethics of theological attention, the question of which themes or topics warrant exploration in theology. At a time when theology was not considered political, around the same time feminist theologians began to suggest that women's particular experiences warranted theological reflection, liberation theologians began to suggest that the experiences of those oppressed by class structures also were in need of further theological consideration.

Thus liberation theology brings together a class analysis informed by Marxism with a deeply spiritual and specifically Christian awareness of the privilege the Bible affords the "poor" and the likeness they bear to the "Suffering Servant, Jesus Christ": "Service in solidarity with the oppressed also implies an act of love for the suffering Christ."[68] This is never just a materialist endeavor, but one that ostensibly stages a confrontation with the divine Other. In the words of Rowland, "the vantage point of the poor is particularly, and especially, the vantage point of the crucified God and can act as a criterion for theological reflection, biblical exegesis, and the life of the Church."[69] Here we should recognize glimmers of the familiar paradox suggested by feminists like Rich and Daly, leftist Christian activists like Dorothee Sölle, and black liberation theologians of redemptive suffering: those who suffer experience the privilege of a life that uniquely figures forth divine suffering, and as a result of their suffering they have special insight to offer the world, but their suffering ought at the same time to give rise to the com-passion that seeks its mitigation. The only suffering that ought to be chosen is suffering that results from work for justice. In other words, the only good (?) suffering is suffering offered in a sort of sacrifice on the altar of struggle for something better.

In response to those who believe that Christianity has nothing to contribute to the "here and now," liberation theologians offer a reenvisioned Christianity that denies any separation between spiritual and material love, seeing Jesus Christ as a radical liberator. As *mujerista* theologian Isasi-Díaz asserts, "Justice is a Christian requirement: one cannot call oneself a Christian and not struggle for justice."[70] Such a theological paradigm is predicated on a certain *hermeneutic,* variously called a "hermeneutic of liberation"[71] or a "hermeneutical privilege for the poor and marginalised."[72] Liberation theology implies "a new way of reading the Bible,"[73] one wherein the holy text and the faith tradition are interpreted through the experience of those who suffer: the result is that these texts, for years read through the experiences of the privileged and dominant (understood to be a universal perspective) give rise to altogether different interpretations, as the portions of the Bible with "intrinsically liberating content,"[74] especially the prophets like Isaiah or the Gospels that paint a picture of Jesus Christ's ministry to the poor and oppressed, take on new significance. In similar fashion, the movements of church history that have overlooked or even caused the suffering of the vulnerable are highlighted in this reading, opening up a way of critique. Boff and Boff call this dynamic a "hermeneutical circle" where "the poor" and "the word" read each other.[75] We might even characterize this hermeneutic as radically intertextual: the *experience* of those who suffer oppression is put into subversive conversation with the tradition's holy book, and the result is a shifted understanding of the Christian faith.

But the result of this reading practice can never be a settled sense of a superior understanding. In fact, many liberation theologians further complicate this hermeneutical circle by insisting that liberation theology is *never* limited to the realm of ideas. Gutiérrez famously described liberation theology in 1964 as "a critical reflection on praxis."[76] Theologians following him argue that liberation theology is not a content but a *method,* one where theological reflection only ever follows action in community: "Liberation theology," writes Rowland, "is above all a new way of *doing* theology rather than being itself a new theology"; it is "a way, a discipline, an exercise."[77] In other words, liberation theology refuses the binaries not just of spiritual/material but also of mind/body: it fundamentally links embodied action with metaphysical contemplation, "practice" before "reasoning."[78] Liberation is a practice undertaken in community, and theology is the result of reflection *on* that practice, for the sake of furthering the conversation and the work for a transformed world.[79]

Liberation theology is not a final solution to the question of how Christian faith relates to human suffering. It originated within a powerful institution that at turns has supported the efforts of liberation theology in various Latin American countries or opposed it as too political, too subversive, too focused on grassroots efforts and forgetful of established hierarchical structures. It has hardly redeemed the Catholic Church, from this perspective. Nor is it an easy path, for as focused as its champions are on the praxis oriented, it can easily be accused of idealism and has to work hard against paternalism in the process of *conscientization*. It has also, much like black liberation theology, been subject to critique for overlooking gender oppression and for its problematic relation to indigenous populations. A best-case scenario is that these critiques have been noted and attended to, consistent with a methodology so concerned with dialogue and openness to the other. Gustavo Gutiérrez includes these concerns in his 2008 essay "The Task and Content of Liberation Theology," acknowledging the history that required revision based on these critiques, so that "factors of race, culture and gender have become increasingly important in helping to draw a more accurate picture of the condition of the poor in Latin America."[80]

This description of liberation theology presents a Catholic theological paradigm that is a far cry from the disengaged Catholicism doña Felicia rejects as a child for not "help[ing] the destitute all around her despite their devotion" (60). It also does not bear much similarity to the liberation theology Castillo critiques in "Saintly Mother and Soldier's Whore." At its best, liberation theology as a methodology seeks justice in conversation with the Christian tradition, reevaluating the structures that have contributed to oppression, opening up dialogue, transforming the material and social conditions of the oppressed, and transforming human understanding of the Divine. It is open and receptive to otherness even as it is critical of the powerful structures that lead to oppression, at once suspicious and hospitable. This is the sense in which all feminist theology, not just Latin American feminist theology, can be called "a critical theology of liberation."[81] Castillo's concerns about dualisms, hierarchy, the commodification of women, and the undervaluing of spirituality, thus, would seem not to apply, especially to the feminist liberation theology she cites. Nevertheless, we are confronted again by the hermeneutical circle, Paul Ricoeur's famous "you must believe in order to understand, but you must understand in order to believe": Latin American liberation theology, like black liberation theology, and feminist liberation theology, begins—and generally ends—with a commitment to reevaluating, and revaluing, the Christian tradition. For those who have found the faith tradition inescapably guilty of causing and exacerbating suffering, such a hermeneutical circle may have no appeal and no entrance.

Still, as Castillo herself notes, the majority of Mexican American women have remained faithful to a syncretic but recognizable Catholicism: they are already within the hermeneutical circle. This may be the reason Castillo chooses to engage so closely, if ambivalently, with the Catholic tradition in some of her writings. Such a perspective sheds light on the characterizations of La Loca, Francisco, and doña Felicia discussed earlier: they implicitly critique but do not destroy or signal an escape from the context of Catholicism. Understanding liberation theology as a methodology, a hermeneutic, offers us a way to read the relation of Christianity and suffering in *So Far from God*. The "liberation theological" elements of the novel cohere not just in Sofi's community organizing, Esperanza's Chicana activism, or even the Way of the Cross Procession near the novel's end (although the Procession does seem almost a textbook example of the praxis Isasi-Díaz proposes). Rather, the novel's force in relation to liberation theology arises from its exemplary exercise of a hermeneutic of liberation, the way the text of the novel rereads the biblical text and the text of the Catholic and indigenous spiritual traditions in light of its characters' myriad experiences of suffering, even as it reads those experiences in light of the religious traditions.

The groundwork of this hermeneutic of liberation is the novel's representation of sufferings not often considered by the mainstream media of North America, which is foundational to its ethics of literary representation. In telling the story of Sofi and her daughters—of their pain and ultimate deaths caused by economic poverty, gender scripts, sexual violence, war, capitalist greed and chemically devastating sweat-shop labor, sexual obsession, homophobia, and AIDS—the novel draws attention to the sufferings of the marginalized whose perspective "offers another story."[82] Within the novel itself, these contemporary tales of woe are mixed into the ancient stories of Christian martyrs: Castillo's source material for Sofi and her daughters, as she has noted in interviews, came from *The Lives of the Saints*. In the classic tale—which is arguably a Christian appropriation of a Greek myth, or a literalization of Sophia as Divine Wisdom from whom Faith, Hope, and Love are born—Sophia is a second-century mother. She raises her daughters, Pistis (Faith), Elpis (Hope), and Agape (Love) to be deeply committed Christians, and when the Emperor Hadrian hears news of their devotion he calls them to him to test their faith out of apparently sadistic curiosity, torturing the three adolescent girls to the point of death. Sophia, who encourages them through their trials, soon dies of a broken heart at their tomb: "In the Christian legend concerning Sophia, she suffered the deep sadness of losing all three daughters to martyrdom."[83] Although La Loca is not part of the original tale of Sophia and her daughters, Castillo also discovered her in *Butler's Lives of the Saints* in the story of Christina the Astonishing, a thirteenth-century Frenchwoman. Christina is said to have had a seizure and was proclaimed dead, then awoke at her own funeral and flew to the rafters.[84] Like La Loca, Christina claimed to have been to hell, purgatory, and heaven, couldn't handle the scent of people, preferred to spend time by the river, underwent surgery, and even stuffed herself into a stove.

Yet Castillo's novel rereads these stories from the Christian tradition in light of her contemporary characters' experiences of suffering, after the mode of the hermeneutics of liberation. To begin with, although the young women in *The Lives of the Saints* typically are listed with the label "virgin," implying that such sexual chastity further emphasizes their holiness, Esperanza, Caridad, and Fe certainly are *not* virgins. Nor is their mother the devoted celibate widow of the Christian legend, but rather a woman who sends away her good-for-nothing husband—twice—and ultimately divorces him, rejecting the church's teachings on marriage. Although the stories of these Christian saints, which offer so few details about their lives that the only important elements of their experience appear to be their death-for-faith and chastity, function within the church tradition to pass on such values to women, the stories of "saints" in *So Far from God* suggest very different norms, undermining the virgin/whore and material/spiritual dichotomies and representing the complex political imbrication of suffering's sources.

Indeed, the novel recasts the entire concept of "martyrdom" or sacrifice for a greater cause. In the original story of Sophia and her daughters, their martyrdom results from their tenacious commitment to the Christian faith; in Sofi's story, this could not be farther from the truth. Esperanza dies as a reporter in the Middle East, perhaps standing for truth, but she would not have to be there were it not for the U.S. drive for war. The heroism of her death is compromised by the nation's politics. Caridad dies (we think) jumping off a cliff with her would-be lover in terrified flight from Francisco's obsessive chase—mysteriously, at the same time, entering into an indigenous creation myth and allowing, through her sacrifice, for the flourishing of the world. Caridad's death is no Christian martyrdom, but rather an ambiguous end in the face of twisted Christianity and exalted indigenous sacrifice. Fe's death is clearly the result of the capitalist system's use of vulnerable bodies for its dirtiest jobs as well as her unfortunate embrace of the American Dream. And La Loca Santa, in her mysterious case of AIDS, does not choose her fate and does not stand for anything but the suffering of the innocent, subverting the typical association of AIDS with the guilty: in this way, she appears to be a revision not just of Christina the Astonishing but also of Jesus Christ. In the end, all four of Sofi's daughters revise the typical concept of Christian martyrdom, rewriting sacrifice through the lens of realistic and unjust contemporary sufferings.

Sofi, too, reinterprets the expected pattern: *So Far from God* does not dwell on the story of the passive, self-sacrificing Catholic mother. "La pobre Sofi," "la abandonida," while pitied by her community for her many losses, does not suffer as a woman simply because of her status within a patriarchal Christian society. Her suffering is not primarily the result of church teachings on submission and emulation of *la Virgen*: indeed, Sofi's life story is one of hard work and survival. The novel glosses over her nearly superhuman feat of running a butcher shop (including raising the animals herself) and raising her four daughters, telling little of their childhoods. Her community organizing work apparently goes on while she experiences all of her devastating losses. In contrast to those middle-class women whose suffering and self-sacrifice, as described by Rich in *Of Woman Born,* occur primarily in relation to their husbands and children in the private sphere of the home, Sofi's class and race positions cause her altogether different suffering. Her nearly helpless witnessing of her daughters' diverse sufferings and untimely deaths appears to be Sofi's primary source of pain. These result, as I have argued, from a complex array of sources, including gender roles, social expectations regarding sexuality, and certain church teachings, as well as the politics of nationalism and war, the abuses of capitalism, and the inescapable nature of disease.

The represented experiences of Sofi, Esperanza, Fe, Caridad, and La Loca raise questions about the helpfulness of a religious economy of sacrifice for higher purposes. In the real world of material vulnerabilities, how many women are likely to face only the challenge of standing up for their religious beliefs? Who actually benefits from their lives and their deaths? What good can martyrdom possibly do? These questions relate to the novel's final chapter, another source of critical dissonance. In it, we are told that Sofi, unlike the Sofia of *The Lives of the Saints,* does not lie down on her daughters' graves and die of a broken heart, but instead lives for nearly four more decades, organizing a group called M.O.M.A.S.—Mothers of Martyrs and Saints.[85] Is this ending sincere or farcical? Some elements of Sofi's organization are magical, requiring an enchanted imagination: the martyrs and saints appear to their mothers, as Esperanza has in the text after her death (250–51). Other elements are outrageous: M.O.M.A.S.'s annual meetings grow to be bigger than the World Series or the Olympics (249). And the gathering is also swept up into the commodifying movement of capitalism, with all sorts of trinkets sold at the annual conventions (249). Still, the narrator's tone shows awareness of the ridiculous, calling the vendors' products "useless" (249), and asserting (against the claims of the participants), that "this was more or less of a 'circus' than mitoteros always went back home reporting, because as I said, the conference of M.O.M.A.S. was very serious business, hombre!" (250). If the narrator is sarcastic here, he or she seems to be mocking the mothers. But if the narrator is a participant-observer sharing a bit of gossip, shaped by the enchanted Catholic imagination that takes such postdeath appearances in stride (which he or she does), we might read the tone as both aware of the silliness and also quite sincere. After all,

M.O.M.A.S. is a group of bereaved mothers gathering for community and mutual support; its massive size, while outrageous, also implies the volume of suffering in the world, the number of children "martyred" not for their faith but sacrificed to the various systems of domination. Indeed, the name M.O.M.A.S., when spoken, implies that all "mamas" are mothers of martyrs and saints, in this sense. Finally, this last chapter also offers another rereading of church tradition in light of the mothers' experiences, explicitly contrasting the practices of M.O.M.A.S. with those of the Catholic hierarchy, especially in relation to gender: rather than testing members to be sure they are biological women, the organization trusts their word to be mothers who have experienced loss. The novel ends, "After all, just because there had been a time way back when, when some fregados all full of themselves went out of their way to prove that none among them had the potential of being a mother, did it mean that there *had* to come a time when someone would be made to *prove* that she did?" (252). The fact that it ends with an unanswered question, phrased in the negative, further intensifies the text's ambivalence, leaving its readers with this questioning, uncertain taste in their mouths.

This humorous but, I think, also partly sincere vision of a group of women who can support each other—humanly, imperfectly—through their losses, and look to their dead children for wisdom, critiques Catholic misogyny (calling Saint Augustine a "malcriado" [252]). It suggests, as I have argued, an altogether different definition of "martyrs"—not as those who die for the faith, as if that were the most important thing, but those who are sacrificed like lambs in the slaughterhouse of various oppressions. But it does not abandon popular Mexican Catholicism altogether: not in vocabulary, nor in ritual (a Mass is still said at the beginning of M.O.M.A.S. gatherings), nor in belief in saints (defined, unlike martyrs, as capable of performing miracles), nor in its economy of redemptive suffering, with the understanding that out of the martyrdom can come something good in the wisdom that the dead children are able to offer their gathered mothers (251). The fact that M.O.M.A.S. exists at all could even be said to support the claim that the spiritually inclined seek organization, even institutions. Yet although the masses of women at these gatherings do not abandon Catholicism, theirs is a critically transformed syncretic Catholicism—critiquing past gender oppressions and seeking not to replicate them in inverse, hearing Mass said by women priests, and not just virginal ones (250). Such a transformation is achieved through the praxis empowered by a hermeneutic of liberation.

I am not the first to note that Castillo rewrites earlier stories of exemplary womanhood; however, my argument links this re-vision to the hermeneutic of liberation, which rereads the Christian tradition through the text of contemporary experiences of oppression and asks how this intertextual reading *matters*. This hermeneutic does not originate with liberation theology: rather, it parallels the interpretive double move of critique and embrace that I am identifying throughout this project, present in numerous liberation movements. Yet considering Castillo's texts in light of a critically feminist Latin American liberation theology provides us with a context and vocabulary for addressing their dogged engagement with, yet ambivalence toward, Catholicism, their ethics of literary representation, their mystical-political edge, and their reenvisioning of the ethical force of caring mothers. Such a vocabulary is immensely helpful not just in reading *So Far from God* but also in reading *The Guardians* and its difficult, layered representation of material suffering, Catholicism, and mother-love.

The Guardians and Co-Madres, or "The Mother-Bond Principle"

> Look into your children's faces. They tell you the truth. They are our future.
> Pero no tendremos ningún futuro si seguimos siendo víctimas.
> —Cherríe Moraga, *Heroes and Saints and Other Plays*

I end this chapter with a tentative, gestural reading of Castillo's 2007 novel *The Guardians*.[86] My experience of reading this novel for the first time, more recently and on no particularly marked day and with no particularly vivid correlating experience, was as disorienting as my readings of *So Far from God*. The first time through, and then the times after that, I put down the book heavy-hearted and bewildered. What to think? What to do? But it is precisely this haunting that, I think, constitutes the novels' invitation to readers to engage in a reading practice that interprets their own material context through the representations of the literary text, confronting them with textual strangeness as well as representations of injustice. Which is to say, while both these texts manifest a hermeneutic of liberation as they re-vision religious texts in light of contemporary suffering (the ethics of literary representation), they also, through their ambivalences and mysteries, challenge readers to an ongoing, intertextual engagement for the sake of ethical praxis (the ethics of readerly attention). In *The Guardians*, this ethical force underlies the entire narrative, with its dramatized sufferings and textual mysteries, but it is especially driven by the character Regina, whose embodiment of a re-visioned Queen of Heaven exemplifies the "mother-bond principle" Castillo forwards in *Massacre of the Dreamers*.

Like *So Far from God*, *The Guardians* confronts readers with heartrending oppressions, occurrences one wishes to believe as fantastical but knows to be realistic, like body part harvesting along the Mexican American border, adolescent gang violence, the separation of families by immigration laws, and kidnapping and sexual slavery. Also like *So Far from God*, *The Guardians* pairs too-awful-to-be-true truths of human suffering with too-strange-to-be-true religious miracles, yet it does so against a backdrop of class-, race-, gender-, and religiously linked oppressions and inextricable complexities. It is also a love story.

The Guardians is narrated by its four central characters, Regina, her nephew Gabriel (Gabo), her coworker and love-interest Miguel (Michael), and Miguel's Abuelo Milton. Their various voices (the three adults speak in present tense, and Gabo writes letters to a father-saint) manifest their personalities: these different narrative perspectives read each other, rendering each character a little suspicious as we recognize the limitations of their own self-perceptions. No one is heroic; everyone is mixed. And nothing is simple. Everything is complicated by layers of cause and effect as well as layers of literary allusion and intertextuality: Milton the grandfather is blind and long-winded, not unlike the literary forebear John Milton. To cement the allusion, John Milton's classic *Paradise Lost* includes the characters of archangels Uriel, Gabriel, Michael, and Rafael—four names in *The Guardians*. Unlike *So Far from God*, this is a text obsessed with reading and writing: Regina studied Latin as a child and has read such books as Gabriel García Márquez's *One Hundred Years of Solitude*; Gabo grew up with his father's library of radical socialist texts traveling with them from migrant job to migrant job and is a voracious reader of these texts and of those in the priest's library, as well as Harry Potter (37–39); Miguel is a teacher of history, a wide reader, and a writer, compiling an overwhelming array of notes for a book on the oppressions of his people (151). The text comments on its own textuality, with Miguel's accounts of his research strangely eliding the distinction between his own book and Castillo's, as their shared ethics of literary representation results in a shared representation of the sufferings of classed, raced, and gendered humans from violence and ecological degradation.

Castillo often creates ties between her novels, even sharing characters among them, and *The Guardians* opens an intertextual conversation with *So Far from God* early on as Regina muses on what it takes to be a martyr or saint: "it seems it would be very, very hard to become one these days. It isn't because we don't have diehard virgins, but because these days the pope is not about to proclaim every girl who fights a rapist a saint. As for the martyrs—you don't get thrown in the den of lions for refusing to renounce your faith as in early Christian times" (9). She admits to daydreaming about becoming such a martyr. Regina's comments highlight the sexualization of sainthood, as well as the degree to which her imagination is shaped by the stories of such martyrs and saints, emphasizing their importance as a cultural discipline. They also comment on *So Far from God*, supporting its questioning of church-sanctioned saints and martyrs and suggesting the power of alternate myths. Second, *The Guardians* alludes to *So Far from God* in the letters of its religiously obsessive young male character, who writes to "Santo Franciscano," recalling the name of Francisco el Penitente. Gabo's asceticism, his troubled relationship to a young woman, and his early loss of a mother also link him to Francisco el Penitente. Yet an important contrast occurs between Francisco and Gabo in their ultimate ends: Francisco el Penitente chases Caridad and Esmeralda off a cliff and ultimately hangs himself like a Judas figure. Gabo, on the other hand, is killed, stabbed in the lungs and the heart from behind by the drugged object of his affection (Tiny Tears, whose given name is, significantly, María Dolores), and wrongfully shot from the front by police officers in search of justice for Gabo's parents (or, perhaps more important to the police, a drug ring).[87]

These intertextual ties suggest a link between the two narratives, a continued exploration of what it means to be a "saint" or a "martyr" and how Catholicism relates to the suffering of Mexican Americans living in the borderlands. *The Guardians* is much less concerned than *So Far from God* with indigenous spirituality: although Miguel is a self-identified Chicano skeptical of the Catholic church, who claims a Native American cosmology and participates in dual-gender sweat lodges (108–109, 195), this is not a story populated by *curanderas* and native myths. Instead, Regina manifests a deeply ambivalent popular Catholicism: not only is her imagination shaped by the stories of martyrs and saints, she is also afraid of purgatory (4), has a Virgin of Guadalupe plaque over her bed (21), calls on archangels (27), dreams of heaven (28), and imagines manna (120). Yet she also avoids church, has a contentious relationship with the local priest Juan Bosco (97), accuses the church of hypocrisy (99), and repeatedly worries that Gabo will become a priest, disappointing his father, whose Marxist critique she shares (7, 21, 147).

Gabriel, on the other hand, is deeply religious, and his religiosity in the novel is open to competing interpretations. Gabriel is committed to his faith, even through struggle, as is evidenced by his letters to "el Santo Franciscano, Padre Pío" (a twentieth-century Capuchin monk famous for his stigmata and his theology of salvation through suffering and pain). On the one hand, Regina, Miguel, Abuelo Milton, and Gabo's school principal all question the extent of Gabo's religious devotion. Regina notes that developmentally he seems traumatized by his mother's death (4) and expresses repeated concern that her nephew's clinging to the church is a result of his early trauma and loss: "He calls it passion. I say obsession" (121). Gabo's behaviors are certainly unusual: he limits his food intake, asserting, "Little sacrificios prepare me daily for the course I have chosen" (19) and "trie[s] not to enjoy [his food] too much" (19), seeks to avoid "extravagances" like "celebrating" by going out for dinner (20), and prays for stigmata (20). Readers are introduced to Gabo in these terms from his first chapter in the novel. He casts his experiences with peers entirely in light of the spiritual, confesses sins most people would not bat an eyelash at, and eventually steals a robe from the church to wear it like a monk at school and preach apocalyptic warning from atop a cafeteria table. Gabo also narrates in his letter a mystical experience one morning when he is helping with Mass, as he sees drops of blood falling down the statue of Jesus and hears a message from God (64). The various characters' doubts, and Gabo's own letters, effectively cast him as a troubled boy.

Yet even as his elders question Gabo's extreme piety, they also recognize him as special, even holy. Father Bosco acts as a mentor, and Abuelo Milton insists he sees a "halo" around Gabo's head (94) (Milton is nearly blind, and the boy has red hair). When Milton asks the deputy Sofia whether she can see this halo, she laughs and agrees that he's "special"; Milton further comments that the boy has "all but grown wings on him" (133). Regina, too, characterizes her nephew in these terms, even when just referring to the speed of the car ahead of her in a high-speed chase: "We were still on the ground. My boy, he was flying" (202). Gabo's extraordinary nature is further emphasized by his actions, including his care for his Aunt Regina, whose swollen feet he soaks and rubs in an act reminiscent of Christ's washing of his disciples' feet (137), and his giving his shoes away to a needy person on the street in Mexico (139).

Traumatized or not, Gabriel seems to find strength for his own suffering in the story of Christ's suffering, reading the two together in an implicit practice of liberation hermeneutics. Hiding in a garbage bin during his stakeout search for his father who has gone missing while crossing the border, Gabo finds himself in a situation that calls to mind both Christ's passion and the boy's previous experiences crossing the border with his parents:

> Tears came to my eyes from the stench, the pain in my back and knees, and so much unsureness de todo.
>
> *Eli, Eli, lema sabachthani?* Jesus had cried on the cross. All I ever have to do is remind myself what Our Savior suffered for us to know what I am capable of enduring, Padre Pío. I did not dare move, just like I used to have to do when we were crossing el desierto and helicopters were hovering over us. "Stay put," my dad would say, pushing my head down between my knees, hoping I would blend in with a nopal.
>
> "Shhh." (85–86)

Gabo's letter ends there, implying a pause in the writing before he takes up his story again in another letter that begins after a white-space break. Perhaps he has reached the limits of his words at that moment of recollected fear and pain. When he does, later, continue his narration of the search for his father, he also continues to describe his experiences crossing the desert with his parents, including one time his sister "became so dehydrated we were sure she was going to die," and "all [he] could see was white": the children's parents carried them until they couldn't, and ultimately the family had to drink their own urine: "It is disgusting to admit, but it saved us" (87). This is a young man who has known suffering, who finds strength to pursue justice for his father in the concept of a suffering God: Gabo exemplifies liberation theology's insight of the special connection between the oppressed and Christ.

And the narrative doesn't just link Gabriel's devotion to the suffering Christ to his own experiences of suffering; it also seems to rewrite some traditional gendered scripts through his mysticism. On Gabriel's first Sunday as an acolyte, he observes the crowd at Mass: the "roasted pecan faces," many of them very young mothers. "All the women, young and old, came to church to kneel before la Virgencita. All of them with frowns and tears seemed to whisper, 'Someone in heaven, give me a break'" (64). Gabo notes the gendered divide here: the women come to church, along with only "very few young or able men": "I always wonder—is it not considered manly to fear God?" It is in the midst of these reflections on men's and women's relations to the church and to their own suffering that Gabriel experiences the text's first miracle: "I turned to face the altar, tan nervioso, as I said, and as I was looking high above, at the life-size crucifix that hangs there, the wisdom de Su Reverencia came to me: '*The One who is keeping you nailed to the Cross loves you and is breathing into you the strength to bear the unbearable martyrdom and the love to love divine Love in bitterness*'" (64). After these words of paradox (quoted from a historical letter of Padre Pío), Gabo sees the drops of blood rolling down Jesus's face. For Gabo, suffering love is not just a call of the church to women, but a call to everyone: the lessons to be learned in suffering (unavoidable or chosen) are not specifically intended for those women who kneel before the Virgin.[88]

Gabo's mystical experiences are further corroborated by the doubt and belief of characters in the text when he finally receives his prayed-for stigmata. Although the young man's preoccupation with suffering is troubling to a modern reader possessed of a disenchanted imagination, Gabo's apparent nail wounds appear after his sermon in the cafeteria wearing Franciscan robes,[89] a sermon in which he names not just typical religious concerns but also environmental contamination and nations warring "in the name of peace" (165). Gabo's concerns are not just spiritual wickedness but also material injustices: the mystical stigmata are inextricably linked to his political awareness. The scene is not entirely clear: Gabriel falls from the table and wakes up in the school nurse's office with bandaged hands: he remembers hearing a "choir" yelling *His hands are bleeding*," but as he can neither open his eyes nor stand, this may well be a hallucination.

Yet while one might expect the skeptical Regina to be the last person to believe Gabo's miracle, she stands up for him when Father Juan Bosco asks whether he inflicted the wounds on himself: "I am the one who wraps them," Regina relates (172). And Father Bosco ultimately believes, vouching for Gabo with Miguel, who recalls his own brief period of "desiring holiness": "Are you sure?" Miguel asks, twice, and twice Juan Bosco nods (196). In this scene, Miguel also reflects on the changes in Father Bosco, whom Regina has always criticized for hypocrisy and who even attempts to leave the priesthood to marry a woman in the community. Bosco appears to return from his hiatus not only more humble, as Regina notes (172), but also with a subversively political consciousness. Miguel comments, "J. B. had come around since the days when he only cared about the longtime residents who supported the parish in Cabuche. 'My superiors advised me to keep out of political issues in the States. But I don't think like that anymore'" (196). Father Bosco checks up on migrant workers, even under threat of gunfire, and ultimately joins Gabo's risky search for his father among a dangerous border-crossing drug ring. Political commitment and openness to the mystical are manifestly united in these scenes, as in Latin American liberation theology.

A final scene that supports the mystical elements of an otherwise painfully realist narrative, undermining a reading of Gabo as a crazy or traumatized fanatic, comes after the confrontation between Regina and the returned Father Bosco. A short chapter follows, narrated as one of Gabo's letters. He recalls a childhood memory, his experience as an eight-year-old witnessing the "Dancing of the Sun," an "official milagro of the Church," with his Tía Regina. Gabo recounts their day, planting tomatoes, when wind, followed by a darkening sky, gave way to a sun, "flat like a disk" and "whirling," then "soaring fast toward the earth" and turning everything golden (175). This is a memory filled with laughter and joy—both before and after the miracle. Gabriel's parents were not dead, just away for work. Regina recognizes the miracle first ("That is how I know she is so blessed," Gabo asserts) and is in her nephew's memory not afraid but joyful (175). Indeed, the miracle, which she counsels Gabo to keep to himself (though he does tell Father Bosco in confession), does not seem to shock Regina, at least in Gabo's recollection. She accepts it with joy. And when it fades, they go "back to [their] planting" (176). It is significant that this scene arrives 175 pages into the novel: the back-and-forth tug of doubt and belief in the novel's fantastical elements has been waged, and so when Regina and Gabo's early shared miracle finally comes out, it reads back with authority on the prior ambivalences. Regina may critique the institutional church, but she is a woman of faith, her imagination wide open to the miraculous.

Regina's dual stance of critique and embrace stands at the center of the narrative, alongside the text's ambivalence about Gabo's religious devotion. Regina, as is noted by numerous characters in the text, is named after the Queen of Heaven, Mary the Mother of Jesus, and is, at least according to Abuelo Milton, like a queen—or a goddess (69). In fact, Regina is named "Regina Ana," carrying both the name of Heaven's queen and that of the patron saint of late-in-life mothers, as she herself notes (152). In a further liberation hermeneutic re-visioning, Regina is a virgin widow, married to a casualty of Vietnam, who proceeds into middle age without children or romantic attachments. Regina struggles financially, has a troubled relationship with her own mother (references to the deceased woman appear at the start of many of Regina's chapters) resulting in low self-esteem, and, according to her nephew, has a rather coarse vocabulary. She troubles the idealized Virgin Mary paradigm. On the other hand, Regina does, to a notable degree, embody a caring mother. "Loving care is what I try to bring to whatever I do," she asserts at one point, in direct reference to her flourishing garden—"otherwise why bother?" (48).

Indeed, while Regina's own difficult experience as a daughter and her self-doubt color her narrations, Gabo honors her as a mother, an exemplar of profound lessons of forgiveness and hospitality. In the scene in which Regina stands up for him and his stigmata to Father Bosco, Gabo responds to her assertion that the priest had left when the boy needed him by first hugging her, then whispering, "don't you know?" He goes on, "'You have been more mother to me than I could have ever asked for . . . more than I deserved. Our friend was wrong, Tía Regina'—Gabo put my hand against his cool cheek—'yet, you let him in your home, just as you made room here for me. Don't you know how many lessons you taught us both?'" (173). Regina further exemplifies this forgiveness and hospitality in her radical choice at the narrative's end to care for Tiny Tears (María Dolores), who is responsible for her nephew's death, and to take in María Dolores's little girl when no one else will, despite what everyone thinks (209–10). Regina attributes this act, in part, to her reading of the Gospel of Matthew,

"Gabo's favorite book of all" (210), and its teaching on forgiveness: "For if ye forgive men their trespasses, your heavenly Father will also forgive you" (210).[90] This radical act of forgiveness and love cements Regina as a virgin-widow-mother, a jeans-wearing, gun-toting, trouble-surviving re-vision of the Mother of God. "*Victim,*" she says on the novel's last page, in reference to María Dolores but also certainly in reference to herself, "is not a word in my vocabulary" (211).[91]

As Regina stands as a re-visioning of the Virgin Mary, read in the her-meneutic of liberation through the experiences of material oppression and suffering of a contemporary woman, Gabo's death rereads the story of Padre Pío and the script of martyrdom. In response to *So Far from God*'s interrogation of martyrdom, and in response to Regina's comments on how hard it is to be a saint or martyr in contemporary life, Gabo dies not because he refuses to renounce his Christian faith but in active pursuit of justice and love. He seeks his father, and Miguel's kidnapped wife Crucita, and ultimately also Tiny Tears, in the house of their oppressors. He is killed, simultaneously, by Tiny Tears (whom he seems to love) and by the police: Tiny Tears shoves a piece of glass first into his lungs and then into his heart, and the police pump him full of bullets when, shocked by Tiny Tears's attack, he fails to put up his hands when he exits the house. In one sense, Gabriel is a sacrificial stand-in, a scapegoat: Tiny Tears is drugged, terrorized by captivity and sexual assault, and she may very well think she is defending herself against her attacker. In any case, her actions are misguided and undeserved. The police mistake Gabo as a violent threat, even a member of the very group that killed his father. Gabo dies like a blood sacrifice to the entire wicked system of border exploitation, a mar-tyr inspired by faith, even amidst his own suffering, to seek to end the suf-fering of those he loved. His death is both deeply spiritual and inescapably political.[92]

The Guardians is a troubling novel. Its representations of human suf-fering caused by interlocking systems of oppression at the border of the United States and Mexico, its engagement with the miraculous, its ambiv-alence about Gabo's perspective on suffering, even its ending all leave one—leave *me*—unsettled. We might even ask whether the novel simply reinforces the same old stories: suffering as a spiritual good, the self-sac-rificing mother as the ideal for women. Do Gabriel and Regina support these conservative positions, or do they call them into question?

The risk with the paradox of critique and embrace is that it is possible to overlook one element or the other, especially because we as readers are motivated by our desires. My response to this question about Gabo and Regina, the mystical-political duo at the heart of this novel, relies on an essay from *Massacre of the Dreamers*, "The Mother-Bond Principle." In this essay, Castillo offers an argument that parallels that of Rich, Morrison, myriad other feminists, and the Latin American liberation theologians cited earlier: the characteristics that have been problematically expected of the oppressed (and that warrant serious critique) are precisely those that offer hope for a transformed society. Castillo asserts in her introduction to the essay collection, "by using the Mother as our model to guide us in place of an abstract, amaterial, distant Father God (that all Christians are called to obey, if not to attempt to emulate in his incarnation as Jesus), it may be possible to have a vision of a truly nurturing society." The argument of the essay is fairly straightforward: Mexican American culture, following its Catholic paradigm and celebration of the Virgin of Guadalupe, both idealizes and demeans mothers and associates all women with motherhood (183). Yet traits like "nurturing, serviceability, and selflessness," associated with mothers and "encouraged in women," "are denigrated, deemed worthless, seen as liabilities within the value system in which we live" (185). These, however, are exactly the traits necessary for building a just and healthy society, and so developing the habits and skills of mothering at all levels of society—not just among women, but among men and women in public and private spheres—could "radically change our world" (186–87). Women, too, need to be mothered (or cared for), even as adults; "co-madre," Castillo reminds her readers, traditionally understood as close friend, literally means "co-mother" (192). Castillo critiques the understanding of a mother as "self-sacrificing or the martyr sufrida madre that tradition has often mandated" (204), nevertheless suggesting that "caring selflessly" and taking responsibility for others' "material, spiritual and emotional needs" are key practices for society to learn from motherhood (187).

Castillo's suggestions may be viewed as idealistic; they are certainly utopian. But they are, I think, at work in *The Guardians*, even amid all its suffering and its revised vision of the mother. In fact, there are no biological mothers as main characters in this novel, and those secondary character mothers who come up frequently are either dead or problematized.

Regina is a woman who takes on the *practices* of mothering: first her nephew Gabo and then, more radically, his killer and his killer's child. But, subverting the impulse to place Regina on a Virgin Mary–size pedestal, I would argue that the novel is full of mother-nurturers, perhaps renamed to avoid this dangerous association of the ethical ideal with only the mother. This assertion relates to the title of the novel and the question it raises: who are "the Guardians"? The first answer the narrative offers, three pages in, is that the guardians are los Franklins, the mountain range that looks down on the happenings of the narrative, which Regina has faith in even when she can't see them. She compares them to giants, shape-shifters, and even self-sacrificing, personified figures that "let the devoted climb up along their spines to crown them with white crosses and flowers and mementos. They give themselves that way, those guardians between two countries" (5). (In this image, like Moraga's, they allow others to walk along their backs.) Yet other options soon arise, as Regina compares Miguel to her "favorite archangel," on whom she calls "whenever I need serious help"—so perhaps the "guardians" are guardian angels (27). On the same page, Regina names herself as her nephew's possible legal guardian (27). Furthermore, she persists in comparing Miguel to her favorite archangel, implying that perhaps the extremely helpful man (and would-be lover) is a "guardian" (57, 66). And the possibilities extend, as we see Gabriel, Miguel, and Milton join forces to gift Regina—so used to caring for others—with the best day of her life (147). Indeed, the guardianship is expansive: Milton actively cares on numerous occasions for both Gabo and Miguel. Father Bosco cares, at points better than others, for Gabo. And Gabo cares not only for his father and Tiny Tears but also for his aunt.

Rather than just celebrating a virginal, self-sacrificing mother figure, the novel dramatizes the mutual, self-giving nurturing—the mother-bond principle—of a collection of guardians, each at points giving (like mothers, like fathers, like angels) and at points receiving care within lives shaped by gendered, raced, classed, and religious sufferings. Some of them end up martyrs, but they are all, to some extent, saints in life, if a saint is understood as one who embodies the mysterious miracle of love with skin on. Rereading the texts—of Catholic tradition, of Mexican American motherhood, of the Bible—in light of contemporary experiences of material oppression, vulnerability, and suffering, *The Guardians* engages a hermeneutic of liberation that ultimately suggests an ethical practice of risky, attentive reading (of both the literary text and the text of life, in light of each other) and loving action. Unsettling with its ambivalences and mysteries, it invites the reader into further contemplation and, ideally, praxis. In the end, Regina's embrace of a critically reappropriated Christian model of forgiveness and active, caring love is not unfamiliar: she chooses to sacrifice herself, her freedoms and emotional distance, in order to care for the young child of a girl she could have perceived as an enemy. But, as I have been suggesting throughout this chapter, from Moraga's "bridge" analogy forward, this is a hard-earned conclusion. Whether it is satisfying to you, as a reader, may very well depend on which circles you are part of, which tools you are willing to work with, which houses you are seeking to dismantle, and which houses you are seeking to build.

Reading in *The Guardians*, like political organizing in *So Far from God*, does not prevent children from dying. Knowing Latin doesn't keep Regina from living a hand-to-mouth life; reading Marxist theory doesn't save Rafael from having to work as a migrant farmer; reading statistics on injustice and sexism does not keep Miguel from losing his marriage, or keep the environmental racism from continuing, or protect his ex-wife from kidnapping and sexual violence. But reading, especially reading from the perspective of the poor and oppressed, can give courage, as with Gabo in his emotional suffering at the loss of his parents. Reading can spur on activism, as it does in Miguel. And reading, even reading from a text used at points to dominate and oppress, as in Regina's reading of the Gospel of Matthew, can inspire the kind of love necessary to break the cycles of violence and oppression. Reading is not enough, it does not complete the work of justice, but it does *matter*.

5

Silent (in the Face of) Suffering?

Chimamanda Ngozi Adichie and Postcolonial Cultural Hermeneutics

> It is a particular academic arrogance to assume any discussion of feminist theory in this time and in this place without examining our many differences, and without a significant input from poor women, black and third-world women and lesbians.
> —Audre Lorde, "The Master's Tools Will Never Dismantle the Master's House," *Sister Outsider*

> I wanted to write a novel. I had no interest in writing a polemic.
> —Chimamanda Ngozi Adichie, "African 'Authenticity' and the Biafran Experience"

> But I will say that fiction is true.
> —Chimamanda Ngozi Adichie in Susan VanZanten, "A Conversation with Chimamanda Ngozi Adichie"

Again and again in postcolonial discourse the same questions are posed: Who speaks? Who listens? Who represents suffering? What is the responsibility of the writer? Of the literary critic? Of the reader?

Such questions also dominate this book, from Adrienne Rich's concern with "voice" and language (*this is the oppressor's language / yet I need it to talk to you*) to Toni Morrison's dedication to the six million and more whose stories she seeks to re-member in *Beloved* to Ana Castillo's double-edged ambivalence. Can the master's tools—of discourse, of language, of faith—dismantle the master's house? Can gaining subjectivity and voice, naming one's own experience, do any good in a time when subjectivity, voice, experience have fallen into fragmentation and suspicion?

In this selective study of four writers, I end with Chimamanda Ngozi Adichie because her fiction offers profound contemporary comment on the questions of voice and representation. Adichie completes my constructed history as a member of a new generation of writers: born in 1978, first publishing after 2000, Adichie is the literary granddaughter of figures like Rich and Morrison. She also completes my trajectory by highlighting the "global" scale of these questions of suffering and sacrifice and their relation to gender, religion, race, and politics: because of the history of colonization, the association of redemptive suffering with women in a Christian frame is a matter of interest in both Western and non-Western literatures, in both Western and non-Western cultures. This concluding turn to a writer publishing in a moment of postcolonial awareness or even globalization does not imply, however, that the other texts in my study have not been the product of global exchanges: indeed, the histories that stand behind much of the particular suffering represented by all the writers in this book are histories of global movements, movements of bodies, goods (sometimes bodies *as* goods), and ideas. But Adichie, as a Nigerian writer with a postcolonial consciousness and an impressive U.S. educational pedigree, suggests in her fiction and her own theorizing a perspective that reminds us that questions of Christian connections to gendered sacrifice and suffering are not just important in an American or British context, and that in postcolonial locations they pose particular complications of their own. She also reminds us that a twenty-first-century consideration of suffering demands attention to local specificity and a global acknowledgment of our interimplications.

I argue in this chapter that Adichie's first novel, *Purple Hibiscus*, highlights the complexly caused and myriad sufferings of postcolonial subjects in late twentieth-century Nigeria, associating suffering with gender and religion as well as the specific colonial history of Nigeria and its ongoing political effects. Adichie repeatedly associates such suffering with silence, and she links healing only ambivalently to suffering as self-sacrificial redemption. The novel's undecidability, I argue—its engagement of readers in a difficult act of interpretation and judgment—aligns with many of the other texts in this project, as does its paradoxical critique and embrace of Christianity.

I link this paradox to the West African theologian Mercy Amba Oduyoye's concept of cultural hermeneutics, relying as well on the postcolonial feminist theological writings of Kwok Pui-lan. These theologians illuminate the paradoxes at work in postcolonial women's practice of finding within their colonial oppressors' religion a source of strength and empowerment that also allows them to reevaluate their own traditional cultures. Such an interpretive stance can aid Western readers in the task of doing justice to novels like Adichie's, which pose challenges to readers seeking to attend ethically to their representations of a different location, negotiating both similarities and important differences of sufferings on a global scale.

Yet these theologians also remind us of the temptation to read literature as sociology, associating writing with experience and taking it as representative not only aesthetically but also politically. The questions of which stories are told, who tells them, and who listens—questions that are central to both feminist and postcolonial theorizing and that undergird my exploration of an ethics of literary representation—take on special importance in Adichie's 2009 TED Talk, distributed widely on the Internet, titled "The Danger of a Single Story." Reading this speech back onto *Purple Hibiscus*, I then understand Adichie's next novel, *Half of a Yellow Sun,* as a corrective to the danger of *Purple Hibiscus* as a stand-alone literary representation of gendered, classed, religious, and political suffering in Nigeria. *Half of a Yellow Sun*, with its multiple points of view, its retrieval of a widely elided national history with colonial roots, and its self-reflexive formal comments on *who* does the telling—and the writing—invites readers into a dynamic partnership, demonstrating the linked ethical workings of literary representation and readerly attention. Its complexities also highlight the moral ambiguities of war and humanness, demonstrating, like *Purple Hibiscus*, the complexly woven sources of suffering and the capacity for humans to cause each other pain that accompanies their capacity for love and connection. The novel interrogates the questions of *whose* story, *whose* suffering, *whose* voice, *whose* representation gains attention. It also, I argue, thematically explores and stylistically engages its readers in the question of Westerners' attention and ethical responsibility, the obligation to respond, suggesting both the difficulty of these challenges and also a possible model of the always risky, imperfect, and ongoing process of responsible attention.

"Speaking with Our Spirits": *Purple Hibiscus*

Analyses of the sacred have been one of the most neglected, and may be one of the most rapidly expanding areas of postcolonial study.
—Bill Ashcroft, Gareth Griffiths, and Helen Tiffin, *The Empire Writes Back*

Purple Hibiscus is a difficult text.[1] Like many of the poems, stories, and essays I've read in this book, Adichie's first novel confronts readers with ambiguity, with multitudinous interlocking sufferings, with questions of culpability, with a double move of critique and optimism. The text thematizes silence, linking it to suffering and self-abnegation caused by a tangled web of colonialism, patriarchy, Christianity, and traditional Igbo culture. This complexity, combined with the novel's ultimate ambiguity on the ethical force of redemptive suffering, demands of readers a difficult reckoning.

The novel is narrated by teenage Kambili Achike, a shy young woman whose narration of her past stands in contrast to her quietness within that past, a quietness characterized by stuttering and silences that only gradually shift to a capacity to speak. At the center of Kambili's existence is her father Eugene, whom she calls Papa, a powerful patriarch who rules his home with a set of conservative Roman Catholic ideals. Eugene is a successful Nigerian businessman, a "Big Man" in the local parlance, who in addition to snack factories owns a newspaper that bravely prints criticisms of the corrupt national regime; he gives generously to his impoverished relatives and to charitable causes; he wins human rights awards. Yet he is also emotionally and physically abusive, punishing his children by burning their skin and breaking their bones, and beating his wife to the point of repeated miscarriages.

Purple Hibiscus traces the critical events that catalyze Kambili's growing freedom from her father's overbearing rule, including a series of visits to her Aunty Ifeoma's household and a friendship with a young priest. Set in the early nineties, the novel fictionalizes the Nigerian government of the eighties and early nineties, combining actual events of different eras into one backdrop to construct a realist political setting of corruption and mismanagement against which the family drama unfolds.[2] As many commentators note, in representing a family story against the backdrop of Nigerian politics, Adichie engages the Nigerian literary tradition of politically allegorical writing, although I agree with those who argue that the novel resists one-to-one allegorical associations between the domestic and political spheres. Eugene, in particular, both parallels and actively resists the dictatorial rule of Nigeria, and this complexity further complicates the narrative's exploration of suffering as a personal and political reality.[3]

Indeed, the novel is woven with instances of public, political suffering brought about by a corrupt and violent government. Ade Coker, the editor of Eugene's paper the *Standard,* is kidnapped early in the narrative by government agents displeased with the paper's critical stance on the nation's politics (37). Aunty Ifeoma, a university lecturer, lacks money for gas and food because of government mismanagement of public funds. After a series of student uprisings, the university closes, and Ifeoma's house is ransacked by a "special security unit" claiming to have heard she was collaborating with the rioting students (231). Ultimately unable to provide for her children in Nigeria, she chooses to try her luck with a much less respectable position in the United States. Ultimately, too, Ade Coker does not escape the government's critique. After taking him away a second time and destroying the newspaper printing operation, the government sends its final message via a letter bomb that kills Coker in front of his family at the breakfast table (206).

Running parallel to these political oppressions is the suffering Eugene causes his wife and children, which marks the text from the very first page. Early in Kambili's narration, she recounts the Sunday when Eugene grows angry with his wife for asking whether she can stay in the car while the family visits the priest after Mass (29–30). Beatrice feels nauseated in the early stages of pregnancy, but she goes anyway to please her husband. Later, Eugene targets his wife in the long prayer after their lunch: "When Papa started the prayer, his voice quavered more than usual. He prayed for the food first, then he asked God to forgive those who had tried to thwart His will, who had put selfish desires first and had not wanted to visit His servant after Mass. Mama's 'Amen!' resounded throughout the room" (32). The prayer—and Mama's response to it—exemplifies Eugene's spiritual and emotional manipulation of his family, persistent throughout the novel, his strong opinions on even the smallest details of his family's life, his legalistic adherence to a series of traditions (saying the Hail Mary nonstop during car rides, twenty-minute prayers after meals, women wearing only skirts and dresses and keeping their hair fully covered in church). Eugene's rule over his family is profoundly ideological, as he teaches them to *desire* to please him in a mixture of fear and love.

This combination of fear, love, and pain is perhaps most strongly pictured in the ritual of "love sips," as he gives his children each a drink of his Sunday after-Mass tea while it is still near the boiling point:

A love sip, he called it, because you shared the little things you loved with the people you loved. Have a love sip, he would say, and Jaja would go first. Then I would hold the cup with both hands and raise it to my lips. One sip. The tea was always too hot, always burned my tongue, and if lunch was something peppery, my raw tongue suffered. But it didn't matter, because I knew that when the tea burned my tongue, it burned Papa's love into me. (8)

As the tale progresses, it becomes clear that this burned tongue is not incidental: disciplined to be a passive and self-abnegating daughter, to fear her father's punishments and long for his approval, Kambili seldom speaks, and when she does she often stutters or whispers. She does not laugh or smile. Throughout her story, she repeats the phrase, "My words would not come" (48, 97, 139, 141). The young woman's tongue is literally scorched and figuratively bound by the rule of her father, whose power mixes pain and love.[4] Indeed, Eugene's persistent emotional and physical abuse is suffused with the vocabulary of love and faith: when he pours boiling water over Kambili's feet, he tells her, "Kambili, you are precious" (194).

Further complicating the matter of speech and silence with postcolonial particularity, Eugene prefers that his children not speak Igbo: "We had to sound civilized in public, he told us; we had to speak English" (13). He likewise disapproves of Igbo-language Christian praise songs being sung at church (28), changes his accent to sound British when speaking with white people (46), and doesn't allow "worshiper[s] of idols" in his house, even when they are the elders of his village to whom he owes respect (70). Eugene has deeply imbibed of the hatred and fear of traditional African culture, and especially religion, in his conversion to an implicitly white mode of Christianity. The novel emphasizes this association, highlighting the "blond life-size Virgin Mary" (4) and the "blond Christ hanging on the burnished cross" (178) at the Achike family's church, Kambili's association of heaven with the "creaminess" of Papa's white-decorated bedroom (41), and her imagination of God having "wide white hands, crescent moon-shadows underneath his nails just like Father Benedict's" (131) and a "British-accented" voice (179). Borrowing from the Nigerian writer Wole Soyinka's concept of self-negation in the face of superior colonial culture, Sophia Ogwude labels Eugene's perspective "cultural hostility."[5]

As numerous commentators have noted, Eugene's abuses connect Christian fundamentalism with a fear of the body and sexuality related to the colonial association of Africanness with the bodily and the sexual. This self-hating version of colonial Christianity is devastatingly critiqued by the novel as a whole.[6] Yet the narrative also complicates its picture of Eugene as a violent patriarch. The man is abusive but also generous, broken and suffering in his own ways. The novel is self-aware in this regard, as Kambili relates her aunt's comment that Eugene is "too much of a colonial product" (13): Eugene's violence toward his wife and children has a clear source in his own subjugation to the colonial mission. For instance, after the boiling water punishment, he tells the children that he learned such a punishment from a missionary priest who soaked the young man's hands in boiling water after catching him masturbating. And in an important scene of later abuse, when Eugene punishes Kambili for hiding a painting of the "heathen" grandfather she is not allowed to love, his kicking and belt-whipping are accompanied by an unhinged verbal refrain: "He talked nonstop, out of control, in a mix of Igbo and English, like soft meat and thorny bones. Godlessness. Heathen worship. Hellfire" (210–11). Eugene's psyche is marked by fear; his violence manifests his brokenness.

But national politics and patriarchal Christianity, both traceable to colonial influences, are not the only sources of suffering exposed in the novel. At several points, the text also emphasizes the problematic elements of traditional Igbo culture as well, especially in regard to women. In addition to an allusion to Achebe's *Things Fall Apart* in its very first line—an allusion that suggests comparisons between Eugene and that other novel's violent Igbo patriarch—Adichie's text hints at traditional Igbo attitudes toward gender in the character of Papa-Nnukwu, Kambili's grandfather. At one point, Papa-Nnukwu speaks of his sadness over letting Eugene "follow those missionaries" and ultimately losing him as a son; his daughter, Ifeoma, challenges this mourning by reminding her father that she did not abandon him, but Papa-Nnukwu (perhaps teasingly) replies, "But you are a woman. You do not count" (83). These Igbo gender distinctions are later emphasized at a traditional cultural event during which Papa-Nnukwu tells his grandchildren that women *mmuo*, or spirits, "are harmless" (85), whereas women "cannot look" at the powerful male *mmuo* (86). When Jaja asks a naïve question about the festival, Papa-Nnukwu scolds him, "Don't speak like a woman!" (87). This section, with its condensed series of references to women within Igbo culture, seems almost calculated to highlight the devaluation of women as more than simply a colonial importation.

Such hints of Igbo gender expectations are further highlighted by the fact that Kambili's mother honors her abusive husband for not choosing to take another wife to bear more children, as the cultural tradition mandates and as people from their village have strongly suggested (20, 75). Beatrice's decision to stay with her violent husband, likewise, seems tied to the traditional view that a "husband crowns a woman's life" (75). The Igbo expectation of women's self-abnegation is perhaps most vividly confirmed in the novel by the folk story Papa-Nnukwu tells his grandchildren, in which a famine leads all the animals in the land to resort to killing and eating their mothers, one by one, to stay alive. Papa-Nnukwu reassures the children, "The mothers did not mind being sacrificed" (158). In a certain sense, this folktale might be read as a key to the puzzle of how we are to read Beatrice's compliance with her husband's abuse and also her ultimate decision to end it by poisoning him. The folk story also complicates the question of the source of its characters' redemptive view of suffering that dominates the novel's ending—a question that, as I will discuss, contributes importantly to the novel's ultimate ambivalence.

Yet while Christianity and Igbo culture are both exposed within *Purple Hibiscus* as sources of serious suffering, especially for women, they are also sources of healing and hope. The narrative may begin by representing the devastating effects of Eugene's abuse, but as it progresses it develops a contrasting, though admittedly more subtle, version of Igbo-Christian faith. Kambili's Aunty Ifeoma represents such an alternative mode of Christianity. Ifeoma is Eugene's sister, a widowed university professor who raises three children on a very small salary and whose parenting style appears to contrast with Kambili's domineering father and frightened mother in almost every way. As Kambili repeatedly notes, Ifeoma wears red lipstick and trousers, signs of feminine confidence Eugene disapproves of even in the nineties. Her house is full of laughter; her children feel free to speak their minds and even discuss Christianity's ties to imperialism. Papa-Nnukwu, whom Eugene condemns as a pagan, is welcome and honored in Ifeoma's home, and Kambili's cousins take part in numerous traditional Igbo rites. Yet Ifeoma's family is also devoutly Catholic: they attend Mass, kneel together for evening prayers (125), and maintain a close friendship with the local priest Father Amadi, who is a frequent dinner guest.

Aunty Ifeoma and Father Amadi both practice critical, joyful, and complexly negotiated versions of Catholicism. Although Eugene disapproves of any Igbo songs in Christian worship, Aunty Ifeoma and Father Amadi both break into Igbo Christian song in between decades of the rosary (125, 138), in church services (28, 241), and along with a tape in the car (178). In contrast to Kambili's predominantly white and British images of God, Father Amadi asserts that he sees the image of Christ in the faces of poor black boys (178). Father Amadi also functions in Kambili's life as an alternative "father," as many critics have noted, offering along with his different Catholicism a markedly different mode of care for Kambili, getting her to run (176), to smile (177), and to laugh (179). Kambili begins to realize that he motivates through encouragement rather than fear (226), drawing her own comparisons, and after he tells her, "You can do anything you want, Kambili," she joins him in singing to the Igbo tape in his car: "I lifted my voice until it was smooth and melodious like his" (239). Kambili emerges from silence into a voicing that is significantly Igbo-language Christian praise.

Indeed, throughout the narrative Kambili increasingly *wishes* she could speak with ease and freedom. She is attracted to her aunt's abundant laughter, her "fearlessness" and smile (76). She is jealous of her cousins, who grow up around "a table where you could say anything at any time to anyone, where the air was free for you to breathe as you wished" (120). Showing her longing and admiration for such a capacity, Kambili says of Father Amadi, "He spoke so effortlessly, as if his mouth were a musical instrument that just let sounds out when touched, when opened" (138). Kambili also observes her brother coming into language before she does: "How did Jaja do it? How could he speak so easily? Didn't he have the same bubbles of air in his throat, keeping the words back, letting out only a stutter at best?" (145). As the story progresses, Kambili does gain language, gain "a voice," to borrow the popular phrase of many earlier feminist writings. Perhaps the strongest evidence of this coming-into-language is the very existence of the narration itself, which through its temporal organization presumes a present-tense Kambili who tells her story with the perspective of one who has already lived through it. Kambili's ability to narrate her past with a critically engaged perspective demonstrates a new facility with words and self-expression that develops in that narrated past.

Kambili's ownership of her voice—and that voice's conflict with her father—are most strongly manifested in the terrible scene that follows Eugene's discovery that Kambili has kept a painting of her grandfather in his house. For the first time in the novel, Kambili stands up to her father with both her actions and her voice. After her father tears the painting to bits, she "shriek[s]," "No!", then refuses to get up after curling her body around the painting (210). In many ways, this scene is a climax, a confrontation between Eugene's patriarchal authority and Kambili's newfound voice and agency. Importantly, Kambili responds with both her voice and her body, seeking through language and action to honor her grandfather (and his—or her—Igbo culture) and to resist her father's domination: this is an act with linguistic and religious implications.

Under the care of her two surrogate parents, Kambili's burned tongue begins to heal. For many contemporary Western readers, the novel may present enough evidence of the suffering caused by the colonially inherited Roman Catholicism in Kambili's family for us to desire repudiation of that faith. But the marked development in her confidence, and her eventual final voicing of "No" to her father, develops not as Kambili rejects Christianity altogether, but as she affirms another version of Christianity, one that values the body and Igbo language and culture. This affirmation is powerfully represented in a scene near the novel's end that often goes unaddressed in critical commentary: Kambili goes on pilgrimage with her aunt's family and Father Amadi to see an apparition of the Virgin Mary. While the others in her party claim not to see anything, Kambili has a holy experience:

> We stood underneath a huge flame-of-the-forest tree. It was in bloom, its flowers fanning out on wide branches and the ground underneath covered with petals the color of fire. When the young girl was led out, the flame-of-the-forest swayed and flowers rained down. The girl was slight and solemn, dressed in white, and strong-looking men stood around her so she would not be trampled. She had hardly passed us when other trees nearby started to quiver with a frightening vigor, as if someone were shaking them. The ribbons that cordoned off the apparition area shook, too. Yet there was no wind. The sun turned white, the color and shape of the host. And then I saw her, the Blessed Virgin: an image in the pale sun, a red glow on the back of my hand, a smile on

the face of the rosary-bedecked man whose arm rubbed against mine. She was everywhere.

. . .

"I felt the Blessed Virgin there. I felt her," I blurted out. How could anyone not believe after what we had seen? Or hadn't they seen it and felt it, too? (274–75)

Kambili's experience of the mother of God, as Cheryl Stobie has argued, is importantly first reported by a young African girl in the village, undoing associations of Christian spirituality with hierarchy, patriarchy, and Western institutions and also challenging denials of women's participation in traditional Igbo religious ceremonies.[7] Even further, Kambili's experience bears the marks of Christian mysticism in its unifying vision of the Virgin's presence all around. Importantly, too, Kambili's vision links her to the people around her and to her own embodied experience, for not only does she see the Virgin in the (white) host, the body of Christ, but also on the back of her own hand—in her own skin—and in the smile on Father Amadi's face that highlights a Christianity marked by love and joy rather than anger and fear, a presence of the divine in African bodies and faces. This scene challenges any reading of the novel that would pin Kambili's faith solely on an acceptance of oppressive ideology: it is profoundly personal, experiential, and embodied.

In Aunty Ifeoma, Father Amadi, and her deeply personal mystical vision of the Virgin, Kambili discovers an alternative mode of Christian belief, one that stands in stark contrast to the patriarchal, colonial, African- and body-hating, fearful fundamentalism of her father. Yet this optimistic vision does not ultimately reign: both critics who have published on *Purple Hibiscus* and students in my classes have offered starkly competing readings of the novel's critique and embrace of patriarchal, postcolonial Christianity, with some insisting on its final skepticism and others on its final hope. Indeed, the text is marked throughout with ambiguity.

One primary source of this ambiguity is Kambili's relationship with Father Amadi, who quickly becomes the object of Kambili's maturing affection. Her crush does not seem to be entirely one sided, as numerous characters comment on the priest's affectionate care. Several scenes between the two also carry sensual overtones, including one in the garden: "Father Amadi walked over to me, standing so close that if I puffed out my belly, it would touch his body. He took my hand in his, carefully slid one flower off my finger and slid it onto his" (269). In another scene, though they do not kiss, after Kambili tells him she loves him Father Amadi "lean[s] over the gear and presse[s] his face to [hers]" before moving it away (276). The sensual accounts of these scenes may be a function of the fact that Kambili herself narrates them, and it is even possible that the observers who comment on the priest's attention to Kambili may be exaggerating to tease her, but an element of sexual tension certainly is evident in the narrative as well as a disproportionate degree of care from Father Amadi, whatever his motivations. Some commentators choose to ignore this, emphasizing instead his religious influence on Kambili. Others acknowledge but minimize the romantic element of the relationship. Still others, like Stobie, read Father Amadi's attention as a safely unexplored but possible sexual relationship that "speaks to a conception of religion which is not steeped in sexual shame and taboos (as it is for Eugene) but which acknowledges the erotic life as deeply spiritual, and conversely, the spiritual life as deeply erotic."[8]

My own reading of Kambili and Father Amadi's attraction emphasizes the novel's open-endedness: the possibility of a positive reading rests on Father Amadi's example of fearlessness and love for the human body (also manifested in his soccer games with the young boys of the neighborhood) in contrast to Eugene's fear and shame. The priest easily *could have* taken advantage of young Kambili's affection, but he does not. This, in itself, may be one of the most positive lessons of their interactions, demonstrating to Kambili that a relationship with a man does not necessarily have to end in abuse or sex. On the other hand, one might read the relationship between Kambili and Father Amadi as already hurtful, already taking advantage, based on their power differential. Furthermore, one could read the relationship—and the longing that Kambili expresses and reads suppressed but present in the priest—as a criticism of expected celibacy among Catholic priests. This ambiguity invites readers into an ethical grappling that is doubtless informed by their own locations and perspectives.[9]

And even as Kambili gains voice and confidence, she lives a life marked by struggle. At the narrative's end, she admits that she still has nightmares about her life in the past, nightmares in which the oppressive silence "mixes with shame and grief and so many other things that I cannot name, and forms blue tongues of fire that rest above my head, like Pentecost, until I wake up screaming and sweating" (305). In light of Kambili's literally and figuratively burned tongue, these nightmares are especially disturbing. The Pentecost image, in a more positive frame, would signify the arrival of God's Spirit to dwell within human bodies, as well as the cross-cultural communication of Spirit-empowered speech. Within Kambili's uncanny nightmares, however, such flaming tongues emphasize the overdetermined symbols at work in Kambili's faith and psyche and leave readers at the novel's end with a sense that her work negotiating that faith is far from finished. After the silence brought about by her suffering, Kambili has gained speech, and the narrative as a whole may be understood as a witness to that suffering, even a lament, but there are still, as she says, many things she cannot yet name. *Purple Hibiscus*, thus, suggests hope, but not any tidy final answer to the very real pains of linked colonial, religious, and patriarchal domination.

The narrative's ambivalence ultimately is played out not just in Kambili's development but also in the plot's final movements, as Eugene is finally stopped from harming his family by his unexpected death. This is no supernatural intervention, however, but rather the result of his wife's choice finally to protect her children and herself: she poisons his British tea with tribal medicine. This choice leaves readers with an ethical quandary: How do we judge Beatrice's act? Is this an admirable choice? Is it an act of love? She risks her own suffering to end the unjust suffering of her children, but is her self-sacrifice fully redemptive?

The problematics of suffering and redemption are complicated even further by Kambili's brother Jaja, whose psyche remains a mystery throughout most of the narrative. Kambili's flourishing in a renegotiated faith is subverted by Jaja's alternate experience. Very near the novel's end, after learning of their father's death, Kambili and Jaja have an uncharacteristic conversation about their faith, one that emphasizes how far apart their perspectives have grown during their time in Aunty Ifeoma's household:

> "God knows best," I said. "God works in mysterious ways." And I thought how Papa would be proud that I had said that, how he would approve of my saying that.
>
> Jaja laughed. It sounded like a series of snorts strung together. "Of course God does. Look what He did to his faithful servant Job, even to His own son. But have you ever wondered why? Why did He have to murder his own son so we would be saved? Why didn't He just go ahead and save us?" (289)

Kambili's narration of this scene shows an awareness of the deeply felt influence of her father as she reflects on his ongoing role in her understanding of God. Still, her faith by this point in the narrative is not *just* the faith of her father: it has undergone a critical transformation, or at least it has begun the process. Jaja, on the other hand, has not been able to find the good in a religion taught to him by the father who has abused him. Jaja's critical stance questions suffering more vehemently, wondering why suffering should have to happen at all. His theological perspective here shows a classic struggle with the problem of evil, with the conundrum of why the innocent should suffer, why, within the Christian imagination, redemption should have to be the result of sacrifice. Jaja's angry questions allude to his own experience as both a "faithful servant" and "son" of his own father, a father who caused his son pain while teaching him of a father God with a similar penchant for violence toward those who love and serve him. Jaja's brief comments here give voice to the agony of those who have been made to suffer in the name of redemption, whether that suffering is the result of familial, religious, or colonial oppression. These comments destabilize the narrative as a whole, inviting readers into a difficult reckoning, subverting a too-optimistic reading of Kambili's renegotiated faith.

Yet although Jaja openly questions the value of redemptive suffering, in the scene that immediately follows, Jaja's *actions* challenge his own theological grapplings. Their mother confesses her crime to her children and is apparently ready to offer herself up to the law in motherly self-sacrifice, a stance that, as noted earlier, is emphatically associated in the novel with both Igbo folk stories about mothers and Christian teachings about the cross. Jaja steps in, however. Just a few hours after his conversation with Kambili—just a single page later in the text—Jaja confesses committing a crime he did not commit in order to save his mother from the consequences of her actions. In other words, Jaja sacrifices himself to redeem his mother, effectively stepping into the role of the Christ whose sacrifice he has so recently and passionately challenged. Or, from another perspective, Jaja steps into the role of the Igbo son, responsible to care for his widowed mother's well-being. It is impossible to say which of these cultural modes of sacrifice is the source of Jaja's choice, and that impossibility is itself part of the point: the novel's postcolonial location renders questions of redemption untraceable to a single source. The complexity is inescapable.

Jaja's theological musings challenge Kambili's redemption of Christianity as a source to resist the oppression that causes her suffering, yet his self-giving action further challenges his own words. The multivoiced text confronts its readers with ambiguity, with ambivalence. Such ambivalence is finally emphasized by the question of whether Jaja's sacrifice has any clearly laudable effect: the text's brief final section portrays a devastated and broken mother and an emaciated son suffering after years of imprisonment in terrible conditions. Yet Kambili, while she has her nightmares, continues to accept grace as it comes to her, recognizing the mixed reality of her existence. Although she still does not have language to bear witness to all her sufferings, this last section is the present setting from which she tells the story of the past, and the very existence of her narrative manifests her healing. The narrative ends with the news that Jaja will soon be released from prison on political grounds, and the last pages suggest a subtle increase of hope for mother and daughter, the promise of a new garden to plant, and coming rain, even the sound of Kambili's laughter. But it is a tenuously happy ending, far from triumphant. A stance of skepticism seems to war with a stance of hopeful commitment, leaving readers with the responsibility of judging for themselves, of wagering an interpretation in the face of such mixed and nuanced modes of suffering and reclamation. Perhaps most important, this ambiguity challenges readers accustomed to comfort with the *experience* of tensions and struggle that shape the work of redemption in a postcolonial location.

Location: Postcolonial Feminist Theology

> As we claim the prophetic heritage of Christianity, we begin to weave new myths for ourselves from the old myths.
> —Mercy Amba Oduyoye, *Daughters of Anowa*

> The idea of Christianity as a triumph of colonialism might be too simplistic.
> —Chimamanda Ngozi Adichie in Susan VanZanten, "A Conversation with Chimamanda Ngozi Adichie"

The ethical ambivalence challenging readers' interpretations of *Purple Hibiscus* highlights the importance of an awareness of *location* in our reading practices. Our conclusions about Eugene, Beatrice, Jaja, and Kambili are indelibly marked by our cultural assumptions, and the differences in our locations matter. In a speech that became her 1984 essay "Notes Towards a Politics of Location," Rich expresses her realization that generalizing for all women from her own white, middle-class experience elided important differences. She learned of this need to revise her earlier feminist theorizing of women's shared, even global, oppression, she writes, from women of color like Audre Lorde and Barbara Smith, from the Combahee River Collective's famous statement, from collections like *This Bridge Called My Back*.[10] One lesson arising from these writings by feminists of color is that statements beginning with "Women have always . . . " are problematic; "'always' blots out what we really need to know: when, where and under what conditions has the statement been true?"[11] *When, where, and under what conditions* become the important questions for a politics of location, a self-aware interpretive practice that asks not just what women share across times and cultures but also what differences characterize their experiences. Another lesson, Rich writes, is the fact that women in Africa and other parts of the so-called Third World have been active in political resistance, active in ways that are often left out of male-written histories, and that such women's activity subverts the assumption that such women are victims while white, economically privileged Westerners are those with agency and the capacity to theorize.[12] In other words, Rich challenges the widely held idea that Western scholars are uniquely able to represent the suffering of postcolonial others.

Rich's essay in particular reminds us of the danger of reading various "other" women's experiences simply in light of our own. Cynthia Ward, in the essay "Reading African Women Readers," even more explicitly highlights the problematics of Western women reading African women's texts, as such texts often are "decontextualized from their material circumstances of production."[13] Ward argues that reading practices in a Western location often pose questions about African texts that are really about "ourselves," whether those questions are based on identity or on deconstruction.[14] West African theologian Oduyoye warns that Western women have tended to understand African women as either wholly different from themselves or wholly similar: "either they assumed that African women experienced the obverse of all that Western women were supposed to have achieved, or they read all of their own sufferings into the

African woman's life."[15] The dangers of reading African women's writing from a Western location are manifold.

These dangers attend Westerners' readings of *Purple Hibiscus,* especially in its paradoxical critique of colonial Roman Catholicism and redemptive sacrifice accompanied by a re-visioned alternative faith. To negotiate the sameness and difference we can read in the suffering represented in Adichie's novel, I will argue again that our interpretive work should be informed by contextually particular intertexts that can guide us: in this case, I suggest we learn from African women's and postcolonial feminist theology. Although it is tempting to emphasize the novel's critique of Christianity as a racist, patriarchal, body-hating effect of colonization, especially from within the Western context of a secular academy, postcolonial feminist theology reminds us that such assumptions of agnosticism and critique are not the prevalent attitude among the postcolonial Christians of West Africa. Postcolonial feminist theology and especially the writing of Oduyoye provide a theoretical discourse and a critical practice, the practice of "cultural hermeneutics," that allow Western readers to encounter *Purple Hibiscus*'s paradoxical representation of religion within a context that is at once critical, informed by both feminist theory and postcolonial theory, and also faithful to the living faith of living people.

Postcolonial feminist theology, according to Kwok, was still only a nascent discipline as of 2005.[16] In much postcolonial theory, gender is an underconsidered element, and postcolonial nationalist political movements are famous for their rhetorical use of woman or mother as a bastion of traditional culture and national nurturance.[17] At the same time, many women in postcolonial, nation-building situations have been wary of Western feminisms as yet another imported cultural and imperialist product, and "postcolonialists are apt to be critical of mainstream (Western) feminism, focusing further on its failure or inability to incorporate issues of race, or its propensity to stereotype or over-generalize the case of the 'Third-World woman.'"[18] Writing specifically of West Africa, Oduyoye notes that many African men, in particular, critique "women's lib" as coming from the "cracked pot of Western decadence, unbecoming to Young Africa."[19] "Western feminism," she further reports, "has stirred fears in Africa of a disruption in the family."[20] Still, as Peter Hitchcock writes,

It is no coincidence that some of the most significant postcolonial theorists work from feminist lessons on gender inequality in socialization.
It is not that Africa has been "Othered" in identical ways to women in
patriarchal and sexist societies; it is, rather, a recognition that the massive upheavals of colonization and decolonization cannot be adequately
understood outside the functions of gender for local, national, and international social relations.[21]

A temptation into which many scholars have fallen is to begin with
their starting point—either gender or postcolonial theory—and to read
the other element allegorically or through the point of origin.[22] So, for
instance, early second-wave feminists like Mary Daly read patriarchy as
the original, universal, and primary mode of oppression on which other
oppressions were modeled. Or some postcolonial theorists read gender-
based oppressions as the product of the master-slave dialectic. Hitchcock
and others argue, however, that the best postcolonial theorizing recognizes the ways these different modes of oppression work together, not in
a hierarchy or narrative of origins but through their mutually constituting
interactions.

The challenge of bringing together postcolonial theory, feminist theory, and *theology*, however, is especially serious. As Kwok asserts, one typically sees two of the three: "Some of the intellectual projects that make
the crucial connection between religion and colonialism have left out the
gender dimension; others that investigate the relationship between gender
and colonialism have not taken note of the role of religion in sustaining colonial ideologies."[23] In the 2001 collection *Postcolonialism, Feminism,
and Religious Discourse*, Kwok and Laura Donaldson are among the first to
argue that "the triadic elements" must be considered together to do justice to their complex interplays.[24] Acting on this call, Kwok's *Postcolonial
Imagination and Feminist Theology* is an almost virtuosic performance of
interdisciplinarity, drawing extensively on postcolonial and globalization
theory, feminist theory, contemporary theology (including feminist, womanist, *mujerista* and liberationist, queer, and so-called Third World), and
literary theory, to weave a theological vision that attends to the collusions
and conflicts among these various discourses.

One of Kwok's greatest contributions in this project is her call to fellow
theologians to re-member the erased history not just of Christian missions'

partnership with political and economic colonizing in the past few centuries but also of the origins of presumed-neutral theologies within histories of colonialism. Indeed, she argues, the Christian church from very early on developed as a marginalized community under imperial Roman rule, although before long its history—especially beginning with the Emperor Constantine—became one of problematic alignment with political states.[25] Such imperialism, Kwok argues, which was also strongly masculinist, affected church doctrine, for instance through the First Council of Nicaea in 325 C.E., which produced the imperialist and masculinist Nicene Creed used to this day in Roman Catholic worship.[26] These origins have ramifications for anyone interested in studying the relation of the Christian church to more recent colonization and postcolonial movements. One important insight is that the church is always already bound up in imperialism, first as a marginalized group living under colonization and later as a bedfellow with nationalism and colonialism. The nineteenth century, during which "colonial desire and imperialistic violence were masked and reconstituted in a blatant reversal as 'civilizing mission,'" to the point that "Christianization and Westernization became almost a synonymous process,"[27] importantly is *not* the primary instance of Christianity's relation to colonization, and contemporary rapprochements between theology and postcolonial theory function against a long, shameful, and overlooked history.[28]

On the matter of feminism, Christianity, and colonialism, Kwok also writes bitingly of what she calls "colonialist feminism," the "compassionate" criticism of native women's situations and assumptions that white women could "elevate" them through education and Christianization:[29]

> The subordination of women was often cited as symptomatic of the inferiority of indigenous cultures, and saving colonized women from their oppression, ignorance, and heathenism became an integral part of the colonialist discourse. Shuttled between tradition and modernity, indigenous women were seen either as victims of male aggression or as pitiful objects of Westerners' compassion.[30]

In her essay "Feminist Theology as Intercultural Discourse," Kwok further argues not just that many women missionaries of the nineteenth and early twentieth centuries held this attitude and motivation, but that their new-found freedom in missionary work—either as missionary wives who could uniquely work with women or as single "lady missionaries"—was actually one of the material conditions that contributed to first-wave feminism.[31] In other words, colonization granted Western women new influence in the church and new independence: the nineteenth- and twentieth-century women's movements were built, in part, on the colonialist disparagement of native cultures and the "gunboats and cannons" with which Christianity entered the so-called Third World.[32] Women missionaries' "voluminous" writings on their experiences in foreign lands also contributed significantly to the Western perception of women of the Global South as "groping in the dark, waiting for the light to be brought to them," and so even an occasion for Western women to find "public voice" in popular publications also relied on the exoticizing of women in non-Western cultures.[33] This historical insight raises the chilling question: at what cost do we find our voices, whoever "we" might be?

Yet the challenge that Kwok and other feminist theologians writing in a postcolonial register must contend with is that the work of colonialist Christian missionaries was both patronizing *and* potentially empowering for some colonized women. Kwok argues, for instance, that "the introduction of the Bible to other cultures was a mixed blessing for women," in that although it did instill harmful lessons of the superiority of colonizing cultures and their gender norms, it also led to the building of girls' schools, women's classes, and literacy.[34] Teresa M. Hinga likewise argues that although the Christ who was introduced to Africans was an imperialistic warrior figure who came to conquer and displace African traditions, this Christ also offered Africans, and African women in particular, a kernel of hope and freedom when read from a different perspective.[35] Oduyoye writes explicitly of the misconception that Christianizing colonial missions offered women better positions in relation to patriarchal rule: "There is a myth in Christian circles that the church brought liberation to the African woman"; rather, "the sexist elements of Western culture have simply fueled the cultural sexism of traditional African society."[36] She argues, along with others, that colonizing missionaries actually brought a vision of British Victorian womanhood that was passed off as universally Christian and arguably restricted West African women. Various ethnic groups within Ghana and Nigeria practiced different gender norms within their traditional cultures: Oduyoye, for instance, grew up within a matrilineal culture in Ghana but married a Nigerian man whose Yoruban family's strong patriarchal structure came as a shock. In contexts in which women had relative freedom, colonizers' gender expectations were a debilitation; in those cultures in which women already were expected to be self-abnegating or submissive, the colonial behavioral norms were doubly restrictive.[37]

And so, as Oduyoye, Kwok, and others point out, formerly colonized women seeking liberation from patriarchal oppression must contend with both the colonialist feminism of patronizing Western sisters and the question of whether their traditional cultures offered them greater freedom (as often is argued in masculinist nationalist rhetoric), if such authentic traditional cultures are even accessible. In response to this challenge, Oduyoye and other African women theologians offer *cultural hermeneutics*, an interpretive practice applied to traditional cultural myths and folktales, contemporary social structures, and inherited Christian beliefs, alike. Kwok summarizes cultural hermeneutics as involving "a hermeneutics of liberation,"[38] which, as we saw in connection to Castillo's work, involves the rereading of traditional and Christian stories in light of the experiences of the oppressed, resulting in re-visioned tales that empower work toward liberation. It also involves "a hermeneutics of suspicion,"[39] which allows postcolonial women to challenge received norms and histories, and "a hermeneutics of commitment,"[40] a devotion to seeing the interpretations through to the point of action and, ultimately, transformation. In her essay "Cultural Hermeneutics: A Postcolonial Look at Mission," Letty M. Russell explicitly links the project of cultural hermeneutics to Rich's politics of location, noting how the social location of the theologian, or the reader of literature, matters in the interpretive practice.[41] In the case of African women, the project of cultural hermeneutics arises from specifically postcolonial situations and results in a paradoxical stance of critique and embrace differently located but similar to the paradoxical stances manifested throughout the texts I read in this book.

Oduyoye's *Daughters of Anowa: African Women and Patriarchy* (1995) exemplifies cultural hermeneutics. In it, Oduyoye takes on a project of detailed interpretation of West African myths, folktales, and proverbs, reading their disciplining force in women's lives, especially the valuation of women primarily as mothers and self-sacrificers. Oduyoye also turns her cultural hermeneutics to reading the West African Christian church, which she argues "shows how Christianity reinforces the cultural

conditioning of compliance and submission and leads to the depersonali-
zation of women."[42] The (male) African theological tradition has ignored
gender as an important category,[43] at points even using the Western-
imported Christian tradition to bolster patriarchal power. Yet despite her
strong critique, Oduyoye continues to write as a theologian and practice
as a Christian, because cultural hermeneutics, turned back on the Christian scriptures, offer her a vision of liberation that paradoxically empowers a critique of the very colonialism that introduced Christianity to her
African forebears. Writing of West African women's motivation for staying within the church, she claims, "Women continue to be clients of the
church because of the insuppressible hope that the Christian community
will bring liberation from brokenness. Women continue in the church in
order to appropriate the healing powers of the Christ who cared so much
for the community that he died for it."[44]

Turning her critical hermeneutics to both the Christian and West African traditions, Oduyoye asserts that African traditional culture may have
a great deal to teach global Christianity about hierarchy and rule, may be
able to contribute to the "redemption" of Christianity. Applying a hermeneutics of suspicion and liberation to the biblical text, Oduyoye reads that
"Jesus Christ as Lord does not permit *any* priest, man or woman, to lord
it over the church. Jesus specifically excluded oppressive hierarchies that
were operated by a self-serving leadership"[45]: both in society and in the
church. Such a structural challenge to the powers-that-be can be supple-
mented, in Oduyoye's view, by a critically retrieved African tradition of
leadership structures that, unlike imported Western systems of rule, relied
much more strongly on democratic, dialogic processes of decision making: "We need to share our traditional African understandings of democ-
racies in which Ruler-in-Council is not an individual acting alone, but one
who pronounces 'what is good' after consulting on all levels and reaching
a consensus. . . . we might redeem both King and Kingdom."[46] Critical of
both Christian and African traditions for their oppressive elements, particularly their oppression of women, Oduyoye at the same time locates
liberative kernels that should be retrieved, re-membered, re-visioned.

This, it seems to me, is the impulse at the core of the ambiguities of
Purple Hibiscus. The novel engages in a practice of cultural hermeneutics, critiquing the life-stealing elements of colonial religious heritage,
and critiquing life-stealing elements of Nigerian traditional culture and

contemporary nationalism, even while suggesting that neither Christianity (expressed as Roman Catholicism), Igbo culture, nor Nigerian nationalism is entirely to blame or entirely to be rejected. Western readers, in particular, need the insight of Oduyoye's cultural hermeneutics to appreciate the paradoxical critique and revision of Catholicism at work in *Purple Hibiscus*. If Kwok's "colonialist feminism" is a "compassionately" ("cosuffering") patronizing belief that African women require Western women's Christian missionary intervention, the contemporary moment of secularization in a Western location suggests a similar temptation of "neo-colonialist feminism," a patronizing belief that African women require Western feminists' anti-Christian evangelization. *Purple Hibiscus* certainly represents the suffering caused by a strictly legalistic and colonial-minded Catholicism: this is the critiquing element of cultural hermeneutics. But it also represents the hopeful possibilities at work in another mode of Catholicism, one that embraces positive elements of the Igbo cultural tradition as well and resists the colonial devaluing of Africanness (in language, in race, in images of God, in music and other cultural expressions). In the theological vocabulary of Oduyoye, Kambili witnesses and learns from Aunty Ifeoma and Father Amadi as "crossroads Christians," a term that highlights "the fluid interface and interaction between African culture and Western forms of Christianity."[47] As crossroads Christians, Father Amadi and Aunty Ifeoma encourage the younger generation to engage in a practice of cultural hermeneutics, inviting the children into conversations about the problematics of Christianity and engaging in self-aware dialogues about the colonial elements of their Catholicism. Thus, *Purple Hibiscus* both exemplifies cultural hermeneutics as a whole and represents characters engaged in its interpretive process. It represents the suffering colonial Christianity can cause and also represents engaged Christianity as a possible way to resist that suffering, most clearly manifested in Kambili's voice and the strength she gains from her sincere belief in the Virgin's mystical apparition. For Western readers to justly interpret the novel's ambiguities from their quite different location, these cultural differences must be acknowledged.

We must also acknowledge the inextricable mix of suffering's causes in the practice of cultural hermeneutics, the impossibility of pinning blame wholly on Christian or Igbo traditions in our troubled ethical reckonings.

An excerpt from *Daughters of Anowa* exemplifies this difficulty. Oduyoye writes,

> We African women have been brought up, and folktalk has been part of our education, to be devoted daughters, sisters, wives, and mothers, to always love others more than self. It seems to me that in this process we have also learned to vote against the self, always preferring others and loving them more than we love ourselves, doing for them what we decline to do for ourselves because we consider ourselves unworthy of such attention. We have been content to work for, rather than with, children, spouse, and other relatives.[48]

The challenge here is to separate out the "traditional" West African teaching from the Christian teaching of feminine self-abnegation. In many ways, this passage reads as though it could have come from Rich's *Of Woman Born* or Daly's *Beyond God the Father*. The language of "loving" and "preferring" others more than self is biblical language. Oduyoye is familiar with both the Bible and with Daly's text, raising the question of theology's inevitable constitution in language, from pieces of the already-said. Is Oduyoye's characterization of African culture here even separable from the earlier colonial heritage and from Oduyoye's education in English (the colonizer's language) and in Western theology? Western African dialects are notoriously resistant to literal translations into English: Is it even possible for Oduyoye to write in English, or for a Western audience, without our hearing biblical allusions even where she intends to speak of a pre-Christian traditional African culture? (*This is the oppressor's language.*) And what are the effects of these inescapable linguistic associations for cross-cultural understanding and clarifying distinctions between the effects of traditional patriarchy and colonialist patriarchy? How do we distinguish between the womanly self-sacrifice taught by West African tradition and that taught by Western Christian tradition?

These questions matter for Western readers in part because of the dangers of reading our own suffering into African women's stories, a danger Oduyoye herself names.[49] The challenge is to negotiate the aporia: to balance in the ethical space that recognizes both difference and sameness. In this project, I seek to practice such a balance by reading contextually and intertextually, finding theoretical paradigms that provide particular explanatory force for a repeated and paradoxical phenomenon of answering suffering with self-sacrifice. My intention in this project is to trace the repeated paradigm in various women's texts of different locations and times in the past fifty years, but also to trace their differences. The fact that *Purple Hibiscus* poses impossible questions about the sources of Beatrice's suffering and its effects on her children, that it presents competing visions of a rejection of the colonizer's religion in Jaja and a re-visioned embrace in Kambili, that it ends with uncomfortable ambivalence, underlines such difference.

The Danger of a Single Story: Literature Resisting Sociology

> I'm interested in the question of how much literary fiction really does represent reality.
> —Chimamanda Ngozi Adichie and Michael Ondaatje, "In Conversation"

The danger of reading our own suffering into the sufferings of women represented in literature is accompanied by another danger, one central to the ethics of literary representation. This is the temptation to read literature as sociology or anthropology, representing not just individual stories in a stylized, literary, and politically interested way, but representing the "real" experiences and social realities of a group of people. In many ways, the writings of postcolonial feminist theologians could be read as a gloss on *Purple Hibiscus*, allowing us to affirm our sense of its sociological realism. For instance, Oduyoye writes, "To make where she lives a home, an African woman is ready and willing to adopt the style of 'putting up with,' for her style of life is directed by working things out and smoothing over domestic conflict. If need be, she becomes the sacrifice."[50] Such a statement could be applied perfectly to Mama in *Purple Hibiscus*. Applying Oduyoye's claim about African women to Adichie's novel bolsters the novel with an affirmation of its sociological explanatory force. Beatrice's behavior—her putting up with Eugene's emotional and spiritual manipulation and physical violence, her habit of setting things to rights after a domestic conflict, her excuses for her husband, even her final choice to risk punishment for the murder to which she openly confesses—aligns her with Oduyoye's description.

On the one hand, some generalizations are necessary: the social expectation in West African cultures that women behave a certain way, passed down through myths, folktales, and proverbs, must be recognized and named for it to be rectified, and this is one of the projects of Oduyoye's theology.[51] Contemporary literature, too, can be looked to as an example of realist portrayals of narratives that have their origins in the real-life experiences of women. The ethics of literary representation at work in books like Adichie's (and Castillo's, and Morrison's, and Rich's) involve a representing of sufferings that otherwise might go untold, unconsidered. Readers are confronted with stories that they otherwise might be wholly unaware of, and with a burden of response arising from the ethics of readerly attention. This ethico-political force is one of the important features of twentieth-century literary writing by marginalized groups. In response to a tradition of literary writing that represents only the stories of the dominant group, and in response to a tradition of popular stories that are used primarily to discipline certain groups, the sharing of stories that reveal the complexity of variously located subjects' sufferings, and the sharing of stories that provide alternatives to those disciplining myths and inherited "wisdom," play an important ethical role.[52]

These questions of representation (as reference and as legal surrogacy) are central to both postcolonialism and feminism, as Deepika Bahri argues: "Fields such as women's studies and postcolonial studies have arisen in part in response to the absence or unavailability of the perspectives of women, racial minorities, and marginalized cultures or communities in historical accounts or literary annals. This lack of representation is paralleled in the political, economic, and legal spheres."[53] As discussed in chapter 2, this emphasis on experience and voice was central to early second-wave feminism, and it also has been important in the work of womanists and Chicana activists. Likewise, the politics of postcolonial publishing also has emphasized the need for formerly colonized peoples to have the opportunity to represent themselves to others around the world. And, as Bahri asserts, fictional representations (and constructions of history not considered to be fiction) do have real-life effects.[54]

Yet there is a serious danger in reading literature *as* sociology, in generalizing from literary representation under the assumption that the text one reads stands in for wider social truths. This is a concern Adichie herself has named repeatedly in interviews and essays, a concern that has arisen from the reception of her novels and comments that readers have made to her about them. She often gives the following example:

> At an Oklahoma university where I spoke not too long ago, a well-meaning student expressed sadness that most Nigerian men were like the physically abusive father in my novel *Purple Hibiscus* (2003). I replied that I had just read Bret Easton Ellis's *American Psycho* (1991) and that perhaps all American twenty-something-year-olds were serial murderers.[55]

Literature, Adichie argues (along with Oduyoye, Drucilla Cornell, Ewa Płonowska Ziarek, and many others), is one of the best ways "to combat stereotypes," to introduce readers to stories that challenge metanarratives and the most-often-spread representations controlled by those with power. Yet Adichie writes, "I am wary of the idea of literature as anthropology," including the problem of "generalizing from the particular" that her quip about *American Psycho* illustrates.[56]

The risk of Adichie's texts being read as anthropology is compounded by the politics of location. The questions of *which* stories are being told and attended to, *who* is doing the telling, *who* is doing the listening—questions that involve both the ethics of literary representation and the ethics of readerly attention—are especially important in a global context where African stories have not been disseminated to the degree that Western stories have been. And when stories of Africa *are* disseminated, they often are used as examples to confirm Western conceptions. One of the results of this paucity of African stories in the public sphere is the risk writers run of having their characters turned into stereotypes. If she wrote simply based on her politics, Adichie claims elsewhere, "all [her] books would have strong women who were proud and independent"[57]: heroes who model what *ought* to be. But reality is more mixed and complicated, and as a writer, Adichie claims to feel a responsibility to interact in her writing with the truth of the real world, both its strong women and its weak ones, both its violent fathers with extraordinary generosity and its grace-giving priests with sexual vulnerability. Still, because so few stories of Africa are known, Adichie claims again and again, "writing truthfully about what interests [her]," including war, patriarchal violence, and religious fundamentalism, becomes a risk, a risk that Western readers will take her literary representations as more broadly *representative* of the total reality of Nigeria.[58]

This problem is perhaps most vividly discussed in Adichie's 2009 TED Talk, titled "The Danger of a Single Story." In this talk, Adichie highlights the risks inherent in Western-located readers having access to non-Western stories, but only limited access. This is an issue of power, an issue of media resources that allow the United States to send its many stories all around the world while other parts of the globe have many fewer stories known about them, and often the stories are chosen and told by those in the West. The answer, however, is not simply for postcolonial nations to work harder to spread positive stories of themselves (a version of political propaganda), but for readers to seek out multiple stories, to resist the urge to generalize from the stories or create tidy pictures of "difference." The ethics of literary representation and the ethics of readerly attention work together, as literary representations of many stories dovetail with readers' commitment to read contextually, intertextually, with sensitivity to differences of location, suspending their own supremacy. Such acts of interpretive resistance—such an ethics of readerly attention—aligns with the plea implicit in postcolonial theorist Chandra Talpade Mohanty's famous essay "Under Western Eyes: Feminist Scholarship and Colonial Discourses" (1988) for Western feminists to resist the propensity to recolonize so-called Third-World women by reducing their pluralities of difference to a homogenized same. Mohanty names, as well, the problem of Western women defining African and other Third-World women primarily as *victims* of male violence.[59] This is a particular risk of reading *Purple Hibiscus* without a self-conscious awareness of one's own location and the text's status as a *single story*. Adichie recognized this danger in her first novel not long after it was published and began to worry that Beatrice would be read simply as a stereotype of the "familiar Battered Woman."[60] If we are not careful, Western readers may find ourselves with an impulse not unlike Kwok's "colonialist feminism," one of pity for the African woman who is abused by her husband, or, to revise a famous phrase of Gayatri Spivak's, we may feel responsible to act as "white [women] saving brown women from brown men."

I have argued that *Purple Hibiscus* does resist this colonizing impulse through its ambivalence, inviting readers into an ethical interpretive practice of attention to the complexities of its characters and its resistance to final, comfortable conclusions. Yet the novel still is vulnerable to a colonialist feminist reading. In light of her claims since its publication in essays, interviews, and the TED Talk, I believe that we can read Adichie's subsequent novel *Half of a Yellow Sun* as a corrective, even a formal self-revision, to the danger of reading *Purple Hibiscus* as a single story of contemporary Nigeria. I end this chapter by offering a brief reading of *Half of a Yellow Sun* to suggest its even stronger interaction between the ethics of literary representation and the ethics of readerly attention, its literary performance of the need to recognize both the sameness and difference of suffering in a global scope.

"Careful Not to Draw Parallels": *Half of a Yellow Sun*

> remember: the body's pain and the pain on the streets
> are not the same   but you can learn
> from edges that blur   O you who love clear edges
> more than anything   watch the edges that blur
> —Adrienne Rich, "Contradictions: Tracking Poems,"
> *Your Native Land, Your Life*

Adichie's second novel in many ways stands in contrast to her first: whereas *Purple Hibiscus* is a first-person account of one young woman's coming-into-voice in a domestic and deeply religious struggle, with politics in the background, *Half of a Yellow Sun* offers a third-person narration traversing a decade, with explicit attention to the political sphere as well as the domestic. If the personal in *Purple Hibiscus* can be read allegorically for politics, *Half of a Yellow Sun* allows for no such allegorical reading, weaving the personal and political through one another. The second novel is much less concerned with religion and is set nearly fifty years into the past, before its author's lifetime. Adichie has claimed that this second novel required significant research, and it is more than twice as long. The novel does not interrogate women's, and especially mothers', suffering and sacrifice, nor does it expose and explore the paradigm of redemptive suffering, to the degree that *Purple Hibiscus* and many of the other texts in this book do, but it is a novel steeped in the complexities of suffering and the question of whether different sufferings can be linked and compared for ethical purposes. It also explicitly thematizes the feminist and postcolonial questions of who speaks, who listens, and from where. These contributions to a literary ethics are performed, especially, through *Half of a Yellow Sun*'s narration. The third-person narrative is focalized through three distinct characters: Ugwu, the teenaged houseboy who comes from a poor village family; Olanna, the university professor, daughter of a wealthy business-man, and lover of Ugwu's master Odenigbo; and Richard, an expat British writer fascinated by Igbo art and history, who is also lover to Kainene, Olanna's twin sister. The fact that the novel is constructed dialogically of the perspectives of characters with such different subject positions disal-lows any straightforward interpretation of the narrative's events, which often appear quite different to Ugwu, Olanna, and Richard. This narrative technique results in a novel that undermines the single story, highlighting by its form the fact that stories are always multiple, with competing ver-sions and various possible interpretations.[61]

Half of a Yellow Sun also corrects the single story by challenging a widely reproduced single image from the Biafran War, which it recounts, and by breaking a silence brought about by the erasure of history. As Mad-elaine Hron articulates, the Biafran War (the civil war in Nigeria primar-ily between the Hausa of the North and the Igbo of the South, lasting from 1967 to 1970) was the event "that first introduced the world with the mediatized image of starving children with bloated stomachs, suffering of kwashiorkor" (44). In other words, the Biafran War resulted in a story—captured in a single, now-familiar image of a big-bellied, emaciated brown child—of abject poverty in Africa, a story that became commonplace in the decades that followed and carried an undertone of African nations' inability to rule themselves, to maintain peace, to provide for their peo-ples. The fact that the troubles in Africa arise, in part, from imported colo-nial systems and illogically drawn borders that create single nation-states of different people groups is an uncomfortable reality that often goes unacknowledged.

The Biafran War is an underdiscussed war in Nigeria, according to Adichie, but one that was especially devastating to Igbo people and affected Adichie's family in numerous ways: her two grandfathers died in the war, one in a refugee camp, and her parents lost all their possessions.[62] Grow-ing up in Nigeria, Adichie recognized the war as a gap, a silence, and she eventually sought to go into that silence, to read earlier books about the war and ask family members to share their stories. Critics recognize the resulting novel as a trauma narrative, one that articulates a woundedness that those in power would rather have covered over and that asks Western audiences for their attention, uncomfortable as it may make them.[63]

The suffering represented in *Half of a Yellow Sun* is complexly caused: by politics, class, gendered vulnerability, religious prejudices. No one is exempt: in the war, both poor villagers and the privileged academic class face violence, hunger, the death of loved ones. Nor is anyone a pure victim, wholly incapable being the *cause* of others' suffering: Olanna and Richard, otherwise sympathetic characters, cause Kainene great anguish by having a brief affair. Ugwu, the young houseboy, whose keen attention to other characters and insights into their lives highlight his unusual capacity for human understanding, participates in a gang-rape while he is a soldier. Ugwu's participation in this violation, which comes near the end of the novel, wraps him up in a web of crimes that the narrative implicitly compares through juxtaposition and Ugwu's own realization of their similarities. This interrogation of linked sexual abuses constitutes one of the novel's invitations to readers to attend to the ethics of sex and the ethics of war, the personal and the political, and their many connections.

Ugwu, kidnapped as a child soldier to fight on the side of Biafra, finds himself in trench warfare, and though he dreams of leaving, he also knows he won't "because a part of him wanted to be [there]" (453). After a successful mission, Ugwu and his peers walk to a nearby bar, and on the way the soldiers insist on commandeering the car of a civilian couple looking for their son, mostly because they don't want the long walk. Ugwu manifests the sort of integrity he has shown throughout most of the preceding story, interrupting the soldiers when they slap the man with "It is enough!" (456). Ugwu's distance from the other men is also clear in his defense of the bar girl when the men insist that she give them beer after she has told them there is none, his anger at one of the men for tearing a page out of his book to roll a cigarette, and his escape outside the bar for fresh air (456–57). And when he returns inside and sees the bar girl "lying on her back on the floor, her wrapper bunched up at her waist, her shoulders held down by a soldier, her legs wide, wide ajar," "sobbing" (457), Ugwu does not wish to participate. The narration, told from his point of view, describes the first rapist's movements as "jerky," after which he "groan[s]" and "collapse[s]," hardly a positive portrayal (457–58). Yet although Ugwu "back[s] away" when the others tell him he's next, when they challenge him by suggesting he's afraid, he "move[s] forward" instead, his bodily movement betraying his vulnerability to his peers' challenges, "aren't you a man?" (458). And so Ugwu rapes the girl, "surprised at the swiftness of his erection," without looking at her. Again, the sexual act is described negatively: Ugwu doesn't look at the girls' face, but he does feel that she is "dry and tense," and his climax arrives as "a self-loathing release" (458). The scene ends against a backdrop of his fellow soldiers clapping: "Finally he looked at the girl. She stared back at him with a calm hate" (458).[64]

This scene of sexual violence is bookended by scenes of grisly military violence. Ugwu has not chosen to fight, and while he is on the side of Biafra—theoretically fighting to put an end to the suffering of the starving and displaced Igbo people—Ugwu does not conceptualize his war experience in these terms. Instead, Ugwu's experience of the war is characterized by both his pervasive fear and by his desire to please and impress his peers and superiors. Before too long, however, Ugwu is himself wounded by a bomb in a violation of his body that, in some ways, parallels the gang-rape of the bar maid: "Then Ugwu felt himself lifted up above the trench, helplessly, haplessly. And when he landed, it was the force of his own weight, rather than the pain firing up his whole body, that stunned him into silence" (460). Ugwu's helplessness, the way his body is co-opted by another, harmful force he can't resist mimics the helpless co-optation of the girl in the bar; his stunned silence (these words end the section and the chapter) echoes the young woman's silent "calm hate" that ends the section only two pages before, just before a white-space break. Ugwu's bodily vulnerability as a participant in war correlates, somehow, to the girls' bodily vulnerability as a participant in a gender-divided society, a point emphasized by the two scenes' immediate juxtaposition.

Importantly, however, these two experiences of suffering are not the same, and the particular horror of sexual violence is emphasized by another juxtaposition within the novel, for when Ugwu finally returns to his village, in addition to discovering that his mother has died, he learns that his sister Anulika was raped during the war in an act of violence startlingly similar to the one in which he participated (526). Anulika "looked most changed" of all the family to Ugwu, her beauty lost in her transformation to "an ugly stranger who squinted with one eye," her habitual wit and energy traded for terse answers and distance: "She looked away often, as if she felt uncomfortable sitting with him, and Ugwu wondered if he had imagined the easy bond they had shared" (524, 525). It is only after noting all these changes that Ugwu learns their cause, and the consequences inscribed in his sister's body and personality confront Ugwu with the results of his own act of violence. Neither side of the war is guiltless on this charge: political rightness does not prevent men of either side from perpetrating sexual violence. He later wanders to the stream, the site of Anulika's violation, and "sob[s]" (526), and one has a sense that it is not only his sister Ugwu is weeping for. Importantly, Ugwu chooses to keep silent about his sister's experience when he returns to his master's house, although the narrative's comment on his *not* telling Olanna is also the novel's first and only use of the word "rape" (526).

Yet even before he learns of his sister's suffering, Ugwu is ashamed of himself: recovering from his war wound (perhaps significantly, a wound to his buttocks, the same body part he had fantasized about in his would-be girlfriend Eberechi), he dreams of the scene at the bar, recalling "the dead hate in the eyes of the girl" whose face he cannot even remember. In these dreams, we are told, the girl turns to Eberechi, and Ugwu "w[akes] up hating the image and hating himself" (497). Ugwu's unconscious association of the girl he raped and the girl with whom he had sought a relationship highlights his shame, the strange continuum of mutual sexuality and abusive sexuality that questions Ugwu's persistent, seemingly innocent, sexual fantasies that mark the narrative up to this point. Ugwu's uncomfortable negotiations of sexual ethics also are related by proximity in the narrative to Kainene's realization only two pages later that the two priests helping with the refugee camp she is overseeing have been demanding sexual favors before distributing food (499). Kainene sends the priests away, and Ugwu, who is already hoping for "redemption" (497), somehow fittingly takes their place distributing food in the camp. Ugwu is self-consciously aware of the irony of the situation: "Ugwu felt stained and unworthy as he went about his new duties after the priests left. . . . He wondered what Kainene would say, what she would do to him, feel about him, if she ever knew about the girl in the bar. She would loathe him. So would Olanna. So would Eberechi" (499). In his sister, Ugwu recognizes the horrible effects of his own sexual crime; in this earlier scene, he recognizes the outrage felt by women he admires and even loves, outrage against a sexual violation that, again, is not unlike the one in which he participated. Although Ugwu's feelings about his act are the most explicitly explored, the links between the bar girl's rape, Anulika's rape, the abuses of the women and young girls in the refugee camp, and even—more distantly— the pain Olanna and Odenigbo cause with their infidelities, demonstrate the myriad manifestations of suffering caused by ethically suspect sexual acts. These multiple sufferings function within the novel to demonstrate the complexity of experience, the linked and yet quite separate ethical quandaries of sex, the vulnerability of those in disparate social positions and also the capacity of nearly everyone to cause others pain. The ethical upshot is one of complexity: Who is most guilty? Whose pains and traumas are the least open to healing? Why do otherwise decent people hurt each other? What role does war play in these crimes? Who can we condemn? How do we respond?

Ugwu's guilt and shame at his sexual violence is, importantly, linked to another central feature of *Half of a Yellow Sun*'s ethics of literary representation. In addition to representing the mixed complexity of suffering in domestic and political spaces, across various subject positions and from competing perspectives, the novel also thematizes the question of representation itself, and it does so from a particularly postcolonial perspective. Who gets to tell the stories? Whose voices are heard? Who gets to be the writer? In terms of material publishing, of course, Adichie, a Nigerian woman, gets to tell the stories, to be the writer, and she subverts expectations by portraying not only a Nigerian woman but also a village-raised houseboy and even a white British man. Resisting the dictum that allows Western white male authors to construct a variety of characters different from themselves but expects nonmale, nonwhite, non-Western authors (those often defined by their "difference") to write from "experience" in creating characters who closely resemble themselves, Adichie's realist fiction brings different characters into dialogical interaction. Yet within the narrative itself, the ethics of representation also are explored in a formal play that, as multiple critics have noted, borrows and inverts the metafictional ending of Chinua Achebe's famous *Things Fall Apart*.

Scattered throughout *Half of a Yellow Sun* are eight sections describing a book-within-the-book. These sections come at the ends of chapters, primarily those focalized through Richard, and are set apart by their sans-serif typesetting and bold, numbered headings that always read, "The Book: The World Was Silent When We Died." These sections function in part to provide readers with a history of colonial and postcolonial Nigeria, as many of the book summaries describe events in the nation's past: for instance, its origins in "the Berlin Conference of 1884 where Europeans divided Africa," the missionary history bound up in colonizing forces, and the fact that when ethnically divided North and South were joined in 1914, the British governor-general's wife picked the nation's name (146–47). Against the personal and political events of the main story, these snapshots of a book overviewing Nigeria's history from a postcolonial perspective provide rather opinionated commentary on the events leading up to and during the war and school readers who are likely unfamiliar with this history, telling, for example, about Independence (195), economics and massacres of the Igbo (256–57), starvation in the Biafran War (296–97), and the politics that kept other nations from helping Biafra during its terrible fight for independence (324). The second-to-last of these book sections is a poem, written as an epilogue, that is explicitly directed to Western readers familiar with the photos of bloated, starving children and accuses them of their apathy in the face of such images (470). In a way, the snapshots of the book *The World Was Silent When We Died* acts as an ethical commentary throughout the novel, not so much on the personal responsibility of the readers but on the relationship of so-called First World to so-called Third World nations and subjects more generally. Whereas in *Purple Hibiscus* one of the central concerns is Kambili's silence in her suffering and her need to come into voice as a speaking subject capable of self-representation, the poem and book-within-the-book of *Half of a Yellow Sun* interrogate *Western* silence in response to representations of African suffering. The "world's" "silence" named here is both verbal silence and a metaphor for a lack of embodied response in the form of material help for war-ravaged, starving human beings represented through journalistic texts and photographs. The question of colonial and postcolonial subjects' silence is a matter of the ethics of representation, but the question of the world's silence in the face of suffering is a matter of the ethics of readerly attention: To whom do we truly attend? Through what hermeneutics do we interpret? How do we *reply*? How do we respond?

Throughout the novel, the reader is led to believe that this book-within-the-book is Richard's. The summaries appear, as I have said, mostly at the ends of his chapters. Richard is a writer, is in Nigeria to write about it, is represented repeatedly in the act of writing. As the novel progresses, he struggles with his topic, moving gradually from an interest in writing about ancient Igbo art to writing about politics; during the war, Richard writes pieces to send back to the West in attempts to correct the Western media's characterization of the war, which does not favor the Biafran cause. The book sections at points stand in contrast to these writing projects, as Richard's project and title change. Yet the reader has every reason to believe that this book—*The World Was Silent When We Died*—is the final result of Richard's politicization, his struggle to find his subject.

Ugwu learns of Richard's book late in the narrative, when Richard visits him in the hospital after he has been wounded. Ugwu tells him about reading *Narrative of the Life of Frederick Douglass*,[65] which made him "sad and angry for the writer," and Richard takes notes, telling Ugwu, "I shall use this anecdote in my book" (495). When Ugwu asks him about the book, Richard tells him that it is about "the war, and what happened before, and how much should not have happened. It will be called 'The World Was Silent When We Died'" (496): the topic and title confirm the reader's assumption that the book woven throughout the text is Richard's. Interestingly, this title is significant for Ugwu: Richard means the silence of the world's leaders that allowed Biafrans to starve and die in mass numbers for dubious political reasons arising from colonial history, but Ugwu translates that silence into his own ethical culpability: "Later, Ugwu murmured the title to himself: *The World Was Silent When We Died*. It haunted him, filled him with shame. It made him think about that girl in the bar, her pinched face and the hate in her eyes as she lay on her back on the dirty floor" (496). As I have argued, Ugwu's silence in his suffering and the girl's silence in hers create a link between their traumas that does not elide their differences. A similar logic is at work here, as Ugwu recognizes the silence in Richard's title not just as a critique of Western culpability for the terrible events in Biafra, but also Ugwu's own ethical culpability for not speaking and acting against the terrible event in the bar.

It is after this wounding that Ugwu himself begins to write, apparently inspired by the example of Frederick Douglass and spurred on by Richard's title. He writes literally in the margins, "in small careful letters on the sides of old newspapers, on some paper Kainene had done supply calculations on, on the back of an old calendar" (497–98). After writing bad imitative poetry and small details of life, he begins to record events from the war: "Finally, he started to write about Aunty Arize's anonymous death in Kano and about Olanna losing the use of her legs, about Okeoma's smart-fitting army uniform and Professor Ekwenugo's bandaged hands" (498). Ugwu's writing becomes for him a sort of healing, for while he struggles to represent the horrors of the war (a struggle he recognizes will never be fulfilled), his own nightmares begin to diminish: "He would never be able to depict the very bleakness of bombing hungry people. But he tried, and the more he wrote the less he dreamed" (498).

Richard, who notices that Ugwu has begun to write, seeks out his papers and asks him about the writing (508). Olanna, too, notices Ugwu's writing when she mentions to him a scene she saw earlier in the war on a train, a scene of a mother carrying her daughter's severed head in a covered basket (512). Olanna describes the experience to him in detail, realizing that Ugwu is taking notes and that this recording has an effect on her: "Ugwu was writing as she spoke, and his writing, the earnestness of his interest, suddenly made her story important, made it serve a larger purpose that even she was not sure of, and so she told him all she remembered about the train full of people who had cried and shouted and urinated on themselves" (512). Ugwu's act of writing—his act of listening, his act of *attention*—grants Olanna a sort of healing, allowing her to break a silence that has followed her after this traumatic experience. It is also, in a subtle way, an act of redemption, for while Ugwu could not look in the face of the girl in the bar as he caused her trauma, while he was silent when he witnessed her violation and caused her silence when he participated in it, in this scene Ugwu's attention allows for another woman to end her silence, invites her testimony, and brokers some form of healing. In this way, Ugwu's act of writing could be read as thematizing the ethics of readerly attention. This scene also hints at a shift that is about to come and upend the reader's perspective on the book sections throughout the narrative, for the very first one is an account of Olanna's experience on the train with the woman carrying her daughter's head (103). A reader with a very good memory—good enough to remember a paragraph from 400 pages earlier—may wonder about this correlation.

After the war ends, after Ugwu has visited his family and learned of his sister's rape, after he has returned to Olanna and Odenigbo's household, Richard finds Ugwu's writings and tells him they're "fantastic": what he finds is Ugwu's story about the woman carrying the head on the train (530). Ugwu tells him, "It will be part of a big book. It will take me many more years to finish it and I will call it 'Narrative of the Life of a Country'" (530). Ugwu then asks Richard about his own book:

"Are you still writing your book, sah?"

"No."

" 'The World Was Silent When We Died.' It is a good title."

"Yes, it is. It came from something Colonel Madu said once." Richard
  paused. "The war isn't my story to tell, really."

Ugwu nodded. He had never thought that it was. (530–31)

This scene effects a reversal, as Richard gives up the challenge of writing
the story of Nigeria and the Biafran War, and Ugwu comes into his own as
the writer whose place it is to tell the tale.

The novel ends in an ambiguity not unlike the ambivalence with which
Purple Hibiscus ends. The characters have all suffered, and although the war
is over, they have lost most of their possessions, have changed dramatically,
and have undergone traumatic experiences that will take serious time to
heal. Kainene is missing, and the final pages have Olanna doing everything
she can to find her. The final sentences read, "She had started to cry softly.
Odenigbo took her in his arms." But then we read the final section describing the book-within-the-book—"8. The Book: The World Was Silent When
We Died. Ugwu writes his dedication last: *For Master, my good man*" (541).

The reversal is complete: Ugwu is the writer of the book, Ugwu the
Igbo houseboy. The previous seven fragments are ostensibly his work,
not Richard's. The political commentary guiding readers' interpretations of the entire novel is Ugwu's. The poem that confronts Westerners
with their culpability in the face of Biafran suffering is Ugwu's, as are the
nuanced historical and economic accounts that one would not expect from
an underprivileged African village boy. Ugwu's dedication to his master
Odenigbo, himself a far from perfect though principled character, plays on
the joke of Odenigbo's favorite mode of address throughout the narrative,
calling his houseboy "my good man." It has seemed like a strange quirk
of British language, even a leftover of colonization, but Odenigbo has also
treated Ugwu as though he believed him to be a good man, one worthy of
respect, by enrolling him in school, giving him clothes, and treating him
with unusual equity despite Ugwu's status as a servant. Ugwu's decision
to dedicate the book to Odenigbo highlights the ethical question: What is
a good man? What makes for a good man?

Is Ugwu himself a good man? His shame over his participation in the
rape, his longing for redemption, his recognition of the ethical judgment
of himself inherent in the phrase "The World Was Silent When We Died,"

all demonstrate that, at the very least, Ugwu is capable of recognizing his own wrong, of lamenting it, of changing. This stance is also manifested less explicitly in Richard, whose implicit racism is with him to the end, recognizing that the Biafran story is not his to tell, and Olanna, who pours herself into seeking the sister she'd betrayed and from whom she'd been estranged. The mixedness of all the novel's characters suggests that all are capable of silence in the face of others' deaths, whether they are literal or figurative, but also that change is possible. And so the critique Ugwu's epilogue-poem levels at Westerners silent in the face of Biafran suffering, with its insistent question, "Did you see?" (470)—a critique that very well may encompass the contemporary Western reader of Adichie's novel as well—is softened, somewhat, by the suggestion that another response is possible through the ethics of readerly attention.

Realizing, perhaps as late as the last page, that *The World Was Silent When We Died* is Ugwu's book, not Richard's, the reader may choose to find those snippets to reread them in light of this new information, confronted by the realization that her own partnership with the text involves a reconfiguration based on her partial knowledge at any given point. The first section is especially instructive for the argument I have been making here that location matters, that an ethical paradigm of responses to suffering requires both the willingness to risk generalizations and the capacity to name differences. After writing in vivid detail about the head in the calabash on the train, Ugwu "mentions the German women who fled Hamburg with the charred bodies of their children stuffed in suitcases, the Rwandan women who pocketed tiny parts of their mauled babies. But he is careful not to draw parallels" (104). The global sufferings of people undergoing genocide—the traumatized responses of women whose children are devastated in the strife—bear marked similarities, and the similarities of such sufferings invite telling. There is something at work in the repetition, some significance to the links. But these sufferings are not the same. Their particularity begs representation and hermeneutically sensitive attention. It is up to those of us who read the sufferings from our various locations, then, to answer the question, "Did you see?" It is up to those of us who attend to the representations to answer the question, "Did you feel sorry briefly / Then turn round . . . ?"

Conclusion

Learning to Learn

> And the news from Biafra (doesn't make the headlines,
> not in today's paper at all)
> doesn't even get in past our eyes.
> —Denise Levertov, "Biafra"

Only days after finishing a first draft of the chapter on Chimamanda Ngozi Adichie, I stumbled quite accidentally across a poem by Denise Levertov, in a book published in 1970, on Biafra.[1] I read it with surprise, then read it again: the world was not quite silent when they died. But Levertov's poem, while its existence breaks through the silence Adichie explores in *Half of a Yellow Sun*, thematizes that very silence, naming both the dearth of journalistic coverage of the Biafran War and the fatigue of peace activists who had poured themselves into anti–Vietnam War work and were overwhelmed at yet another global crisis. Levertov describes the famous photos of starving Biafran children in Western magazines and the fact that even those who learned the "overdue statistics" about the "Massacre / of the Ibos" were left without any energy to act in ethical response.

The poem provides a powerful image of the relationship between text and ethically responsive action, a relationship that has been my concern throughout this book. Beginning the poem's second section with a repetition of its first line, Levertov writes:

> Biafra, Biafra, Biafra.
> Hammering the word against my breast:
> trying to make room for more knowledge
> in my bonemarrow.

This image concretizes the relationship between language and material reality, a word and the body: knowledge needs a space not in the mind but deep inside the bones. Language must enter the body to bring the body to act. It also calls to mind the behavior of a mourner, not just in the rhythmic repetition of the name but also in the practice of beating one's breast; it is fitting that the poem appears in a section of Levertov's *Relearning the Alphabet* called "Elegies."

Despite the efforts of the poetic speaker to internalize knowledge of Biafra for the sake of an embodied response, the poem ends without hope for such action. Levertov imagines the televised 1968 presidential nomination of Hubert Humphrey as a scene from Hieronymus Bosch, perhaps his most famous painting of a fantastical "Garden of Earthly Delights," signifying excess and oblivion to the hellish conditions in another place. She juxtaposes the starving Biafran child against this oblivious U.S. political scene that takes the bulk of journalistic attention. In response to this political context and the dying African child, the poetic speaker concludes with hopelessness and inaction:

And know
no hope: Don't know
what to do: Do nothing:

Levertov here connects hope to knowledge to action, or, more specifically, a lack of hope to a lack of knowledge to a lack of action. Confronted with the image of the dying child in Biafra, with the knowledge that the war is happening there and that United States politics are progressing as they do, oblivious to far-off suffering, the poetic persona does not know what to do. The first problem is the lack of information, but even as it comes ("overdue"), the speaker cannot find the wherewithal to assimilate the information, the energy to act. The poem's final punctuation is perhaps its only hopeful gesture, as a colon indicates that something follows, that this "Do nothing:" is not the end. On the other hand, we might read the white space that follows it *as* the phrase that follows the colon and completes the statement, a white space of wordlessness and inaction that offers no remedy for the atrocities happening in Biafra. The question of whether the reader interprets this ending as a hopeful invitation or a hopeless emptiness has a great deal to do with the reader's location.

But then, Levertov does engage the ethics of literary representation by choosing to write a poem about the Biafran War, about the suffering of its massacred Igbos and starving children, about the lack of Western media attention and governmental aid. The very existence of the poem in a book published in 1970, the year the short war ended, stands as a witness, a challenge. And unlike the character Richard in *Half of a Yellow Sun*, Levertov as a Western writer does not seek to stand as a representative for the Biafran people, telling their stories; instead, she narrates her own distance. Indeed, the poem represents not so much the Biafran people but the Western lack of awareness and response, and in so doing, it *raises* awareness of the situation. In this way, the poem, while in a certain sense representing Biafra, could be said also to thematize the ethics of readerly attention, implicitly raising the questions, To whom do we give our attention? To whom do we give our care? To whom are we responsible? How, in a modern era of televised and reported violence, injustice, and suffering from across the globe, can we both demand to have the truly important stories reported but then also learn how to divide our attention and our resources to respond?

In addition to asking these questions, "Biafra" highlights the fact that attention to representations—whether they are on television or in magazines or in literature—does not necessarily result in ethical response. Scholars are often optimistic about the effects of reading texts that participate in an ethics of literary representation,[2] but the partnership of the reader and the text in the making of meaning does not necessarily lead to embodied ethical action. Information does not always work its way into our bone marrow; knowledge of a situation, however new and attitude-changing, does not always lead to knowledge about what to do in response, and knowledge itself does not always lead to action.

I began this project not with a definitive argument I wanted to support but with a series of premises that built to a hypothesis. One of those premises was that several recent theoretical discourses—in theology, feminism, philosophy, and literary criticism—have championed a version of redemptive suffering as an ethical model: typically without acknowledging that other discourses are doing a similar thing, and typically eliding either the gendered or religious history of redemptive suffering in Western culture, or both. The second premise was that multiple contemporary women writers *also* engaged redemptive suffering in their literary texts, but with an unflagging attention to the imbricated and particular causes of that suffering, including gender and religion as well as race, class, place, and politics, as well as an exploration of the problematics of language. The hypothesis that arose from these premises was that the women's literary texts I chose for this study offer a uniquely literary and much more adequately nuanced ethics of suffering, one that is predicated on paradox and invites readers into an ethical relationship with both the text and the material world.

In this conclusion, I lay out the model of literary ethics that has developed through my textual encounters over the course of this project, an ethics predicated on the interactions of writer, text, and reader, specifically understood through the dynamic relationship of literary representation and readerly attention. First, I elaborate on representation, then turn to attention, discussing my theory of an ethical reading practice that arises from the intertextual conversation I have forged between theoretical and literary texts. Next, I concern myself with the theme of suffering, the *content* of ethical attention that has haunted my reading and that limns the gap between textual representations and material women. I struggle, in my writing here, to make sense of the overdetermined relationship between that theme of suffering and the practice of ethical reading I present, read in the pages of the books in my hands and in the pains of my own flesh and bones. I end with a meditation on the dangers and risks of the interpretive practices I advocate for, settling finally on the need for an ongoing reflection on pedagogy, embodied responsive action, and communities of interpretation and activism.

Representation

> That is what I work to do: to produce stories that save our lives.
> —Toni Cade Bambara, "Salvation Is the Issue"

By the ethics of literary representation, I have meant, first of all, the ethical and political valence of writers' choices and intentions about content as well as form. The decision to write about this or that cause, to explore the life experiences of a group not typically recognized in mainstream culture, to break silences about tacitly approved abuses, to introduce readers to various "other" groups or issues—these are risky choices made by writers. In choosing to represent certain content to their readers—in the senses of artistic mimesis, legal counsel, and a form of substitution that I borrow from Gayatri Spivak and expand—these writers take an ethico-political stand, and one that has not always been popular. For instance, in notes for an unpublished review, Elizabeth Bishop criticized Lever-tov's "Biafra," posing the question, "When have politics ever made good poems?"[3] I have discussed similar resistance to the work of Adrienne Rich and Toni Morrison, in particular. The reception history of Rich's poetry is marked by institutional resistance to her feminist writings, both *Of Woman Born* and poems of the seventies, leading, I and others have argued, to a strange forgetfulness about her recent work in the academy. Yet the whole scope of Rich's writing manifests risky representations of women's sufferings and other ethically significant realities: of the domestic sphere of motherhood and its many ambivalences, of the insidious prevalence of rape, of institutionalized racism and sexism, of global injustices against sweatshop workers and marginalized ethnic groups. Morrison likewise has claimed to have explicitly ethico-political aims for her writing, seeking to represent the elided horrors of the Middle Passage and the complexity of cross-gender, cross-generational, and cross-color relations within black communities, to bear witness to the "six million and more" destroyed by the slave trade. Yet she has famously been criticized for overemphasizing suffering, and it wasn't until the nineties that her novels began to be more widely read and studied within the academy. Although Ana Castillo and Adichie have primarily published in decades more open to explicitly political writing by women, they have faced scrutiny for their representations, especially from within their respective communities. They also have commented on the risks of their literary representations being taken as wholly representative of entire cultures.

Literary representation is an ethical practice in more than one way, and these different understandings of representation have led to serious critical debates. One widely held view—popular among feminists and womanists in the seventies but also among twenty-first-century readers—is that writers' choices to represent otherwise under-represented identity groups in their literature allows for increased personal and political recognition. This perspective relates closely to identity politics and played a role in a Women in Literature course in which I taught *So Far from God*. Most of the forty students did not identify with the characters in the novel, but two young Latina women expressed gratitude for the text's inclusion on the syllabus. One of them made the note in a piece of in-class writing, and the other approached me after class to say, "I know the rest of the class didn't really like this book, but I did. I felt like I knew the women in it. I felt like I was reading about my mom or my aunts or my grandma." These two students expressed their gladness to study a text that, unlike the Shakespeare or Ernest Hemingway or even Toni Morrison encountered in other classes and conversations, reminded them of their own experiences.

The idea is that recognizing ourselves within artistic representations allows for both healthier psychological development and a broader cultural revaluing of "normal" for the sake of increasingly egalitarian political and social relations. Yet although this understanding of representation has clearly affected cultural production in the past few decades, and in many instances for the better, it often is accompanied by a pressure for *positive* representations. So, for instance, African American writers are criticized if their representations of African American characters in any way confirm stereotypes. Or, as was prevalent in much feminist literary criticism of the seventies, activists demanded representations of heroic or idealized figures for women to take as representative and emulate. Then, of course, there is the problem of readers: just because a text represents characters in whom certain traditionally "othered" people can recognize themselves, the broader society will not necessarily appreciate the representation. My Women in Literature class sadly exemplifies this possibility, as the dominant voices raised in the classroom—a dominance supported perhaps by white middle-class students' sense of their experience being normative, or perhaps by simple solipsism—ultimately silenced the opposing views of the two women in the class who *did* recognize themselves in the novel. These two women expressed their identification with the text in private rather than raising their voices to contradict the opinion repeated by their classmates that the novel's representation of Southwestern Chicana women was irrelevant for their experience of the world, too depressing, and "not relatable." In the face of this pedagogical challenge, which felt to me like a failure to engage my students in the practice of ethical reading, I struggled to imagine a way to better help students consider the value of literary representations of cultural locations different from their own. My example provides a good reminder of the need for the ethics of literary representation to be accompanied by the ethics of readerly attention, including a reading practice that is self-aware about one's location, pre-conceived ideas, and the work it takes to be open to changing those ideas.

Yet another, possibly competing, understanding of representation stems from the legal sense of the term: in this view, literary representa-tion is not primarily writers' presentations of under-represented groups for the sake of self- and cultural recognition. Instead, in this view, writers seek to represent under-represented *sufferings* or *injustices,* for the sake of bearing witness, for the sake of possible reparations, and even for the sake of encouraging readers toward responsive political action. With writer or text as lawyer, advocate, or even witness, the reader is put into the position of judge or jury. From this perspective, literary texts complicate comfort-able lethargy or oblivion. They may raise readers' awareness of phenom-ena like the horrific labor practices that claim Fe's life in *So Far from God* or the traffic in body parts and drugs that cause such pain in *The Guard-ians*; they may explore the complexity of gender relations and highlight the common practices that lead to oppressions. This is the understanding of literary representation that emphasizes "breaking silences," not just of under-recognized "voices" but also of injustices and sufferings, that seeks to bring that which was hidden into the light. And so, Rich writes poems and essays about the contentious and difficult struggle to recognize her part in the oppression of women of color within the women's movement, and she implicitly asks her readers to consider their own culpability. And so, too, Morrison tells a nearly untellable tale of an escaped-slave-mother's violent act to free her children from a return to bondage, and she implic-itly asks her readers to struggle with the questions, What would you have done? And what should you do now?

These two modes of representation certainly work together; indeed, their differences may arise primarily from readers' locations, as some may recognize themselves in a text while others recognize their responsibility to an other. For instance, Adichie's novels give Igbo readers the chance to read books in which their own mangoes and harmattans, rather than apples and snowstorms, provide a recognizable setting for human drama (she often makes this point in interviews). They also serve to alert West-ern readers to the complexity of life in twentieth-century Nigeria, the pains as well as beauties of an Africa Westerners often see represented as a continent of starving, dusty brown people in need of Western aid. In other words, Adichie's books challenge the single story and encourage a new understanding. They also, however, represent certain particular modes of suffering that *do* demand some sort of ethical response, or that *did*. It would be hard to argue that *Purple Hibiscus* asks for Western intervention into the lives of the Nigerian middle class, but *Half of a Yellow Sun* highlights the ways in which the Biafran War—a war decades in the past—needed to be represented, needed Western response. Whereas Levertov's poem "Biafra," written during the war, challenged her readers with the question of responsibility as the war continued, Adichie's novel represents suffering and interrogates responsibility perhaps in an effort to warn against future silences in the face of genocide. In this way, Adichie's writing all at once represents Nigeria as a much more nuanced and lovely place than Westerners usually see (providing for her Nigerian readers a representation in which they can recognize themselves and their history), acts as witness to oft-elided suffering, and also represents Nigeria as a nation that poses difficult ethical questions about global responsibility for human suffering.

As postmodern literature, however, these texts challenge their own representations, both invoking and problematizing referentiality, to borrow Linda Hutcheon's terminology. They do so through their own marked textuality, their epigraphs and allusions to other literature, their poetic form, their self-aware thematizing of representation and language. They do so through their play with readers' conceptions of reality: their reliance on the mysterious, miraculous, or magical, their irony and humor, their collapsing of events from different eras into one setting. They do so through their gaps and ambiguities, their dogged resistance to straightforward or singular interpretations. The writings I have been studying both do and do not represent in any sense of the term, and that is one of their primary ethical lessons: the limitations of any reader's reading, the way justice is called for, again and again, and yet continues to slip just over the horizon. We both can and cannot recognize ourselves in texts. We both can and cannot learn from them what we ought to do.

The challenges of ethical literary representation provoke discussion of a problem that has accompanied me throughout these pages. Many scholars paint the relation of literature to the material world as either straightforwardly mimetic or as wholly separate. Rather than accepting one side or the other of these claims, I have argued that while literature does do something unique in its literary use of language, our experience of the real world is *always* mediated by the symbolic order; thus, although we almost inevitably make the leap of associating literary representations with the material world, we also are confronted by their distance from it, by the ways their language functions. In other words, literature both means something about the world in which we live and also means something about what it is to mean anything at all. There is no clear one-to-one, straightforward representation—language is always more nuanced, always more rich than that, as is human experience itself—but we take the risk of believing that a connection exists. Such a perspective is also embraced by Drucilla Cornell, whose ethical feminism rests on a vision of a utopian future brought about, in part, through the human imagination inspired by literature. Rich famously makes a similar claim, that literature functions in part to exercise our imaginations so that we might envision a better future.

I have struggled with the resulting question of whether it is more important for literature to represent things as they *are* or to represent things as they *ought to be*. I am influenced, for instance, by the argument of Mercy Amba Oduyoye that West African culture needs new myths and proverbs to effect positive cultural change for women, by the oft-repeated claim that our ethical dilemmas will be answered only by the creation of something *new*. Yet we cannot recognize the suffering and do something about it until it has been represented to us; we cannot make sense of it until we have worked through it in creation and interpretation. As numerous scholars have noted, literature that represents human suffering, through the specifically literary distance of artistic creation, allows us to struggle with our emotional and ethical quandaries in potentially productive ways. Moreover, literary language itself is *always* creating something new, even when it represents some past or present sorrow: because the structure of metaphor opens up the space of the "as if," because every writerly expression is really a figuration, a new creation.[4]

Ultimately, it seems to me that the texts I have been discussing in these pages have shown the both–and duality of literature as both a space for representing things *as they are* and for hinting at the imaginative potential of how things *could be*. So, for instance, Rich ends her incisive *Of Woman Born* by painting a hopeful picture of how mothering could be, and she thematizes and formally concretizes in the poem "Splittings" not only the pain of separation but also the possibility of learning to learn from that pain. Similarly, in *A Mercy* Morrison not only represents the evils of slavery and prejudice but also gives a glimpse of the goodness of a household of diverse women bringing their various gifts and experiences into a harmonious community. The novel does not end with a utopian vision; it is a sliver of light in the midst of the text, a hint at what could be that is too quickly occluded by what is. But the seed is planted through imaginative representation of some possible created good. Castillo's novels, too, share this glimpse of hope (again, in the form of a community of women): *So Far from God* ends with Sofi's creation of M.O.M.A.S., and *The Guardians* ends with Regina's care for María Dolores's child. Although the two narratives could be said to end happily, this is hardly the case: both women have suffered the unjust deaths of their children, losses that nearly overshadow the hope of their endings.[5] Adichie's novels, similarly, present a gamut of sorrows and sufferings but end with perhaps incongruous hope: Kambili looks forward to the rains, and Ugwu has taken up his pen.

Ugwu's writing is perhaps emblematic of a commonality across all the texts in my study, for not only do my writers represent suffering—or, rather than the abstract and general "suffering," myriad sufferings—they also represent writing and reading, language and interpretation. Indeed, from Rich's insistent exploration of words and speech to the secret "idigay" talk of the girls in Morrison's *Love* and its thematization of speech and silence, to the powerful image of Florens covering her Master's house with writing during the night, to the voracious reading of Gabo in *The Guardians* and the importance of his aunt's reading of the Gospel of Matthew for her final ethical choice, to Kambili's developing voice and Ugwu's replacement of Richard as rightful recorder of his people's stories, these texts repeatedly, insistently, and explicitly interrogate the function of language in human relations and political justice. They highlight the role of the writer as witness and representer (or representative?), the power of words to both oppress and relieve, and—almost always—the role of interpretation in the author-text-reader triad.

Attention

In order to respect the transcendence or the heterogeneity of the other, we have to pay attention. Sometimes, however, attention is not sufficient to surmount hallucination. But in order to overcome hallucination we have to pay attention to the other, that is, to listen to the other and to closely read the other. Reading, in the broad sense which I attribute to this word, is an ethical and political responsibility.

—Jacques Derrida, "Hospitality, Justice and Responsibility"

Not every piece of literature is about writing, although many of them are, in part because they are written by writers who have an inevitable interest in the topic. The fact that the narratives, essays, and poems I focus on in this book are so interested in language, both in writing and in interpretation, further complicates the relationship of the ethics of literary representation with the ethics of readerly attention. Again, not all texts thematize ethical interpretive practices or school readers in them through their formal literary features, but those that do provide an especially compelling study.

The ethics of readerly attention, again, has several valences, valences that overlap with each other and the thematics of suffering and thus challenge attempts to sort them out. The word "attention" is a nominalization of the verb "to attend": "attention," or "the act of attending to," is an abstraction of an action that always has an object. As the *Oxford English Dictionary* defines it, the verb "to attend," which derives from the Old French *attendre*, meaning "to stretch to," carries the following primary definition: "to direct the mind or observant faculties, to listen, apply oneself; to watch over, minister to, wait upon, follow, frequent; to wait for, await, expect." The first cluster of meanings focuses primarily on the mental work we might call "paying attention"; the second emphasizes the actions of service or servitude, care, and accompanying; and the third highlights the act of waiting, of expecting, of focusing with hope (or dread) on the future. All three divisions of signification imply a certain self-abnegation or opening of the self: first, in the work of noting details, accepting information, welcoming insights or stimuli; second, and more literally, in the act of following in the path of the other or seeking to comfort or provide for the other; and, third, in the forward-looking but otherwise inactive act of waiting for the other whose own agency must bring herself or himself to the waiting subject. In all these cases, attending is an act that places the object of the attention in some sort of primary position and places the self in a secondary or receptive position.[6]

Thus, attention as an ethical practice of receptive, open, even self-abnegating care or focus relates closely to the redemptive suffering so problematized throughout the preceding pages. As my discussion in chapter 1 of the uncanny resonances between the writings of contemporary ethical literary critic Derek Attridge and the philosopher-mystic Simone Weil demonstrates, an ethical stance of attention—an open and caring direction of energies—strongly resembles the self-sacrificing stance associated with Christian ethics or with motherly care. The irony of suggesting such a practice in the ethics of readerly attention does not escape me. Yet I have shown throughout this project that my advocacy for an ethical reading practice of close, careful, and open attention to texts does not derive solely from the theoretical texts—whether they are theological, feminist, philosophical, or literary. Instead, such a practice is a hard-earned insight reached through particular interactions with particular literary texts, texts that paradoxically seem to advocate such a stance even as they highlight the specific dangers of the gendered and religiously mediated ethics of redemptive suffering or sacrifice.

Indeed, the second valence of attention at work here is the way the texts themselves, through their complexities, ambiguities, and resistances to closure, seem to school readers in such a practice, to invite them into a relationship of focusing on the details of the text, following the text, waiting for the text. Such features include the ambivalence of Rich's description of motherhood as causing "exquisite suffering" and her mingling of forms, the open end of *Love* that leaves readers wondering who is alive and who is dead and whom is to blame. The question of how to understand the mystical or miraculous in *The Guardians*, *So Far from God*, and *Purple Hibiscus* is another instance of the texts inviting readers into an uncertain place that makes them reconsider their notions of the divine and material worlds, that leaves them wondering how to understand the texts' overall meaning. Yet another example is the revelation, only at the end of *Half of a Yellow Sun*, that Ugwu has been the writer of the book *The World Was Silent When They Died* all along, causing a seismic shift in reader perceptions after more than 400 pages of the novel and perhaps sending them back to the early pages to reinterpret the way these excerpts comment upon the narration. Again and again, such formal tactics remind readers: you do not know everything; you must pay closer attention; you may be surprised; you will have to struggle with this ethical question, with this ending, with this openness, because you cannot judge everything by your own experience, and yet now the book has ended and you are responsible. Morrison's novel *Jazz* is beautifully instructive here. After a difficult tale of pain and love conveyed by a mysterious narrator, the book concludes with a crescendo that ends in a whisper to leave one thinking:

> I envy [the people I observe] their public love. I myself have only known it in secret, shared it in secret and long, aw longed to show it—to be able

to say out loud what they have no need to say at all. *That I have loved only you, surrendered my whole self reckless to you and nobody else. That I want you to love me back and show it to me. That I love the way you hold me, how close you let me be to you. I like your fingers on and on, lifting, turning. I have watched your face for a long time now, and missed your eyes when you went away from me. Talking to you and hearing you answer—that's the kick.*

But I can't say that aloud; I can't tell anyone that I have been waiting for this all my life and that being chosen to wait is the reason I can. If I were able I'd say it. Say make me, remake me. You are free to do it and I am free to let you because look, look. Look where your hands are. Now.[7]

The final revelation, by a popular reading of this passage, is that the narrator is *the book*. The passage concisely summarizes what I am discussing here: not just the surprise at the end of the novel that reminds the reader she isn't such a master after all and sends her back looking for clues, but also the relationship between text and reader. The book presents itself here as vulnerable, "surrendered," desirous of love: and one more understanding of love, as an act, is attention and care.

The relative vulnerability of the book in this image, as it rests in the reader's hands (and not just "the reader's" hands, but "my" hands as I read its second-person address), relies on an implicit understanding of the reader as powerful and responsible. This power is an important component of my vision of a literary ethics; such an ethics is not comprised solely of the textual features themselves, or of the author's representations, no matter their ethical force. Unless the reader picks up the book, opens it, lifts and turns its pages, grants them *attention*, the text is nothing. As Paul Ricoeur argues, the interaction between the text and the reader is absolutely necessary for the creation of meaning in the space of reception. And as I have been claiming, the reader's location, the reader's imagination, the reader's interpretive paradigms all contribute to that meaning: the reader has every capacity to "make" and "remake" the text. Thus, a literary ethics must be aware both of literary representation, what a text represents and how it does so, and also readerly attention, not only the fact that the reader picks up the book and "pays attention" to it but also how the reader does so.

But are all books vulnerable in the way *Jazz* claims to be? Are all books powerless in the hands of a powerful reader who must deign to partner in their meaning? It is certainly the case that readers always bring their own locations and meanings to their interpretations of texts, but I would argue that certain texts—and at points certain widely disseminated interpretations of texts—can bring their own force to the meeting. Political propaganda, fairy tales intended for disciplining, books that celebrate violence or oppression: do these texts warrant a stance of openness, of hospitality, of care? This question parallels the challenges posed to many Christian, feminist, and philosophical models of care and redemptive suffering: is it really ethically exemplary to provide endless service or humble obeisance to one's oppressor?

The literary texts we have been discussing are again instructive here, for these books repeatedly demonstrate not only the paradoxical championing of a generalized self-giving ethics always challenged (or attended) by their representations of the particular dangers of such an ethics in particular cultural locations, but also an alternative hermeneutics. Rich advocates for and practices a tireless dynamic not just of open acceptance and close reading but also of critique and revision. And especially in their engagement with Christian texts and traditions, all my project's literary writers manifest a both–and stance of critique and embrace, one predicated on a hermeneutic of liberation or suspicion that rejects received interpretations in favor of a rereading that seeks to find the liberatory, the justice-producing, the life-giving elements of those texts and traditions. Within the texts, characters exemplify these reading practices: Regina finds a liberatory word in Matthew's Gospel in *The Guardians*, and both Rebecca Vaark of *A Mercy* and Jaja of *Purple Hibiscus* struggle against the popular understandings of the book of Job. At another level, the literary texts themselves enact such practices, as their writers take biblical texts, or church traditions, or tales of martyrdom, and rewrite them from the perspective of the oppressed for subversive, liberatory purposes. Such a practice paradoxically combines an open embrace of the text or tradition—a willingness to follow it, or wait for it, or otherwise focus on it—with a commitment to critique if such critique is necessary for justice. Which is to say, while these texts again and again disrupt readerly mastery and invite (or demand) careful attention, they also thematize the dangers of naïve reading and the benefits of attention to context, location, and power differentials.

The ethical readerly attention that I have learned from Rich, Morrison, Castillo, and Adichie is all at once a stance that parallels a self-sacrificial openness and care, and also a stance that requires awareness of the danger of wholly submitting to the text-as-other, wholly trusting it and welcoming it and following it. Ethically attentive reading is not only a practice that readers learn in the singular interaction with a particular text and apply in that case, but a practice that readers can choose to bring to various texts. In other words, we do not approach texts as blank slates, with nothing but openness and attentiveness. Instead, we carry with us our entire socialization as readers. There is no such thing as neutral reading. Even as children, we are taught to read in certain ways: looking for information, looking for ourselves or for points of identification, looking for points with which to argue, or even simply looking for escape. Thus, to read ethically, we must again engage in self-reflection, awareness of our location, of what we bring to texts, of those texts' locations and material histories and cultural contexts. We must *choose* an interpretive paradigm, practice it, learn it. I have argued throughout this book that certain texts—often recent texts of the marginalized and oppressed—can school us in practices that hold in tension the general and the particular, the attitude of embrace and the attitude of critique. This is Ricoeur's hermeneutic circle: the meaning we make in interpretive partnership with any given text moves with us into future creations of meaning, whether we work with the next text as writer or as reader. Again, location is key, and I mean this in culturally material terms: the relative power of a given reader and a given text within their social contexts will determine the ratio of open, receptive attention versus attentive suspicion that the reader ought to bring to that text.

The reading practice I am advocating for here is one that tempers a stance of openness, receptivity, and care for detail, a certain hermeneutic humility and even sacrifice of the self, with an awareness, learned from attention to prior literary representations, that not every text is liberatory, that not every use of language brings life, that the most ethically attentive approach to certain texts, based on their functions within their contexts, is to read them against the grain. This suspicion especially applies to texts that are powerful, but it also applies to the texts of the vulnerable or marginalized. For if we learn nothing else from the history of the women's movement, we should remember that the text of a white woman struggling to represent the sufferings and value of women for the sake of justice can reinscribe racism and classism, and the text of an African American man (or woman) seeking to represent the sufferings and value of black folk can reinscribe sexism. The liberation-seeking text of a Chicana can reinscribe homophobia, and the representation of a writer from the Global South can reinscribe Western paternalism. And on and on. Our self-giving openness therefore must be attended by a careful suspicion—of both oppression and of ourselves—if we are to engage in a fully ethical practice of attentive reading.

From Pain:

> The affirmation of particularity tends to a type of universality, universal accountability, that precludes universally true interpretations of the human condition or final strategies for social change. Particular stories call us to accountability.
> —Sharon Welch, *A Feminist Ethic of Risk*

The foregoing chapters have explored the ethical practices of literary representation and readerly attention as arising from and opening up and inextricably intertwined with the theme of women's suffering. I have struggled with the liberatory or ethical power of literature in the real world, wondered what good it does, whether the subaltern can speak, whether the master's tools can ever dismantle the master's house, whether it is better to sit silent and still. As I piece together this conclusion, I am haunted by all my texts, by the sufferings they represent, by the question of what I ought to do, in my body, in my life-world, in response. I am haunted by the "Do nothing:" that ends Levertov's poem.

The day I found this poem, I was reading Levertov as one reads poetry in life's lulls that demand it, in the low points that beg for a bit of beauty or a drop of hope or understanding. I pulled the slim volume down from a shelf on a day when I was in the throes of a miscarriage at nearly fourteen weeks pregnant, my entire self surprised and pained, from burning eyes to cramped uterus to throbbing back muscles. I sat in a low chair and ran my fingers over the taupe book-cloth and caressed the thick pages of "Elegies" with eyes shadowed by tear-clumped lashes.

Throughout the years that I have devoted to this project, I have thought a great deal about the pains of childbirth, about the biblical tale of Eve's curse and its cultural afterlife, about feminist responses to this story that crystallized especially in the later nineteenth century but that pepper literary history. With the hubris of the uninitiated, I theorized about the chosen or unchosen suffering of a woman bearing a child, the self-giving literalized in breastfeeding and sleepless nights, the daily tasks of providing for, cleaning and feeding, attending to an other. I began this book with pregnancy, childbirth, and mothering in part because this is where women writers throughout history began their meditations on suffering, and later first-wave and second-wave feminists began much of their feminist engagement, but also because in the Christian tradition pregnancy, childbirth, and mothering have been so linked to women's suffering and sacrifice: through the figures of Eve and the Virgin Mary, and through Mary's son who, in the Christian imagination, wrought redemption through sacrifice of his body and very life (*surely he hath borne our grief*). I also began with these experiences because the scenario of pregnancy, childbirth, and mothering is a widely shared experience of women around the globe. As my literary readings have demonstrated, however, these experiences *always* are mediated through the cultural symbolic, given significance by the particular language and attitudes of a cultural location. Which is to say that women in different times and places experience childbirth in radically different ways. Thus, this biological reality both unifies women across space and time and also separates them. In the literary texts I have read for this project, a shared stake in the Christian tradition and its texts has contributed to the cultural symbolic of all the writers (and characters), adding another commonality of significance. But even Christianity and its scriptures have been shaped in complex ways by the distinct contexts of their application. And so we see, for example, the heightened role of Mary in Castillo's writing and the social location of its production, or the significance of Hagar for womanist theologian Delores Williams and Morrison's use of the biblical name in one of her novels. Even within a shared Catholic imagination, childbearing means something significantly different in the Roman Catholic Igbo location of Adichie's writing than it does in the Mexican Catholic location of Castillo's. Amid shared vocabularies and parallel experiences, distinctions abound.

A literary ethics that is attentive to women's suffering, then, must take literary representations of pregnancy, childbirth, and mothering as a source of insight and a correction to the theoretical celebrations of redemptive suffering that are so forgetful of its history. The literary and theoretical texts I have turned to in this book, however, repeatedly confront readers with the particularity of cultural locations and the inevitable interplay of similarities and differences between texts' and readers' locations. A literary ethics of suffering, as I have sought to discover and construct in these pages, can make few generalized pronouncements and judgments of women's activities that bring them suffering. I certainly cannot proclaim, as some have, that all suffering is "bad" and to be avoided, resisted, or fought against. The texts with which I have spent my days these past years have taught, through the content and forms of their literary representations, that suffering brought about by injustice and oppression is to be condemned and struggled against—but that the chosen struggle for justice itself may result in suffering, reconfirming the structure of redemption through self-sacrificial, chosen suffering. Yet more difficult is the repeated lesson that even the sufferings that do result from oppression may provide precisely the special insight needed to empower resistance to that oppression, that strength may grow from certain instances, although not every instance, of suffering. The texts to which I have given myself these past years have also, in their very existence, argued for their own importance, for their unique capacity to represent the unrepresented, to engage readers in a practice of attention—and attention *to a particular suffering*—that just might bring readers not only to catharsis through identification with their own suffering, or empathy through an awakening of their affective and embodied sensibilities, but also to a sense of responsibility, a longing to work for some utopian vision, as well as a humility about their capacity to do so without ongoing self-revision and input from others. I have concluded, am concluding, we need these poems and stories. We need to read them, and to teach them, and to find still more that can challenge us with representations of cultural difference, representations in which we both do and do not recognize ourselves and our own suffering, representations that both are and are not clearly related to the material world, representations that teach us both about some other's experience and also about the dangers of taking that representation as too real, too representative, about the need to give the book sustained, careful, and also critical attention and then—and then—to look up from it.

We learn about suffering from our reading, and we learn about reading from our suffering. As I wrote and read about pregnancy and childbirth and mothering, about pain and suffering, I did not think much of miscarriage. But then, just as I finished these pages, just as I turned to revision, my own vision shifted. This shift was manifested not in red ink but in blood, in the professional control of a midwife and a doctor in a dim ultrasound room, in the carefully blank face of the physician's assistant also present as a training shadow, and the way she clutched her three-ring binder to her chest and wrote no notes but watched.

I carried that little one with shock and joy for three full months, and right at the cusp of the second trimester, when the statistics told me I was safe from the ever-present fear of an early loss, just days after sharing the good news with friends, the midwife and then the doctor found no heartbeat. With their impressive technology, they saw a fetus that had ceased to grow. They pointed to the electronic screen and I saw not a babe I would hold and cherish but a tiny death mask, smaller than a plum.

I attended a birth in the early days of this project, and I saw its pain. Its pain was an otherworldly thing, seeming to arise both from the self and from some foreign source, wrenching to observe, but it was a productive pain. At the end of the labor, Annie held her little girl and welcomed her with words of such tender surprise that the room felt to me a holy place. "Hello!" she gasped, breathless and awed. "Hello there! You're here! You're finally here! Welcome! Hello!"

My pain was not productive, did not welcome an other into the world through the paradox of letting her go from within me: the contractions that wracked my body were for death, not life.

Women's suffering, I decided in those gasping, desperate days, is from fragility. We suffer because we are vulnerable to cultural norms, to social expectations, to bodily limitations. We suffer because death lurks and threatens, and we are battered by forces beyond our control. We suffer because so often, we cannot hold the babies we long for, or we are made to bear the babies we never asked for. We are permeable, open, and find our control and agency so often a mirage. Even the grief that overtook me surprised me: I did not ask for it, did not welcome it, but it pinned me to my bed, filled my head with fog, spun me into a dance of suffering beyond what I ever could have anticipated.

I know that I interpret my pain at this loss, the pain of my clenched and contracting body and of my lost hopes and dissolved dreams and nipped-in-the-bud love, through the texts I have spent these years attending to. I know that my claim about the source of suffering, crystallized in these days of most acute pain, holds true with what I've read and reread, though I'd never used this language before. The suffering represented in Rich's writing, and Morrison's, and Castillo's, and Adichie's, and the writings of countless other writers, is a suffering produced by vulnerability within experiences of embodiment and culture (read: language). We live amid power hierarchies, violence, and suspicion of difference, and our cultures sustain and are sustained by these impulses and structures, and render them significant in various and sundry ways. We live toward death, and our cultures make meaning of that death and its related illness and pains.

And what can literary representation do in the face of such human frailty? What can readerly attention do?

When I couldn't work or eat or put my fingers to piano keys, I sat crossways in a chair and I pulled down a book of poems. And when I talked to Annie—the Annie whose second birth I attended like the most precious of texts, the Annie whose miscarriage I reference in the first chapter of this book—she told me that the two things that most helped in her own healing were crafting a liturgy and reading a collection of other women's miscarriage stories, which, she said, through their similarities and differences from her own, alleviated her sense of isolation and strengthened her sense of her own particular experience. Which is to say, Annie told me to create something with language and to read literary narratives of other women's experiences. She told me that in response to my suffering I should write and I should read.

I did. I clutched my journal like a life vest. I tacked words together into sentences and paragraphs and mailed them off to friends like an emergency light, and I cherished their replies. I constructed myself, my meaning, in e-mails, made myself calm and coherent through drafting and revision. I made something. On the day the doctor's ultrasound showed only a void, a blank space inside me the medical books label a "successful miscarriage," he asked me about my manuscript. I told him its topic, and his eyes grew wide: "It seems you've learned a bit more these past few weeks," he said. I thought to myself, I'm not sure how much I've *learned*. Am I learning? But I waved my hand the length of my own torso like a game-show hostess in an evening gown, and smiled a pained smile, not quite ironic, not quite a grimace: "This is my last chapter." My body, the text.

Do I learn from pain? Do I learn from the pain in my own bones and flesh, the pain of my jaw clenched at night that signifies stress or sorrow and spreads to my forehead and shoulders as the day wears on? Can I choose to learn from it? Can some good come of it?

Does the pain of my miscarriage change my reading of the miscarriages in *Purple Hibiscus*, or the miscarriages of embodied women who, like the character Beatrice, lose babies at the hands of abusive partners? Does my reading of *Purple Hibiscus* change my experience of miscarriage within my own body?

Yes, I will say. Yes, I believe it does. The wordless throb and thrum of my suffering is part of my life-world now, part of the resources I bring to any interpretation of any text. And the words woven over the pages of fiction I have read are also part of my life-world, part of the resources I bring to any interpretation of my own fraught life-text.

Early in the journey of this project, several colleagues warned me not to elide the difference between sufferings, not to make of "suffering" the noun a grand and encompassing thing, not to slide the relatively minor chosen suffering (or self-sacrifice) of readers into the relatively short and even good suffering of women in labor into the suffering of those afflicted with long-term illnesses or social oppressions or war. As my chosen literary sources have manifested again and again, the negotiation of similarity and difference is a tenuous one. It's a delicate dance to bring our own suffering into conversation with the suffering of others: for as humans, I believe along with philosophers like Arne Vetlesen and Judith Butler, we all do suffer. But my lost pregnancy, painful as it is, and mediated as it is through the cultural matrix that gives it its meaning, is not the result of any injustice or oppression, and this is an important distinction. The character Beatrice in *Purple Hibiscus*—and women like Beatrice, who suffer abuse—face a different pain altogether when they lose their unborn children at the hands of a violent oppressor. The questions, then, become: What meaning will I make of my suffering, unchosen yet not a violence or an oppression? And how will I respond to that other suffering, when confronted by it, that suffering of violence or oppression wrought by body or language? How will such literary representations shape my attention to other texts, even to texts that do harm? For whose sake will I choose to suffer, for what justice will I harness this energy of my own pain?

Again and again, in so many forms and with so many nuances, I have read this meaning: The suffering that results from injustice ought not to be, and it is worth choosing to suffer, oneself, to struggle against that injustice. The suffering that results from the human condition of limitation and frailty, or the suffering that is inescapable, cannot be assuaged by someone else's suffering, but redemption can be found in the *meaning* we derive from our own suffering: we can buy back the good by learning to learn from pain. Finally, an ethics based on self-giving care, care that at points stretches toward suffering on behalf of the other, is not an easy thing; it is a dangerous thing, a risky thing. But it can be a beautiful and necessary thing. I have read these meanings, again and again, until they have seeped into the marrow of my bones. The question now is, how will I move those bones, this body, in response to all that I have read and felt and known?

Risk

There is always more to write.
—Drucilla Cornell, *Beyond Accommodation*

Still, at some moment the book will be closed.
—Susan Sontag, *Regarding the Pain of Others*

Rereading the rhythms of the foregoing paragraph, I recognize its uncanny resonance with that paragraph at the end of Morrison's novel *A Mercy*, the words of Florens's mother, her authoritative moral claims: "to be given dominion over another is a hard thing; to wrest dominion over another is a wrong thing; to give dominion of yourself to another is a wicked thing" (167). My tidy summation of a contemporary literary ethics, this meaning I have read, ought to be challenged in the same way I challenge that last page of Morrison's novel and readers' (even Morrison's) propensity to read it as a key to the whole narrative. A literary ethics can never be adequately summarized; its incarnation in literary language, in the form of the novel or the poem, subverts such an attempt at extracting and naming its significance. The particularity of the whole exceeds any attempt at generalizing: I have said this over and again, and it holds true for my own writing here. The literary ethics of suffering is not in this conclusion; the ethics is in the chapters, in the readings, in the textual encounters and the writing itself. The ethics is in the invitation to read the novels and theory and to respond, to read these pages of my own writing and respond, with speech or writing, and carry on the work. The ethics is also in the invitation to do something with your hands, once the book is back on the shelf, to attend more ethically to some human other, to join some community of action.

But still, I risk the generalizing claims, the inevitably failed attempt at articulating an ethics, for the sake of this ongoing conversation. And the ethical paradigm I am forwarding here is in the end not so different from the one I found in the theoretical texts that first provoked this project. With theologians and feminist theorists and philosophers, I am advocating an ethics of self-giving, even self-sacrificing care; I am arguing that chosen suffering can be redemptive, and that unchosen suffering can be redeemed through the lessons sought within it. Yet my argument is distinctive in that I am asserting that such an ethics never should be forwarded apart from the stories that challenge it, apart from awareness of the gendered and religious (and raced and classed) histories and connotations that accompany it in Western culture broadly and in different cultural locations more specifically. In a sense, I have argued in each chapter of this book that to *do justice* to the paradoxes and nuances of an ethical model predicated on suffering, we must locate it within texts like the ones I have attended to. In other words, when we speak of an ethics of suffering, conceptually, when we struggle with the question of how to attend to the cultural phenomena of women's chosen and mandated self-giving care, we should turn for guidance to literary texts that represent situations of such suffering and sacrifice in all their particularity, highlighting the role language and culture play in imbuing such experiences with significance.

In broadest strokes, I could be said to be arguing for the value of literature, period. More pragmatically, I am advocating for syllabi that are self-conscious in their inclusion of texts that explore these complexities, for scholarship that looks to illuminating intertexts to aid in readings that are neither sociology-lite nor personal applications. I am challenging the field of poststructuralist literary ethics, in particular, to remember where its theory has come from and to consider the challenging contributions of women's literary writing to a theory of literary ethics.

One of the final paradoxes of my proposed literary ethics—an ethical model that provides a way to interpret and respond to suffering both within texts and within the material world—is that it encourages both openness and caution, a starting point that unabashedly values women's flourishing and liberation. I am suggesting that radical humility goes hand in hand with courageous commitment to an ethical ideal of an egalitarian society of transformed social structures.[8]

The risk of this paradox, like the wager of the other paradoxes that contribute to a literary ethics of suffering, is of falling too far to one side or the other. Those who read, as I do, in a culture dominated by avoidance and negative evaluations of suffering, by *apatheia*,[9] also read in a culture of risk management and risk avoidance, as Zygmunt Bauman argues in *Postmodern Ethics*.[10] We read and relate in a culture shaped, as Sharon Welch asserts, by an ethic of control that emphasizes success and results over process and intentions.[11] We are disciplined to value being *right*, being our *best*, and we are embarrassed by lapses and failures.

But I am calling for us to *try*. I am calling for us to admit that we will be wrong at times. We will approach texts that may do us harm, that may trick us, as not every book is for the world's good, and the language available to us belongs just as much—and more—to the oppressor. I am calling us to approach texts knowing that we may misinterpret, make mistakes that are innocuous and mistakes that later cause us shame or cause someone else pain. I am calling those of us who teach to walk into our classrooms, create our syllabi, humbled by the fact that there is always more we are leaving out of the reading list or the lecture or the discussion, usually without even realizing it. The ever-present *differend* will haunt us, as will the inevitable need to face limitations and say, "enough for now," for the human condition of limitations that brings us suffering also shapes our capacity to respond to it. I am calling us to bring the ethics of readerly attention to each text, attempting to be self-aware and hopeful and open but also a tad suspicious, seeking liberation and justice, even as we know that our definitions of liberation and justice will have to continue to shift and change. I am calling us to try not to be paralyzed by the need to be *right*, by the need to be *best*, by the endless array of choices that confront us. I am advocating for us to seek communities (or to seek to create communities) that will bring together differences and allow us to challenge each other: in classrooms, in women's circles, in reading groups, around our dining tables, and in activist networks. I am suggesting that we seek to listen more than we speak, seek to read more than we write, reading and rereading and also *acting*: with a vote, with a campaign, with a friendship, with a casserole, with a story, with a song.

As for me, I will try to have another baby, knowing the pain of miscarriage that has wracked my body and my spirit. I will be terribly afraid of conceiving and eventually, wrapped in my partner's arms, jump into the unknown, open myself wide to the possibility of another loss, another sorrow. I will do this for the sake of life, knowing in my bone marrow that life and death, joy and suffering, are two sides of passion's coin. I will hold the news of a new pregnancy deep and silent in my heart, breathe it in my lungs, and I will live in terror every day of a cramp, a stain, a sign. I will pray. I will read books that tell the truth and also give me hope. I will read poems aloud, before the tiny little one even has ears to hear. I will cling to the faith that she or he will hear.

And again I will look up and out and face the world, even when the news stories haunt and overwhelm. I will risk action, risk overidentification and underidentification, risk misinterpretation and missteps for the sake of the ethical response, for the sake of the alleviation of that suffering that ought not be, with hope for the blank white space on the page beneath Levertov's "Do nothing:" In response to the private pain that could threaten to draw all my attentions and sympathies to myself, I will write the words again: we learn about suffering from our reading, and we learn about reading from our suffering. My suffering is *not* the suffering of any other woman, but my suffering inevitably colors my interpretation, and it can empower my work for justice. I will read and reread from Rich's "Contradictions: Tracking Poems," the lines that have accompanied me through these pages:

> remember: the body's pain and the pain on the street
> are not the same   but you can learn
> from the edges that blur   O you who love clear edges
> more than anything   watch the edges that blur[12]

Even when it hurts, even when it requires a giant leap, even though the task will never be fully completed, I will seek, in a circle of books and bodies, of texts and contexts, to choose, over and again, to *try* to learn to learn from pain.

What will you do, once your hands are again free?

NOTES

Preface

1. Andrew Gibson, "Ethics," in *The Johns Hopkins Guide to Literary Theory and Criticism,* 2nd ed., ed. Michael Groden, Martin Kreiswirth, and Imre Szeman (Baltimore, MD: Johns Hopkins University Press, 2005), n.p.

2. By "redemptive suffering" here I do not refer specifically to the Roman Catholic practice of "offering up" one's suffering with Christ's for the sake of one's own or another's spiritual health or the Protestant doctrine of penal substitutionary atonement, but instead the broader perspective that suffering can bring about restoration, salvation, or some other good. Jesus's suffering and death that freed us from slavery to sin and death is the paradigmatic instance of redemptive suffering within Christianity, although its theological nuances remain hotly contested. Redemptive suffering is not a unique feature of Christianity, however, and is present in many world religions.

3. Geoffrey Galt Harpham, "Ethics," in *Critical Terms for Literary Study,* 2nd ed., ed. Frank Lentricchia and Thomas McLaughlin (Chicago: University of Chicago Press, 1995), 387–405.

4. Adam Zachary Newton, "Versions of Ethics; Or, The SARL of Criticism: Sonority, Arrogation, and Letting-Be," *American Literary History* 13, no. 3 (2001): 606–37.

5. Chela Sandoval, *Methodology of the Oppressed* (Minneapolis: University of Minnesota Press, 2000).

6. Barbara Christian, "The Race for Theory," *Cultural Critique* 6 (1987): 51–63.

1. History (Herstory) and Theory, or Doing Justice to Redemptive Suffering

1. Julian of Norwich, *Revelation of Love*, trans. John Skinner (c. 1400; New York: Image, 1997), 4–5. Subsequent citations appear in the text.

2. C. S. Lewis quoted in Skinner's preface to *Revelation of Love*, vii.

3. Dame Julian was not alone in using feminine language or calling Jesus mother; instead, she participates in a trend that grew among monks during the twelfth and thirteenth centuries. See Carolyn Walker Bynum, *Jesus as Mother: Studies in the Spirituality of the High Middle Ages* (Berkeley: University of California Press, 1984).

4. Liz Herbert McAvoy, *Authority and the Female Body in the Writings of Julian of Norwich and Margery Kempe* (Cambridge, England: Boydell & Brewer, 2004), 19.

5. In appealing to the language of wounding, Julian participates in a mystical tradition often traced to Bernard of Clairvaux and also taken up by Catherine of Siena.

6. Diane Watt, *Medieval Women's Writing* (Cambridge, England: Polity, 2007), 104.

7. Again, Julian was by no means the first to participate in this potentially dangerous, potentially good association of women's bodiliness with Christ's suffering, and I am certainly not the first to comment on it. For an introduction to much of the recent scholarship on medieval women's spirituality, see Amy Hollywood, "Feminist Studies," in *The Blackwell Companion to Christian Spirituality*, ed. Arthur Holder (Oxford: Blackwell, 2005), 363–86.

8. As Laurie Finke writes, "Without a doubt, the largest single genre of women's writing throughout the Middle Ages was devotional" (*Women's Writing in English: Medieval England* [New York: Longman, 1999], 125). Erica Longfellow notes a similar trend in early modern English women writers (*Women and Religious Writing in Early Modern England* [Cambridge: Cambridge University Press, 2004], 3).

9. Katherine Parr, *Prayers or Medytacions The Early Modern Englishwoman—A Facsimile Library of Essential Works. Part 1, Printed writings, 1500–1645*, Vol. 3., ed. Janel Mueller (1545; Brookfield, VT: Ashgate, 1996).

10. Anne Vaughan Lock, *The Collected Works of Anne Vaughan Lock*, ed. Susan Felch (Tempe, AZ: Arizona Center for Medieval and Renaissance Studies in conjunction with the Renaissance English Text Society, 1999), ll. 333–34.

11. Aemelia Lanyer, *Salve Deus Rex Judaeorum*, in *The Poems of Shakespeare's Dark Lady*, introduction by A. L. Rowse (1611; New York: Clarkson N. Potter, 1979), 77.

12. Ibid., 117.

13. Ibid., 69.

14. See Carolyn Walker Bynum, *Fragmentation and Redemption: Essays on Gender and the Human Body in Medieval Religion* (New York: Zone, 1991), for a discussion

of the ways in which medieval women writers discovered power in their era's emphasis on Christ's suffering and embodiment.

15. Helen Wilcox, *Women and Literature in Britain, 1500–1700* (Cambridge: Cambridge University Press, 1996), 41.

16. Anne Finch, *Poor Man's Lamb*, UPenn Digital Library, 1713, http://www.digital .library.upenn.edu/women/finch/1713/mp-lamb.html; Elizabeth Hands, *The Death of Amnon* (N. Rollason Coventry, 1789); Anne Yearsley, *Poems on Various Subjects* (1787; New York: Woodstock Books, 1994).

17. George Eliot, *Adam Bede* (1856; New York: Modern Library, 2002), 365.

18. Christina Rossetti, *The Complete Poems of Christina Rossetti*, ed. R. W. Crump (Baton Rouge: Louisiana State University Press, 1979).

19. Florence Nightingale, *Cassandra and Other Selections for Thought,* ed. Mary Poovey (1859; Washington Square: New York University Press, 1992), 227, 230.

20. Elizabeth Barrett Browning, *A Drama of Exile* (New York: Henry G. Langley, 1845), 107. Subsequent citations appear in the text.

21. Annie Dillard, *Holy the Firm* (New York: Perennial, 1977), 36.

22. Ibid., 72.

23. Ibid.

24. Derek Attridge, *The Singularity of Literature* (London: Routledge, 2004), 124.

25. See, especially, Lawrence Buell, "Introduction: In Pursuit of Ethics," *PMLA* 114, no. 1 (1999): 7–19; Lawrence Buell, "What We Talk About When We Talk About Ethics," in *The Turn to Ethics*, ed. Marjorie Garber, Beatrice Hanssen, and Rebecca L. Walkowitz (New York: Routledge, 2000), 1–14; Robert Eaglestone, *Ethical Criticism: Reading After Levinas* (Edinburgh: Edinburgh University Press, 1997); Andrew Hadfield, Dominic Rainsford, and Tim Woods, "Introduction: Literature and the Return to Ethics," in *The Ethics in Literature* (New York: St. Martin's Press, 1999), 1–14; Geoffrey Galt Harpham, *Shadows of Ethics: Criticism and the Just Society* (Durham, NC: Duke University Press, 1999), 18–37; Dominic Rainsford and Tim Woods, eds., *Critical Ethics: Text, Theory, and Responsibility* (New York: Macmillan, 1999), 1–20; Marjorie Garber, Beatrice Hanssen, and Rebecca L. Walkowitz, eds., *The Turn to Ethics* (New York: Routledge, 2000), vii–xii; and Michael Eskin, "Introduction: The Double 'Turn' to Ethics and Literature?" *Poetics Today* 25, no. 4 (2004): 557–72.

26. Zygmunt Bauman, *Postmodern Ethics* (Oxford: Blackwell, 1993). For more on theorists' ethical turns and linguistic turns, see Baker, *Deconstruction and the Ethical Turn* (Gainesville: University Press of Florida, 1995), and Rajchman, *Truth and Eros: Foucault, Lacan, and the Question of Ethics* (New York: Routledge, 1991).

27. Andrew Gibson, "Ethics," in *The Johns Hopkins Guide to Literary Theory and Criticism*, 2nd ed., ed. Michael Groden, Martin Kreiswirth, and Imre Szeman (Baltimore, MD: Johns Hopkins University Press, 2005), n.p.

28. Wayne C. Booth, *The Company We Keep: An Ethics of Fiction* (Berkeley: University of California Press, 1988).

29. J. Hillis Miller, *The Ethics of Reading: Kant, de Man, Eliot, Trollope, James, and Benjamin* (New York: Columbia University Press, 1987), 1.

30. Hadfield, Rainsford, and Woods, *The Ethics in Literature*, 2; Baker, *Deconstruction and the Ethical Turn*, 1.

31. Consider Elizabeth Ammons, *Brave New Words: How Literature Will Save the Planet* (Iowa City: University of Iowa Press, 2010).

32. John D. Caputo, *Philosophy and Theology* (Nashville, TN: Abingdon Press, 2006), 50.

33. Jacques Derrida, "Hospitality, Justice and Responsibility: A Dialogue with Jacques Derrida," in *Questioning Ethics: Contemporary Debates in Philosophy*, ed. Richard Kearney and Mark Dooley (London: Routledge, 1999), 67.

34. A number of other critics influenced by poststructuralist theory have proposed models of humility, receptivity, redemptive substitution, and self-emptying or -sacrifice as ideals for human behavior (beyond the interpretation of texts) in recent years. These include Pamela Caughie's discussion in *Passing and Pedagogy: The Dynamics of Responsibility* (Urbana: University of Illinois Press, 1999) of "self-divestment through passing" as a postmodern answer to the modern privileging of the self (12–13) and Kearney's emphasis on radical hospitality and *kenosis* in *Anatheism: Returning to God After God* (New York: Columbia University Press, 2010).

35. Simon Critchley, "The Original Traumatism: Levinas and Psychoanalysis," in *Critical Ethics: Text, Theory, and Responsibility*, ed. Dominic Rainsford and Tim Woods (New York: Macmillan, 1999), 89.

36. Emmanuel Levinas, *Totality and Infinity: An Essay on Exteriority*, trans. Alphonso Lingis (1961; Pittsburgh: Duquesne University Press, 1969).

37. Norman Ravvin, "Have You Reread Levinas Lately? Transformations of the Face in Post-Holocaust Fiction," in *Ethics in Literature*, ed. Andrew Hadfield, Dominic Rainsford, and Tim Woods (New York: St. Martin's Press, 1999), 52.

38. Emmanuel Levinas, "No Identity," in *Collected Philosophical Papers*, trans. Alphonso Lingis (Dordrecht, The Netherlands: Martinus Nijhoff, 1987), 146.

39. Emmanuel Levinas, "Useless Suffering," in *Entre Nous: Thinking of the Other*, trans. Michael B. Smith and Barbara Harshav (New York: Columbia University Press, 1998), 80.

40. Emmanuel Levinas, *Otherwise Than Being: or, Beyond Essence.* 1974. Trans. Alphonso Lingis (Dordecht, The Netherlands: Kluwer Academic, 1991), 40.

41. Ewa Płonowska Ziarek, *An Ethics of Dissensus: Postmodernity, Feminism, and the Politics of Radical Democracy* (Stanford, CA: Stanford University Press, 2001), 102.

42. Ibid.

43. Erin Lothes Biviano, *The Paradox of Christian Sacrifice: The Loss of Self, The Gift of Self* (New York: Crossroad, 2007), 139.

44. Simone De Beauvoir, *The Second Sex*, trans. H. M. Parshley (1949; New York: Vintage, 1952); Luce Irigaray, "The Fecundity of the Caress: A Reading of Levinas, *Totality and Infinity*, 'Phenomenology of Eros'," in *The Ethics of Sexual Difference*, trans. Carolyn Burke and Gillian C. Gill (1984; Ithaca, NY: Cornell University Press, 1993), 185–217; Tina Chanter, ed., *Feminist Interpretations of Emmanuel Levinas* (University Park: Pennsylvania State University Press, 2001).

45. Levinas, *Otherwise than Being*, 79.

46. Said, "Traveling Theory Reconsidered," in *Reflections on Exile and Other Essays* (Cambridge, MA: Harvard University Press, 2000), 436–52.

47. Harpham, *Shadows of Ethics*, 11.

48. Ravvin, "Have You Reread Levinas Lately?" 55.

49. Adam Zachary Newton, "Versions of Ethics; Or, The SARL of Criticism: Sonority, Arrogation, and Letting-Be," *American Literary History* 13, no. 3 (2001): 604, 606.

50. Adrienne Rich, *Of Woman Born: Motherhood as Experience and Institution*, tenth anniversary ed. (1976; New York: Norton, 1986), 270.

51. For examples of this critique, see Scott Lash, "Postmodern Ethics: The Missing Ground," *Theory, Culture, and Society* 13, no. 2 (1996): 91–104. Lash argues that the ethics propounded by the likes of Levinas "reproduces the shortcomings, especially the abstraction, already present in liberal, high modernist ethics" (92). Terry Eagleton offers a similar critique in *Trouble with Strangers: A Study of Ethics* (Hoboken, NJ: Wiley-Blackwell, 2009), 223–72. To be fair, I should mention that Levinas is cited in several places as claiming that his ethics was practiced in the simple act of opening a door and saying, "After you."

52. Andrew Gibson, *Postmodernity, Ethics, and the Novel: From Leavis to Levinas* (New York: Routledge, 1999), 161–85.

53. Linda Hutcheon, *A Poetics of Postmodernism: History, Theory, Fiction* (New York: Routledge, 1988).

54. Ibid., 53, 125.

55. Ibid., 40.

56. Ibid., 4, 178, 179.

57. Arne Johan Vetlesen, *A Philosophy of Pain*, trans. John Irons (2004; London: Reaktion, 2009).

58. Elaine Scarry, *The Body in Pain: The Making and Unmaking of the World* (New York: Oxford University Press, 1985), 4.

59. Simone Weil, *Waiting for God*, trans. Emma Craufurd (1951; New York: Harper and Row, 1973), 120, 125.

60. Dorothee Sölle, *Suffering*, trans. Everett R. Kalin (Philadelphia: Fortress Press, 1975), 68.

61. Ibid., 69, 71.

62. Ibid., 72.

63. Kristine M. Rankka, *Women and the Value of Suffering: An Aw(e)ful Rowing Toward God* (Collegeville, MN: Liturgical Press, 1998), 19.

64. Sölle, *Suffering*, 35, 38.

65. Sharon Welch, *A Feminist Ethic of Risk* (Minneapolis, MN: Fortress Press, 1990), 40.

66. Matilda Joslyn Gage, *Woman, Church, and State* (1893; Watertown, MA: Persephone Press, 1980), 293.

67. Ibid., 209.

68. Elizabeth Cady Stanton, *The Woman's Bible*, Vol. I–II, foreword by Maureen Fitzgerald (1895; Boston: Northeastern University Press, 1993), 84.

69. Carol Gilligan, *In a Different Voice* (Cambridge, MA: Harvard University Press, 1982). Gilligan's study—now three decades old—is enmeshed in a history of criticism of essentializing tendencies and methodological problems. My purpose here is not to rehash these debates, however, but to acknowledge the strong influence of Gilligan's work on later feminists, especially its place within the discursive tradition of debating women's role as sufferers.

70. Ibid., 73, 87.

71. Ibid., 149.

72. Ibid., 174.

73. Ruth E. Groenhout, *Connected Lives: Human Nature and An Ethics of Care* (Lanham, MD: Rowman and Littlefield, 2004), 80.

74. Ziarek, *An Ethics of Dissensus*, 79–80.

75. Key players in this debate include Nel Noddings, Sarah Ruddick, Nancy Chodorow, and Virginia Held (all of whom present different constructions of an ethics of care). Such an ethics, however, has been questioned by Sandra Lee Bartky, Claudia Card, Marilyn Friedman, Kate Millett, and others. For more on these debates see Hilde Lindemann, *An Invitation to Feminist Ethics* (Boston: McGraw Hill, 2006); Groenhout, *Connected Lives*; Biviano, *The Paradox of Christian Sacrifice*; and Virginia Held, *Feminist Morality: Transforming Culture, Society, and Politics* (Chicago: Chicago University Press, 1993).

76. Stanton, *The Woman's Bible*, 7.

77. Lindemann, *An Invitation to Feminist Ethics*, 96.

78. Joseph Amato, *Victims and Values: A History and Theory of Suffering* (New York: Greenwood, 1990), 83.

79. Charles Taylor, *A Secular Age* (Cambridge, MA: Harvard University Press, 2007), 623.

80. Vetlesen, *A Philosophy of Pain*, 156.

81. Susan Sontag, *Regarding the Pain of Others* (New York: Picador, 2003), 80, 99.

82. Valerie Saiving Goldstein, "The Human Situation: A Feminine View," *Journal of Religion* 40, no. 1 (1960): 100.

83. Ibid., 101.

84. Ibid.

85. Ibid., 108–109.

86. Sölle, *Suffering*, 13.

87. Johann-Baptist Metz, "The Future in the Memory of Suffering," in *Faith and the Future: Essays on Theology, Solidarity, and Modernity*, by Johann-Baptist Metz and Jürgen Moltmann (1972; Maryknoll: Orbis, 1995), 6.

88. Ibid., 11, 8.

89. Ibid., 10.

90. Attridge, *The Singularity of Literature*, 80.

91. Weil, *Waiting for God*, 111.

92. Attridge, *The Singularity of Literature*, 23. Drucilla Cornell finds similar language in both Theodor Adorno's and Luce Irigaray's concepts of *mimesis* as "an ethical relation to otherness" (*Beyond Accommodation: Ethical Feminism, Deconstruction, and the Law*, new ed. [Lanham, MD: Rowman and Littlefield, 1999], 148) and in fact remarks on the gendering of the language. This form of openness, "housewarming," "embrace," Cornell notes, is very difficult to describe in phallic language but rather lends itself to feminine linguistic connotations of receptivity, acceptance, and care. Thus, it is one of many instances of the feminization of postmodern ethics that links it, in certain ways, to feminist care ethics.

93. Weil, *Waiting for God*, 147–48.

94. Adrienne Rich, *Blood, Bread, and Poetry: Selected Prose 1979–1985* (New York: Norton, 1986), 213, 217, 223.

95. Adrienne Rich, "Notes Towards a Politics of Location," in *Feminist Postcolonial Theory: A Reader*, ed. Reina Lewis and Sara Mills (1984; New York: Routledge, 2003), 31.

96. Paul Ricoeur, *Time and Narrative* (Chicago, University of Chicago Press, 1984), 71.

97. Martha C. Nussbaum, *The Fragility of Goodness: Luck and Ethics in Greek Tragedy and Philosophy* (Cambridge: Cambridge University Press, 1986), 170–71.

98. Roxanne Harde, "Making of Our Lives a Study: Feminist Theology and Women's Creative Writing," *Feminist Theology* 15, no. 1 (2006): 55.

99. Ibid., 59, 60, 61.

100. Ibid., 49.

101. Ibid., 59.

102. Cornell, *Beyond Accommodation*, 132.

103. Miller, *The Ethics of Reading*, 50, 56.

104. Caughie, *Passing and Pedagogy*, 140.

105. Attridge, *The Singularity of Literature*, 118–19.

106. W. J. T. Mitchell, "Representation," in *Critical Terms for Literary Study*, 2nd ed., ed. Frank Lentricchia and Thomas McLaughlin (Chicago: University of Chicago Press, 1995), 11.

107. Ella Shohat, "The Struggle Over Representation: Casting, Coalitions, and the Politics of Identification," in *Late Imperial Culture,* ed. Román de la Campa, E. Ann Kaplan, and Michael Sprinker (London: Verso, 1995), 166.

108. Gayatri Spivak, "Can the Subaltern Speak?" in *Marxism and the Interpretation of Culture*, ed. Cary Nelson and Lawrence Grossberg (Urbana: University of Illinois Press, 1988), 275.

109. Gayatri Spivak, "Practical Politics of the Open End," in *The Postcolonial Critic: Interviews, Strategies, Dialogues,* ed. Sarah Harasym (New York: Routledge, 1990), 108.

110. It is not incidental that the first definition of "advocate" listed in the *OED* originates in the Christian Church, as "A person or agent believed to intercede between God and sinners; spec. Christ or the Virgin Mary." The Western grammar of representation—which is perhaps not so far off from sacrifice—is threaded with Christian references.

111. Diana Tietjens Meyers's "Narrative Structures, Narratives of Abuse, and Human Rights," in *Feminist Ethics and Social and Political Philosophy: Theorizing the Non-Ideal,* ed. Lisa Tessman (New York: Springer, 2009), 253–70, provides just one example of recent work in feminist narrative ethics that considers the role formal expectations play in how victims tell—and witnesses hear—their stories of suffering.

112. My comparison here, while helpful for explaining my use of "representation," is fraught, in part because one of the functions of the literary texts I read in this project is to disrupt the prevailing formal expectations of legal cases. As I have noted earlier in this chapter, the relation of suffering to language, and the question of whether existing language can ever adequately "represent" suffering, parallels the concern of many feminist legal scholars who argue that prevailing idioms are not sufficient for the representation of women's sufferings within the courtroom.

113. Drucilla Cornell, "What Is Ethical Feminism?" in *Feminist Contentions: A Philosophical Exchange,* ed. Seyla Benhabib, Judith Butler, Drucilla Cornell, and Nancy Fraser (New York: Routledge, 1996), 81.

114. Cornell, *Beyond Accommodation*, xxxii.

115. Ibid., xxv–xxvii.

116. Ibid., 3.

117. Ibid., 131.

2. Adrienne Rich and the "Long Dialogue Between Art and Justice"

1. Adrienne Rich, *Of Woman Born: Motherhood as Experience and Institution*, tenth anniversary ed. (1976; New York: Norton, 1986), n.p. Subsequent citations appear in the text.

2. By "justice" in my discussion of Rich and in my understanding of her use of the term, I mean social justice, that admittedly vague concept of some future egalitarian (even utopian) structure of personal–political relations. Yet as the *Oxford English Dictionary* reminds us, the earliest uses of the adjective "just" in the English language are specifically religious: that which is just is "morally right," "righteous in the sight of God." In the context of secularization, justice is more properly posed as a question than understood as a property: What is the "morally right" act characterized as just? What is "ethical"? Thus, the vocabulary of "justice" recalls Geoffrey Harpham's claim that ethics is about posing questions rather than mandating proper behaviors: "Ethics does not solve problems, it structures them" ("Ethics," in *Critical Terms for Literary Study*, 2nd ed., ed. Frank Lentricchia and Thomas McLaughlin [Chicago: University of Chicago Press, 1995], 404). In keeping with my project of questing after a literary ethics, in this book I understand "justice" as one more signifier the content of which must be worked out in the particulars of language and concrete locations.

3. Cheri Colby Langdell, *Adrienne Rich: The Moment of Change* (Westport, CT: Praeger, 2004), 1.

4. Liz Yorke, *Adrienne Rich: Passion, Politics, and the Body* (London: Sage, 1997), 2.

5. She discusses these experiences in detail in the essay "Teaching Language in Open Admission" (1972), collected in Rich, *On Lies, Secrets, and Silence: Selected Prose 1966–1978* (New York: Norton, 1979), 51–68.

6. Rich narrates her own autobiography more fully in "Split at the Root: An Essay on Jewish Identity" (1982) (in Rich, *Blood, Bread, and Poetry: Selected Prose 1979–1985* [New York: Norton, 1986], 100–12). For critics' overviews of Rich's history, see the introductions to Yorke, *Adrienne Rich*; Craig Werner, *Adrienne Rich: The Poet and Her Critics* (Chicago: American Library Association, 1988); Alice Templeton, *The Dream and the Dialogue: Adrienne Rich's Feminist Poetics* (Knoxville: University of Tennessee Press, 1994); or Claire Keyes, *The Aesthetics of Power: The Poetry of Adrienne Rich* (Athens: University of Georgia Press, 1986).

7. See, for instance, the foreword to Adrienne Rich, *Blood, Bread, and Poetry* (vii–xiv), where Rich explains how "the radical-feminist claim to identify with all women was to undergo severe challenge" (x) in light of black women's objections, rising awareness of "the simultaneity of oppressions" (xii) and other forces within the movement and within the broader culture. She does similar work in the introduction to the tenth-anniversary edition to *Of Woman Born*, ix–xxxv; the

preface to *What Is Found There: Notebooks on Poetry and Politics* (New York: Norton, 1993), xiii–xv; and the foreword to *Arts of the Possible: Essays and Conversations* (New York: Norton, 2001), 1–9.

8. Werner, *Adrienne Rich.*

9. Rich, *On Lies, Secrets, and Silence,* 260.

10. In making this argument, Rich gets at the dynamics working in literary representation, where the "representative" (in this case, herself) both stands for and does not stand for the referent. In writing of her own experience in *Of Woman Born*, Rich does not address the parallel incommensurability of language and reality and the fact that her writings about her experience are not a straightforward presentation of the real but rather a textual construction. This more tenuous understanding of language arises in her later work, however, and it is predicted in her assertion of herself as both representative and not of a "women's reality."

11. I follow Rich in listing composition dates for her poems and essays out of respect for her desire to mark their particular temporal origins.

12. Rich, *Collected Early Poems 1950–1970* (New York: Norton, 1993), 270.

13. Rich, *A Wild Patience Has Taken Me This Far: Poems 1978–1981* (New York: Norton, 1981), 10–15.

14. Rich, *The Dream of a Common Language: Poems 1974–1977* (New York: Norton, 1978), 3.

15. Rich writes of the token woman in her famous essay "When We Dead Awaken: Writing as Re-Vision" (1971), collected in *On Lies, Secrets, and Silence,* 38.

16. The phrase "powerless responsibility" suggests a challenge to Emmanuel Levinas's ethics of infinite responsibility: What of the subject who finds herself "responsible" for an other but without the means to enact that responsibility? What of the subject whose location in the social structure precludes action, choice?

17. Simone Weil, *Waiting for God*, trans. Emma Craufurd (1951; New York: Harper and Row, 1973).

18. As I discuss in chapter 1, Weil's (and Attridge's) writing on *attention* is also implicitly gendered. Rich's recognition and exploitation of this implicit gendering in *Of Woman Born* serves as another proof of its functioning within the symbolic.

19. For more on the critical debates surrounding *Of Woman Born*, particularly the charges of essentialism and biologism, see Yorke's discussion of Elaine Showalter, Hester Einstein, and Diana Fuss (*Adrienne Rich,* 14), and her treatment of Janet Sayer's misreading of Rich as a biological essentialist (65). Doubtless influenced by these earlier readers, Emily Jeremiah also labeled *Of Woman Born* as essentialist in a 2004 publication ("Murderous Mothers: Adrienne Rich's

Of Woman Born and Toni Morrison's *Beloved*," in *From Motherhood to Mothering: The Legacy of Adrienne Rich's* Of Woman Born, ed. Andrea O'Reilly [Albany: SUNY Press, 2004], 60).

20. Templeton, *The Dream and the Dialogue*, 6.

21. Andrea O'Reilly describes this action as "blending, blurring, and bending the conventional oppositions of theory and experience" (*From Motherhood to Mothering: The Legacy of Adrienne Rich's* Of Woman Born [Albany: SUNY Press, 2004], 3), and Krista Ratcliffe notes that Rich "critiques the separation of theory and practice" (*Anglo-American Feminist Challenges to the Rhetorical Traditions: Virginia Woolf, Mary Daly, Adrienne Rich* [Carbondale: Southern Illinois University Press, 1996], 117).

22. Mary Daly, *Beyond God the Father: Toward a Philosophy of Women's Liberation* (Boston: Beacon, 1973).

23. Ibid., 77.

24. Ibid., 101.

25. Ibid., 102.

26. Valerie Saiving Goldstein, "The Human Situation: A Feminine View," *Journal of Religion* 40, no. 1 (1960): 100–12.

27. Ibid., 100.

28. Ibid.

29. Ibid., 101.

30. Ibid., 108.

31. Ibid., 109.

32. Ibid., 111.

33. Rich, *Collected Early Poems*, 15.

34. Ibid., 10, 13, 36.

35. Ibid., 89, 94, 103.

36. Ibid., 75.

37. Rich, *On Lies, Secrets, and Silence*, 30.

38. See, for instance, in *On Lies, Secrets, and Silence*, the implicit negative valuation of churches in "The Antifeminist Woman" (1972, 70–84); the critique of religion (and its association with women and self-sacrifice) in "Jane Eyre: The Temptations of a Motherless Woman" (1975, 89–106); and the assumed religious heterodoxy that Rich admits informs her reading in "Vesuvius at Home: The Power of Emily Dickinson" (1975, 157–83).

39. Rich, *Blood, Bread, and Poetry*, 100–123.

40. Charles Taylor, *A Secular Age* (Cambridge, MA: Harvard University Press, 2007), 494–95, 500–503.

41. Although such a stance has recently been challenged by feminists like Leela Fernandes, who argues in *Transforming Feminist Practice: Non-Violence, Social Justice*

and the Possibilities of a Spiritualized Feminism (San Francisco: Aunt Lute Books, 2003)
for a reappraisal of the importance of spirituality within activist movements (10).

42. Daly, *Beyond God the Father*, 18, 155.

43. Rosemary Radford Ruether, *Sexism and God-Talk* (Boston: Beacon, 1983); Elisabeth
Schüssler Fiorenza, *In Memory of Her: A Feminist Theological Reconstruction of
Christian Origins* (New York: Crossroads, 1984); Elizabeth Johnson, *She Who Is:
The Mystery of God in Feminist Theological Discourse* (New York: Crossroad, 1994).

44. Heather Walton, *Literature, Theology, and Feminism* (Manchester: Manchester
University Press, 2007), 45–48.

45. Carol Christ, *Diving Deep and Surfacing: Women Writers on Spiritual Quest* (Boston:
Beacon, 1980), 1.

46. Roxanne Harde, "Making of Our Lives a Study: Feminist Theology and
Women's Creative Writing," *Feminist Theology* 15, no. 1 (2006): 48–69.

47. Alison Jasper, "'The Past Is Not a Husk Yet Change Goes On': Reimagining
(Feminist) Theology," *Feminist Theology* 15, no. 2 (2007): 204.

48. Rich, *On Lies, Secrets, and Silence*, 35.

49. Rich, *Blood, Bread, and Poetry*, 100–123.

50. Rich, *Arts of the Possible*, 144.

51. Rich, *Blood, Bread, and Poetry*, 159.

52. Ibid., 194.

53. Nick Halpern, *Everyday and Prophetic: The Poetry of Lowell, Ammons, Merrill, and
Rich* (Madison: University of Wisconsin Press, 2003), 228.

54. Daly's commitment to her position is vividly exemplified by her famous
failure to reply to Audre Lorde's "Open Letter to Mary Daly," in which Lorde
questioned Daly's assertion of global oppression in *Gyn/Ecology: The Metaethics
of Radical Feminism* (1978; Boston: Beacon, 1990) and her failure to mention the
agency and survival of African women. Daly's silence in response to Lorde's
critique caused this exchange (or lack thereof) to symbolize, even decades later,
the tension between early, implicitly white, radical feminism and the concerns
of feminists of color.

55. Daly, *Beyond God the Father*, 8.

56. This claim complicates Rich's argument in a way that critics have not always
appreciated, for it refuses a clear division between insidious "institution" and
pure "experience": within the institution of male dominance, even the experience
of motherhood is colored by institutional norms and available language. In
making this assertion, Rich forwards an argument notably similar to Jacques
Lacan's concept of the Symbolic or Louis Althusser's of interpellation, both of
which rely on language as a structuring force for subjectivity.

57. Rich, *Collected Early Poems*, 363–66.

58. Rich, *On Lies, Secrets, and Silence*, 63.

59. Ibid.

60. Ibid., 67.

61. Ibid.

62. Kaja Silverman, *The Subject of Semiotics* (Oxford: Oxford University Press, 1984).

63. Rich, *Of Woman Born,* 249.

64. Rich, *On Lies, Secrets, and Silence,* 245.

65. Rich, *A Wild Patience Has Taken Me This Far,* 3–5.

66. Rich, *The Fact of a Doorframe: Poems Selected and New 1950–1984* (New York: Norton, 1984), 324–28.

67. Lisa K. Perdigao, "'The Words I'd Found': The Poetics of Recovery in Adrienne Rich's Poetry," in *"Catch if you can your country's moment": Recovery and Regeneration in the Poetry of Adrienne Rich,* ed. William S. Waddell (Newcastle, England: Cambridge Scholars, 2007), 144–45.

68. Alex Blazer, *I Am Otherwise: The Romance Between Poetry and Theory After the Death of the Subject* (Champaign: Dalkey Archive Press, 2007), 38.

69. Yorke, *Adrienne Rich,* 15, 46–47, 67, 103.

70. Rich, *On Lies, Secrets, and Silence,* 247.

71. Rich, *What Is Found There,* 234.

72. Again, in using this term I invoke the feminist claim that the personal is political; structures of relating map onto social structures, and Rich's concern has insistently been to highlight the way personal domestic relations (figured as ethics) are intertwined with structural justice.

73. Robert Boyers, "On Adrienne Rich: Intelligence and Will," in *Adrienne Rich's Poetry,* ed. Barbara Charlesworth Gelpi and Albert Gelpi (New York: Norton, 1975), 156.

74. Helen Vendler, "Ghostlier Demarcations, Keener Sounds," in *Adrienne Rich's Poetry,* ed. Barbara Charlesworth Gelpi and Albert Gelpi (New York: Norton, 1975), 165.

75. Keyes, *The Aesthetics of Power,* 181.

76. Ibid., 182.

77. Rich, *Blood, Bread, and Poetry,* 173.

78. Ibid., 179.

79. Ibid., 182. The phrase "pushing at the limits of experience reflected in literature" seems to place Rich on the side of expressivist, mimetic understandings of literature, but her emphasis on language elsewhere mediates against such a straightforward reading of "reflection" in this phrase. Rich's commitment to widening the scope of representation in poetry (her ethics of literary representation) was not just a commitment to using neutral words to refer to women's experiences, but resignifying language to "push the limits" of referentiality itself.

80. Ibid., 184.

81. Kathleen Barry, "Reviewing Reviews: *Of Woman Born,*" in *Reading Adrienne Rich: Reviews and Re-Visions 1951–81,* ed. Jane Roberta Cooper, 300–3. (1977; Ann Arbor: University of Michigan Press, 1984), 302.

82. Gretchen Mieszkowski, " 'By a Miracle, a Twin': Helen Vendler's Reviews of Adrienne Rich's Recent Poetry," *South Central Review* 5, no. 2 (1988): 72–86.

83. Werner, *Adrienne Rich,* 5.

84. Alice Templeton, "Contradictions: Tracking Adrienne Rich's Poetry," *Tulsa Studies in Women's Literature* 12, no. 2 (1993): 335.

85. Susan Sheridan, "Adrienne Rich and the Women's Liberation Movement: A Politics of Reception," *Women's Studies* 35 (2006): 19.

86. Ibid., 28–29.

87. Rich, *A Human Eye: Essays on Art in Society, 1997–2008* (New York: Norton, 2009), 93.

88. Rich, *Arts of the Possible,* 117–18.

89. Rich, *Blood, Bread, and Poetry,* 88.

90. Ibid., 214.

91. Rich, *Time's Power* (New York: Norton, 1989), 45.

92. Yorke, *Adrienne Rich,* 11; Werner, *Adrienne Rich,* 12.

93. Yorke, *Adrienne Rich,* 52.

94. Werner, *Adrienne Rich,* 122.

95. Ibid., 125.

96. Ibid., 126.

97. Ibid., 127.

98. Ibid.

99. Elizabeth Hirsch, "Another Look at Genre: *Diving into the Wreck* of Ethics with Rich and Irigaray," in *Feminist Measures: Soundings in Poetry and Theory,* ed. Lynne Keller and Christanne Miller (Ann Arbor: University of Michigan Press, 1994), 122.

100. Ibid.

101. Miriam Marty Clark, "Human Rights and the Work of Lyric in Adrienne Rich," *Cambridge Quarterly* 38, no. 1 (2009): 52, 57.

102. Ibid., 59.

103. Perdigao, "The Words I'd Found," 142.

104. As I note in chapter 1, however, many poststructuralist thinkers have defended themselves against accusations that their emphasis on language in practices like deconstruction led away from ethical or political engagement in the material world. For instance, see Derrida's interviews collected in Richard Kearney and Mark Dooley's volume *Questioning Ethics: Contemporary Debates in Philosophy* (London: Routledge, 1999); or consider Judith Butler's title *Bodies That Matter: On the Discursive Limits of "Sex"* (New York: Routledge, 1993).

105. Walton, *Literature, Theology, and Feminism*, 2.

106. Rich, *The Dream of a Common Language*, 10–11.

107. Werner, *Adrienne Rich*, 37.

108. Rich, *Arts of the Possible*, 1, 3.

109. Rich, *Your Native Land, Your Life* (New York: Norton, 1986), 111.

110. Drucilla Cornell, *Beyond Accommodation: Ethical Feminism, Deconstruction, and the Law*, new ed. (Lanham, MD: Rowman and Littlefield, 1999); Ewa Płonowska Ziarek, *An Ethics of Dissensus: Postmodernity, Feminism, and the Politics of Radical Democracy* (Stanford, CA: Stanford University Press, 2001).

111. A reader familiar with the topics of women's suffering and self-sacrifice, ethics, writing, and activism may very well wonder why Kristeva and Irigaray (and Cixous) have not played a larger role in this chapter. I simply couldn't fit them in, but numerous critics have noted the similarities. Especially interesting is Hirsch's essay "Another Look at Genre: *Diving into the Wreck* of Ethics with Rich and Irigaray," which examines parallels between Rich and Irigaray relating to the interworkings of gender, genre, ethics, and embodiment. Although it doesn't treat Rich extensively, Walton's book *Literature, Theology, and Feminism* offers one chapter each on Kristeva, Irigaray, and Cixous exploring their importance in discussions of literature, feminist ethics, and theology.

112. Rich, *Collected Early Poems*, 205.

3. Love and Mercy

1. Thanks to Amy Hollywood for reminding me that this material reading of *Beloved* is important to maintain as a possibility—and all the more terrible to think of in light of the novel's later exorcism scene that then would seem to perpetuate the systemic violence against a vulnerable black woman.

2. I hesitate to name Stanley Crouch simply because doing so further amplifies his role in discussions of Morrison's writing, But the notorious review in which he argues that *Beloved* is "a blackface holocaust novel" that "seems to have been written in order to enter American slavery into the big-time martyr ratings contest" is worth mentioning because Crouch seems to suspect any literary representation of black female suffering as emotionally manipulative and dangerously reliant on a vision of redemptive suffering whereby the sufferer possesses a moral superiority ("Aunt *Medea*," *New Republic*, 19 Oct. 1987, 40). For more on these dynamics in response to Crouch, see Lars Eckstein, *Re-Membering the Black Atlantic On the Poetics and Politics of Literary Memory* (Amsterdam: Editions Rodopi B.V., 2006), 224–28; Carl Plasa, ed., *Toni Morrison, Beloved* (New York: Columbia University Press, 1998), 25–31; Shirley Samuels, *The Culture of Sentiment: Race, Gender, and Sentimentality in Nineteenth-Century America* (New York: Oxford University Press, 1992), 334, note 39; and

Rebecca Wanzo, *The Suffering Will Not Be Televised: African American Women and Sentimental Political Storytelling*. (Albany: SUNY Press, 2009), 94–98.

3. I recognize the awkwardness of the parenthetical modifiers here but find that they stand in for an important ambivalence: while we may generalize "suffering" and even take black women's experiences as more broadly representative of a human condition, such generalizing also must be attended by the lesson of particularity. Black women's stories both do and do not represent the wider scope of human experience, just as white men's or women's stories both do and do not represent human experience.

4. Barbara Christian, "The Race for Theory," *Cultural Critique* 6 (1987): 51.

5. Ibid., 52.

6. Ibid., 55, 57.

7. Lawrence Buell, "Introduction. In Pursuit of Ethics," *PMLA* 114, no. 1 (1999): 8.

8. Christian, "The Race for Theory," 61.

9. Cherríe Moraga and Gloria Anzaldúa, eds., *This Bridge Called My Back: Writings by Radical Women of Color*, 2nd ed. (1981; Lanham, NY: Kitchen Table Press, 1983); Gloria T. Hull, Patricia Bell Scott, and Barbara Smith, eds., *All the Women Are White, All the Blacks Are Men, But Some of Us Are Brave: Black Women's Studies* (Old Westbury, NY: The Feminist Press, 1982).

10. Combahee River Collective, "A Black Feminist Statement," 13.

11. Hull, Scott, and Smith, *All the Women*, xviii.

12. Ibid., xix.

13. Barbara Smith, "Toward a Black Feminist Criticism," in *All the Women Are White, All the Blacks Are Men, But Some of Us Are Brave: Black Women's Studies*, ed. Gloria T. Hull, Patricia Bell Scott, and Barbara Smith (1978; Old Westbury, NY: Feminist Press, 1982), 157–75.

14. Farah Jasmine Griffin, "That the Mothers May Soar and the Daughters May Know Their Names: A Retrospective of Black Feminist Literary Criticism," *Signs* 32, no. 2 (2007): 491.

15. The question of whose suffering receives attention continues to be an important question, as Wanzo's *The Suffering Will Not Be Televised* exemplifies. Certain "stories about suffering bodies" (3), she argues, align with popularly accepted conventions and thus are published or publicized—typically stories that don't make listeners too uncomfortable or stories that support prominent political ideologies (10).

16. Toni Morrison, "The Site of Memory," in *Inventing the Truth: The Art and Craft of Memoir*, ed. William Zinsser (Boston: Houghton Mifflin, 1987), 106.

17. Ibid., 113.

18. Christian, "The Race for Theory," 54.

19. Marc C. Connor, "Introduction: Aesthetics and the African American Novel," in *The Aesthetics of Toni Morrison: Speaking the Unspeakable*, ed. Marc C. Connor

(Jackson: University Press of Mississippi, 2000), x; Wanzo, *The Suffering Will Not Be Televised*, 109.

20. Nellie McKay, "An Interview with Toni Morrison," in *Conversations with Toni Morrison,* ed. Danielle Taylor-Guthrie (1983; University Press of Mississippi, 1994), 151.

21. Ben Naparstek, "Mercy in a Time of Slavery: An Interview," *Sydney Morning Herald*, 22 November 2008), n.p.

22. Morrison, "Nobel Lecture, 7 December 1993," *The Georgia Review* 49, no. 1 (1995): 318–23. Subsequent citations appear in the text.

23. See Mar Gallego, "Love and the Survival of the Black Community," in *The Cambridge Companion to Toni Morrison*, ed. Justine Tally (Cambridge: Cambridge University Press, 2007), 92–100; and Anissa Janine Wardi, "A Laying on of Hands: Toni Morrison and the Materiality of *Love*," *MELUS* 30, no. 3 (2005): 201–18.

24. Morrison, *Love* (New York: Knopf, 2003), 3. Subsequent citations appear in the text. The segments of L's narration are italicized in the text, marking them out as differently voiced (we eventually discover that L is humming/speaking from beyond the grave—the relation of the musical nonverbal/verbal is a mysterious and unexplained phenomenon). This mystery serves as one more reminder that "literary representation" is never just a reflection of any straightforward reality.

25. Morrison herself has admitted in several interviews that while she ultimately decided to name L "Love" and to give the book this name, the attention to love is inseparable from attention to language, an effect she heightened by going back through the manuscript and removing the word "love" itself so that when it finally comes at the end, it has a powerful effect (Michael Silverblatt, "Michael Silverblatt Talks with Toni Morrison About Love," in *Toni Morrison: Conversations,* ed. Carolyn C. Denard [Jackson: University Press of Mississippi, 2008], 214).

26. The fact that Romen doesn't know the girl's name—the indeterminacy of the word within the text—links his lack of attention to the verbal particularity of her self-representation to his near-participation in a profoundly unethical act. It may thus imply a connection between ethical choices and practices of attention.

27. It also highlights their wrongful sense of responsibility for someone else's behavior, suggesting that "responsibility," championed in postmodern ethics, can be a damaging burden, especially in situations structured by power differentials like the one between a well-respected middle-age man and two young girls. This challenge to the valorization of responsibility parallels Rich's concern over "powerless responsibility," that condition of socially mandated responsibility without the means to enact the responsible behavior.

28. Susana Vega-González, "Toni Morrison's Water World: Watertime Writing in *Love*," *The Grove* 11 (2004): 217.

29. Heed and Christine's use of "idigay" to tell secrets is another textual feature that highlights language: they create the language as an act of resistance and private communication, but when Christine uses the language to hurt Heed (or at least to express her own frustration), she widens the rift in their friendship.

30. According to L, Police-heads are the Up Beach community's explanation for natural disasters that occur to punish "loose women" and "disobedient children" (5). They are "dirty things with big hats who shoot up out of the ocean," and Sweeney connects them to the wide-hatted schoolteacher in *Beloved* (Megan Sweeney, "'Something Rogue': Commensurability, Commodification, Crime, and Justice in Toni Morrison's Later Fiction," *MFS Modern Fiction Studies* 52, no. 2 [2006]: 467).

31. This scene is also reminiscent of the "exorcism" scene near the end of *Beloved* in which the town's women gather and raise their voices in a shared, musical sound, "wide enough to sound deep water and knock the pods off chestnut trees" (261). Their sound, too, has powerful effects and interrogates the power of certain kinds of language. Karen Baker-Fletcher names a longer tradition of black women's linguistic sound when she cites the important nineteenth- and early twentieth-century figure Anna Julia Cooper's description of "the initial vocalization among Black women as being 'with no language but a cry'" of elemental pain and longing ("'Soprano Obligato': The Voices of Black Women and American Conflict in the thought of Anna Julia Cooper," in *A Troubling in My Soul,* ed. Emilie Townes [Maryknoll: Orbis, 1993], 177).

32. As Connor notes, Morrison's concerns about "dead" or oppressive language in her Nobel speech could be read as problematically restrictive, conflicting with the commitment she voices elsewhere to resist censorship and promote freedom of speech ("Introduction: Aesthetics," xxi). This tension calls to mind a similar underlying problematic whereby postmodern ethics—often described as groundless and understood in the matrix of relativism—assumes an ethically positive value for difference and limitless responsibility: we still assume good and bad.

33. Ernesto Javier Martínez argues that Judith Butler's interpretation of this speech in *Excitable Speech* is a gross misreading and exemplifies a propensity among poststructuralist theorists to use writers of color for their own purposes. I would agree with Martínez's claim that Morrison does not seem to join Butler in a radically indeterminate, nonreferential view of language, but Morrison does assert in her speech and thematize in her fiction the slipperiness of referents and difficulties of interpretation. See Martínez, "On Butler on Morrison on Language," *Signs* 35, no. 4 (2010): 821–42.

34. Geoffrey Galt Harpham, "Ethics," in *Critical Terms for Literary Study,* 2nd ed., ed. Frank Lentricchia and Thomas McLaughlin (Chicago: University of Chicago Press, 1995), 390.

35. Morrison, "Rootedness: The Ancestor as Foundation," in *Black Women Writers (1950–1980): A Critical Evaluation*, ed. Mari Evans (Garden City, NY: Anchor Press/ Doubleday, 1983), 341.
36. Morrison, "Unspeakable Things Unspoken: The Afro-American Presence in American Literature," *Michigan Quarterly Review* 28, no. 1 (1989): 29.
37. Many critics simply assume one way or the other, and their disagreement highlights the ambiguity. Wen-ching Ho, for instance, asserts that L found the 1958 will ("'I'll Tell'—The Function and Meaning of L in Toni Morrison's *Love*," *EurAmerica* 36, no. 4 [2006]: 659), whereas Sweeny asserts that L wrote the 1958 will herself in 1971 ("Something Rogue," 458).
38. Vega-González, "Toni Morrison's Water World," 217.
39. This quotation is actually B. C. Hutcheon's paraphrase of the subject's assumed mastery Emmanuel Levinas wishes to disrupt (*Levinas: A Guide for the Perplexed* [New York: Continuum, 2004], 14).
40. Morrison, "Nobel Lecture," 320.
41. Ewa Płonowska Ziarek, *An Ethics of Dissensus: Postmodernity, Feminism, and the Politics of Radical Democracy* (Stanford, CA: Stanford University Press, 2001), 1.
42. Emilie Townes, *In a Blaze of Glory: Womanist Spirituality as Social Witness.* (Nashville: Abingdon Press, 1995), 49.
43. Andrea O'Reilly, ed., *Toni Morrison and Motherhood: A Politics of the Heart* (Albany: SUNY Press, 2004), 45.
44. John A. McClure, *Partial Faiths: Postsecular Fiction in the Age of Pynchon and Morrison* (Athens: University of Georgia Press, 2007), 107.
45. Dwight N. Hopkins, *Heart and Head: Black Theology—Past, Present, and Future* (New York: Palgrave, 2002), 7.
46. As Hopkins points out, James Hal Cone published his early works of black liberation theology at the same time Gustavo Gutíerrez was publishing his own *A Theology of Liberation: History, Politics, and Salvation* (1971; Maryknoll: Orbis, 1973). Cone has served as professor at Union Theological Seminary for decades. His important early books include *Black Theology and Black Power* (New York: Harper & Row, 1969), *A Black Theology of Liberation* (1970; Maryknoll: Orbis, 1986), *The Spirituals and the Blues: An Interpretation* (1972; Maryknoll: Orbis, 1991), and *God of the Oppressed* (1975; Maryknoll: Orbis, 1997).
47. Cone, *God of the Oppressed*, 287.
48. Ibid., 288–291.
49. Ibid., 293. In other words, passivity, or openness to outside influences and feelings, is tied to (even causes) passion, devoted commitment to a cause. Experiences of suffering do not necessitate political passivity or inactivity. Which is to say, within black theology (and other models of redemptive suffering), an acceptance and resignification of suffering is not the same as passive acquiescence.
50. Ibid., 295.

51. Martin Luther King, Jr., "Suffering and Faith," *Christian Century* 77 (April 27, 1960), reprinted in *Moral Evil and Redemptive Suffering: A History of Theodicy in African-American Religious Thought*, ed. Anthony B. Pinn (Gainesville: University Press of Florida, 2002), 225.

52. This position is structurally similar to Mary Daly's assertion that women's experience of oppression gives them the unique capacity to stare down nonbeing and thus is an important existential contribution to modern life.

53. Anthony B. Pinn, ed., *Moral Evil and Redemptive Suffering: A History of Theodicy in African-American Religious Thought* (Gainesville: University Press of Florida, 2002), 8.

54. Phillis Wheatley, "On Being Brought from Africa to America," in *The Norton Anthology of American Literature*, shorter 5th ed., ed. Nina Baym (New York: Norton, 1999), 360. Wheatley's use of "mercy" highlights its significance in Christian teaching: whereas the "benighted soul" deserves punishment or divine justice, God's mercy subverts that generalized fairness through the individual application of grace. The Christian tradition is shaped by a tension between this understanding of justice and mercy and the more prophetic call for God's justice to right structural social wrongs, specifically the oppression of vulnerable peoples. In other words, justice is both something to fear and something to call out for.

55. This perspective has frustrated many; one notable example is Alice Walker's notorious disappointment in Wheatley expressed in *In Search of Our Mothers' Gardens: Womanist Prose* (Orlando, FL: Harcourt, 1983).

56. Jacquelyn Grant, "Black Women and the Church," in *All the Women Are White, All the Blacks Are Men, But Some of Us Are Brave: Black Women's Studies*, ed. Gloria T. Hull, Patricia Bell Scott, and Barbara Smith (Old Westbury, NY: Feminist Press, 1982), 148.

57. Delores S. Williams, *Sisters in the Wilderness: The Challenge of Womanist God-Talk*. (Maryknoll: Orbis, 1993), 153.

58. Indeed, Williams rejects redemptive suffering paradigms, arguing that the way a community "image[s] redemption" (*Sisters in the Wilderness*, 161) can have dangerous effects. Because the image of the cross gives rise to an interpretation of Jesus as the "ultimate surrogate figure" (162), surrogacy "takes on an aura of the sacred" (162) and therefore can be insidiously glorified, leading to an oppressive glorification of black women's surrogacy and the suffering it causes. As an alternative, Williams advocates a reimagined story of Jesus's life that emphasizes his resistance to sin (and conquering of it) in life, in his wilderness testing and ministry, rather than in death—or activity rather than passivity. Although I seek in this book to avoid a wholesale rejection of the

nuanced (and undeniably risky) possibilities of passivity and even suffering, Williams offers an indispensible reminder of the risks.

59. M. Shawn Copeland, "'Wading Through Many Sorrows': Toward a Theology of Suffering in Womanist Perspective," in *A Troubling in My Soul: Womanist Perspectives on Evil and Suffering*, ed. Emilie M. Townes (Maryknoll: Orbis, 1993), 109.

60. Ibid., 122.

61. Ibid., 119.

62. Womanists not only take on black theologians for failing to attend to the specific experiences of black women, they also offer a body of scholarship devoted to the question of black women's suffering and its particular status in the community. Frances E. Wood, for instance, names the problematic "idealization and romanticization of Black women's suffering" as an "insidious habit in the African-American community" ("'Take My Yoke Upon You': The Role of the Church in the Oppression of African-American Women," in *A Troubling in My Soul: Womanist Perspectives on Evil and Suffering,* ed. Emilie M. Townes [Maryknoll: Orbis, 1993], 39).

63. Layli Phillips, ed., *The Womanist Reader* (New York: Routledge, 2006), xx.

64. Ibid., xx–xxi. For a concise introduction to the contestations of womanism (and an exemplary appeal to *Beloved*), see the 1989 roundtable discussion between Cheryl J. Sanders, Katie G. Cannon, Emilie M. Townes, M. Shawn Copeland, bell hooks, and Cheryl Townsend Gilkes ["Roundtable Discussion: Christian Ethics and Theology in Womanist Perspective," in *The Womanist Reader*, ed. Layli Phillips (1989; New York: Routledge, 2006), 126–57].

65. "Womanism" apart from Walker's also has been developed by Chikwenye Okonjo Ogunyemi and Clenora Hudson-Weems, but they have not been as central to the literary and theological developments of womanism that I address here.

66. Katie Geneva Cannon, in *Black Womanist Ethics* (Atlanta: Scholars Press, 1988), for instance, highlights the specificity of black women's experiences, especially under slavery and its aftermath, that led to an alternative system of ethics.

67. For a reading of *Paradise*, see the third chapter of John A. McClure, *Partial Faiths: Postsecular Fiction in the Age of Pynchon and Morrison* (Athens: University of Georgia Press), 2007, 100–30. His introduction is also a helpful resource exploring the formal and thematic characteristics of postmodern/postsecular fiction.

68. For one close reading that demonstrates Morrison's biblical engagement and her specifically raced and gendered revisions of Christ, consult Carolyn A. Mitchell, "'I Love to Tell the Story': Biblical Revisions in *Beloved*," *Religion and Literature* (Autumn 1991): 27–42, which explicates the novel's numerous associations between characters and Christ, particularly Christ's suffering and redemptive work.

69. Phillips, *The Womanist Reader*, xxxii, xxxi.

70. Ibid., xxxi.

71. As Linda Hutcheon argues in *A Poetics of Postmodernism: History, Theory, Fiction* (New York: Routledge, 1988), while postmodern theory (at least as of 1988) often ignores women and African Americans, their "explorations of narrative and linguistic form have been among the most contesting and radical" (16). Hutcheon's claim that theory and practice are not so easily separable as many of the debates would seem to indicate informs my discussion here and my reading of Morrison's literary ethics.

72. On womanist disruption of binaries, see Cheryl A. Kirk-Duggan, "African-American Spirituals: Confronting and Exorcising Evil Through Song," in *A Troubling in My Soul: Womanist Perspectives on Evil and Suffering*, ed. Emilie M. Townes (Maryknoll: Orbis, 1993), 156; Cannon, *Black Womanist Ethics*, 104, 109; and Townes, *In a Blaze of Glory*, 48.

73. Townes, *Womanist Ethics and the Cultural Production of Evil* (New York: Palgrave Macmillan, 2006), 4.

74. Ibid., 5.

75. Townes, *In a Blaze of Glory*, 47.

76. Ibid., 54.

77. Ibid., 50, 65.

78. Morrison, *A Mercy* (New York: Knopf, 2008), 3. Subsequent citations appear in the text.

79. Already, *A Mercy* suggests an allegory of reading: First, in its disruption of expectation that "reading" is a solely linguistic or immaterial practice (reminiscent of Adrienne Rich's implicit deconstruction of the binary between material and symbolic). Second, in its narrator's admission that even those skilled in reading should admit that they are "missing much," that the practice of reading requires keen attention and an awareness that the text's otherness escapes the best attempts to sum up its meaning in a conclusive reading.

80. As an embodied ghost, Beloved confronts readers as a concretization of the sufferings of the Middle Passage and slave-mothering. Florens, on the other hand, as an embodied woman-slave writing her sufferings, is impossible within her context and can be understood only by its other occupants as a ghost. We might read this image of Florens as a direct response to Audre Lorde's claim about the master's tools and house: can Florens dismantle his house through language? Is the house simply the wooden structure? If so, she can take it down with fire. Is his house the community of its inhabitants? If so, it seems their various sufferings have already dismantled it. Is Florens's use of the master's language to voice her own suffering—or literally to write it—a means of dismantling the master's house in the eyes of the readers? Or is her project

more properly a resignification than a dismantling, as she literally uses the house as her paper, covering it in her own meanings? Rather than giving an answer to Lorde's question, Morrison's novel provides a challenging narrative and haunting image to engage readers in puzzling through it.

81. By this reading, the destruction of the priest-school-master's language and the dead-slave-master's house are inextricable.

82. This example of chosen wounding reminds us that even suffering that is chosen for the sake of some ultimate good can be necessitated by oppression rather than fully and freely elected.

83. Rebecca's feminist critique of the Job theodicy is structurally similar to feminist critiques of postmodern sacrificial ethics, which ask a similar question: What good does it do to tell someone who is already expected to substitute her own suffering for the suffering of the other that this act is an ethical ideal? What comfort does it offer, Rebecca similarly asks, to tell a woman that she is nothing when this is already a common message to her? It also parallels Cannon's critique of "dominant [white] ethics," which assumes that

> one is free to choose whether or not she/he wants to suffer and make sacrifices as a principle of action or as a voluntary vocational pledge of crossbearing. In dominant ethics a person is free to make suffering a desirable moral norm. This is not so for Blacks. For the masses of Black people, suffering is the normal state of affairs. (*Black Womanist Ethics* 2–3)

84. This pained insistence is reminiscent of Sethe's ethical dilemma in *Beloved*: in the horrifically vulnerable situation of slavery, mothers are without reasonable options for caring for their own children. The choices that they make to do so may seem like an abdication of ethical responsibility and even render them guilty within dominant ethical paradigms (and readers' estimations), but the structure itself, its powerless responsibility, is ultimately responsible for their terrible ethical choices.

4. Ana Castillo, Mexican M.O.M.A.S., and a Hermeneutic of Liberation

1. Ana Castillo, *So Far from God* (New York: Norton, 1993), 242. Subsequent citations appear in the text.

2. An important note on terminology: the terms "Chicana," "Latina," and "Hispanic" are widely contested, and they carry different meanings for different writers at different points in time. By "Latina" I mean the broad category of women of Latin American origin or descent; by "Chicana" I mean women of specifically Mexican descent in North America (the term originated as a slur but has since been reappropriated by Castillo and many others). Castillo does

not prefer the term "Hispanic" to describe Chicanas, as it elides the indigenous heritage of a mixed people, and I follow her usage.

3. For more on the transgression of these boundaries, especially the parallels between liberation movements like third-world feminism and postmodern theory, see Chela Sandoval, *Methodology of the Oppressed* (Minneapolis: University of Minnesota Press, 2000). Gloria Anzaldúa also has been widely discussed in these terms.

4. Castillo joined Cherríe Moraga in translating *This Bridge Called My Back: Writings by Radical Women of Color*, 2nd ed. (1981; Lanham, NY: Kitchen Table Press, 1983) into a Spanish edition published in 1987.

5. Moraga, "Preface," in *This Bridge Called My Back*, xvi.

6. Anzaldúa, "Foreword" in *This Bridge Called My Back*, n.p.

7. Moraga, "Preface," in *This Bridge Called My Back*, xix.

8. Ibid., xv.

9. Ibid. In offering this image, Moraga employs the body as metaphor for language, as her work of "bridging" at the conference is ostensibly a verbal one, a work of conversation and explanation. Moraga thus participates with Adrienne Rich and Toni Morrison in poetically challenging a division of symbolic and material.

10. It may be significant that this self-sacrifice is not particularly gendered: it's not a nursing, or a birth-giving, or some other mother work.

11. Of course, another musical intertext is the song "Bridge Over Troubled Water" (1970), in which the poetic persona promises a friend in need, "Like a bridge over troubled water / I will lay me down."

12. Moraga, "Preface," in *This Bridge Called My Back*, xix.

13. Ibid., xviii.

14. Ibid., xvii; Mirtha Quintanales, "I Paid Very Hard for My Immigrant Ignorance," in *This Bridge Called My Back*, 156.

15. María Pilar Aquino, Daisy L. Machado, and Jeanette Rodríguez, eds., *A Reader in Latina Feminist Theology: Religion and Justice* (Austin: University of Texas Press, 2002), xiii.

16. Ibid., xv, xviii.

17. These three were not the first Chicana feminists, but the popularity of their writings in the eighties and nineties gives rise to a certain understanding of their importance in history.

18. Bryce Milligan, "An Interview with Ana Castillo," *South Central Review* 16, no. 1 (1999): 23.

19. For examples of Latina/Chicana scholars turning to black/womanist precedent, see Aquino, "Latina Feminist Theology: Central Features," in *A Reader in Latina Feminist Theology: Religion and Justice*, ed. María Pilar Aquino, Daisy L. Machado, and Jeanette Rodríguez (Austin: University of Texas Press, 2002), 135; Emma Pérez, "Sexuality and Discourse: Notes from a Chicana Survivor,"

in *Chicana Critical Issues,* ed. Norma Alarcón, Rafaela Castro, Emma Pérez, Beatríz Pesquera, Adaljiza Sosa Riddell, and Patricia Zavella (Berkeley, CA: Third Woman Press, 1993), 60; Beatríz M. Pesquera and Denise A. Segura, "There Is No Going Back: Chicanas and Feminism," in *Chicana Critical Issues,* ed. Norma Alarcón, Rafaela Castro, Emma Pérez, Beatríz Pesquera, Adaljiza Sosa Riddell, and Patricia Zavella (Berkeley, CA: Third Woman Press, 1993), 105; Laura Gillman and Stacy M. Floyd-Thomas, "Con un pie a cada lado / With a Foot in Each Place: Mestizaje as Transnational Feminisms in Ana Castillo's *So Far from God,*" *Meridians: Feminism, Race, Transnationalism* 2, no. 1 (2001): 159–60; and Carmela Delia Lanza, "Hearing the Voices: Women and Home and Ana Castillo's *So Far from God,*" *MELUS* 23, no. 1 (1998): 65. Note also the number of womanist texts listed in the works cited of Ada María Isasi-Díaz, *En la Lucha/In the Struggle: A Hispanic Women's Liberation Theology* (Minneapolis, MN: Fortress Press, 1993).

20. Castillo, *Massacre of the Dreamers: Essays on Xicanisma* (New York: Plume, 1994), 90.

21. Anzaldúa, *Borderlands/La Frontera: The New Mestiza,* 2nd ed. (1987; San Francisco: Aunt Lute Books, 1999), 39.

22. Tey Diana Rebolledo, *Women Singing in the Snow: A Cultural Analysis of Chicana Literature* (Tucson: University of Arizona Press, 1995), 49.

23. I use the term "Mexican Catholic" to refer to the specific cultural formation of Roman Catholicism within Mexico, which has traveled with migrants into the United States and continues to shape Mexican American culture. The self-described Latina theologians I cite in this chapter include Mexican Catholicism within the scope of Latin American religious practice, although of course aspects of it are distinct from other social locations in Latin America.

24. Anzaldúa, *Borderlands/La Frontera,* 53; Castillo, *Massacre of the Dreamers,* 116–17.

25. Rebolledo, *Women Singing in the Snow,* 53.

26. Aquino, "Latina Feminist Theology," 151.

27. Hector A. Torres, *Conversations with Contemporary Chicana and Chicano Writers* (Albuquerque: University of New Mexico Press, 2007), 154.

28. Elsa Saeta, "A MELUS Interview: Ana Castillo," *MELUS* 22, no. 3 (1997): 135.

29. Gloria Inés Loya, for instance, argues that mestiza women show a marked attraction to figures like the Virgin of Guadalupe ("Pathways to a *Mestiza* Feminist Theology," in *A Reader in Latina Feminist Theology: Religion and Justice,* ed. María Pilar Aquino, Daisy L. Machado, and Jeanette Rodríguez [Austin: University of Texas Press, 2002], 219). For more on Guadalupe, La Malinche (the traitor woman), and La Llorona (the weeping woman), and how Chicanas reinterpret these mythological figures as empowering examples of female and indigenous agency instead of archetypal instances of feminine weakness or Catholic hegemony, see Rebolledo, *Woman Singing in the Snow,* 49–81. Rita Cano

Alcalá also discusses the three figures in relation to *So Far from God* ("A Chicana Hagiography for the Twenty-First Century: Ana Castillo's *Locas Santas*," in *Velvet Barrios: Popular Culture and Chicana/o Sexualities,* ed. Alicia Gaspar de Alba [New York: Palgrave Macmillan, 2003], 9–12). An even more sustained engagement is Castillo's edited collection of essays on the Virgin of Guadalupe, *Goddess of the Americas: Writings on the Virgin of Guadalupe* (New York: Riverhead, 1996), the introduction to which asserts the indigenous and even more broadly spiritual goddess significance of the Virgin of Guadalupe over against the official Roman Catholic understanding.

30. Rodríguez, "Latina Activists: Toward an Inclusive Spirituality of Being in the World," in *A Reader in Latina Feminist Theology: Religion and Justice,* ed. María Pilar Aquino, Daisy L. Machado, and Jeanette Rodríguez (Austin: University of Texas Press, 2002), 126.

31. For examples of the qualitative, interview-based method (traceable to the influence both Paulo Freire's *Pedagogy of the Oppressed,* trans. Myra Bergman Ramos [1968; New York: Continuum, 1984] and Carol Gilligan's *In a Different Voice* [Cambridge, MA: Harvard University Press, 1982]), see Isasi-Díaz, *En la Lucha,* 86–134; Rodríguez, "Latina Activist"; and Loya, "Pathways."

32. Aquino and others employ Elisabeth Schüssler Fiorenza's term "kyriarchy": the Greek "kyrios" (lord or master) is here joined with "archo" (to lead, rule, govern) to signify a "rule of the lords/masters." Schüssler Fiorenza began to forward this term in the early nineties as a more nuanced alternative to "patriarchy," one that implies the linked systems of oppression, including race and class. Such a view parallels the womanist goal of a more holistic critique.

33. Aquino, "Latina Feminist Theology," 151.

34. Isasi-Díaz, *En la Lucha,* 45–49.

35. These are hotly contested issues: in Anzaldúa's chapter "Entering the Serpent" in *Borderlands/La Frontera,* for instance, she does not share her theologian sisters' optimism when she asserts, "The Catholic and Protestant religions encourage fear and distrust of life and of the body; they encourage a split between the body and the spirit and totally ignore the soul; they encourage us to kill off parts of ourselves" (59).

36. Anzaldúa, *Borderlands/La Frontera,* 69, 97.

37. Castillo, *Massacre of the Dreamers,* 11.

38. Ibid., 12.

39. Suzanne Bost, *Encarnación: Illness and Body Politics in Chicana Feminist Literature* (New York: Fordham University Press, 2010), 27.

40. Ibid.

41. Carmela Delia Lanza, "'A New Meeting with the Sacred': Ana Castillo's *So Far from God,*" *Romance Languages Annual* 10 (1999): 658.

42. Castillo, *So Far from God*, 22.

43. New Revised Standard Version.

44. Gail Pérez, "Ana Castillo as *Santera*: Reconstructing Popular Religious Praxis," in *A Reader in Latina Feminist Theology: Religion and Justice,* ed. María Pilar Aquino, Daisy L. Machado, and Jeanette Rodríguez (Austin: University of Texas Press, 2002), 57, 59.

45. Ralph E. Rodriguez, "Chicana/o Fiction from Resistance to Contestation: The Role of Creation in Ana Castillo's *So Far from God*," *MELUS* 25, no. 2 (2000): 63–82; Gillman and Floyd-Thomas, "Con un pie a cada lado / With a Foot in Each Place," 158–75.

46. Lanza, "A New Meeting."

47. Alcalá, "A Chicana Hagiography."

48. Colette Morrow, "Queering Chicano/a Narratives: Lesbian as Healer, Saint and Warrior in Ana Castillo's *So Far from God*," *Journal of the Midwest Modern Language Association* 30, no. 1/2 (1997): 63–80.

49. Michelle M. Sauer, "'Saint-Making' in Ana Castillo's *So Far from God*: Medieval Mysticism as Precedent for an Authoritative Chicana Spirituality," *Mester* 29 (2000): 72–91.

50. Gillman and Floyd-Thomas, "Con un pie a cada lado."

51. Daniel Cooper Alarcón, "Literary Syncretism in Ana Castillo's *So Far from God*," *Studies in Latin American Popular Culture* 23 (2004): 145–52.

52. Theresa Delgadillo, "Forms of Chicana Feminist Resistance: Hybrid Spirituality in Ana Castillo's *So Far from God*," *Modern Fiction Studies* 44, no. 4 (1998): 888.

53. Alcalá, "A Chicana Hagiopgraphy," 6.

54. Ibid., 3.

55. Ibid., 7.

56. Delgadillo, "Forms of Chicana Feminist Resistance," 902–904.

57. Caminero-Santangelo, "'The Pleas of the Desperate': Collective Agency Versus Magical Realism in Ana Castillo's *So Far from God*," *Tulsa Studies in Women's Literature* 24, no. 1 (2005): 86.

58. Ibid., 88–89.

59. Boff and Boff borrow this term from Freire's *Pedagogy of the Oppressed*, as do Castillo and Moraga in their Spanish translation of *This Bridge Called My Back*. In Latin American liberation theology, Freire's influence produces a methodology that is based on grassroots gatherings, questions that open up discussion, ongoing dialogue, and mutual empowerment.

60. Leonardo Boff and Clodovis Boff, *Introducing Liberation Theology*, trans. Paul Burns (Maryknoll: Orbis, 1987), 5.

61. Ibid., 39.

62. Ibid., 64–65.

63. Castillo, *Massacre of the Dreamers*, 87. Subsequent citations appear in the text.

64. In this section, unless otherwise specified, by "liberation theology," I refer to Latin American liberation theology, which of course bears many similarities to black liberation theology like James Hal Cone's, the liberation theology of German Johann Baptist Metz, and the theology that arose from the women's liberation movement, although these various perspectives develop in distinct locations. Latin American liberation theology is a wide umbrella likewise arising from various different locations—for instance, the Boffs in Brazil and Gustavo Gutiérrez in Peru—and addressed primarily to the inhabitants of those particular locations. Still, the discourse crossed national boundaries as it developed, and theory travels: I follow many others in recognizing the resonance of liberation theology for Mexican Americans.

65. Christopher Rowland, "The Theology of Liberation," in *The Cambridge Companion to Liberation Theology*, ed. Christopher Rowland (Cambridge: Cambridge University Press, 2008), 6.

66. Aquino, Machado, and Rodríguez, *A Reader in Latina Feminist Theology*, xix.

67. Boff and Boff, *Introducing Liberation Theology*, 2–3.

68. Ibid., 4.

69. Rowland, "The Theology of Liberation," 7.

70. Isasi-Díaz, *En la Lucha*, 41. Although Isasi-Díaz is an important early voice among Latina theologians, her term "mujerista theology" has not been widely embraced, and her perspective is sometimes critiqued for being inattentive to indigenous elements of Latina women's spirituality. As Aquino, Machado, and Rodríguez explain, "mujerista" was used for an antifeminist splinter sect in Peru during the seventies and thus carries connotations these theologians wish to avoid (*A Reader in Latina Feminist Theology*, xiv). See also Aquino, "Latina Feminist Theology," 138–39.

71. Boff and Boff, *Introducing Liberation Theology*, 32.

72. Rowland, "The Theology of Liberation," 12.

73. Boff and Boff, *Introducing Liberation Theology*, 32.

74. Ibid., 33.

75. Ibid.

76. Ibid., 69.

77. Rowland, "The Theology of Liberation," 3, 4.

78. Gutiérrez, "The Task and Content of Liberation Theology," in *The Cambridge Companion to Liberation Theology*, trans. Judith Condor, ed. Christopher Rowland (Cambridge: Cambridge University Press, 2008), 29.

79. Particularly in their emphasis on openness to difference or otherness, the subversion of binaries, intertextuality, and an endless openness to revision, these practitioners of liberation theology echo (or predict) the theoretical

insights of poststructural theorists. Sandoval recognizes this crossover in *Methodology of the Oppressed*.

80. Gutiérrez, "The Task and Content of Liberation Theology," 24.

81. This is Schüssler Fiorenza's phrase from her 1975 article "Feminist Theology as a Critical Theology of Liberation," *Theological Studies* 36, no. 4 (1975): 606–26. For a more recent overview of feminist theology as a mode of liberation theology, see Mary Grey, "Feminist Theology: A Critical Theology of Liberation," in *The Cambridge Companion to Liberation Theology,* ed. Christopher Rowland (Cambridge: Cambridge University Press, 2008).

82. Rowland, "The Theology of Liberation," 6.

83. Matthew Bunson, Margaret Bunson, and Stephen Bunson, *Our Sunday Visitor's Encyclopedia of Saints* (Huntington, IN: Our Sunday Visitor, 2003), 763.

84. Alban Butler, *Butler's Lives of the Saints*, ed. Michael J. Walsh (New York: Harper, 1991), 225.

85. Castillo has admitted that she originally ended the novel like the martyr's tale, with Sofi "on the grave crying for her three martyred daughters." Her agent reminded her that she'd promised Norton a book with a happy ending, however, so Castillo claims, "I thought, 'what would she [Sofia] do to change that, particularly as a religious figure. What would she do?' She takes over. She doesn't submit to that point in history when patriarchy took over her authority" (Saeta, "A MELUS Interview," 147).

86. Castillo, *The Guardians* (New York: Random House, 2007). Subsequent citations appear in the text.

87. Another intertextual oddity here is the possibility that the deputy Sofia who offers Gabriel mercy when he gets taken in with his gang-member friends might be the Sofi of *So Far from God*. She tells Milton that she's "from up around Albuquerque, quesque some lil village nearby there" (94)—right in the vicinity of Tome. Regina, who is approaching middle age, notes to herself when the two women meet, "She looked like she might be a little older than me but la diputada moved like one of Charlie's Angels" (201): so perhaps la pobre Sofi, with her dreams of becoming a mayor, does enter into a public service career in those thirty-eight years after her children die? Even more telling, Regina recognizes their shared experiences: "She was someone like me. We get to witness a whole lot of things before it's our time. Things people wouldn't believe" (201).

88. Such a reading aligns with Rich's or Castillo's own claim that the com-passion and love typically associated with women would be well applied to all society, men and women alike. But this reading still does not fully account for the quotation of Padre Pío, which implies a God who causes suffering, not just one who suffers-with.

89. The Franciscans were the original order from which Padre Pío's order, the Capuchins, derived. Saint Francis was the first recorded person to receive the stigmata.

90. Matthew also offers us an intertext in Jesus's parable of the sheep and the goats in chapter 25, which tells a tale of the judgment day, when the "righteous" and "unrighteous" will be separated, not on the basis of their claimed religion but on the basis of their actions toward the hungry, the thirsty, the stranger, the naked, the sick, and the imprisoned, with the famous last lines, "Inasmuch as you have done it unto the least of these my brethren, ye have done it unto me" (Matthew 25:42). This is the sort of passage highlighted in the Bible by a hermeneutic of liberation, and Regina's care of María Dolores and her little girl falls within these parameters.

91. María Dolores also rewrites the script of the Sorrowing Virgin after whom she is named: she shares in common the status of unwed teenage mother and a life characterized by sorrow, but her sorrow arises not from some cosmic scheme of redemptive sacrifice, or even simply from the death of her own child, but through the very material system of gang violence, family apathy (her mother chooses not to care for her grandchild), and sexual vulnerability. She reminds us, again, that not all suffering leads to something good: in María Dolores's case, her own suffering simply leads her to inflict more suffering, a structure of perpetuation Arne Johan Vetlesen argues in *A Philosophy of Pain*, trans. John Irons (2004; London: Reaktion, 2009), can be stopped only through creation, through resignification in art.

92. In another strange parallel, Tiny Tears's puncturing of Gabo's lungs and heart with a shard of glass recalls Padre Pío's miracle of "transverberation," a spiritual piercing of the side with God's love that was so overwhelming it left him devastated and also actually physically marked with blood. In Gabo's death, Castillo rewrites the tale by significantly literalizing and politicizing it: Gabo is pierced by Tiny Tears, not an invisible God, and this suffering-unto-death is not a result of divine love but instead of a young woman's own agony, fear, and anger, which itself is wrapped in a web of gendered, classed, raced, and specifically placed vulnerabilities.

5. Silent (in the Face of) Suffering?

1. Chimamanda Ngozi Adichie, *Purple Hibiscus* (New York: Anchor, 2003). Subsequent citations appear in the text.

2. Adichie and Michael Ondaatje, "In Conversation," *Brick* 79 (2007): 44.

3. There is an established history of reading African women's writing in English allegorically. See, for instance, Susan Z. Andrade, "Rewriting History,

Motherhood, and Rebellion: Naming an African Women's Literary Tradition," *Research in African Literatures* 21, no. 1 (1990): 91–110 and her more recent "Gender and the 'Public Sphere' in Africa: Writing Women and Rioting Women," *Agenda* 54 (2002): 45–59.

4. In this familial quietness, *Purple Hibiscus* illustrates Simone Weil's, Dorothee Sölle's, and Elaine Scarry's claims that suffering is language-stealing, relationship-barring.

5. Sophia O. Ogwude, "History and Ideology in Chimamanda Adichie's Fiction," *Tydskrif vir Letterkunde* 48, no. 1 (2011): 110–23.

6. Several scholars have documented the relation of *Purple Hibiscus* to the history of the Christian missionary project in Nigeria. As Susan Strehle argues, it is significant that the colonial history of Nigeria began in the mid-nineteenth century with Christian missionaries, "long before it became a British colony and protectorate in 1914," which means that "Nigeria first encountered Western domination in the spiritual realm" ("The Decolonized Home: Chimamanda Ngozi Adichie's *Purple Hibiscus*," in *Transnational Women's Fiction: Unsettling Home and Homeland* [New York: Palgrave Macmillan, 2008], 102). The Christianizing mission in Nigeria created a strong relationship among education, the English language, and Roman Catholicism, which, as Lily Mabura articulates, distinguished itself from Protestant missions by teaching rather than withholding English from Africans ("Breaking Gods: An African Postcolonial Gothic Reading of Chimamanda Ngozi Adichie's *Purple Hibiscus* and *Half of a Yellow Sun*," *Research in African Literatures* 39, no. 1 [2008]: 212). The mission also insisted on an abandonment of African culture, which was demonized as backward, bestial, and even literally demonic.

7. Cheryl Stobie, "Dethroning the Infallible Father: Religion, Patriarchy and Politics in Chimamanda Ngozi Adichie's *Purple Hibiscus*," *Literature and Theology: An International Journal of Religion, Theory, and Culture* 24, no. 4 (2010): 429.

8. Ibid., 433.

9. Teaching the novel and discussing it with peers, I've come across only a few readers (and no critics I've read) who express discomfort at the possible similarity between Father Amadi's relationship to Kambili and the many terrible cases of sexual abuse of vulnerable minors perpetrated by Roman Catholic priests. Most have instead admitted how desperately they *wanted* a consummation for Kambili and Father Amadi. The question of whether the novel is constructed to bring about this desire is one that can't quite be answered, but it certainly does seem to have that effect among many readers, for better or worse. Kambili's ongoing longing seems to be their own, and this adds to the lasting effect (and romance) of the novel.

10. Rich, "Notes Towards a Politics of Location," in *Feminist Postcolonial Theory: A Reader*, ed. Reina Lewis and Sara Mills (1984; New York: Routledge, 2003), 41.

11. Ibid., 31.

12. Ibid., 39–40.

13. Cynthia Ward, "Reading African Women Readers," *Research in African Literatures* 27, no. 3 (1996): 78.

14. Ibid., 78–79.

15. Mercy Amba Oduyoye, *Daughters of Anowa: African Women and Patriarchy* (Maryknoll: Orbis, 1995), 85.

16. This is not the same as claiming that women in formerly colonized locations have not been doing theology from those locations. The collection *Inheriting Our Mothers' Gardens: Feminist Theology in Third World Perspective* (Louisville, KY: Westminster John Knox Press) was published in 1988, bringing together the work of several theologians cited throughout this project, including Kwok Pui-lan, Oduyoye, Ada María Isasi-Díaz, Katie Cannon, and Letty M. Russell. In 1989, Oduyoye helped convene the Circle of Concerned African Women Theologians at Trinity College in Accra, Ghana, which has been marked as a turning point in the history of African theology which had, until that point, been largely masculinist.

    To claim that "postcolonial feminist theology" is a still-developing field in the early decades of the twenty-first century is, rather, to claim that an explicit, interdisciplinary *theoretical* conversation between postcolonial theories, feminist theories, and theologies is still not widely practiced and is slowly growing in academic circles.

17. See Deepika Bahri, "Feminism in / and Postcolonialism," in *Cambridge Companion to Postcolonial Studies* (Cambridge: Cambridge University Press, 2006), 201; Ania Loomba, "Dead Women Tell No Tales: Issues of Female Subjectivity, Subaltern Agency and Tradition in Colonial and Postcolonial Writings on Widow Immolation in India," in *Feminist Postcolonial Theory: A Reader*, ed. Reina Lewis and Sara Mills (1993; New York: Routledge, 2003), 215–17.

18. Bahri, "Feminism in / and Postcolonialism," 202; see also Andrade, "Rewriting History," 93.

19. Oduyoye, *Daughters of Anowa*, 3.

20. Ibid., 87.

21. Peter Hitchcock, "Postcolonial Africa? Problems of Theory," *Women's Studies Quarterly* 25, no. 3/4 (1997): 239.

22. Andrade, "Rewriting History," 94.

23. Kwok, *Postcolonial Imagination and Feminist Theology* (Louisville, KY: Westminster John Knox Press, 2005), 7.

24. Kwok and Laura Donaldson, eds., *Postcolonialism, Feminism, and Religious Discourse* (New York: Routledge, 2001), 7.
25. Kwok, *Postcolonial Imagination*, 9.
26. Ibid., 10–11.
27. Ibid., 17.
28. Africa as a continent was not first introduced to Christianity in the colonizing missions' movements of the past several hundred years: African Christianity began from the beginning of Christian history, as in the first-century C.E. Christianity spread into Egypt and North Africa. There is a rich tradition of syncretic Coptic and Ethiopian Orthodox churches [see Kwok, "Mercy Amba Oduyoye and African Women's Theology," *Journal of Feminist Studies in Religion* 20, no. 1 (2004): 12].
29. Kwok, *Postcolonial Imagination*, 18.
30. Kwok, "Mercy Amba Oduyoye," 8.
31. Kwok, "Feminist Theology as Intercultural Discourse," in *Cambridge Companion to Feminist Theology*, ed. Susan Frank Parsons (Cambridge: Cambridge University Press, 2006), 25.
32. Mary Daly's *Gyn/Ecology: The Metaethics of Radical Feminism* (1978; Boston: Beacon, 1990) is often cited in postcolonial feminist theologians' discussions of this Western impulse to speak with "compassion" of the unique "oppressions" leveled upon women in traditional non-Western cultures, like foot-binding, female circumcision (or female genital mutilation), and *sati* (or widow-burning). Audre Lorde, Kwok, and Oduyoye all critique Daly for offering only stories of African women's oppression, and not their strength, in her global exposé of patriarchy.
33. Kwok, *Postcolonial Imagination*, 62.
34. Ibid.
35. Teresa M. Hinga, "Jesus Christ and the Liberation of Women in Africa," in *The Will to Arise: Women, Tradition, and the Church in Africa,* ed. Mercy Amba Oduyoye and Musimbi R. A. Kanyoro (Eugene: Wipf and Stock, 1992), 187.
36. Oduyoye, *Daughters of Anowa*, 172, 183.
37. On Igbo women's reduced freedom under colonial Christianity, see also Musa W. Dube, "Postcoloniality, Feminist Spaces, and Religion," in *Post-Colonialism, Feminism, and Religious Discourse*, ed. Laura E. Donaldson and Kwok Pui-lan (New York: Routledge, 2002), 100–120.
38. Kwok, "Mercy Amba Oduyoye," 15.
39. Ibid.
40. Ibid., 16.
41. Letty M. Russell, "Cultural Hermeneutics: A Postcolonial Look at Mission," *Journal of Feminist Studies in Religion* 20, no. 1 (2004): 26.

42. Oduyoye, *Daughters of Anowa*, 9.

43. Ibid., 180.

44. Ibid., 187.

45. Ibid., 193.

46. Ibid., 180.

47. Kwok, "Mercy Amba Oduyoye," 12. For more on crossroads Christianity, see Oduyoye, "Christianity and African Culture," *International Review of Mission* 84, no. 332–33 (1995): 77–90.

48. Oduyoye, *Daughters of Anowa*, 195.

49. Ibid., 85.

50. Ibid., 205.

51. Oduyoye's generalizations about "African" women (by which she says she means West African, and especially Ghanaian and Nigerian women) may themselves raise questions about accuracy. Throughout her text, the theologian does cite sociologists and other sources in footnotes, although she also supports some of her generalizations with appeals to personal experience (phenomena she has witnessed repeatedly) and anecdotes.

52. Oduyoye's emphasis on crafting *new* stories echoes—or rather, predicts—the claims of poststructuralist feminist theorists like Drucilla Cornell, whose utopian feminism is based on a similar re-imagining of stories and myths.

53. Bahri, "Feminism in/and Postcolonialism," 204.

54. Ibid., 205.

55. Adichie, "African 'Authenticity' and the Biafran Experience," *Transition: An International Review* 99 (2008): 46–47.

56. Ibid., 46.

57. Aminatta Forna, "New Writing and Nigeria: Chimamanda Ngozi Adichie and Helen Oyeyemi in Conversation," *Wasafiri: The Transnational Journal of International Writing* 47 (2006): 57.

58. Adichie, "African 'Authenticity,'" 47. The other side of this risk is that Western readers will insist that her writings are not "authentically African," as some have done, comparing her stories of middle-class Nigerian life to images of Africa as a draught- and plague-riddled continent of total poverty. Adichie's frustration with this dynamic is devastatingly recorded in the story "Jumping Monkey Hill" in *The Thing Around Your Neck* (New York: Anchor, 2009). Adichie discusses her motivation for this story in an interview with Renee H. Shea, "A Slender Hope," *Poets and Writers* (July/August 2009): 47.

59. Chandra Talpade Mohanty, "Under Western Eyes: Feminist Scholarship and Colonial Discourses," in *Feminist Postcolonial Theory: A Reader*, ed. Reina Lewis and Sara Mills (New York: Routledge, 2003), 54.

60. Adebanwi, "Nigerian Identity Is Burdensome: The Chimamanda Ngozi Adichie Interview," NigeriaVillageSquare.com (12 May 2004), n.p.

61. Adichie, *Half of a Yellow Sun* (New York: Anchor, 2006). Subsequent citations appear in the text. Adichie's next book, *The Thing Around Your Neck*, furthers this formal refusal of the single story through its multiplicity: as a short-story collection, the book is able to forge a dialogical play of differently located characters—women and men, in Nigeria and the United States, in cities and villages, of various class positions and ages. Within many of the stories, too, Adichie stages confrontations of difference between characters of different locations. The collection also manifests her ongoing concern with decolonization, gender and sex, and religion.

62. Kera Bolonik, "Memory, Witness, and War: Chimamanda Ngozi Adichie Talks with BookForum," *BookForum: The Review for Art, Fiction, and Culture* 14, no. 4 (2007): n.p.; Adichie, "African 'Authenticity,'" 50.

63. See Amy Novak, "Who Speaks? Who Listens? The Problem of Address in Two Nigerian Trauma Novels," *Studies in the Novel* 40, no. 1–2 (2008): 31–51, for an especially strong explication of the difference gender and race make in colonial traumas.

64. This scene parallels in many ways the gang-rape scene in Morrison's *Love* (New York: Knopf, 2003), discussed in chapter 3, both in its protagonist's ambivalence and in its victim's resulting silence.

65. This is one of the few places in Adichie's texts before *Americanah* (New York: Knopf, 2013) that links the experiences of African subjects to the differently located African Americans whose experience often dominate Western readers' understandings of "race." The particularity of Adichie's settings as postcolonial rather than post-U.S-slavery is one reason I choose to read her texts together with African theology rather than black liberation or womanist theology, the particular Americanness of which it is tempting to overlook.

Conclusion

1. Denise Levertov, "Biafra," in *Relearning the Alphabet* (New York: New Directions, 1970), 17–18.

2. Consider, for example, Sharon Welch's claim that Toni Morrison's "stark depiction of unnecessary human suffering evokes in her readers outrage and an impassioned search for avenues of overturning and transforming the cause of that suffering" (*A Feminist Ethic of Risk* [Minneapolis, MN: Fortress Press, 1990], 83). Does it? I have taught Morrison's novel *Love* (New York: Knopf, 2003) and have seen no such reaction grip all my students, although it does a few.

3. Quoted in Eric L. Haralson, *Reading the Middle Generation Anew: Culture, Community, and Form in Twentieth-Century American Poetry* (Iowa City: University of Iowa Press), 2006, 55.

4. The phrase "new creation" is, of course, biblical. It also echoes Hille Haker's claim that in the configuration of the text, "The narrative takes up elements of reality and passes them on by way of a new creation" ("Narrative and Moral Identity in Paul Ricoeur," *Concilium* 2 [2000]: 64).

5. It is also significant that both Morrison and Castillo have named their publishers' pressure as the reasons for some of their happier endings. The literature we read is not shaped just by writers' ethical visions but also by the market-driven needs of publishers who want to sell books.

6. This is not to say that attention is always positive. Plenty of people pay attention to political rivals, for instance, to debate with them or debunk their claims. In the second sense of the word, I am confident that plenty of disgruntled "attendants" (for instance, underpaid servants) have rendered service with ill will. And in the third sense, it is entirely possible to attend on someone, to wait for his or her arrival, with violent intentions, as in an ambush. One may certainly attend to, on, or for another, even placing oneself in a secondary or receptive position, under duress or for one's own self-serving purposes.

7. Morrison, *Jazz* (New York: Knopf, 1992), 229.

8. In this regard, my ethics recalls Chela Sandoval's meditation on Donna Haraway's claim that "theorists who subscribe" to a "decolonizing postmodern mode of oppositional consciousness must learn to be 'more generous and more suspicious—both generous *and* suspicious, exactly the receptive posture' we must all seek in 'political semiosis generally'" (*Methodology of the Oppressed* [Minneapolis: University of Minnesota Press, 2000], 175).

9. Dorothee Sölle, *Suffering*, trans. Everett R. Kalin (Philadelphia: Fortress Press, 1975), 36.

10. Zygmunt Bauman, *Postmodern Ethics* (Oxford: Blackwell, 1993), 199.

11. Sharon Welch, *A Feminist Ethic of Risk* (Minneapolis, MN: Fortress Press, 1990), 14.

12. Adrienne Rich, "Contradictions: Tracking Poems," *Your Native Land, Your Life* (New York: Norton, 1986), 111.

BIBLIOGRAPHY

Achebe, Chinua. *Things Fall Apart*. New York: Fawcett Crest, 1959.

Adebanwi, Wale. "Nigerian Identity Is Burdensome: The Chimamanda Ngozi Adichie Interview." NigeriaVillageSquare.com. 12 May 2004.

Adéèkó, Adéléke. "Power Shift: America in the New Nigerian Imagination." *Global South* 2, no. 2 (2008): 10–30.

Adichie, Chimamanda Ngozi. "African 'Authenticity' and the Biafran Experience." *Transition: An International Review* 99 (2008): 42–53.

——. *Americanah*. New York: Knopf, 2013.

——. "The Danger of a Single Story." TED Talks. July 2009. http://www.ted.com/talks/chimamanda_adichie_the_danger_of_a_single_story.

——. *Half of a Yellow Sun*. New York: Anchor, 2006.

——. *Purple Hibiscus*. New York: Anchor, 2003.

——. *The Thing Around Your Neck*. New York: Anchor, 2009.

Adichie, Chimamanda Ngozi, and Michael Ondaatje. "In Conversation." *Brick* 79 (2007): 38–48.

Adorno, Theodor. *Negative Dialectics*. 1966. New York: Continuum, 1983.

Alarcón, Daniel Cooper. "Literary Syncretism in Ana Castillo's *So Far from God.*" *Studies in Latin American Popular Culture* 23 (2004): 145–52.

Alarcón, Norma. "Chicana's Feminist Literature: A Re-Vision Through Malintzin / or Malintzin: Putting Flesh Back on the Object." 1981. In *This Bridge Called My Back: Writings by Radical Women of Color*, edited by Cherríe Moraga and Gloria Anzaldúa, 182–90. Foreword by Toni Cade Bambara. 2nd ed. Lanham, NY: Kitchen Table Press, 1983.

Alarcón, Norma. "The Sardonic Power of the Erotic in the Work of Ana Castillo." In *Chicana Critical Issues*, edited by Norma Alarcón Rafaela Castro, Emma Pérez, Beatríz Pesquera, Adaljiza Sosa Riddell, and Patricia Zavella, 5–19. Berkeley, CA: Third Woman Press, 1993.

Alarcón, Norma, Rafaela Castro, Emma Pérez, Beatríz Pesquera, Adaljiza Sosa Riddell, and Patricia Zavella, eds. *Chicana Critical Issues*. Berkeley, CA: Third Woman Press, 1993.

Alcalá, Rita Cano. "A Chicana Hagiography for the Twenty-First Century: Ana Castillo's *Locas Santas*." In *Velvet Barrios: Popular Culture & Chicana/o Sexualities*, edited by Alicia Gaspar de Alba, 3–15. New York: Palgrave Macmillan, 2003.

Als, Hilton. "Ghosts in the House: How Toni Morrison Fostered a Generation of Black Writers." *New Yorker* (27 Oct. 2003): 64–75.

Amato, Joseph. *Victims and Values: A History and Theory of Suffering*. New York: Greenwood, 1990.

Ammons, Elizabeth. *Brave New Words: How Literature Will Save the Planet*. Iowa City: University of Iowa Press, 2010.

Andrade, Susan Z. "Adichie's Genealogies: National and Feminine Novels." *Research in African Literaturesi* 42, no. 2 (2011): 91–101.

——. "Gender and 'the Public Sphere' in Africa: Writing Women and Rioting Women." *Agenda* 54 (2002): 45–59.

——. "Rewriting History, Motherhood, and Rebellion: Naming an African Women's Literary Tradition." *Research in African Literatures* 21, no. 1 (1990): 91–110.

Anzaldúa, Gloria. *Borderlands/La Frontera: The New Mestiza*. 1987. 2nd ed. San Francisco: Aunt Lute Books, 1999.

——. "Foreword to the Second Edition." In *This Bridge Called My Back: Writings by Radical Women of Color*, 2nd ed., edited by Cherríe Moraga and Gloria Anzaldúa, n.p. Lanham, NY: Kitchen Table Press, 1983.

——. "now let us shift . . . the path of conocimiento . . . inner work, public acts." In *This Bridge We Call Home: Radical Visions for Transformation*, edited by Gloria Anzaldúa and Ana Louise Keating, 540–78. New York: Routledge, 2002.

——. Preface. In *This Bridge Called My Back: Writings by Radical Women of Color*, 2nd ed., edited by Cherríe Moraga and Gloria Anzaldúa, xiii–xx. Lanham, NY: Kitchen Table Press, 1983.

——. "Speaking in Tongues: A Letter to 3rd World Women Writers." 1981. In *This Bridge Called My Back: Writings by Radical Women of Color*, 2nd ed., edited by Cherríe Moraga and Gloria Anzaldúa, 165–73. Lanham, NY: Kitchen Table Press, 1983.

Aquino, María Pilar. "Latina Feminist Theology: Central Features." In *A Reader in Latina Feminist Theology: Religion and Justice*, edited by María Pilar Aquino, Daisy L. Machado, and Jeanette Rodríguez, 134–60. Austin: University of Texas Press, 2002.

Aquino, María Pilar, Daisy L. Machado, and Jeanette Rodríguez, eds. *A Reader in Latina Feminist Theology: Religion and Justice.* Austin: University of Texas Press, 2002.

Ashcroft, Bill, Gareth Griffiths, and Helen Tiffin. *The Empire Writes Back: Theory and Practice in Post-Colonial Literatures.* 2nd ed. New York: Routledge, 2002.

Attridge, Derek. "Ethical Modernism." *Poetics Today* 25, no. 4 (2004): 653–71.

——. *The Singularity of Literature.* London: Routledge, 2004.

Bahri, Deepika. "Feminism in/and Postcolonialism." In *Cambridge Companion to Postcolonial Studies,* 199–220. Cambridge: Cambridge University Press, 2006.

Baker, Peter. *Deconstruction and the Ethical Turn.* Gainesville: University Press of Florida, 1995.

Baker-Fletcher, Karen. "'Soprano Obligato': The Voices of Black Women and American Conflict in the thought of Anna Julia Cooper." In *A Troubling in My Soul,* edited by Emilie Townes, 172–85. Maryknoll, NY: Orbis, 1993.

Bambara, Toni Cade. Foreword. In *This Bridge Called My Back: Writings by Radical Women of Color,* 2nd ed., edited by Cherríe Moraga and Gloria Anzaldúa, vi–viii. Lanham, NY: Kitchen Table Press, 1983.

——. "Salvation Is the Issue." In *Black Women Writers (1950–1980): A Critical Evaluation,* edited by Mari Evans, 71–84. New York: Anchor, 1984.

Barry, Kathleen. "Reviewing Reviews: *Of Woman Born.*" 1977. In *Reading Adrienne Rich: Reviews and Re-Visions 1951–81,* edited by Jane Roberta Cooper, 300–303. Ann Arbor: University of Michigan Press, 1984.

Bauman, Zygmunt. *Postmodern Ethics.* Oxford: Blackwell, 1993.

The Bible. English Standard Version. Wheaton, IL: Crossway, 2001.

——. New Revised Standard Version. Washington, DC: The National Council of Christian Churches, 1989.

——. Today's New International Version. Colorado Springs, CO: Zondervan, 2005.

Biviano, Erin Lothes. *The Paradox of Christian Sacrifice: The Loss of Self, The Gift of Self.* New York: Crossroad, 2007.

Blazer, Alex E. *I Am Otherwise: The Romance Between Poetry and Theory After the Death of the Subject.* Champaign, IL: Dalkey Archive Press, 2007.

Boff, Leonardo, and Clodovis Boff. *Introducing Liberation Theology.* Trans. Paul Burns. Maryknoll, NY: Orbis, 1987.

Bolonik, Kera. "Memory, Witness, and War: Chimamanda Ngozi Adichie Talks with BookForum." *BookForum: The Review for Art, Fiction, and Culture* 14, no. 4 (2007): n.p.

Booth, Wayne C. *The Company We Keep: An Ethics of Fiction.* Berkeley: University of California Press, 1988.

Bost, Suzanne. *Encarnación: Illness and Body Politics in Chicana Feminist Literature.* New York: Fordham University Press, 2010.

Boyers, Robert. "On Adrienne Rich: Intelligence and Will." In *Adrienne Rich's Poetry*, edited by Barbara Charlesworth Gelpi and Albert Gelpi, 148–60. New York: Norton, 1975.

Brown, Amy Benson. *Rewriting the Word: American Women Writers and the Bible.* Westport, CT: Greenwood Press, 1999.

Browning, Elizabeth Barrett. *Aurora Leigh and Other Poems.* New York: James Miller, 1872.

——. *A Drama of Exile.* New York: Henry G. Langley, 1854.

Buell, Lawrence. "Introduction. In Pursuit of Ethics." *PMLA* 114, no. 1 (1999): 7–16.

——. "What We Talk About When We Talk About Ethics." In *The Turn to Ethics*, edited by Marjorie Garber, Beatrice Hanssen, and Rebecca L. Walkowitz, 1–14. New York: Routledge, 2000.

Buley-Meissner, Mary Louise, Mary McCaslin Thompson, and Elizabeth Backran Tan. *The Academy and the Possibility of Belief.* Cresskill, NJ: Hampton Press, 1998.

Bunson, Matthew, Margaret Bunson, and Stephen Bunson. *Our Sunday Visitor's Encyclopedia of Saints.* Huntington, IN: Our Sunday Visitor, 2003.

Butler, Alban. *Butler's Lives of the Saints*, edited by Michael J. Walsh. New York: Harper, 1991.

Butler, Judith. *Bodies That Matter: On the Discursive Limits of "Sex."* New York: Routledge, 1993.

——. *Precarious Life: The Powers of Mourning and Violence.* London: Verso, 2004.

Bynum, Carolyn Walker. *Fragmentation and Redemption: Essays on Gender and the Human Body in Medieval Religion.* New York: Zone, 1991.

——. *Jesus as Mother: Studies in the Spirituality of the High Middle Ages.* Berkeley: University of California Press, 1984.

Caminero-Santangelo, Marta. "'The Pleas of the Desperate': Collective Agency Versus Magical Realism in Ana Castillo's *So Far from God.*" *Tulsa Studies in Women's Literature* 24, no. 1 (2005): 81–103.

Cannon, Katie Geneva. *Black Womanist Ethics.* Atlanta, GA: Scholars Press, 1988.

——. "'The Wounds of Jesus': Justification of Goodness in the Face of Manifold Evil." In *A Troubling in My Soul: Womanist Perspectives on Evil and Suffering*, edited by Emilie Townes, 219–31. Maryknoll, NY: Orbis, 1993.

Caputo, John D. *Philosophy and Theology.* Nashville, TN: Abingdon Press, 2006.

Castillo, Ana, ed. *Goddess of the Americas: Writings on the Virgin of Guadalupe.* New York: Riverhead, 1996.

Castillo, Ana. *The Guardians.* New York: Random House, 2007.

——. *Loverboys.* 1996. New York: Plume. 1997.

——. *Massacre of the Dreamers: Essays on Xicanisma.* New York: Plume, 1994.

——. *The Mixquiahuala Letters.* 1982. New York: Anchor, 1986.

——. *Peel My Love Like an Onion.* New York: Anchor, 1999.

———. *Sapogonia*. 1990. New York: Anchor, 1994.

———. *So Far from God*. New York: Norton, 1993.

Caughie, Pamela. *Passing and Pedagogy: The Dynamics of Responsibility.* Urbana: University of Illinois Press, 1999.

Chanter, Tina, ed. *Feminist Interpretations of Emmanuel Levinas.* University Park: Pennsylvania State University Press, 2001.

Christ, Carol. *Diving Deep and Surfacing: Women Writers on Spiritual Quest.* Boston: Beacon, 1980.

Christian, Barbara. "The Race for Theory." *Cultural Critique* 6 (1987): 51–63.

Cixous, Hélène. "Sorties: Out and Out: Attacks/Ways Out/Forays." In *The Newly Born Woman*. Trans. Betsy Wing, 63–129. Minneapolis: University of Minneapolis Press, 1986.

Clark, Miriam Marty. "Human Rights and the Work of Lyric in Adrienne Rich." *Cambridge Quarterly* 38, no. 1 (2009): 45–65.

Collins, An. *Divine Songs and Meditacions.* London: R. Bishop, 1653. Early English Books Online.

Combahee River Collective. "A Black Feminist Statement." 1978. In *All the Women Are White, All the Blacks Are Men, But Some of Us Are Brave: Black Women's Studies,* edited by Gloria T. Hull, Patricia Bell Scott, and Barbara Smith, 13–22. Old Westbury, NY: Feminist Press, 1982.

Cone, James Hal. *Black Theology and Black Power.* New York: Harper & Row, 1969.

———. *A Black Theology of Liberation.* 1970. Maryknoll, NY: Orbis, 1986.

———. *God of the Oppressed.* 1975. Maryknoll, NY: Orbis, 1997.

———. *The Spirituals and the Blues: An Interpretation.* 1972. Maryknoll, NY: Orbis, 1991.

———. "Suffering in the Black Religious Tradition." 1975. In *God of the Oppressed*, 1983–94. New York: Harper and Row. Reprinted in *Moral Evil and Redemptive Suffering: A History of Theodicy in African-American Religious Thought,* edited by Anthony B. Pinn, 285–97. Gainesville: University Press of Florida, 2002.

Connor, Marc C. "Introduction: Aesthetics and the African American Novel." In *The Aesthetics of Toni Morrison: Speaking the Unspeakable,* edited by Marc C. Connor, ix–xxviii. Jackson: University Press of Mississippi, 2000.

Connor, Steven. *Theory and Cultural Value.* Oxford: Blackwell, 1992.

Cooper, Jane Roberta, ed. *Reading Adrienne Rich: Reviews and Re-Visions 1951–81.* Ann Arbor: University of Michigan Press, 1984.

Copeland, M. Shawn. "'Wading Through Many Sorrows': Toward a Theology of Suffering in Womanist Perspective." In *A Troubling in My Soul: Womanist Perspectives on Evil and Suffering,* edited by Emilie M. Townes, 109–29. Maryknoll, NY: Orbis, 1993.

Cornell, Drucilla. *Beyond Accommodation: Ethical Feminism, Deconstruction, and the Law.* New Edition. Lanham, MD: Rowman and Littlefield, 1999.

———. "What Is Ethical Feminism?" In *Feminist Contentions: A Philosophical Exchange*, edited by Seyla Benhabib, Judith Butler, Drucilla Cornell, and Nancy Fraser, 75–106. New York: Routledge, 1996.

Critchley, Simon. "The Original Traumatism: Levinas and Psychoanalysis." In *Critical Ethics: Text, Theory, and Responsibility*, edited by Dominic Rainsford and Tim Woods, 88–104. New York: Macmillan, 1999.

Crouch, Stanley. "Aunt *Medea.*" *New Republic* (19 Oct. 1987): 38–43.

Cullinan, Colleen Carpenter. *Redeeming the Story: Women, Suffering, and Christ.* New York: Continuum, 2004.

Daly, Mary. *Beyond God the Father: Toward a Philosophy of Women's Liberation.* Boston: Beacon, 1973.

———. *Gyn/Ecology: The Metaethics of Radical Feminism.* 1978. Boston: Beacon, 1990.

De Beauvoir, Simone. *The Second Sex.* 1949. Trans. H. M. Parshley. New York: Vintage, 1952.

Delgadillo, Theresa. "Forms of Chicana Feminist Resistance: Hybrid Spirituality in Ana Castillo's *So Far from God.*" *Modern Fiction Studies* 44, no. 4 (1998): 888–916.

Denard, Carolyn C. *Toni Morrison: Conversations.* Jackson: University Press of Mississippi, 2008.

De Rosa, Deborah. "Womanist." In *The Toni Morrison Encyclopedia*, edited by Elizabeth Ann Beaulieu, 29–49. Westport, CT: Greenwood Press, 2003.

Derrida, Jacques. "Hospitality, Justice and Responsibility: A Dialogue with Jacques Derrida." In *Questioning Ethics: Contemporary Debates in Philosophy*, edited by Richard Kearney and Mark Dooley, 65–83. London: Routledge, 1999.

Dillard, Annie. *For the Time Being.* New York: Knopf, 1999.

———. *Holy the Firm.* New York: Perennial, 1977.

———. *The Writing Life.* New York: Perennial, 1989.

Dixie, Quinton Hosford, and Cornel West, eds. *The Courage to Hope: From Black Suffering to Human Redemption.* Boston: Beacon, 1999.

Dube, Musa W. "Postcoloniality, Feminist Spaces, and Religion." In *Post-colonialism, Feminism, and Religious Discourse*, edited by Laura E. Donaldson and Kwok Pui-lan, 100–120. New York: Routledge, 2002.

DuBois, W. E. B. "Criteria of Negro Art." 1926. In *Within the Circle: An Anthology of African American Literary Criticism from the Harlem Renaissance to the Present*, edited by Angelyn Mitchell, 60–68. Durham, NC: Duke University Press, 1994.

———. "The Damnation of Women." 1920. *The New Crisis* 107, no. 6 (2000): 1–8.

DuPlessis, Rachel Blau. "The Critique of Consciousness and Myth in Levertov, Rich, and Rukeyser." *Feminist Studies* 3, no. 1/2 (1975): 199–221.

Eaglestone, Robert. *Ethical Criticism: Reading After Levinas.* Edinburgh: Edinburgh University Press, 1997.

Eagleton, Terry. *After Theory*. Cambridge: Basic Books, 2003.

——. *Trouble with Strangers: A Study of Ethics*. Hoboken, NJ: Wiley-Blackwell, 2009.

Eckstein, Lars. *Re-Membering the Black Atlantic: On the Poetics and Politics of Literary Memory*. Amsterdam: Editions Rodopi B.V., 2006.

Eliot, George. *Adam Bede*. 1856. New York: Modern Library, 2002.

Eskin, Michael. "Introduction: The Double 'Turn' to Ethics and Literature?" *Poetics Today* 25, no. 4 (2004): 557–72.

Eugene, Toinette M. "Moral Values and Black Womanists." In *Feminist Theological Ethics: A Reader*, edited by Lois K. Daly, 160–71. Louisville, KY: Westminster John Knox Press, 1994.

Ezell, Margaret. *Writing Women's Literary History*. Baltimore, MD: Johns Hopkins University Press, 1993.

Fernandes, Leela. *Transforming Feminist Practice: Non-Violence, Social Justice and the Possibilities of a Spiritualized Feminism*. San Francisco: Aunt Lute Books, 2003.

Finch, Anne. *Poor Man's Lamb*. 1713. UPenn Digital Library. http://www.digital .library.upenn.edu/women/finch/1713/mp-lamb.html.

Finke, Laurie. *Women's Writing in English: Medieval England*. New York: Longman, 1999.

Fiorenza, Elisabeth Schüssler. *But SHE Said: Feminist Practices of Biblical Interpretation*. Boston: Beacon, 1992.

——. "Feminist Hermeneutics." In *Dictionary of Feminist Theologies*, edited by Letty M. Russell and J. Shannon Clarkson, 99–100. Louisville, KY: Westminster John Knox Press, 1996.

——. "Feminist Theology as a Critical Theology of Liberation." *Theological Studies* 36, no. 4 (1975): 606–26.

——. *In Memory of Her: A Feminist Theological Reconstruction of Christian Origins*. New York: Crossroads, 1984.

Forna, Aminatta. "New Writing and Nigeria: Chimamanda Ngozi Adichie and Helen Oyeyemi in Conversation." *Wasafiri: The Transnational Journal of International Writing* 47 (2006): 50–57.

Freire, Paulo. *Pedagogy of the Oppressed*. 1968. Trans. Myra Bergman Ramos. New York: Continuum, 1984.

Gage, Matilda Joslyn. *Woman, Church, and State*. 1893. Watertown, MA: Persephone Press, 1980.

Gallego, Mar. "Love and the Survival of the Black Community." In *The Cambridge Companion to Toni Morrison*, edited by Justine Tally, 92–100. Cambridge: Cambridge University Press, 2007.

Garber, Marjorie, Beatrice Hanssen, and Rebecca L. Walkowitz, eds. *The Turn to Ethics*. New York: Routledge, 2000.

Gelpi, Albert. "Adrienne Rich: The Poetics of Change." In *Adrienne Rich's Poetry*, edited by Barbara Charlesworth Gelpi and Albert Gelpi, 130–48. New York: Norton, 1975.

Gelpi, Barbara Charlesworth, and Albert Gelpi, eds. *Adrienne Rich's Poetry*. New York: Norton, 1975.

Gibbs, Robert, and Elliot R. Wolfson, eds. *Suffering Religion*. London: Routledge, 2002.

Gibson, Andrew. "Ethics." In *The Johns Hopkins Guide to Literary Theory and Criticism*, 2nd ed., edited by Michael Groden, Martin Kreiswirth, and Imre Szeman. Baltimore, MD: Johns Hopkins University Press, 2005.

——. *Postmodernity, Ethics, and the Novel: From Leavis to Levinas*. New York: Routledge, 1999.

——. "Sensibility and Suffering in Rhys and Nin." In *The Ethics in Literature*, edited by Andrew Hadfield, Dominic Rainsford, and Tim Woods, 184–211. New York: St. Martin's Press, 1999.

Gilkes, Cheryl Townsend. "'Some Folks Get Happy and Some Folks Don't': Diversity, Community, and African American Christian Spirituality." In *The Courage to Hope: From Black Suffering to Human Redemption*, edited by Quinton Hosford Dixie and Cornell West, 200–213. Boston: Beacon, 1999.

Gilligan, Carol. *In a Different Voice*. Cambridge, MA: Harvard University Press, 1982.

Gillman, Laura, and Stacy M. Floyd-Thomas. "Con un pie a cada lado / With a Foot in Each Place: Mestizaje as Transnational Feminisms in Ana Castillo's *So Far from God*." *Meridians: Feminism, Race, Transnationalism* 2, no. 1 (2001): 158–75.

Goldstein, Valerie Saiving. "The Human Situation: A Feminine View." *Journal of Religion* 40, no. 1 (1960): 100–112.

Grant, Jacquelyn. "Black Women and the Church." In *All the Women Are White, All the Blacks Are Men, But Some of Us Are Brave: Black Women's Studies*, edited by Gloria T. Hull, Patricia Bell Scott, and Barbara Smith, 141–52. Old Westbury, NY: Feminist Press, 1982.

——. "The Sin of Servanthood: And the Deliverance of Discipleship." In *A Troubling in My Soul: Womanist Perspectives on Evil and Suffering*, edited by Emilie M. Townes, 199–218. Maryknoll, NY: Orbis, 1993.

Grey, Mary. "Feminist Theology: A Critical Theology of Liberation." In *The Cambridge Companion to Liberation Theology*, edited by Christopher Rowland, 105–22. Cambridge: Cambridge University Press, 2008.

Griffin, Farah Jasmine. "That the Mothers May Soar and the Daughters May Know Their Names: A Retrospective of Black Feminist Literary Criticism." *Signs* 32, no. 2 (2007): 483–507.

Groenhout, Ruth E. *Connected Lives: Human Nature and An Ethics of Care*. Lanham, MD: Rowman and Littlefield, 2004.

———. "I Can't Say No: Self-Sacrifice and an Ethics of Care." In *Philosophy, Feminism, and Faith,* edited by Ruth Groenhout and Marya Bower, 152–74. Bloomington: Indiana University Press, 2003.

Groenhout, Ruth, and Marya Bower, eds. *Philosophy, Feminism, and Faith.* Bloomington: Indiana University Press, 2003.

Gutiérrez, Gustavo. "The Task and Content of Liberation Theology." Trans. Judith Condor. In *The Cambridge Companion to Liberation Theology,* edited by Christopher Rowland, 19–38. Cambridge: Cambridge University Press, 2008.

———. *A Theology of Liberation: History, Politics, and Salvation.* 1971. Maryknoll, NY: Orbis, 1973.

Hadfield, Andrew, Dominic Rainsford, and Tim Woods, eds. "Introduction: Literature and the Return to Ethics." In *The Ethics in Literature,* 1–14. New York: St. Martin's Press, 1999.

Haker, Hille. "Narrative and Moral Identity in Paul Ricoeur." *Concilium* 2 (2000): 59–68.

Hall, Linley Erin. *Who's Afraid of Marie Curie? The Challenge Facing Women in Science and Technology.* Emeryville, CA: Seal Press, 2007.

Halpern, Nick. *Everyday and Prophetic: The Poetry of Lowell, Ammons, Merrill, and Rich.* Madison: University of Wisconsin Press, 2003.

Hands, Elizabeth. *The Death of Amnon.* N. Rollason Coventry. 1789. Downloaded from Google Books.

Hanssen, Beatrice. "Ethics of the Other." In *The Turn to Ethics,* edited by Marjorie Garber, Beatrice Hanssen, and Rebecca L. Walkowitz, 127–80. New York: Routledge, 2000.

Harde, Roxanne. "Making of Our Lives a Study: Feminist Theology and Women's Creative Writing." *Feminist Theology* 15, no. 1 (2006): 48–69.

Haralson, Eric L. *Reading the Middle Generation Anew: Culture, Community, and Form in Twentieth-Century American Poetry.* Iowa City: University of Iowa Press, 2006.

Harpham, Geoffrey Galt. "Ethics." In *Critical Terms for Literary Study,* 2nd ed., edited by Frank Lentricchia and Thomas McLaughlin, 387–405. Chicago: University of Chicago Press, 1995.

———. *Shadows of Ethics: Criticism and the Just Society.* Durham, NC: Duke University Press, 1999.

Held, Virginia. *Feminist Morality: Transforming Culture, Society, and Politics.* Chicago: Chicago University Press, 1993.

Hewett, Heather. "Coming of Age: Chimamanda Ngozi Adichie and the Voice of the Third Generation." *English in Africa* 32, no. 1 (2005): 73–97.

Hinga, Teresa M. "African Feminist Theologies, the Global Village, and the Imperative of Solidarity Across Borders: The Case of the Circle of Concerned African Women Theologians." *Journal of Feminist Studies in Religion* 18, no. 1 (2002): 79–86.

——. "Jesus Christ and the Liberation of Women in Africa." In *The Will to Arise: Women, Tradition, and the Church in Africa,* edited by Mercy Amba Oduyoye and Musimbi R. A. Kanyoro, 183–94. Eugene, OR: Wipf and Stock, 1992.

Hirsch, Elizabeth. "Another Look at Genre: *Diving into the Wreck* of Ethics with Rich and Irigaray." In *Feminist Measures: Soundings in Poetry and Theory,* edited by Lynne Keller and Christanne Miller, 117–38. Ann Arbor: University of Michigan Press, 1994.

Hitchcock, Peter. "Postcolonial Africa? Problems of Theory." *Women's Studies Quarterly* 25, no. 3/4 (1997): 233–44.

Ho, Wen-ching. "'I'll Tell'—The Function and Meaning of L in Toni Morrison's *Love.*" *EurAmerica* 36, no. 4 (2006): 651–75.

Hollingsworth, Andrea. "The Courage to Attune." Ph.D. dissertation, Loyola University, Chicago, 2012.

Hollywood, Amy. "Feminist Studies." In *The Blackwell Companion to Christian Spirituality,* edited by Arthur Holder, 363–86. Oxford: Blackwell, 2005.

hooks, bell. "Choosing the Margins as a Space of Radical Openness." In *Yearning: Race, Gender, and Cultural Politics,* 145–54. Boston: South End Press, 1990.

Hopkins, Dwight N. *Heart and Head: Black Theology—Past, Present, and Future.* New York: Palgrave, 2002.

Houston, Pam. "Pam Houston Talks with Toni Morrison." *Toni Morrison: Conversations,* edited by Carolyn C. Denard, 228–47. Jackson: University Press of Mississippi, 2008.

Hove, Thomas B. "Toni Morrison." In *Postmodernism: The Key Figures,* edited by Hans Bertens and Joseph Natoli, 254–66. Malden, MA: Blackwell, 2002.

Hron, Madelaine. "Ora na-azu nwa: The Figure of the Child in Third-Generation Nigerian Novels." *Research in African Literatures* 39, no. 2 (2008): 27–48.

Hull, Gloria T., Patricia Bell Scott, and Barbara Smith, eds. *All the Women Are White, All the Blacks Are Men, But Some of Us Are Brave: Black Women's Studies.* Old Westbury, NY: The Feminist Press, 1982.

Hutchens, B. C. *Levinas: A Guide for the Perplexed.* New York: Continuum, 2004.

Hutcheon, Linda. *A Poetics of Postmodernism: History, Theory, Fiction.* New York: Routledge, 1988.

Irigaray, Luce. "The Fecundity of the Caress: A Reading of Levinas, *Totality and Infinity,* 'Phenomenology of Eros.'" 1984. In *The Ethics of Sexual Difference.* Trans. Carolyn Burke and Gillian C. Gill, 185–217. Ithaca, NY: Cornell University Press, 1993.

——. "What Other Are We Talking About?" *Yale French Studies* 104 (2004): 67–81.

Isasi-Díaz, Ada María. *En la Lucha/In the Struggle: A Hispanic Women's Liberation Theology.* Minneapolis, MN: Fortress Press, 1993.

Jantzen, Grace. *Julian of Norwich: Mystic and Theologian.* 1987. New Edition. Mahwah, NJ: Paulist Press, 2000.

Jasper, Alison. "'The Past Is Not a Husk Yet Change Goes On': Reimagining (Feminist) Theology." *Feminist Theology* 15, no. 2 (2007): 202–19.

Jeremiah, Emily. "Murderous Mothers: Adrienne Rich's *Of Woman Born* and Toni Morrison's *Beloved*." In *From Motherhood to Mothering: The Legacy of Adrienne Rich's* Of Woman Born, edited by Andrea O'Reilly, 59–71. Albany: SUNY Press, 2004.

Johnson, Barbara. *A World of Difference*. Baltimore, MD: Johns Hopkins University Press, 1987.

Johnson, Elizabeth. *She Who Is: The Mystery of God in Feminist Theological Discourse.* New York: Crossroad, 1994.

Kavka, Misha. "Feminism, Ethics, and History, or What Is the 'Post' in Postfeminism?" *Tulsa Studies in Women's Literature* 21, no. 1 (2002): 29–44.

Kearney, Richard. *Anatheism: Returning to God After God.* New York: Columbia University Press, 2010.

——. "Narrating Pain: The Power of Catharsis." *Paragraph* 30, no. 1 (2007): 51–66.

Kearney, Richard, and Mark Dooley, eds. *Questioning Ethics: Contemporary Debates in Philosophy.* London: Routledge, 1999.

Keniston, Ann. "Beginning with 'I': The Legacy of Adrienne Rich's *Of Woman Born*." In *From Motherhood to Mothering: The Legacy of Adrienne Rich's* Of Woman Born, edited by Andrea O'Reilly, 223–40. Albany: SUNY Press, 2004.

Keyes, Claire. *The Aesthetics of Power: The Poetry of Adrienne Rich.* Athens: University of Georgia Press, 1986.

King, Martin Luther, Jr. "Suffering and Faith." *Christian Century* 77 (April 27, 1960): 510. Reprinted in *Moral Evil and Redemptive Suffering: A History of Theodicy in African-American Religious Thought*, edited by Anthony B. Pinn, 223–26. Gainesville: University Press of Florida, 2002.

——. *Where Do We Go From Here? Chaos or Community?* Boston: Beacon, 1968.

Kirk-Duggan, Cheryl A. "African-American Spirituals: Confronting and Exorcising Evil Through Song." In *A Troubling in My Soul: Womanist Perspectives on Evil and Suffering*, edited by Emilie M. Townes, 150–71. Maryknoll, NY: Orbis, 1993.

Kwok, Pui-lan. "Feminist Theology as Intercultural Discourse." In *Cambridge Companion to Feminist Theology,* edited by Susan Frank Parsons, 23–39. Cambridge: Cambridge University Press, 2006.

——. "Mercy Amba Oduyoye and African Women's Theology." *Journal of Feminist Studies in Religion* 20, no. 1 (2004): 7–22.

——. *Postcolonial Imagination & Feminist Theology.* Louisville, KY: Westminster John Knox Press, 2005.

Kwok, Pui-lan, and Laura Donaldson, eds. *Postcolonialism, Feminism, and Religious Discourse.* New York: Routledge, 2001.

Langdell, Cheri Colby. *Adrienne Rich: The Moment of Change.* Westport, CT: Praeger, 2004.

Lanyer, Aemelia. *Salve Deus Rex Judaeorum.* 1611. In *The Poems of Shakespeare's Dark Lady.* Introduction by A. L. Rowse. New York: Clarkson N. Potter, 1979.

Lanza, Carmela Delia. "Hearing the Voices: Women and Home and Ana Castillo's *So Far from God.*" *MELUS* 23, no. 1 (1998): 65–79.

——. "'A New Meeting with the Sacred': Ana Castillo's *So Far from God.*" *Romance Languages Annual* 10 (1999): 658–63.

Lash, Scott. "Postmodern Ethics: The Missing Ground." *Theory, Culture, and Society* 13, no. 2 (1996): 91–104.

Levertov, Denise. "Biafra." In *Relearning the Alphabet,* 17–18. New York: New Directions, 1970.

——. "This Day." In *Oblique Prayers,* 80–81. New York: New Directions, 1984.

Levinas, Emmanuel. "No Identity." In *Collected Philosophical Papers,* 141–52. Trans. Alphonso Lingis. Dordrecht, The Netherlands: Martinus Nijhoff Publishers, 1987.

——. *Otherwise Than Being: or, Beyond Essence.* 1974. Trans. Alphonso Lingis. Dordecht, The Netherlands: Kluwer Academic, 1991.

——. *Totality and Infinity: An Essay on Exteriority.* 1961. Trans. Alphonso Lingis. Pittsburgh, PA: Duquesne University Press, 1969.

——. "Useless Suffering." In *Entre Nous: Thinking of the Other,* 78–87. Trans. Michael B. Smith and Barbara Harshav. New York: Columbia University Press, 1998.

Lewis, Reina, and Sara Mills, eds. *Feminist Postcolonial Theory: A Reader.* New York: Routledge, 2003.

Li, Stephanie. *Something Akin to Freedom: The Choice of Bondage in Narratives by African American Women.* Albany: SUNY Press, 2010.

Lindemann, Hilde. *An Invitation to Feminist Ethics.* Boston: McGraw Hill, 2006.

Lock, Anne Vaughan. *The Collected Works of Anne Vaughan Lock,* edited by Susan Felch. Tempe, AZ: Arizona Center for Medieval and Renaissance Studies in conjunction with the Renaissance English Text Society, 1999.

Longfellow, Erica. *Women and Religious Writing in Early Modern England.* Cambridge: Cambridge University Press, 2004.

Loomba, Ania. "Dead Women Tell No Tales: Issues of Female Subjectivity, Subaltern Agency and Tradition in Colonial and Postcolonial Writings on Widow Immolation in India." 1993. In *Feminist Postcolonial Theory: A Reader,* edited by Reina Lewis and Sara Mills, 241–62. New York: Routledge, 2003.

Lorde, Audre. *Sister Outsider: Essays and Speeches.* Berkeley: Crossing Press, 1984.

Loya, Gloria Inés. "Pathways to a *Mestiza* Feminist Theology." In *A Reader in Latina Feminist Theology: Religion and Justice,* edited by María Pilar Aquino, Daisy L. Machado, and Jeanette Rodríguez, 217–40. Austin: University of Texas Press, 2002.

Mabura, Lily. "Breaking Gods: An African Postcolonial Gothic Reading of Chimamanda Ngozi Adichie's *Purple Hibiscus* and *Half of a Yellow Sun*." *Research in African Literatures* 39, no. 1 (2008): 203–22.

MacIntyre, Alasdair. *After Virtue: A Study in Moral Theory*. Notre Dame, IN: University of Notre Dame Press, 1981.

Manríquez, B. J. "Ana Castillo's *So Far from God*: Intimations of the Absurd." *College Literature* 29, no. 2 (2002): 37–49.

Martin, Clarice J. "Biblical Theodicy and Black Women's Spiritual Autobiography: 'The Miry Bog, The Desolate Pit, A New Song in My Mouth.'" In *A Troubling in My Soul: Womanist Perspectives on Evil and Suffering*, edited by Emilie M. Townes, 13–36. Maryknoll, NY: Orbis, 1993.

Martin, Wendy. "From Patriarchy to the Female Principle: A Chronological Reading of Adrienne Rich's Poems." In *Adrienne Rich's Poetry*, edited by Barbara Charlesworth Gelpi and Albert Gelpi, 175–89. New York: Norton, 1975.

——. "A Nurturing Ethos in the Poetry of Adrienne Rich." In *Reading Adrienne Rich: Reviews and Re-Visions 1951–81*, edited by Jane Roberta Cooper, 163–70. Ann Arbor: University of Michigan Press, 1984.

Martínez, Ernesto Javier. "On Butler on Morrison on Language." *Signs* 35, no. 4 (2010): 821–42.

McAvoy, Liz Herbert. *Authority and the Female Body in the Writings of Julian of Norwich and Margery Kempe*. Cambridge: Boydell & Brewer, 2004.

McClure, John A. *Partial Faiths: Postsecular Fiction in the Age of Pynchon and Morrison*. Athens: University of Georgia Press, 2007.

McKay, Nellie. "An Interview with Toni Morrison." 1983. In *Conversations with Toni Morrison*, edited by Danielle Taylor-Guthrie, 138–55. Jackson: University Press of Mississippi, 1994.

Metz, Johann-Baptist. "The Future in the Memory of Suffering." 1972. In *Faith and the Future: Essays on Theology, Solidarity, and Modernity*, by Johann-Baptist Metz and Jürgen Motlmann, 3–16. Maryknoll, NY: Orbis, 1995.

Meyers, Diana Tietjens. "Narrative Structures, Narratives of Abuse, and Human Rights." In *Feminist Ethics and Social and Political Philosophy: Theorizing the Non-Ideal*, edited by Lisa Tessman, 253–70. New York: Springer, 2009.

——. *Subjection and Subjectivity: Psychoanalytic Feminism and Moral Philosophy*. New York: Routledge, 1994.

Miesszkowski, Gretchen. "'By a Miracle, a Twin': Helen Vendler's Reviews of Adrienne Rich's Recent Poetry." *South Central Review* 5, no. 2 (1988): 72–86.

Miller, J. Hillis. *The Ethics of Reading: Kant, de Man, Eliot, Trollope, James, and Benjamin*. New York: Columbia University Press, 1987.

Milligan, Bryce. "An Interview with Ana Castillo." *South Central Review* 16, no. 1 (1999): 19–29.

Mitchell, Carolyn A. "'I Love to Tell the Story': Biblical Revisions in *Beloved*." *Religion & Literature* (Autumn 1991): 27–42.

Mitchell, W. J. T. "Representation." In *Critical Terms for Literary Study*, 2nd ed., edited by Frank Lentricchia and Thomas McLaughlin, 11–22. Chicago: University of Chicago Press, 1995.

Mohanty, Chandra Talpade. "Under Western Eyes: Feminist Scholarship and Colonial Discourses." In *Feminist Postcolonial Theory: A Reader*, edited by Reina Lewis and Sara Mills, 49–74. New York: Routledge, 2003.

Moraga, Cherríe. *Heroes and Saints & Other Plays*. Albuquerque: West End Press, 1994.

——. "La Güera." In *This Bridge Called My Back: Writings by Radical Women of Color*, 2nd ed., edited by Cherríe Moraga and Gloria Anzaldúa, 27–34. Lanham, NY: Kitchen Table Press, 1983.

——. *Loving in the War Years: lo que nunca pasó por sus labios*. New York: South End Press, 1983.

——. "Refugees of a World on Fire: Foreword to the Second Edition." In *This Bridge Called My Back: Writings by Radical Women of Color*, 2nd ed., edited by Cherríe Moraga and Gloria Anzaldúa, n.p. Lanham, NY: Kitchen Table Press, 1983.

——. *Waiting in the Wings: Portrait of a Queer Motherhood*. Ithaca, NY: Firebrand Books, 1997.

Moraga, Cherríe, and Gloria Anzaldúa, eds. *This Bridge Called My Back: Writings by Radical Women of Color*. 1981. 2nd ed. Lanham, NY: Kitchen Table Press, 1983.

Morrison, Toni. *Beloved*. 1987. New York: Plume, 1988.

——. *The Bluest Eye*. 1970. New York: Washington Square Press, 1972.

——. "For a Heroic Writers Movement." 1981. In *What Moves at the Margin: Selected Nonfiction*, edited by Carolyn C. Denard, 156–63. Jackson: University Press of Mississippi, 2008.

——. "James Baldwin: His Life Remembered; Life in His Language." *New York Times* (20 Dec. 1987).

——. *Jazz*. New York: Knopf, 1992.

——. *Love*. New York: Knopf, 2003.

——. *A Mercy*. New York: Knopf, 2008.

——. "Nobel Lecture, 7 December 1993." *The Georgia Review* 49, no. 1 (1995): 318–23.

——. *Paradise*. New York: Knopf, 1998.

——. *Playing the Dark: Whiteness and the Literary Imagination*. Cambridge, MA: Harvard University Press, 1990.

——, ed. *Race-ing Justice, En-Gendering Power: Essays on Anita Hill, Clarence Thomas, and the Construction of Social Reality*. New York: Pantheon, 1992.

——. "Recitatif." In *Confirmation: An Anthology of African American Women*, edited by Amiri and Amini Baraka. New York: William Morrow, 1983.

——. "Rootedness: The Ancestor as Foundation." In *Black Women Writers (1950–1980): A Critical Evaluation*, edited by Mari Evans, 339–45. Garden City, NY: Anchor Press/Doubleday, 1983.

——. "The Site of Memory." In *Inventing the Truth: The Art and Craft of Memoir*, edited by William Zinsser, 103–24. Boston: Houghton Mifflin, 1987.

——. *Song of Solomon*. New York: Vintage, 1977.

——. *Sula*. 1973. New York: Plume, 1980.

——. *Tar Baby*. New York: Plume, 1981.

——. "Unspeakable Things Unspoken: The Afro-American Presence in American Literature." *Michigan Quarterly Review* 28, no. 1 (1989): 1–34.

Morrow, Colette. "Queering Chicano/a Narratives: Lesbian as Healer, Saint and Warrior in Ana Castillo's *So Far from God*." *Journal of the Midwest Modern Language Association* 30, no. 1/2 (1997): 63–80.

Naparstek, Ben. "Mercy in a Time of Slavery: An Interview." *Sydney Morning Herald (Australia)* (22 Nov. 2008).

Newton, Adam Zachary. *Narrative Ethics*. Cambridge, MA: Harvard University Press, 1995.

——. "Versions of Ethics; Or, The SARL of Criticism: Sonority, Arrogation, and Letting-Be." *American Literary History* 13, no. 3 (2001): 606–37.

Nightingale, Florence. *Cassandra and Other Selections from Suggestions for Thought*, edited by Mary Poovey. 1859. Washington Square: New York University Press, 1992.

Noddings, Nel. *Women and Evil*. Berkeley: University of California Press, 1989.

Norwich, Julian of. *Revelation of Love*. c. 1400. Trans. John Skinner. New York: Image, 1997.

Novak, Amy. "Who Speaks? Who Listens? The Problem of Address in Two Nigerian Trauma Novels." *Studies in the Novel* 40, no. 1–2 (2008): 31–51.

Nussbaum, Martha C. *The Fragility of Goodness: Luck and Ethics in Greek Tragedy and Philosophy*. Cambridge: Cambridge University Press, 1986.

O'Reilly, Andrea, ed. *From Motherhood to Mothering: The Legacy of Adrienne Rich's Of Woman Born*. Albany: SUNY Press, 2004.

——. *Rocking the Cradle: Thoughts on Feminism, Motherhood, and the Possibility of Empowered Mothering*. Brunswick, ON: Demeter Press, 2004.

——. *Toni Morrison and Motherhood: A Politics of the Heart*. Albany: SUNY Press, 2004.

Oduyoye, Mercy Amba. "Be a Woman, and Africa Will Be Strong." In *Inheriting Our Mothers' Gardens: Feminist Theology in Third World Perspective*, edited by Letty M. Russell et. al., 35–53. Louisville, KY: Westminster John Knox Press, 1988.

——. "Christianity and African Culture." *International Review of Mission* 84, no. 332–33 (1995): 77–90.

——. *Daughters of Anowa: African Women and Patriarchy*. Maryknoll, NY: Orbis, 1995.

Ogwude, Sophia O. "History and Ideology in Chimamanda Adichie's Fiction." *Tydskrif vir Letterkunde* 48, no. 1 (2011): 110–23.

Oliver, Mary. "Singapore." In *House of Light*, 8–9. Boston: Beacon, 1990.

The Oxford English Dictionary. 2nd ed. 1989. 2011. Online Version.

Parr, Katherine. *Prayers or Medytacions.* 1545. *The Early Modern Englishwoman—A Facsimile Library of Essential Works. Part 1, Printed writings, 1500–1645.* Vol. 3, edited by Janel Mueller. Brookfield, VT: Ashgate, 1996.

Perdigao, Lisa K. " 'The Words I'd Found': The Poetics of Recovery in Adrienne Rich's Poetry." In *"Catch If You Can Your Country's Moment": Recovery and Regeneration in the Poetry of Adrienne Rich,* edited by William S. Waddell, 141–57. Newcastle, England: Cambridge Scholars, 2007.

Pérez, Emma. "Sexuality and Discourse: Notes from a Chicana Survivor." In *Chicana Critical Issues,* edited by Norma Alarcón, Rafaela Castro, Emma Pérez, Beatríz Pesquera, Adaljiza Sosa Riddell, and Patricia Zavella, 45–69. Berkeley, CA: Third Woman Press, 1993.

Pérez, Gail. "Ana Castillo as *Santera*: Reconstructing Popular Religious Praxis." In *A Reader in Latina Feminist Theology: Religion and Justice,* edited by María Pilar Aquino, Daisy L. Machado, and Jeanette Rodríguez, 53–79. Austin: University of Texas Press, 2002.

Pesquera, Beatríz M., and Denise A. Segura. "There Is No Going Back: Chicanas and Feminism." In *Chicana Critical Issues,* edited by Norma Alarcón, Rafaela Castro, Emma Pérez, Beatríz Pesquera, Adaljiza Sosa Riddell, and Patricia Zavella, 95–115. Berkeley, CA: Third Woman Press, 1993.

Phillips, Layli, ed. *The Womanist Reader.* New York: Routledge, 2006.

Pinn, Anthony B., ed. *Moral Evil and Redemptive Suffering: A History of Theodicy in African-American Religious Thought.* Gainesville: University Press of Florida, 2002.

Plasa, Carl, ed. *Toni Morrison, Beloved.* New York: Columbia University Press, 1998.

Quintanales, Mirtha. "I Paid Very Hard for My Immigrant Ignorance." In *This Bridge Called My Back: Writings by Radical Women of Color,* 2nd ed., edited by Cherríe Moraga and Gloria Anzaldúa, 150–56. Lanham, NY: Kitchen Table Press, 1983.

Raboteau, Albert J. " 'The Blood of the Martyrs is the Seed of Faith': Suffering in the Christianity of American Slaves." In *The Courage to Hope: From Black Suffering to Human Redemption,* edited by Quinton Hosford Dixie and Cornel West, 22–39. Boston: Beacon, 1999.

Rainsford, Dominic and Tim Woods, eds. *Critical Ethics: Text, Theory, and Responsibility.* New York: Macmillan, 1999.

Rajchman, John. *Truth and Eros: Foucault, Lacan, and the Question of Ethics.* New York: Routledge, 1991.

Rankka, Kristine M. *Women and the Value of Suffering: An Aw(e)ful Rowing Toward God.* Collegeville, MN: Liturgical Press, 1998.

Ratcliff, Krista. *Anglo-American Feminist Challenges to the Rhetorical Traditions: Virginia Woolf, Mary Daly, Adrienne Rich*. Carbondale: Southern Illinois University Press, 1996.

Ravvin, Norman. "Have You Reread Levinas Lately? Transformations of the Face in Post-Holocaust Fiction." In *Ethics in Literature*, edited by Andrew Hadfield, Dominic Rainsford, and Tim Woods, 52–70. New York: St. Martin's Press, 1999.

Rebolledo, Tey Diana. *Women Singing in the Snow: A Cultural Analysis of Chicana Literature*. Tucson: University of Arizona Press, 1995.

Rich, Adrienne. *Arts of the Possible: Essays and Conversations*. New York: Norton, 2001.

——. *An Atlas of the Difficult World: Poems 1988–1991*. New York: Norton, 1991.

——. *Blood, Bread, and Poetry: Selected Prose 1979–1985*. New York: Norton, 1986.

——. *Collected Early Poems 1950–1970*. New York: Norton, 1993.

——. *Diving into the Wreck: Poems 1971–1972*. New York: Norton, 1973.

——. *The Dream of a Common Language: Poems 1974–1977*. New York: Norton, 1978.

——. *The Fact of a Doorframe: Poems Selected and New 1950–1984*. New York: Norton, 1984.

——. *Fox*. New York: Norton, 2001.

——. *A Human Eye: Essays on Art in Society, 1997–2008*. New York: Norton, 2009.

——. "Notes Towards a Politics of Location." 1984. In *Feminist Postcolonial Theory: A Reader*, edited by Reina Lewis and Sara Mills, 29–42. New York: Routledge, 2003.

——. *Of Woman Born: Motherhood as Experience and Institution*. 1976. Tenth Anniversary Edition. New York: Norton, 1986.

——. *On Lies, Secrets, and Silence: Selected Prose 1966–1978*. New York: Norton, 1979.

——. *The School Among the Ruins*. New York: Norton, 2004.

——. *Sources*. Woodside, CA: Heyeck Press, 1985.

——. *Time's Power*. New York: Norton, 1989.

——. *Tonight No Poetry Will Serve: Poems 2007–2010*. New York: Norton, 2011.

——. *What Is Found There: Notebooks on Poetry and Politics*. New York: Norton, 1993.

——. *A Wild Patience Has Taken Me This Far: Poems 1978–1981*. New York: Norton, 1981.

——. *Your Native Land, Your Life*. New York: Norton, 1986.

Ricoeur, Paul. *Oneself as Another*. Trans. Kathleen Blamey. Chicago: University of Chicago Press, 1995.

——. *Time and Narrative*. Chicago: University of Chicago Press, 1984.

Robbins, Jill. *Altered Reading: Levinas and Literature*. Chicago: University of Chicago Press, 1999.

Rodríguez, Jeanette. "Latina Activists: Toward an Inclusive Spirituality of Being in the World." In *A Reader in Latina Feminist Theology: Religion and Justice*, edited by María Pilar Aquino, Daisy L. Machado, and Jeanette Rodríguez, 114–30. Austin: University of Texas Press, 2002.

Rodriguez, Ralph E. "Chicana/o Fiction from Resistance to Contestation: The Role of Creation in Ana Castillo's *So Far from God.*" *MELUS* 25, no. 2 (2000): 63–82.

Rossetti, Christina. *The Complete Poems of Christina Rossetti*, edited by R. W. Crump. Baton Rouge: Louisiana State University Press, 1979.

Rowland, Christopher. "The Theology of Liberation." In *The Cambridge Companion to Liberation Theology,* edited by Christopher Rowland, 1–16. Cambridge: Cambridge University Press, 2008.

Ruether, Rosemary Radford. *Sexism and God-Talk*. Boston: Beacon, 1983.

Russell, Letty M. "Cultural Hermeneutics: A Postcolonial Look at Mission." *Journal of Feminist Studies in Religion* 20, no. 1 (2004): 23–40.

Russell, Letty M. et. al., eds. *Inheriting Our Mothers' Gardens: Feminist Theology in Third World Perspective*. Louisville, KY: Westminster John Knox Press, 1988.

Saeta, Elsa. "A MELUS Interview: Ana Castillo." *MELUS* 22, no. 3 (1997): 133–49.

Said, Edward. "Traveling Theory Reconsidered." In *Reflections on Exile and Other Essays*, 436–52. Cambridge, MA: Harvard University Press, 2000.

Samuels, Shirley. *The Culture of Sentiment: Race, Gender, and Sentimentality in Nineteenth-Century America*. New York: Oxford University Press, 1992.

Sanders, Cheryl J., Katie G. Cannon, Emilie M. Townes, M. Shawn Copeland, bell hooks, and Cheryl Townsend Gilkes. "Roundtable Discussion: Christian Ethics and Theology in Womanist Perspective." 1989. In *The Womanist Reader*, edited by Layli Phillips, 126–57. New York: Routledge, 2006.

Sandoval, Chela. *Methodology of the Oppressed*. Minneapolis: University of Minnesota Press, 2000.

Sauer, Michelle M. "'Saint-Making' in Ana Castillo's *So Far from God*: Medieval Mysticism as Precedent for an Authoritative Chicana Spirituality." *Mester* 29 (2000): 72–91.

Scarry, Elaine. *The Body in Pain: The Making and Unmaking of the World*. New York: Oxford University Press, 1985.

Schweizer, Harold. *Suffering and the Remedy of Art*. New York: SUNY Press, 1997.

Shea, Renee H. "A Slender Hope." *Poets and Writers* (July/August 2009): 42–47.

Sheridan, Susan. "Adrienne Rich and the Women's Liberation Movement: A Politics of Reception." *Women's Studies* 35 (2006): 17–45.

Shohat, Ella. "The Struggle over Representation: Casting, Coalitions, and the Politics of Identification." In *Late Imperial Culture,* edited by Román de la Campa, E. Ann Kaplan, and Michael Sprinker, 166–78. London: Verso, 1995.

Silverblatt, Michael. "Michael Silverblatt Talks with Toni Morrison About *Love*." In *Toni Morrison: Conversations,* edited by Carolyn C. Denard, 216–27. Jackson: University Press of Mississippi, 2008.

Silverman, Kaja. *The Subject of Semiotics*. Oxford: Oxford University Press, 1984.

Skinner, John, ed. and trans. Preface to *Revelation of Love* by Julian of Norwich, vii–xiii. New York: Image, 1999.

Smith, Barbara. "Toward a Black Feminist Criticism." 1977. In *All the Women Are White, All the Blacks Are Men, But Some of Us Are Brave: Black Women's Studies,* edited by Gloria T. Hull, Patricia Bell Scott, and Barbara Smith, 157–75. Old Westbury, NY: The Feminist Press, 1982.

Sölle, Dorothee. *Suffering.* Trans. Everett R. Kalin. Philadelphia, PA: Fortress Press, 1975.

Sontag, Susan. "The Artist as Exemplary Sufferer." In *Against Interpretation and Other Essays,* 39–48. New York: Delta, 1966.

——. *Regarding the Pain of Others.* New York: Picador, 2003.

Spivak, Gayatri. "Can the Subaltern Speak?" In *Marxism and the Interpretation of Culture,* edited by Cary Nelson and Lawrence Grossberg, 271–313. Urbana: University of Illinois Press, 1988.

——. "Practical Politics of the Open End." In *The Postcolonial Critic: Interviews, Strategies, Dialogues,* edited by Sarah Harasym, 95–112. New York: Routledge, 1990.

Stanton, Elizabeth Cady. *The Woman's Bible. Vol. I–II.* 1895. Foreword by Maureen Fitzgerald. Boston: Northeastern University Press, 1993.

Stepto, Robert. "Intimate Things in Place: A Conversation with Toni Morrison." 1976. In *Conversations with Toni Morrison,* edited by Danielle Taylor-Guthrie, 10–29. Jackson: University Press of Mississippi, 1994.

Stobie, Cheryl. "Dethroning the Infallible Father: Religion, Patriarchy and Politics in Chimamanda Ngozi Adichie's *Purple Hibiscus.*" *Literature & Theology: An International Journal of Religion, Theory, and Culture* 24, no. 4 (2010): 421–35.

Strehle, Susan. "The Decolonized Home: Chimamanda Ngozi Adichie's *Purple Hibiscus.*" In *Transnational Women's Fiction: Unsettling Home and Homeland,* 102–25. New York: Palgrave Macmillan, 2008.

Sweeney, Megan. "'Something Rogue': Commensurability, Commodification, Crime, and Justice in Toni Morrison's Later Fiction." *MFS Modern Fiction Studies* 52, no. 2 (2006): 440–69.

Taylor, Charles. *A Secular Age.* Cambridge, MA: Harvard University Press, 2007.

Taylor-Guthrie, Danielle, ed. *Conversations with Toni Morrison.* Jackson: University Press of Mississippi, 1994.

Templeton, Alice. "Contradictions: Tracking Adrienne Rich's Poetry." *Tulsa Studies in Women's Literature* 12, no. 2 (1993): 333–40.

——. *The Dream and the Dialogue: Adrienne Rich's Feminist Poetics.* Knoxville: University of Tennessee Press, 1994.

Torres, Hector A. *Conversations with Contemporary Chicana and Chicano Writers.* Albuquerque: University of New Mexico Press, 2007.

Townes, Emilie M., ed. *A Troubling in My Soul: Womanist Perspectives on Evil and Suffering*. Maryknoll, NY: Orbis, 1993.

——. *In a Blaze of Glory: Womanist Spirituality as Social Witness*. Nashville, TN: Abingdon Press, 1995.

——. *Womanist Ethics and the Cultural Production of Evil*. New York: Palgrave Macmillan, 2006.

VanZanten, Susan. "A Conversation with Chimamanda Ngozi Adichie." *Image* 65 (2010): 86–99.

Vega-González, Susana. "Toni Morrison's Water World: Watertime Writing in *Love*." *The Grove* 11 (2004): 207–20.

Vendler, Helen. "Ghostlier Demarcations, Keener Sounds." In *Adrienne Rich's Poetry*, edited by Barbara Charlesworth Gelpi and Albert Gelpi, 160–71. New York: Norton, 1975.

Vetlesen, Arne Johan. *A Philosophy of Pain*. 2004. Trans. John Irons. London: Reaktion, 2009.

Waddell, William S., ed. *"Catch if you can your country's moment": Recovery and Regeneration in the Poetry of Adrienne Rich*. Newcastle, England: Cambridge Scholars, 2007.

Walker, Alice. "Coming Apart." 1979. In *The Womanist Reader*, edited by Layli Phillips, 3–11. New York: Routledge, 2006.

——. *In Search of Our Mothers' Gardens: Womanist Prose*. Orlando, FL: Harcourt, 1983.

——. "Womanist." 1983. In *The Womanist Reader*, edited by Layli Phillips, 19. New York: Routledge, 2006.

Walton, Heather. *Imagining Theology: Women, Writing, and God*. London: T&T Clark, 2007.

——. *Literature, Theology, and Feminism*. Manchester: Manchester University Press, 2007.

Wanzo, Rebecca. *The Suffering Will Not Be Televised: African American Women and Sentimental Political Storytelling*. Albany: SUNY Press, 2009.

Ward, Cynthia. "Reading African Women Readers." *Research in African Literatures* 27, no. 3 (1996): 78–86.

Wardi, Anissa Janine. "A Laying on of Hands: Toni Morrison and the Materiality of *Love*." *MELUS* 30, no. 3 (2005): 201–18.

Watt, Diane. *Medieval Women's Writing*. Cambridge: Polity, 2007.

Weil, Simone. *Waiting for God*. 1951. Trans. Emma Craufurd. New York: Harper and Row, 1973.

Welch, Sharon. *A Feminist Ethic of Risk*. Minneapolis, MN: Fortress Press, 1990.

Werner, Craig. *Adrienne Rich: The Poet and Her Critics*. Chicago: American Library Association, 1988.

Wheatley, Phillis. "On Being Brought from Africa to America." In *The Norton Anthology of American Literature*, shorter 5th ed., edited by Nina Baym, 360. New York: Norton, 1999.

White, Stephen K. *Sustaining Affirmation: The Strengths of Weak Ontology in Political Theory.* Princeton, NJ: Princeton University Press, 2000.

Wilcox, Helen, ed. *Women and Literature in Britain, 1500–1700.* Cambridge: Cambridge University Press, 1996.

Williams, Delores S. *Sisters in the Wilderness: The Challenge of Womanist God-Talk.* Maryknoll, NY: Orbis, 1993.

——. "A Womanist Perspective on Sin." In *A Troubling in My Soul: Womanist Perspectives on Evil and Suffering,* edited by Emilie M. Townes, 130–49. Maryknoll, NY: Orbis, 1993.

——. "Womanist Theology, Black Women's Voices." 1986. In *The Womanist Reader,* edited by Layli Phillips, 117–25. New York: Routledge, 2006.

Williams, Sherley Anne. "Some Implications of Womanist Theory." 1986. In *The Womanist Reader,* edited by Layli Phillips, 159–64. New York: Routledge, 2006.

Wood, Frances E. " 'Take My Yoke Upon You': The Role of the Church in the Oppression of African-American Women." In *A Troubling in My Soul: Womanist Perspectives on Evil and Suffering,* edited by Emilie M. Townes, 37–47. Maryknoll, NY: Orbis, 1993.

Wu, Yung-Hsing. "Doing Things with Ethics: *Beloved, Sula,* and the Reading of Judgment." *MFS* 49, no. 4 (2003): 780–805.

Yearsley, Anne. *Poems on Various Subjects.* 1787. New York: Woodstock Books, 1994.

Yorke, Liz. *Adrienne Rich: Passion, Politics, and the Body.* London: Sage, 1997.

Ziarek, Ewa Płonowska. *An Ethics of Dissensus: Postmodernity, Feminism, and the Politics of Radical Democracy.* Stanford, CA: Stanford University Press, 2001.

LIST OF CREDITS

292 LIST OF CREDITS

Some materials in chapter 3 first appeared in the article "L as Language: Love and Ethics" in *African American Review*, Vol. 47, No. 2–3, Summer/Fall, 2014, pp. 375–390.

Some materials in chapter 5 first appeared in the article "Chimamanda Ngozi Adichie's *Purple Hibiscus* and the Paradoxes of Postcolonial Redemption" in *Christianity and Literature*, Vol. 61, No. 3, 2012, pp. 465–483.

INDEX

Achebe, Chinua, 174, 201

Adam (biblical figure), 6–7

Adichie, Chimamanda Ngozi: 2009 TED Talk by, 170, 195–96; Africans and African Americans and, 203, 267n65; *Americanah* by, 267n65; background of, 169; childbirth in works of, 223; on Christianity and colonialism, 182; on combating stereotypes with literature, 149; complexities addressed by, 8–9; criticism of, 211; danger of a single story and, 170, 195–96, 213–14; ethics of literary representation and, 193, 211; on fiction, 168, 192; on generalizing from the particular, 193–94; glimpses of hope in works of, 216; "Jumping Monkey Hill" by, 266n58; literature as anthropology and, 194; multiplicity of stories and, 196–97, 267n61; new generation of writers and, 169; postcolonial theory and, xvii, xviii; thematization of readerly attention in works of,

32–33; *The Thing Around Your Neck* by, 267n61; voice and representation and, 168–69. *See also Half of a Yellow Sun* (Adichie); *Purple Hibiscus* (Adichie)

Adorno, Thodor, 19, 239n92

Africa. *See* Biafran War; *Half of a Yellow Sun* (Adichie); imperialism and colonialism; postcolonialism; *Purple Hibiscus* (Adichie)

African American women: absence of black lesbianism in literature and, 89; academy's growing welcome for, 92; black feminist criticism and, 89, 90–91; black liberation theology's inattentiveness to experiences of, 107; Black Women's Studies and, 90; as Christ figures, 110, 253n68; on the cross, 104; idealization of suffering of, 253n62; intellectual traditions of, 90; linguistic sound of, 250n31; mothering for, 103–4; racialized causes of suffering for, 104; representativeness and particularity

African American women (*continued*)
of experiences of, 87, 248*n*3; Rich
and, 59; standpoint theory and, 108;
the supernatural in black women's
fiction and, 104; womanist ethics
and, 111, 253*n*62. *See also* womanist
ethics
Alarcón, Daniel, 140
Alcalá, Rita Cano, 139, 142, 257–58*n*29
Althusser, Louis, 244*n*55
Altieri, Charles, 70
Amato, Joseph, 27
Anthony, Susan B., 24
Anthony of Padua, 131
Anzaldúa, Gloria, 125, 129–33, 136–37,
256*n*3, 258*n*35
Aquino, María Pilar, 134, 258*n*32, 260*n*70
Aristotle, 35
Arnold, Matthew, 47
Ashcroft, Bill, 170
Attridge, Derek: attentiveness and
sacrifice and, 217; ethical turn in
literary scholarship and, 18; ethics
of literary representation and, 35;
gendered writing on attention
and, 242*n*18; new ethical literary
discourse and, 13; readerly attention
and, 31–32; on responsibility for the
other's needs, 11; on self-emptying
receptivity to texts, 14
Augustine (saint), 155

Bahri, Deepika, 193
Baker-Fletcher, Karen, 250*n*31
Baldwin, James, 105, 113
Bambara, Toni Cade, 210
Barrett Browning, Elizabeth, 6–7, 22,
56, 80
Barry, Kathleen, 66
Barthes, Roland, xii

Bartky, Sandra Lee, 238*n*75
Bauman, Zygmunt, 12, 230
Beloved (Morrison): Baby Suggs's
sermon in, 113, 114; *Beloved* as
language-act and, 86–87; as center
of Morrison's oeuvre, 86–87;
concretization of historic suffering
in, 254–55*n*80; criticisms of, 247*n*2;
exorcism scene in, 250*n*31; material
reading of, 247*n*1; powerless
responsibility in, 255*n*84; prizes for,
92; religion in, 110; re-membering
slaves' stories and, 168; sound in,
250*n*31
Bernard of Clairvaux, 234*n*5
Biafran War: "Biafra" (Levertov) and,
207–9, 211, 214, 222; global apathy
about, 207–9, 214; in *Half of a Yellow
Sun* (Adichie), 197–200, 202–5, 209,
214; media coverage of, 197, 202, 207,
208–9
Bishop, Elizabeth, 211
Biviano, Erin, 15
black faith: black liberation theology
and, 105, 107, 135, 148–51, 251*n*46,
259*n*64, 267*n*65; debates about
redemptive suffering and, 106; Job
versus Exodus as paradigm for
suffering and, 120; passivity versus
strength and, 105, 251*n*49; slaves'
redemption of the Bible and, 106–7;
suffering and sacrifice in, 104–5.
See also Christianity and the Bible;
theology and theologians
Black Power movement, 69, 105
Blazer, Alex, 64
bodies: author's body as text and,
226; embodiment and ethics-and-
feminism debate and, 83; one's
back as a bridge and, 131, 256*n*9; as

powerful and powerless, 51; as site for ethical insight, 81; women's hands and, ix

Boff, Clodovis, 30, 144–46, 148, 149, 259n64

Boff, Leonardo, 30, 144–46, 149, 259n64

Booth, Wayne, 13

Bosch, Hieronymus, 208

Bost, Suzanne, 136–37

Bradstreet, Ann, 56

Buell, Lawrence, 12, 89

Butler, Judith, 227, 250n33

Bynum, Carolyn Walker, 234–35n14

Calvin, John, 4

Caminero-Santangelo, Marta, 144–46

Cannon, Katie G., 253n64, 253n66, 255n83, 264n16

Caputo, John, 14

Card, Claudia, 238n75

Castillo, Ana: ambivalence in texts of, 168; Catholicism and, xvii, 134, 136, 138, 146–47, 151; *Chicana* as term and, 255–56n2; childbirth in works of, 223; compassion and gender and, 261n88; complexity and particularity of works of, 129; conscientization and, 259n59; criticism of, 211; critique of self-sacrifice in works of, 129; double moves in works of, 129; ethics of literary representation and, 156, 193, 211; on feminist liberation theology, 138; gaps and mysteries in works of, 129; generational shift in literature and, 132; glimpse of hope in works of, 216; *Goddess of the Americas* and, 257–58n29; hermeneutic of liberation and, 188; on indigenous

religious traditions, 136; liberation theology and, 146–47, 150, 151, 152; magical realism in works of, 144; on Marxism, 146–47; *Massacre of the Dreamers* by, 133, 136, 138–39, 146–47, 157, 165; on misogyny, 125; mother-bond principle and, 157, 165; mothering in works of, xvii; on publisher's pressure to write happy endings, 268n5; "Saintly Mothers and Soldier's Whore" by, 146, 150; on self-giving Chicana mother, 133; sharing between novels of, 158, 261n87; thematization of readerly attention in works of, 32–33; Virgin Mary in writings of, 223; on women's vulnerability as activists, 147; on Xicanisma, 136, 139, 146–47. *See also Guardians, The* (Castillo); *So Far from God* (Castillo)

Catherine of Siena, 234n5

Caughie, Pamela, 35, 236n34

Chanter, Tina, 15

childbirth: chosen and unchosen suffering and, 222–23; chosen versus unchosen pregnancy and, x; creative versus destructive pain and, 51; cultural meaning of labor pain and, 21; death in, 53; Eve's curse and, 222–23; maintenance of patriarchy and, 50–51; midwives as witches and, 53; miscarriage and, x, 222–23, 224–27, 231; painful passivity of, 50; pain in as God's punishment and, 53; purposiveness of suffering in, 50–51; resistance to anesthesia for, 53–54; Rich on suffering and pain-relief in, 75–76; sameness and difference in experiences of, 223

Chodorow, Nancy, 238*n*75

chosen versus unchosen suffering:
affliction versus suffering and, 50;
childbirth and mothering and, x,
222–23; chosen versus imposed, x,
3, 10, 16, 20, 22, 23, 26; necessitated
choice and, 255*n*82; in *Purple Hibiscus*
(Adichie), 175, 181; redemption
of, 228; Rich on, 43, 76, 77–78,
79–80; similarity and difference in
suffering and, 227; in *So Far from
God* (Castillo), 142–43; struggle for
justice and, 107, 149, 224, 227–28, 231;
unchosen, unimposed suffering and,
228; for whites versus blacks, 255*n*83

Christ, Carol, 57–58

Christian, Barbara, xviii, 89–90, 92,
111, 112

Christianity and the Bible:
abandonment of indigenous culture
and, 263*n*6; anthologies of the
early 1980s and, xvi; baptism and,
120; biblical men causing women
to suffer and, 5; as both damaging
and a resource for resistance, 107,
136, 258*n*35; breaking silence about
suffering in, xiv; brother's keeper
in, 11; Catholicism and, xvii, 133,
150, 233*n*2, 262*n*89, 263*n*6; Christ
and Virgin Mary as advocates in,
240*n*110; Christ as mother and, 2,
234*n*3; colonialism and, 174, 182,
185, 186–87, 263*n*6; critique and
embrace and, xiv, 169–70, 177–79,
190, 220; culturally mandated
suffering and self-sacrifice and, xvii,
23–24; dangers of *kenosis* ethics of,
79; direction of influence between
white Western and other writers
and, xviii; ethical turn in, x–xi, xii;

expectation of women's suffering
and, 53–54; feminism in twentieth-
century theology and, 28; first- and
second-wave feminism and, 26–27;
Good Friday and, 125, 127–29;
historic African, 265*n*28; humility
in, 27; inattention to gender and,
xii; Job versus Exodus as paradigm
for suffering and, 120; justification
of masochism and, 29; kyriarchy
in, 136; lessons for Westerners
from African traditions and, 189;
lives of saints in, 152; love and
suffering in, 3–4; love-as-justice
in, 30; Mary Daly's repudiation of,
60; misogyny of Church Fathers
and, 53; in Morrison's works,
109–10, 119, 253*n*68; origins of
women's propensity to suffer
and, 25–26; pain in childbirth
as God's punishment and, 53;
paradoxes inherent in, 111; passion
and passivity in, 20; preference
for qualities viewed as masculine
in, 54; pregnancy, childbirth,
and mothering in, 223; prophetic
heritage of, 184–92, 264*n*16;
redemptive suffering and, xi–xii,
27–28, 233*n*2; religion exiled from,
xii; role of Eve in church teaching
and, 54; self-abnegation and, 32;
self-emptying in, 79; self-hating
in, 172, 173–74; self-sacrifice for
women in, 23–24; sin and, 55, 96,
109; slavery and, 88; social ethics in,
59; as source of political oppression,
28; as source of suffering and of
healing and hope, 175–76, 178, 189;
suffering associated with feminine
gender in, 52; suffering God in, 6;

suffering (*continued*)

as sufferers and, 8; complexity of,
9–10; conversion of, into activism,
75–76; critique and embrace and,
xiv, 19; cultural hermeneutics to
identify causes of, 190; as culturally
mandated for women, xvii; cultural
mediation of meaning of pain and,
21; death and, 23; definitions of,
19–21; denial of, 49; disavowal of,
23–24; in earliest women's literature,
4–5, 234–35n14; expectations in
narratives of, 240n111; exquisite,
43; feminist reevaluation of, 23;
gendering of, 4, 52, 79–80; as
holy duty, 6–7; images of global
suffering and, 23; indifference to, 22;
justification of masochism and, 29;
language and, 10–11, 19–23, 263n4;
learning from, 231; local specificity
and global acknowledgment of, 169;
love and, 3–4; meaning of *borne* and,
47–48; as natural female destiny,
25–26, 45; one's own and others,'
130; for the other, 11, 14–15, 17–18, 24,
28, 30, 131; as an ought, 22; versus
pain, 19, 22; pain management
and, 23; particularity of, xviii,
209–10; as passive experience
versus active engagement, 20,
76, 77–78, 79; passive resistance
and, 45–46; pregnancy, childbirth,
and mothering and, 103, 223;
reappropriation of by Chicana
feminists, 137; refusal to reject
histories of, xviii; in *Revelation of
Love* (Julian of Norwich), 3; Rich
and, xvi, 22, 40, 43, 74; sameness
and difference in, 191–92, 196,
206, 226, 227, 231; in second-wave

feminism, 40; self-sacrifice as
chosen suffering and, x; silence
and isolation and, 21–22, 94–95; as
source of creative energy, 106; as
source of emancipatory action, 30;
substitutionary, 104, 123; subversive
remembering of Christ's suffering
and, 29–30; traumas too disturbing
for literature and, 91–92; traumas
too disturbing to televise and,
248n15; universality of, 227; Western
aversion to, 9–10; willing, 4; as
woman's special means of grace,
6; women's fragility and, 225–26;
women's writing before 1900 and,
5–7. *See also* chosen versus unchosen
suffering; pain; redemptive suffering
suffrage, 23–27

Tarango, Yolangogy, 147
Taylor, Charles, 27–28, 57
Templeton, Alice, 52, 67
temporality: of feminism, 42, 65, 130; of
poetry's social use, 63; Rich and, 42,
242n11
Teresa of Avila, 136–37
theodicy, 2, 106, 121, 122–23, 181
theology and theologians:
Americanness of black liberation
and womanist theology and, 267n65;
black/white racial polarity and, 132;
critical hermeneutics and, 58; ethics
of theological attention and, 148;
faith, hope, and charity and, 147;
hermeneutics of commitment and,
188; hermeneutics of suspicion and,
188; Latina, 147; methodology of, 135,
258n31; *mujerista* theology and, 149,
260n70; politics of location and, 188;
postcolonial feminist, 169, 184–92;

under-reading of literature by, 34; Rich and, 52–60. *See also* black faith; Christianity and the Bible; liberation theology; Mexican Catholicism
This Bridge Called My Back (Moraga and Anzaldúa), 130–32, 148, 167, 183, 259*n*59
Tiffin, Helen, 170
Torres, Hector, 134
Townes, Emilie, 30, 88, 103, 112–14, 253*n*64

Vega-González, Susan, 96, 102
Vendler, Helen, 65, 66
Vetlesen, Arne Johan, 21, 22, 28, 227, 262*n*91
Victorian era, 7, 53
Virgil, 39
Virgin of Guadalupe, 126, 134, 257–58*n*29

Walker, Alice, 90, 108, 252*n*55
Walton, Heather, 34, 57, 72, 247*n*110
Wanzo, Rebecca, 248*n*15
Ward, Cynthia, 183
Watt, Diane, 4
Weil, Simone: on anonymity of the sufferer, 21; attentiveness and sacrifice and, 217; on crucifixion of Christ, 1; gendered writing on attention and, 242*n*18; language and activism and, 61; readerly attention and, 31–32; Rich and, 50, 51; on suffering, silence, and isolation, 94; on suffering as language-stealing, 263*n*4; on suffering versus affliction, 50, 75
Welch, Sharon, 22, 34, 81, 222, 230, 267*n*2
Werner, Craig, 42, 64, 66, 70, 72, 80
Wheatley, Phillis, 106, 252*n*54, 252*n*55

White, Stephen, 71
Wilcox, Helen, 5
Williams, Delores, 30, 107, 223, 252–53*n*58
Wittgenstein, Ludwig, 85
Wollstonecraft, Mary, 53, 85
womanist ethics: Americanness of womanist theology and, 107, 267*n*65; experience and voice in, 193; holistic critique and, 258*n*32; meaning of *womanism* and, 108, 253*nn*64–65; Morrison and, 108, 109–11, 124; origins of, 108, 111, 253*n*66; postmodernism and, 110–11; religion, gender, and race and, 110–11, 114; standpoint theory and, 108; on status of black women's suffering, 253*n*62; womanism versus feminism and, 108; womanist theory and, 88
women writers: before 1900, 5–6; academy's growing welcome for black women writers and, 92; African, 183–84, 262–63*n*3; alternative sacred texts for women and, 57–58; appropriation of biblical discourse by, 5; black women's writing and literary representation and, 89–93; challenges to redemptive suffering by, 11; Christians, women, and writers as sufferers and, 8; erasure of women's thought and, 9; historiographic metafiction and, 18, 19; justification of doing man's task of writing and, 7; new generation of, 169; paradox of redemption and, 22; poststructuralism and postmodernism and, xviii, 229; pregnancy, childbirth, and

women writers (*continued*)
mothering as themes for, 223;
redemptive suffering in texts of,
209–10; responsibility of, 38; Rich
and black women writers and, 82;
self-giving of motherhood and of
creative process and, 7; suffering
in earliest works of, 4–5, 234–35*n*14;
the supernatural in black women's
fiction and, 104; women's poetry

movement and, 60; women's
vulnerability and, 226
Wood, Frances E., 253*n*62
Wright, Richard, 105

Yearsley, Anne, 5
Yorke, Liz, 41, 64, 70, 242–43*n*19

Ziarek, Ewa Płonowska, 15, 25, 82–84,
102–3, 194